The Bare Essentials

Plus

Fourth Edition

The Bare Essentials
Plus

Fourth Edition

Sarah Norton, Brian Green, Nell Waldman

NELSON EDUCATION

NELSON EDUCATION

The Bare Essentials Plus, Fourth Edition

Sarah Norton, Brian Green, and Nell Waldman

Vice President, Editorial Director:
Anne Williams

Executive Editor:
Laura Macleod

Senior Marketing Manager:
Amanda Henry

Developmental Editor:
Rebecca Ryoji

Permissions Coordinator and Photo Researcher:
Natalie Russell

Senior Content Production Manager:
Natalia Denesiuk Harris

Copy Editor:
Cathy Witlox

Proofreader:
Kate Revington

Indexer:
Jin Tan

Senior Production Coordinator:
Ferial Suleman

Design Director:
Ken Phipps

Managing Designer:
Franca Amore

Interior Design:
Greg Devitt

Cover Design:
Peter Papayanakis

Compositor:
Carol Magee

Printer:
RR Donnelley

Library and Archives Canada Cataloguing in Publication Data

Norton, Sarah, [date]
    The bare essentials plus / Sarah Norton, Brian Green, Nell Waldman. — 4th ed.

Includes bibliographical references and index.
ISBN 978-0-17-650217-1

    1. English language— Composition and exercises.
2. English language—Textbooks for second language learners.
I. Green, Brian II. Waldman, Nell, 1949– III. Title.

PE1128.N67 2012   808'.042
C2011-908631-X

ISBN-13: 978-0-17-650217-1
ISBN-10: 0-17-650217-3

CONTENTS

UNIT 6   FOR ESL LEARNERS: A REVIEW OF THE BASICS

UNIT 7   READINGS

APPENDIXES

PREFACE

TO THE INSTRUCTOR

The Bare Essentials Plus, Fourth Edition, is part of the *Essentials* series, the comprehensive set of texts that has helped more than 500,000 Canadian students learn to write for college and the workplace. The book provides students with the knowledge they need to progress from sentence correctness through paragraph development to the preparation of college and university papers. We have tried to present these concepts clearly, in a friendly tone, and to motivate students with encouragement and humour.

The *Plus* in the title refers to information and exercises we have included to meet the needs of second-language learners, a growing segment of the postsecondary population across Canada. Most of this material is concentrated in Unit 6, which can be integrated into classwork or assigned as homework for students who need it, but there are also short, ESL-specific passages throughout the book in places where these students are likely to need extra help.

The "essentials" in *Bare Essentials Plus* are arranged from words (Unit 1) to sentences (Unit 2) to grammar (Unit 3) to punctuation (Unit 4) to paragraphs and essays (Unit 5). Each chapter offers simple (but not simplistic) explanations, copious examples, and plenty of exercises. For students who need even more practice, additional exercises for most chapters are posted on our website (**www.bareplus4e.nelson.com**).

HIGHLIGHTS OF THE FOURTH EDITION

Here is an overview of the major changes to content and organization of *The Bare Essentials Plus*:

- Approximately 30 to 40 percent of the exercises are new (with answers at the back of the book). Most of the exercises can be completed in the text, and the answers, in Appendix C, are easy to find.

- New pre- and post-tests (the Quick Quizzes and Rapid Reviews) and all-new Mastery Tests are provided for skill-based units (Units 1, 2, 3, 4, and 6). These exercises preview and review the contents of each unit and provide practice in editing continuous prose passages. By comparing their results on the preliminary quiz and the final review, students can see for themselves how far they've progressed.
- New material includes a chapter on responsible research (Chapter 27), as well as sections on clichés (Chapter 1), coordination and subordination (Chapter 10), and conditional verbs (Chapter 29).
- Unit 5, "Paragraphs and Essays," includes a more flexible treatment of thesis statements, a more comprehensive overview of outlines, and a new treatment of revision. We have added exercises to each step of the writing process to give students practice in working through a writing project from beginning to end.
- Unit 6, "For ESL Learners," features new cloze procedure exercises for each chapter to provide more hands-on editing, together with suggestions for speaking/listening practice.
- The "Readings" in Unit 7 consist of 11 essays, 8 of them new to this edition, that illustrate the instruction in Units 1 through 6 and exemplify commonly assigned types of essays. This unit concludes with a short documented essay formatted in both MLA and APA styles. Questions for discussion and suggestions for writing follow each essay.
- For the grammatically faithful, Appendix A, "The Fundamentals," provides definitions and examples of the kinds and parts of sentences and the parts of speech.
- The "List of Useful Terms," Appendix B, defines and illustrates terms that appear in bold print in the text. It also offers definitions and examples of other grammatical terms with which you may want your students to be familiar.
- "Spelling Matters," an appendix in previous editions, is now on the Student Resources page of *The Bare Essentials Plus* website.
- New cartoon illustrations can be found throughout the book, and we have added a fresh new design with a new second colour.

The units in *Bare Essentials Plus* are independent of each other, so instructors can present them in any order they choose. The chapters within each unit, however, should be introduced in the order in which they appear. The unit exercises are cumulative: those in later chapters often include questions that assume mastery of skills covered in earlier chapters.

We instruct students to check their answers as soon as they have completed an exercise so that they will get immediate feedback, learn from their mistakes, and avoid reinforcing their errors. **We urge instructors to emphasize the importance of this procedure.** Students who need more practice than the exercises in the text provide will find supplementary, self-scoring exercises on the website. Web icons identify when and where to find this additional material.

Answers to the chapter Mastery Tests are posted on the Instructor Resources page of the website and printed in the *Instructor's Manual*. Both resources also offer an alternative set of Mastery Tests, equivalent in number and difficulty to those in the book.

On the inside front cover is a Quick Revision Guide that students can use as a checklist as they edit their work. Instructors can duplicate the guide, staple a copy to each student's paper, and mark ✓ or ✗ beside each point to identify the paper's strengths and weaknesses. This strategy provides students with comprehensive and consistent feedback. It also saves hours of marking time.

INSTRUCTOR RESOURCES

WEBSITE: www.bareplus4e.nelson.com

The chart below provides an outline of the features on the website. On the Instructor Resources page, "Preventing Plagiarism: Why? What? How?" offers helpful tips on dealing with this perennial problem. "The Creative Classroom" contains teaching tips and classroom activities based on game theory. An introductory essay explains the theory and rationale for these activities, which students find fun to do.

Instructor Resources	Student Resources

How to Use *Bare Essentials Plus*
Preventing Plagiarism: Why? What? How?
The Creative Classroom
Answers to Chapter Mastery Tests
Alternative Chapter Mastery Tests & Answers
Answers to Discussion Questions (Unit 7)
Supplementary Readings
PowerPoint Slides and Transparencies
Essentials *iTests*
Authors' Forum
	Web Exercises (Chapters 2–32)
	More Information
	•Additional Examples for Selected Chapters
	•Spelling Matters
	•ESL Tips
	•Formatting & Documentation
	  • MLA Style
	  • APA Style
	•InfoTrac/Research Skills
	•Student Survival Skills
	More Practice
	•Practice Tests (Chapters 1–21; 28–32)
	•Supplementary Readings
	Ask the Authors

The Student Resources page is divided into three sections. The first, "Web Exercises," contains additional exercises, automatically scored, to supplement Chapters 2 through 32, for students who need extra practice.

The second section of the Student Resources page, "More Information," contains additional examples of the principles explained in the body of the book, instruction on APA and MLA formatting and documentation styles, and other useful information.

The third section, "More Practice," contains practice tests for Chapters 1 to 21 and 28 to 32, along with supplementary readings (posted on both Instructor and Student Resources pages) designed for students who need unambiguous examples of five-paragraph essay development. These essays are less sophisticated in language and structure than those in Unit 7.

Instructor's Manual. The *Instructor's Manual* to accompany *The Bare Essentials Plus*, Fourth Edition, includes teaching tips, classroom activities, and answers to the chapter Mastery Tests; a set of alternative Mastery Tests and answers; additional readings for analysis; and transparency masters that summarize chapter contents. The last 20 slides define and illustrate parts of speech and sentences and provide a quick review of major syntax, grammar, and punctuation errors.

Microsoft® PowerPoint®. Key concepts from *The Bare Essentials Plus*, Fourth Edition, are presented in PowerPoint format, with generous use of figures and samples from the text.

Essentials iTests. The *Essentials iTests*, a self-scoring CD-ROM version of the *Essentials Test Manual*, is now available to support instructors who use any textbook in the *Essentials* series. This comprehensive test bank includes diagnostic tests as well as pre- and post-tests for each unit and chapter. The tests address six principal points of composition: organization, syntax, grammar, punctuation, diction, and spelling. Instructors can select pre-formatted tests, revise ready-made tests, or develop their own tests tailored specifically to their curriculum.

With its easy-to-use assessment and tutorial system, *Essentials iTests* enables you to create and deliver customized tests in minutes. You can choose either Quick Test Wizard or an Online Test Wizard to guide you step by step through the process of creating individualized tests. Each test appears on-screen exactly as it will print or display online.

We have designed *The Bare Essentials Plus*, Fourth Edition, not only for students who need to learn how to write for academic or professional purposes, but also for instructors who are dedicated to helping their students learn as efficiently and painlessly as possible. While *The Bare Essentials Plus* can successfully be used to support self-instruction and independent study, it works best for students lucky enough to have an instructor to guide them enthusiastically through its contents, adjust the pace and level of instruction to the needs of each class, and provide regular feedback and encouragement. We hope this new edition will meet instructors' expectations and help them sustain their joy in teaching.

ACKNOWLEDGMENTS

We are indebted to our reviewers, whose suggestions helped to make this a more useful book:

Veronica Abbass, Seneca College
Prita Sethuram, Centennial College
Mariopi Spanos, Vanier College

We owe special thanks to Valerie Grabove, chair of the Centre for Educational and Professional Development at Niagara College, who developed the teaching strategies and classroom activities that support and enhance this book. We would also like to thank the editors at Nelson Education Ltd.: Laura Macleod, executive editor; Rebecca Ryoji, developmental editor; Natalia Denesiuk Harris, senior content production manager; and Cathy Witlox, copy editor.

Sarah Norton
Brian Green
Nell Waldman

INTRODUCTION

TO THE STUDENT: WHY YOU NEED THIS BOOK

College and university composition courses have always had a public-relations problem. Writing skills is not a core course, and students often wonder why they are required to take it. The fact is that good writing skills are as valuable to career success as any subject you will take. That's why English composition is part of your curriculum: program advisory boards and curriculum committees know that graduates who can communicate well are hired more quickly, advance more rapidly, and climb higher in their professions than graduates with poor communication skills. Companies from Imperial Oil to IBM, from RIM to Ford, from the Royal Bank to Bell Canada, not to mention all levels of government, hospitals, police forces, and the Canadian military, have gone on record as requiring superior communication skills as an essential criterion for promotion.

To any employer, an employee is more valuable if he or she can write well. Fairly or unfairly, no matter what field you're in, employers, peers, and subordinates will judge your professional ability on the basis of your communication skills. In most careers, your ability to write well will be tested every day.

The good news is that writing skills can be learned. There is no reason you can't write clear and correct reports, memoranda, and even emails. This book is intended to help you, just as it has helped hundreds of thousands of Canadian students in the past. If you really want to succeed, you'll invest the time, effort, and care to make this book work for you.

WHAT'S IN THIS BOOK?

There is more to this text than meets the eye. In addition to the book you're holding in your hand, you have access to a comprehensive website that provides extra exercises, information, and practice: **www.bareplus4e.nelson .com**. Together, the book and the website give you all the tools and resources you need to improve your writing.

If you turn to the table of contents (page v), you'll see that the book is divided into seven units. Units 1 through 4 and Unit 6 will help you identify and eliminate errors in your writing. Unit 5 explains and illustrates how to organize and develop your ideas in effective paragraphs, essays, and reports. Unit 6 reviews those aspects of English that second-language students find troublesome. Unit 7 consists of 11 readings on a variety of topics we hope you will find interesting.

Three appendixes follow Unit 7: Appendix A covers basic grammatical points—the kinds and parts of sentences and the parts of speech. Appendix B defines the grammatical and other terms used in the book. Whenever you find a **technical term** in bold type, you can turn to Appendix B to discover its meaning, together with examples of its correct use. Appendix C contains answers to the exercises in the first six units (except for the Mastery Tests), and a comprehensive index concludes the book.

On the website, under "More Information," you'll find additional examples for most of the principles explained and illustrated in the book. A computer icon tells you when and where exercises are available on the website for extra practice. These exercises are electronically scored, which means you can get immediate feedback on your improvement. Also on the website are practice tests that check your knowledge of the principles in Units 1 through 4 and Unit 6. (We suggest you do these practice tests before you try the chapter Mastery Tests.)

If you are required to write a research paper as part of your composition course, the "More Information" section of the website provides explanations and examples of both APA and MLA format and documentation styles. The website also provides a chapter on "Student Survival Skills," with topics ranging from understanding course outlines to overcoming procrastination and writer's block.

A special feature of our website is the "Ask the Authors" button. Click on this button to send us questions that you don't want to raise in class.

"Ask the Authors" questions are emailed to us, and one of us will get back to you with the answer. We welcome your questions as well as messages telling us what you like and don't like about our book.

HOW TO USE THIS BOOK

In each chapter, we do three things: explain a point, illustrate the point with examples, and provide exercises to help you master it. The exercises are arranged in sets that become more challenging as you go along. After some of the exercises, you'll find a symbol directing you to the "Web Exercises" page on *The Bare Essentials Plus* website (**www.bareplus4e.nelson.com**), where we have provided extra exercises for those who need extra practice. By the time you finish a chapter, you should have a good grasp of the skill. Then it's up to you to apply that skill every time you write.

Here's how to proceed:

1. Read the explanation. Make sure you understand the concept, and get help from your teacher if it's not completely clear.
2. Study the highlighted rules and the examples that follow.
3. If you find an explanation easy and think you have no problem with the skill, try the last set of exercises following the explanation. Then check your answers. If you've made no errors, go on to the next point.

   If you're less confident, don't skip anything. Start with the first set and work through all the exercises, including those on the website, until you are sure you understand the point. (As a general rule, getting three exercises in a row entirely correct demonstrates understanding and competence.)
4. **Always check your answers to one set of exercises before you go on to the next.** Only by checking your results after each set can you identify errors and correct them, instead of repeating and reinforcing them.
5. When you find a mistake in an exercise, go back to the explanation and examples. Study them again; then look up the additional examples for that point on the website. If you are still confused, check with your instructor.

You can reinforce your understanding—and prepare for in-class tests—by doing the practice tests posted on the Student Resources page at **www.bareplus4e.nelson.com**.

WHAT THE SYMBOLS MEAN

Go to Web Exercise

This symbol (see left) means that you will find on the website exercises to supplement the material you are working on. Once you've logged on to the website, click on "Web Exercises." The exercises are posted by chapter, so to get to the exercises for the apostrophe, for example, click on Chapter 3 in the list, and then go to the numbered exercise(s) below the icon (e.g., 3.1, 3.2). Web exercises are graded automatically, so you will know instantly whether or not you have understood the material.

This symbol beside an exercise means the exercise is designed to be done by two or three students working together. Sometimes you are instructed to begin working in a pair or group, then to work individually on a writing task, and finally to regroup and review your writing with your partner(s).

This symbol means "note this." We've used it to highlight writing tips, helpful hints, hard-to-remember points, and information that you should apply whenever you write.

An exercise marked with this icon is a Mastery Test. The answers to these exercises are not in the back of the book; your instructor will provide them.

When this symbol appears in the margin beside a paragraph or an exercise, it means that the information is specifically designed to help ESL learners master a point that many find troublesome.

THREE LEARNING TOOLS

Inside the front cover, you'll find a Quick Revision Guide. Use it to help you revise your papers before handing them in. This book is intended to be a practical tool, not a theoretical reference. We can identify writing problems and show you how to solve them, and exercises can give you practice in eliminating errors, but only writing and revising can bring real and lasting improvement.

On pages 586–87, you'll find a Time Line that summarizes verb tenses in a quick, easy-to-read chart.

On the inside back cover, we've provided a list of the most common editing and proofreading symbols. For each error, we illustrate and explain standard marking symbols and also leave space for you to write in your instructor's preferred symbol or abbreviation for each type of error.

UNIT 1

Words

QUICK QUIZ

This Quick Quiz tests your competence in the writing skills covered in Unit 1. Revise the passage below so that it contains no inappropriate language (e.g., slang), no redundancies (i.e., wordiness), and no misused words, incorrect apostrophes, or unnecessary capital letters.

After you've made your corrections, turn to page 501 in Appendix C to see how successful you've been in finding and correcting the 15 errors. For each error you miss, the Answer Key directs you to the chapter(s) you need to work on to eliminate that error from your writing.

[1]Having decided to buy a new stereo system for my car, I went to Awesome Auto Audio, a store who's advertisements in the paper said they're quality and prices are unbeatable. [2]The salesperson could see that I was a more serious customer, then the average car radio buyer and recommended that I consider V3A. [3]Of coarse, I didn't want to let him know that I didn't know what V3A was, so he lead me to a special showroom where I spotted a sign that read "Voice-Activated Auto Audio (V3A)."

[4]The salesperson switched on the system and demonstrated by saying, "louder," which increased the radio's volume. [5]Then he said, "Techno," and the radio immediately switched to a techno station. [6]I thought this was way cool, so, irregardless of the price, I told him to install it in my car. [7]In actual fact, I had convinced myself that its safer to have a radio that doesn't need to be adjusted manually, by hand, while I was driving. [8]Once I had presented my

Credit Card and a peace of identification, I went to the parking lot to wait for

the installation.

[9]Soon I was driving home and calling out, "Louder" and "Oldie's" and

"Classic rock," and the radio was obeying every command. [10]Suddenly, as I

was turning a corner, another driver cut right in front of me. [11]Annoyed, I

yelled, "Stupid!" and the radio suddenly and abruptly switched to a call-in talk

show.

1 Choosing the Right Words

The difference between the right word and the almost right word is

the difference between lightning and the lightning bug.

—Mark Twain

Real estate salespeople say there are three things to consider when buying a property: location, location, location. Good writers know that there are three things to consider when sending a message: audience, audience, audience. Your readers and their expectations—what they need or want to know from you, the writer—should be your constant focus.

Whenever you write, you want your reader
- to understand your message and
- to think well of you as a writer

To achieve these goals, your writing must be both correct and appropriate. If your readers are to understand you, your message must consist of accurate words organized into grammatical sentences and arranged in well-developed paragraphs.

The notion of "correctness" in writing has developed over hundreds of years—and is still changing—to help writers create messages that say what their authors intend. Error-filled writing fails to meet the reader's expectation that a message will be clearly communicated. Mistakes in grammar, sentence structure, spelling, and punctuation mean that a message will not be easy to read.

Another reason to ensure that your writing is correct is that our culture associates correct language with education and intelligence. Careless, ungrammatical writing is often considered a sign of ignorance or laziness—or both.

But that's not all. Accuracy alone will not help you reach your goals. A message that is technically free of errors can still confuse or annoy a reader if it contains inappropriate language. Slang; racist, sexist, obscene, or blasphemous language; and even wordiness can interfere with your message. That's why we call them errors. They divert the reader's attention from what you're saying to how you're saying it. They also lower the reader's opinion of you.

In this chapter, we provide a brief introduction to choosing language that is correct and appropriate for your message and **audience**. We assume that you are writing for readers in an academic or professional environment. Our goals are to help you convey your message clearly and leave your readers with a positive impression of you and your ideas.

Before you get started, you need to equip yourself with a few essential resources and an understanding of the levels of language that are available to you when you write.

1. Buy and use a good dictionary.

A dictionary is a writer's best friend. You will need to use it every time you write, so if you don't already own a good dictionary, you should buy one. For Canadian writers, a good dictionary is one that is Canadian, current, comprehensive (contains at least 75,000 entries), and reliable (published by an established, well-known firm).

For this text, we have used the *Canadian Oxford Dictionary,* 2nd edition (Oxford University Press, 2004). Another convenient reference is the *Collins Gage Canadian Paperback Dictionary,* and, for those whose first language is not English, the *Oxford Advanced Learner's Dictionary*, 8th ed. (Oxford University Press, 2010), is helpful. Unfortunately, no comprehensive Canadian dictionary is available on the Internet.

A good dictionary packs a lot of information into a small space. Take a look at the *Canadian Oxford Dictionary* entry for the word *graduate*, for example. The circled numbers correspond to some of the numbers in the guide that follows the entry.

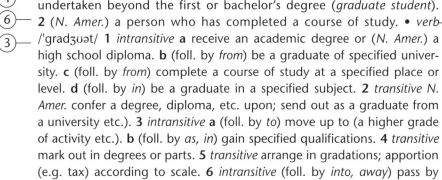

grad·u·ate • *noun.* /ˈɡradʒʊət/ **1 a** a person who has been awarded an academic degree. **b** (*attributive*) designating or involved in education undertaken beyond the first or bachelor's degree (*graduate student*). **2** (*N. Amer.*) a person who has completed a course of study. • *verb* /ˈɡradʒʊət/ **1** *intransitive* **a** receive an academic degree or (*N. Amer.*) a high school diploma. **b** (foll. by *from*) be a graduate of specified university. **c** (foll. by *from*) complete a course of study at a specified place or level. **d** (foll. by *in*) be a graduate in a specified subject. **2** *transitive N. Amer.* confer a degree, diploma, etc. upon; send out as a graduate from a university etc.). **3** *intransitive* **a** (foll. by *to*) move up to (a higher grade of activity etc.). **b** (foll. by *as, in*) gain specified qualifications. **4** *transitive* mark out in degrees or parts. **5** *transitive* arrange in gradations; apportion (e.g. tax) according to scale. **6** *intransitive* (foll. by *into, away*) pass by degrees. [medieval Latin *graduari* take a degree, from Latin *gradus* step]

Source: *Canadian Oxford Dictionary,* 2nd Edition, Edited by Katherine Barber © Oxford University Press Canada 2004. Reprinted by permission of the publisher.

In a dictionary entry, you will find some or all of the following information:

1. **Spelling:** if there are two or more acceptable spellings, the most common one is normally given first
2. **Syllables:** small, centred dots (·) show you where hyphens can go if you need to break a word at the end of a line
3. **Pronunciation:** if there is more than one acceptable pronunciation, the most common one is listed first
4. **Grammatical form(s):** for example, noun (*n.*), verb (*v.*), adjective (*adj.*)
5. Any **irregular forms** of the word, such as the plural form of a noun or the past tense and past participle of a verb
6. **Usage restrictions:** for example, slang, informal, offensive, N. Amer.
7. **Definition(s):** the most common meanings are given first, followed by the technical or specialized meanings; together with phrases or sentences illustrating how the word is used
8. **Idioms** using the word
9. **Origins** of the word (etymology)
10. **Other helpful information:** for example, homonyms (words that sound the same as the entry word); synonyms (words that are similar in meaning to the entry word); antonyms (words opposite in meaning to the entry word); and special variations in grammar, spelling, pronunciation, and usage

 Unless you have already done so (and most people haven't), begin by reading the introduction or guide in the front of your dictionary. This information may not be very entertaining, but it is essential if you want to understand how to read your dictionary accurately. No two dictionaries are alike. Only if you are familiar with your dictionary's symbols, abbreviations, and entry format will you be able to use it efficiently.

Knowing the information in your dictionary's guide will also save you time. For example, you do not need to memorize long lists of irregular plurals. Good dictionaries include irregular plurals in their entries. They also include irregular forms of verbs, adjectives, and adverbs. And if you've forgotten how to form regular plurals, verbs, adjectives, and adverbs, you'll find that information in your dictionary guide as well.

Take the time to read through the front matter in your dictionary. Then do the following sets of exercises. Be sure to check your answers to each set before going on to the next. Answers for exercises in this chapter begin on page 502.

EXERCISE **1.1**

1. Find two pronunciations for *lieutenant* and *schedule*. Which pronunciation of these words is preferred in Canada?
2. What is another spelling of the word *humour*? ~Humor~ Which spelling is used when an ending like *-ous* or *-ist* is added to the root word?
3. The prefix *ir-* at the beginning of some words reverses their meaning. For example, *irregular* is the opposite of *regular*. Find six other words that have this characteristic.
4. Is *tatoo* spelled correctly? Is the word a noun or a verb? Find two different meanings of the word.
5. Find alternative spellings for the words *programme*, *centre*, *skillful*, *traveler*, and *judgement*. In each case, indicate the spelling favoured in Canada.

EXERCISE **1.2**

Write the plural form of each word.

1. ratio*s*   6. data

2. criterion *Criteria*   7. mother-in-law

3. analysis   8. nucleus

4. personnel   9. appendix

5. crisis   10. formula

EXERCISE **1.3**

Combine each root word with the ending given.

1. delay + ed   6. lonely + ness

2. journey + s   7. policy + s

3. play + er   8. easy + er

4. destroy + ing   9. lazy + ness

5. repay + ment   10. necessary + ly

After you have checked your answers to this exercise, go back and look closely at the questions. What do the root words in questions 1 to 5 have in common? What do the root words in questions 6 to 10 have in common? How does this similarity affect the way these words are spelled when an ending is added? Can you write a rule to guide other writers who must deal with words like these?

EXERCISE **1.4**

Using hyphens, show where each word could be divided at the end of a line. (Some words can be divided in two or more places: *pol-it-ic-al*, for example.)

1. discuss   6. create

2. management   7. challenge

3. accommodate   8. technician

4. distribute   9. conscience

5. through   10. business

EXERCISE **1.5**

The following words are not pronounced the way you might expect if you had never encountered them before. Working in teams of two, look them up in your dictionary and, in the space beside each word, write out their pronunciation (the information given in parentheses immediately after the entry). Take turns with your partner sounding out each word, one syllable at a time, using your diction- ary's pronunciation key to help you. No answers are given for this exercise.

1. preferable _____   6. eulogy _____

2. epitome _____   7. indict _____

3. impotent _____   8. irreparable _____

4. comparable _____   9. corps _____

5. subtle _____   10. chassis _____

> 2. Use spelling and grammar checkers responsibly.

- Good spell-check programs can find typing errors and some spelling mis- takes. They have limitations, however. They can't tell if you meant to write "your" or "you're," and they won't flag either word, even if it's used incor- rectly. (You'll learn more about such words in Chapter 2, "Hazardous Homonyms.") Also, since we use Canadian English, our spellings some- times differ from the American spellings used in most word-processing pro- grams. If your word-processing program can be set to Canadian spelling, make that adjustment. If it cannot, be aware that words such as *colour*, *honour, neighbour, centre, travelled,* and *metre*—all correct Canadian spellings—will be flagged as errors.

- Another useful tool is a hand-held spell checker. Pocket-sized and inexpensive, these devices contain a large bank of words and will provide the correct spelling if the "guess" you type in is not too far off. Some checkers even "talk," pronouncing the word for you. Ask your instructor if you can use this device (sound turned off, please) for in-class writing and exams.

- Electronic translating dictionaries are available online and as hand-held devices. Most of these tools pronounce the word as a native speaker would. (Of course, the accuracy of the pronunciation depends on the knowledge and skill of the programmer.) Please do not use the voice feature in class! Most translating dictionaries are limited in their capability, so look for one that is both comprehensive and accurate. And be careful not to seize on the first definition that appears for a word you are looking up. Read through all the options given. Computers cannot grasp ambiguity, irony, or idioms the way the human mind does. Sometimes the convenience of electronic dictionaries can lead to embarrassing language errors; for example, a European vacuum cleaner manufacturer translated its slogan into English as "Nothing sucks like our product." Print dictionaries are usually more reliable than their electronic counterparts, but they won't tell you how to say a word you don't know how to pronounce. Pronunciation websites, such as **www.forvo.com**, provide pronunciations of many words, including "foreign" words for English speakers. (How would you pronounce *ménage à trois*?)

- The best advice we can give you about grammar checkers (they announce their presence by producing a wavy green line under words or sentences on your word processor) is to use them with caution. No grammar checker has yet been able to account for the subtleties of English grammar. A grammar program is as likely to flag a perfectly good sentence, even to suggest an incorrect "fix," as it is to ignore a sentence full of errors. "I done real good on my grammar test," for example, escapes the dreaded wavy green line.

3. Buy and use a good thesaurus.

If you use the same words again and again, you will bore your reader. A thesaurus is a dictionary of synonyms—words with similar meanings. For any word you need to use repeatedly in a document, a good thesaurus will provide a list of alternatives. Note, however, that synonyms are not identical in meaning. Only you (or a knowledgeable friend) can decide which of the words listed in your thesaurus is appropriate for your message. Your dictionary will help you decide which terms are acceptable and which are not.

We recommend that you rely on a print thesaurus rather than on the thesaurus in your word-processing program, even though your computer's thesaurus will provide quick synonyms for words you don't want to repeat. A word-processor thesaurus provides a list of approximate synonyms, but no examples of usage. With unfamiliar or complex words, the information you need is whether the synonyms offered are nouns or verbs and whether they are in general use or are slang, technical, derogatory, or even obsolete. For this information, you probably need a book. Buy a good thesaurus and use it in conjunction with your dictionary.

Two good thesauruses are available in inexpensive paperback editions: *Oxford Paperback Thesaurus* (Oxford University Press, 2006) and *Roget's Thesaurus* (Penguin, 2004).

Inexperienced writers sometimes assume that long, obscure words will impress their readers. In fact, the opposite is true. Most readers are annoyed by unnecessarily "fancy" language (see Pretentious Language, page 16).

NEVER use a word whose meaning you do not know. When you find a possible but unfamiliar synonym, look it up in your dictionary to be sure it means what you need it to say.

LEVELS OF LANGUAGE

Communication occurs on many levels, from grunts and mumbles to inspiring speeches; from unintelligible graffiti to moving poetry. Different levels of language are appropriate for different messages and different audiences. In academic and professional writing, you will be expected to use what is called standard written English.

Levels of language are defined by vocabulary, by length and complexity of sentences and paragraphs, and by tone (how the writing "sounds"). Most of the communication you encounter or are required to write in college will be at the **general level**, whether in postings to online course discussion groups or in voice-mail or email messages you leave for your instructor. Your relationship with your teacher is a professional one, and your language should reflect your understanding of that relationship.

Outside of school and off the job, you normally communicate at the **informal level**, which is used in personal writing and in conversation.[1]

The following chart outlines the characteristics of general and informal English.

---

[1] If you aspire to be a judge, a research scientist, or a professor, you will be required to write formal-level English, which is beyond the scope of this book.

	Informal	**General**
Vocabulary	Casual, everyday; some slang and colloquial expressions; contractions commonly used; written in first and second person	The language of educated persons; non-technical; readily understood by most readers; few if any colloquial expressions; no slang; few contractions; written in first, second, or third person
Sentence and paragraphs	Short, simple sentences; some sentence fragments; dashes acceptable; short paragraphs	Complete sentences of varying lengths; paragraphs usually between 75 and 200 words
Tone	Casual, conversational; sounds like ordinary speech	Varies from light to serious to suit writer's message, audience, and purpose
Typical uses	Personal communications between friends; some fiction; some newspaper columns; much advertising	Most of what we read, including newspapers, magazines, most textbooks, business correspondence

Examples:

Informal: He's not going to go for the job.
General: He will not be applying for the position.
Informal: She's just not that into you.
General: She doesn't really like you.
Informal: We're fed up with you people, so we're getting somebody else.
General: We are not satisfied with your service, so we have decided to use another supplier.

From the chart and these examples, you can see why the general level is preferred for written communication. It's more precise, and it's clear to a wide audience of readers.

In the past few years, text-messaging short forms have been creeping into written assignments, reports, even research papers and resumés. In college writing, "text messagese" is inappropriate. We urge you not to use it except in messages to friends.

EXERCISE 1.6

Write two short reports explaining how you are enjoying your courses so far. One is an email to a good friend; the other is a report required by the director of your program. Adapt your level of language so that it is appropriate to each situation.

We've introduced you to the tools you'll need as a writer and to the levels of language you can choose from when writing a message for a specific audience. Let's now turn to the writing errors you must not commit in any message to any audience: wordiness, slang, pretentious language, clichés, offensive language, and "abusages."

WORDINESS

One of the barriers to clear communication is **wordiness**, the unnecessary repetition of information or the use of two or more words when one would do. As a courtesy to your reader, you should make your writing as concise as possible.

Sometimes wordiness results from careless revision. In the editing stage of writing a paper, you should tighten up your sentences and paragraphs. Wordy or awkward phrasing often pops into your mind when you are struggling to express an idea, and it always appears in a first draft. However, there is no excuse for it to survive a careful edit and make its way into a final draft.

Here's an example of what can happen when a writer fails to prune his or her prose:

> In my personal opinion, the government of this country of ours needs an additional amount of meaningful input from the people of Canada right now.

The writer has chosen impressive-sounding phrases (*meaningful input, this country of ours*) and wordy but meaningless expressions (*personal opinion, an additional amount*) to produce a sentence so hard to read that it isn't worth a reader's effort to decipher. This wordy sentence could be nicely shortened to "In my opinion, our government needs to hear more from the people."

The following list contains some of the worst offenders we've collected from student writing, corporate memoranda, form letters, and advertisements.

Wordy	Concise
a large number of	many
absolutely nothing (*or* everything, complete, perfect)	nothing (*or* everything, complete, perfect)
actual (*or* true) fact	fact
almost always	usually
at that point in time	then
at the present time	now
consensus of opinion	consensus
continue on	continue
could possibly (*or* may possibly, might possibly)	could (*or* may, might)

Wordy	Concise
crisis (*or* emergency) situation	crisis (*or* emergency)
due to the fact that	because
end result	result
equally as good	as good
few and far between	rare
final conclusion	conclusion
for the reason that	because
free gift	gift
I myself (*or* you yourself, *etc.*)	I (*or* you, *etc.*)
I personally think/feel	I think/feel
in actual fact	in fact
in every instance	always
in my opinion, I think	I think
in the near future	soon
in today's society/in this day and age	now (*or* today)
is able to	can
many different kinds	many kinds
mutual agreement (*or* cooperation)	agreement (*or* cooperation)
my personal opinion	my opinion
no other alternative	no alternative
personal friend	friend
real, genuine leather (*or* real antique, *etc.*)	leather (*or* antique, *etc.*)
red in colour (*or* large in size, *etc.*)	red (*or* large, *etc.*)
repeat again	repeat
return back	return (*or* go back)
really, very	*These words add nothing to your meaning. Leave them out.*
8:00 a.m. in the morning	8:00 a.m.
actual (*or* real, true) fact	fact
such as, for example	such as
take active steps	take steps
totally destroyed	destroyed
truly remarkable	remarkable
very (*or* most, quite, almost, rather) unique	unique

By studying these examples, you can see how these and many other phrases add words but not meaning to your message. Teachers and editors call these phrases "fill" or "padding," and they urge students to eliminate them from their writing if they want to build a good relationship with their readers.

EXERCISE **1.7**

Working with a partner, revise these sentences to make them shorter and clearer. Then compare your answers with our suggestions on page 502.

1. A woman has the absolute last word in any argument, and anything a man says to continue on is the beginning of a new argument.
2. Each evening at 10 p.m., we always watch the same identical program on television: *The National* on CBC.
3. How can we completely eliminate our debt when we have no other choice each and every month but to spend more than the two of us together can earn?
4. The city told me that, in actual fact, there was next to nothing they could do about the raccoons that have gathered together in my backyard.
5. My grandfather totally impressed me when I asked him if he had lived his whole entire life in the country of Canada and he replied, "Not yet."

SLANG

Amped, bugdust, and *spacker*: do you know what these words mean? Probably not. **Slang** is "street talk," non-standard language used in conversation among people who belong to the same social group. It's a kind of private speech. Because slang expressions become outdated quickly and are understood by a limited group of people, they are not appropriate for a message intended for a general reader. There are thousands of slang expressions; if you're curious about them, browse through an online dictionary such as **www.slangsite.com**.

If you are in doubt about a word, check your print dictionary. The notation *sl.* or *slang* appears after words that are slang or have a slang meaning. (Some words—for example, *house, cool,* and *bombed*—have both a standard meaning and a slang meaning. Taking the time to choose words and expressions that are appropriate to written English increases your chances of communicating clearly and earning your readers' respect.

EXERCISE **1.8**

- Working in groups of three or four, list five slang expressions that are outdated—they are no longer used by your peers.
- Now identify five current slang expressions that everyone in your group is familiar with.
- Define each current slang term in language appropriate to a general reader. (That is, write each definition in words your teachers would understand.)

PRETENTIOUS LANGUAGE

The opposite of slang is **pretentious language**: words that are too formal for general writing. Never use a long, difficult, or obscure word when a simpler word will do. Your writing will be easier to read and your message clearer and more convincing if you write to inform rather than to impress.

You can recognize pretentious language easily: the words are long, unfamiliar, and unnatural-sounding. If the average reader needs a dictionary to "translate" your words into general English, then your writing is inflated and inappropriate. Consider these examples:

Before we embark on our journey, we must refuel our vehicle.

The refrigerator is bare of comestibles, so it is time to repair to the local emporium and purchase victuals.

After consulting your dictionary, you can translate these pompous sentences into plain English:

Before we leave, we need to put gas in the car.

The refrigerator is empty, so it's time to go to the store and buy some food.

But why would you? It's the writer's job to communicate, and a pretentious writer makes the reader do too much work. Here is a list of some common offenders, together with their general-level equivalents.

Pretentious	Clear
ascertain	find out
commence	begin
endeavour	try
facilitate	help
finalize	finish
manifest	show
reside	live
transmit	send
utilize	use

The cure for pretentious language is simple: be considerate of your readers. If you want your readers to understand and respect you, write in a simple, straightforward style.

Prima facie I concur – viz, a fortiori, I shall therefore accept between one and three portions of sweet crystalline substance in full and final settlement

That'll be two sugars then

EXERCISE **1.9**

Revise the following sentences to eliminate pretentious language in favour of plain English. You may need to use your dictionary to complete this exercise. Compare your answers with our suggestions on page 502.

1. One should exercise diligence when utilizing an axe.

2. We reside at the conjunction of Maple Street and Rue Érable in the metropolis of Sherbrooke.

3. After we finalized our survey of the task we had been assigned, we knew assistance would be necessary.

4. When we detected the presence of storm clouds in advance of our position, we knew that precipitation was imminent.

5. My gym teacher is conscious of the fact that I have an aversion to physical exertion.

CLICHÉS

Pretentious writing requires time and effort; clichéd writing requires neither. It is as easy and as thoughtless as casual talk. A **cliché** is a phrase that has been used so often it no longer communicates a meaningful idea.

> At this point in time, we have no choice but to focus all our efforts where it really counts: on the bottom line.

At this point in time, we have *no choice but, focus all our efforts, where it really counts,* and *on the bottom line*—all these phrases are clichés. They do not create a picture in the reader's mind, and if your reader cannot "see" what you're saying, no communication takes place. After a few cliché-filled sentences, readers will conclude, "There's nothing new here. It's all been said before." And they will stop reading.

Spoken English is full of clichés—we often use them as shortcuts to put our thoughts into words, and if our listener doesn't understand our meaning, we can always explain further. Writers, on the other hand, have time to plan what they want to say. They also have the opportunity to revise and edit. So writers are expected to communicate with more precision and more originality than speakers.

If you are a native speaker of English, clichés are easy to recognize. When you can read the first few words of a phrase and fill in the rest automatically, you know the phrase is a cliché: *live and ___; thinking outside the ___; when push comes to ___; a pain in the ___.*

The solution to a cliché problem involves time and thought, first to recognize the cliché and then to find a better way to express your idea. Think about what you want to say and then say it in your own words, not everyone else's.

EXERCISE **1.10**

Working with a partner, identify the cliché(s) in each sentence. Then rewrite the sentence, expressing the ideas in your own words. When you have finished, exchange your results with another group and check each other's work: have all clichés been eliminated? Have any new ones been introduced? Finally, compare your work with our suggested answers on page 503.

1. I'm just giving you a heads-up about this problem because at the end of the day we're all in this together.

2. Last but not least, we want to thank our support staff, whose thinking outside the box saved the day.

3. This is not rocket science. Ballpark figures reveal that a small investment now will reap huge dividends when all is said and done.

4. If I had cutting-edge graphics programs on a state-of-the-art computer, I could make the grade as a game developer.

5. Just when divorce rates have reached epidemic proportions and loneliness has become a fact of life, psychological experts have agreed that meaningful relationships are critical to mental health.

"Did you remove all the clichés and slang from your term paper?"

"Like, totally, dude!"

OFFENSIVE LANGUAGE

The last thing you want to do when you write is offend your reader, even if you are writing a complaint. As we've seen, some words occasionally used in speech are *always* inappropriate in writing. Swear words, for example, are unacceptable in a written message. So are obscene words, even mild ones.

Offensive language appears much stronger in print than in speech. It can shock and outrage a reader. Racist language and blasphemy (the use of names or objects that are sacred to any religion) are always unacceptable and deeply offensive.

Many writers have suffered the embarrassment of having a message read by someone for whom the message was not intended. What may seem when you write it to be an innocent joke or an emphatic expression could, if it is read by someone other than the person you sent it to, prove shocking to readers and mortifying to you. Before you send an angry email, save it as a draft and reread it later. You may decide to tone it down. And make sure you don't accidentally hit Reply All when you intend to reply only to a message's sender. Always THINK before you click Send.

Language has power. Our language shapes as well as reflects our attitudes and values. People who use racist, blasphemous, sexist, or profane terms reinforce the attitudes reflected by those terms and project a negative image to their readers.

ABUSAGES

Some words and phrases, even ones we hear in everyday speech, are *always* incorrect in written English. Technically, they are also incorrect in speech, but most people tolerate them as part of the casual standard that is common in informal conversation. If these expressions appear in your writing, your reader will assume you are uneducated, careless, or both. In some conversations, particularly in academic and professional environments, these expressions make a poor impression on your listeners.

Carefully read through the following list and highlight any words or phrases that sound correct to you. These are the ones you need to find and fix when you revise.

alot	There is no such word. Use *much* or *many*. (*A lot* is acceptable in informal usage.)
anyways (anywheres)	The *s* on these words betrays the writer as uneducated.
between you and I	A very common error. Use *between you and me*.
can't hardly (couldn't hardly)	The correct expression is *can* (or *could*) *hardly*.
could of (would of, should of)	Using the preposition *of* instead of the auxiliary verb *have* in these verb phrases is a common

	error. Write *could have, would have,* and *should have.*
didn't do nothing	All double negatives are errors. Some familiar examples are *couldn't see nothing, won't go nowhere,* and *can't find nobody.* Write *didn't do anything, couldn't see anything, won't go anywhere,* and *can't find anybody.*
good *used as an adverb*	"How are you?" "I'm good." This all-too-common expression is incorrect (unless you mean to say that you are moral or ethical or saintly). If you want to say that you are healthy, then say, "I'm *well.*"
irregardless	There is no such word. *Regardless* is the word you may want, but check your thesaurus for other, possibly more appropriate, choices.
media *used as singular*	The word *media* is plural. It is incorrect to say, "Television is a mass media." It is a mass *medium.* Newspapers, magazines, and the Internet are mass *media.* Radio is an electronic *medium.*
off of	Use *off* by itself. "I fell *off* the wagon." Or use *from*: "I fell *from* the wagon."
prejudice *used as an adjective*	It is incorrect to write "She is *prejudice* against blonds." Use *prejudiced.*
prejudism	There is no such word. Use *prejudice* (a noun): "He showed *prejudice* in awarding the prize to his daughter."
real *used as an adverb*	*Real good, real bad,* and *real nice* are not acceptable. You could use *really* or *very* and be correct, but such filler words add nothing to your meaning.
the reason is because	Write *the reason is that*: "The reason is that my dog ate my essay."
sort of speak	If you *must* use this expression, get the words right: "So to speak."
suppose to	Like *use to,* this phrase is incorrect. Write *supposed to* and *used to.*

themselfs   Also *ourselfs, yourselfs*. The plural of *self* is
                             selves: ourselves, yourselves, and *themselves*.
                             Theirselves is non-standard English and is not
                             used by educated speakers and writers.

youse   There is no such word. *You* is both the sin-
                             gular and the plural form of the second-
                             person pronoun. While occasionally heard in
                             restaurants or retail stores, "Can I help
                             youse?" labels the speaker as uneducated.

EXERCISE **1.11**

Working with a partner, revise the following sentences to eliminate any
abusages. Then compare your revisions with our suggestions on page 503.

1. Alot of my friends are real happy to be going away to college, but I would
   rather stay home and live with my family.
2. For this party, you are suppose to dress the way you did in primary school.
3. Irregardless of what you say, I think the mass media is generally reliable.
4. Many young people prefer to read the news off of their smartphones.
5. The reason for this preference is because smartphones offer real quick and
   convenient access to information.
6. Between you and I, I rely on television to tell me what's going on in the
   world.
7. The reason youse are failing is because you don't do no homework.
8. Luisa's father isn't prejudice; he can't hardly stand none of her boyfriends.
9. George shouldn't be driving anywheres; we should of taken his car keys
   off of him.
10. Our instructor doesn't have no patience with people who should of been
    coming to class and now can't write real well.

EXERCISE **1.12**

Eliminate the 15 abusages from the following passage. No answers are in the
back of the book for this exercise, but your instructor will provide them.

When I get up, I can barely move until I get my first cup of strong coffee. I
like my coffee real strong—strong enough to peel the glaze off of the cup. Over
the years, I have become use to my morning caffeine jolt, and now my body
depends on it to get going. Between you and me, I could cut back on my

morning coffee, I suppose, but I enjoy the taste of it so much that I don't really want to do nothing that would deprive me of its pleasure.

There are alot of people who are more addicted to caffeine than I am: some of my friends can't hardly get through the day without 10 or more cups. I believe the media is at least partly responsible for our addiction because of how it promotes caffeine-laden drinks. Advertisements imply that these drinks are suppose to be good for us. One of my former classmates always carried high-caffeine soft drinks in her backpack when she could of been carrying fruit juice or water. Halfway through the term, she got sick and had to drop out. I am convinced the reason was because of her caffeine addiction.

I guess caffeine is like anything else: fine in moderation but dangerous in excess. Anyways, until some study proves us wrong, my friends and I will enjoy our caffeine fixes, comforting ourselfs with the knowledge that there are alot of worse addictions.

2 | Hazardous Homonyms

This chapter focuses on **homonyms**—words that sound alike or look alike and are easily confused: *accept* and *except*; *weather* and *whether*; *whose* and *who's*; *affect* and *effect*. Your word processor will not help you find spelling mistakes in these words because the correct spelling depends on the sentence in which you use the word. If you use the wrong one, you'll muddle the meaning of the sentence and throw your reader off-track. For example, if you write, "Meat me hear inn halve an our," no spell checker will find fault with your sentence, and no reader will understand what you're talking about.

Below you will find a list of the most common homonym hazards. Only some of the words in this list will cause you trouble. Careful pronunciation can sometimes help you tell the difference between words that are often confused. For example, if you pronounce the words *accept* and *except* differently, you'll be less likely to use the wrong one when you write. It's also useful to make up memory aids to help you remember the difference in meaning between words that sound or look alike. The list that follows includes several examples that we hope you will find helpful.

 Make your own list of problem pairs and keep it where you can easily refer to it. Tape it inside the cover of your dictionary or post it over your computer. Get into the habit of checking your document against your list every time you write.

accept/ **except**	*Accept* means "take" or "receive." It is always a verb. *Except* means "**ex**cluding." I *accepted* the spelling award, and no one *except* my mother knew I cheated.
advice/ **advise**	The difference in pronunciation makes the difference in meaning clear. *Advise* (rhymes with *wise*) is a verb. *Advice* (rhymes with *nice*) is a noun. I *advise* you not to listen to free *advice*.
affect/ **effect**	*Affect* as a verb means "to change." Try substituting *change* for the word you've chosen in your sentence. If it makes sense, then *af-FECT* is the word you want. As a noun, *AF-fect* means "a strong feeling." *Effect* is a noun meaning "result." If

you can substitute *result,* then *effect* is the word you need. Occasionally, *effect* is used as a verb meaning "to bring about."

> Learning about the *effects* (results) of caffeine *affected* (changed) my coffee-drinking habits.
> Depressed people often display an inappropriate *affect* (feeling).
> Antidepressant medications can *effect* (bring about) profound changes in mood.

**allusion/
illusion**

An *allusion* is an implied or indirect reference. An *illusion* is something that appears to be real or true but is not what it seems. It can be a false impression, idea, or belief.

> Many literary *allusions* can be traced to the Bible or to Shakespeare.
> A good movie creates an *illusion* of reality.

a lot/allot

A lot (often misspelled *alot*) should be avoided in formal writing. Use *many* or *much* instead. *Allot* (*al-LOT*) means "distribute" or "assign."

>   *many*   *much*
> He still has ~~a lot of~~ problems, but he is coping ~~a lot~~ better.
> The teacher will *allot* the marks according to the difficulty of the questions.

are/our

Are is a verb. *Our* shows ownership. Confusion of these two words often results from careless pronunciation.

> Where *are our* leaders?

beside/besides *Beside* is a preposition meaning "by the side of" or "next to." *Besides* means "also" or "in addition to."

> One evening with Mario was more than enough. *Besides* expecting me to buy the tickets, the popcorn, and the drinks, he insisted on sitting *beside* Lisa rather than me.

choose/chose Pronunciation gives the clue here. *Choose* rhymes with *booze,* is a present tense verb, and means "select." *Chose* rhymes with *rose,* is a past tense verb, and means "selected."

> Please *choose* a topic.
> I *chose* to write about fuel-cell technology.

cite/sight/site   To *cite* means "to quote from" or "to refer to."

> A lawyer *cites* precedents; writers *cite* their sources in articles or research papers; and my friends *cite* my texts as examples of comic writing.

Sight means "vision," the ability to see. It can also mean "something that is visible or worth seeing."

> She lost her *sight* as the result of an accident.
> With his tattoos and piercings, Izzy was a *sight* to behold.

A *site* is the location of something: a building, a town, or a historic event.

> The *site* of the battle was the Plains of Abraham, which lie west of Québec City.

coarse/course   *Coarse* means "rough, unrefined." (The slang word *arse* is co**arse**.) For all other meanings, use *course*.

> That sandpaper is too *coarse* to use on a lacquer finish.
> *Coarse* language only weakens your argument.
> Of *course* you'll do well in a *course* on the history of pop music.

**complement/
compliment**   A *complement* completes something. *A compliment* is a gift of praise.

> A glass of wine would be the perfect *complement* to the meal.
> Some people are embarrassed by *compliments*.

**conscience/
conscious**   Your *conscience* is your sense of right and wrong. *Conscious* means "aware" or "awake"—able to feel and think.

> After Ann cheated on the test, her *conscience* bothered her.
> Ann was *conscious* of having done wrong.
> The injured man was *unconscious*.

**consul/council/
counsel**   A *consul* is a government official stationed in another country. A *council* is an assembly or official group. Members of a *council* are *councillors*. *Counsel* can be used to mean both "advice" and "to advise."

> The Canadian *consul* in Venice was helpful.
> The Women's Advisory *Council* meets next month.

Maria gave me good *counsel.*
She *counselled* me to hire a lawyer.

desert/dessert A *DE-sert* is a dry, barren place. As a verb, *de-SERT* means "to abandon" or "to leave behind." *Des-SERT* is the part of a meal you'd probably like an extra helping of, so give it an extra *s*.

The tundra is Canada's only *desert* region.
If you *desert* me, I'll be all alone.
I can't resist any *dessert* made with chocolate.

dining/dinning You'll spell *dining* correctly if you remember the phrase "wining and dining." You'll probably never use *dinning*, which means "making a loud noise."

The dog is not supposed to be in the *dining* room.
We are *dining* out tonight.
The noise from the karaoke bar was *dinning* in our ears.

does/dose Pronunciation provides the clue. *Does* rhymes with *buzz* and is a verb. *Dose* rhymes with *gross* and refers to a quantity of medicine.

Josef *does* drive fast, *doesn't* he?
My grandmother used to give me a *dose* of cod liver oil every spring.

forth/fourth *Forth* means "**for**ward." *Fourth* contains the number **four**, which gives it its meaning.

Please stop pacing back and *forth*.
The Raptors lost their *fourth* game in a row.

hear/here *Hear* is what you do with your **ear**s. *Here* is used for all other meanings.

Now *hear* this!
Ranjan isn't *here*.
Here is your assignment.

it's/its *It's* is a shortened form of *it is*. The apostrophe takes the place of the *i* in *is*. If you can substitute *it is*, then *it's* is the form you need. If you can't substitute *it is*, then *its* is the correct word.

It's really not difficult. (*It is* really not difficult.)

The book has lost *its* cover. ("The book has lost it is cover" makes no sense, so you need *its*.)

It's is also commonly used as the shortened form of *it has*. In this case, the apostrophe takes the place of the *h* and the *a*.

It's been a bad month for new car sales.

knew/new	*Knew* is the past tense of *know*. *New* is an adjective meaning "having recently come into being," "fresh," or "original."

We *knew* our *new* pool would attract friends just as surely as fruit attracts flies.
Who would have thought that cropped pants, a style from the 1950s, would be considered a *new* fashion 60 years later?

know/no	*Know* is a verb meaning "to understand" or "to recognize." *No* can be used as an adverb to express refusal or denial, or as an adjective to express a negative state or condition.

No, we do not *know* the results of the test yet.
Why are there *no* cookies left in the jar?

later/latter	*Later* rhymes with *gator*, refers to time, and has the word *late* in it. *Latter* rhymes with *fatter*, means "the second of two," and has two *t*s. It is the opposite of *former*.

See you *later*, alligator.
You take the former, and I'll take the *latter*.

lead/led	*Lead* is pronounced to rhyme with *speed* and is the present tense of the verb *to lead*. (*Led* is the past tense of the same verb.) The only times you pronounce *lead* as "led" is when you are referring to the writing substance in a pencil or to the metal used to make bullets or leaded windows.

You *lead*, and I'll decide whether to follow.
Your suitcase is so heavy it must be filled with either gold or *lead*.

loose/lose	Pronunciation is the key to these words. *Loose* rhymes with *moose* and means "not tight" or "unrestricted." *Lose* rhymes with *ooze* and means "misplace" or "be defeated."

There's a screw *loose* somewhere.
When Moosehead beer is served, people say, "The moose is *loose!*"
Some are born to win, some to *lose.*
You can't *lose* on this deal.

miner/minor   A *miner* works in a **mine.** *Minor* means "lesser" or "not important" or "a person who is not legally an adult."

Liquor can be served to *miners*, but not if they are *minors*.
For some people, spelling is a *minor* problem.

moral/morale   Again, pronunciation provides the clue you need. *MO-ral* refers to the understanding of what is right and wrong; *mo-RALE* refers to the spirit or mental condition of a person or group.

Most religions are based on a *moral* code of behaviour.
Despite his shortcomings, he is basically a *moral* man.
Low *morale* is the reason for our employees' absenteeism.

passed/past   *Passed* is the past tense of the verb *pass*, which has several meanings, most of which have to do with movement on land or water, but some of which have to do with sports or games. *Past* describes something that happened or existed in an earlier time. *Passed* is always a verb; *past* can be a noun, adjective, adverb, or preposition, but it is never a verb.

George *passed* the puck to Henry, who slammed it *past* the goalie to win the game.

peace/piece   *Peace* is what we want on **Ea**rth. *Piece* means "a part or portion of something," as in "a **pie**ce of **pie**."

Everyone hopes for *peace* in the Middle East.
A *piece* of the puzzle is missing.

personal/ personnel   *PER-sonal* means "priv**a**te." *Personnel* (*person-NEL*) refers to the group of people working for a particular employer or to the office responsible for maintaining employees' records.

The letter was marked "*Personal* and Confidential."
We are fortunate to have highly qualified *personnel*.

principal/ principle   *Principal* means "m**a**in." A *principle* is a ru**le**.

A *principal* is the main administrator of a school.
The federal government is the *principal* employer in
Summerside, P.E.I.
The *principal* and the interest totalled more than I could pay.
(In this case, the principal is the main amount of money.)
One of our instructor's *principles* is to refuse to accept late
assignments.

quiet/quite   If you pronounce these words carefully, you won't confuse
them. *Quiet* has two syllables (kwy-et); *quite* has only one
(kwyt).

The chairperson asked us to be *quiet*.
We had not *quite* finished our assignment.

stationary/   *Stationary* means "fixed in place." *Stationery* is writing paper.
stationery

A *stationary* bicycle will give you a good cardio workout
without stressing your knees.
Please order a new supply of *stationery*.

than/then   *Than* is used in comparisons: bigger than, better than, slower
than, etc. Pronounce it to rhyme with *can*. *Then* refers to
time and rhymes with *when*.

Kim is a better speller *than* I.
I'd rather be here *than* there.
Pay me first, and *then* you can have my notes.

their/there/   *Their* indicates ownership. **There** points out something or
they're   indicates place. It includes the word **here**, which also indicates place. *They're* is a shortened form of *they are*. (The apostrophe replaces the *a* in *are*.)

It was *their* fault.
There are two weeks left in the term.
Let's walk over *there*.
They're late, as usual.

threw/through *Threw* is the past tense of the verb *throw*. *Through* can be used
as a preposition, adjective, or adverb, but never as a verb.

James *threw* the ball *through* the kitchen window. When
he climbed *through* to fetch it, his mother angrily told him
that his days of playing catch in the yard were *through*.

too/two/to The *too* with an extra *o* in it means "more than enough" or "also." *Two* is the number after one. For all other meanings, use *to*.

> It's *too* hot, and I'm *too* tired *to* go for another hike.
> There are *two* sides *to* every argument.
> The *two* women knew *too* much about each other *to* be friends.

wear/were/ where/we're If you pronounce these words carefully, you won't confuse them. *Wear* rhymes with *pear* and can be a noun or a verb. *Were* rhymes with *purr* and is a verb. *Where* is pronounced "hwear," includes the word *here*, and indicates place. *We're* is a shortened form of *we are* and is pronounced "weer."

> After 360,000 km, you shouldn't be surprised that your car is showing signs of *wear* and tear.
> What should I *wear* to the wedding?
> You *were* joking, *weren't* you?
> *Where* did you want to meet?
> *We're* on our way.

weather/ whether *Weather* refers to climatic conditions: temperature and humidity, for example. *Whether* means "if" and is used in indirect questions or to introduce two alternatives.

> We're determined to go camping this weekend, no matter what the *weather* is like. We'll pack enough gear to be prepared *whether* it rains or it shines.

who's/whose *Who's* is a shortened form of *who is* or *who has*. If you can substitute *who is* or *who has* for the *who's* in your sentence, then you have the right spelling. Otherwise, use *whose*.

> *Who's* coming to dinner? (*Who is* coming to dinner?)
> *Who's* been sleeping in my bed? (*Who has* been sleeping in my bed?)
> *Whose* paper is this? ("*Who is* paper is this" makes no sense, so you need *whose*.)

woman/ women Confusing these two is guaranteed to irritate your women readers. *Woman* is the singular form; compare **man**. *Women* is the plural form; compare **men**.

> Only one *woman* responded to our ad.
> Our company sponsors both a *women*'s team and a men's team.

you're/your   *You're* is a shortened form of *you are*. If you can substitute *you are* for the *you're* in your sentence, then you're using the correct form. If you can't substitute *you are*, use *your*.

> *You're* welcome. (*You are* welcome.)
> Unfortunately, *your* hamburger got burned. ("You are hamburger got burned" makes no sense, so *your* is the word you want.)

In the exercises that follow, choose the correct word. If you don't know an answer, go back and reread the explanation. Check your answers after each set. Answers for exercises in this chapter begin on page 504.

EXERCISE **2.1**

1. Biology is a (coarse/course) that I should be able to pass easily.
2. My sister is a (woman/women) who (heres/hears) everything and forgets nothing.
3. (Who's/Whose) stereo is disturbing our (quiet/quite) meditation time?
4. (They're/Their) still in bed because they stayed up (to/too) late.
5. This college values (its/it's/its') students.
6. I'd like to (lose/loose) five kilograms before summer, but I can't resist (deserts/desserts).

EXERCISE **2.2**

1. (Its/It's) the perfect (site/sight) for our annual meeting.
2. Our math teacher won't (accept/except) assignments submitted (later/latter) than Thursday.
3. Our (moral/morale) was boosted by the (compliments/complements) we received.
4. (They're/Their) love of junk food is having an (effect/affect) on their health.
5. It was the (fourth/forth) quarter of the game, and we (lead/led) by 20 points.

EXERCISE **2.3**

1. Is there anyone (who's/whose) (advice/advise) you will pay attention to?
2. (Your/You're) confidence in statistics is an (allusion/illusion).
3. My (conscious/conscience) sometimes troubles me when I send long (personnel/personal) messages on the office computer.

4. It's (your/you're) turn to get more (stationary/stationery) from the store-room.
5. I believe in the (principle/principal) of fairness more (than/then) the deterrent of punishment.

EXERCISE **2.4**

1. We (lead/led) the relief workers to the (sight/site) of the disaster.
2. She (cited/sited) my writing in her new book on the (effects/affects) of poor grammar.
3. If we (except/accept) your (council/counsel), will you guarantee our success?
4. He was dizzy but (conscience/conscious) after falling off his (stationery /stationary) bike.
5. At the checkpoint, I was hit on the head and (than/then) dragged out into the (desert/dessert).

Go to Web Exercises 2.1, 2.2

EXERCISE **2.5**

1. (Choose/Chose) carefully, because the candidate who is chosen is bound to change (are/our) environment.
2. This company makes a better product (then/than) any of (it's/its) competitors does.
3. According to Woody Allen, "The (moral/morale) is that money is better (then/than) poverty, if only for financial reasons."
4. Rita was (conscious/conscience) that Yuri's (compliments/complements) were never sincere.
5. When someone says, "(It's/Its) not the money but the (principle/principal) of the thing," it's the money. (Elbert Hubbard)

EXERCISE **2.6**

Find and correct the 15 errors in the following sentences.

1. Other then hope and pray that voters will chose our candidate, there is not much more we can do.
2. She's quiet sure that the committee will except her resumé, even though its late and written on lined stationary.

3. The streets were desserted, and as we drove threw, we past only a police officer and a stray dog.

4. Not knowing whether to except the company's offer, I asked my lawyer for advise; she sighted previous settlements that convinced me to turn it down.

5. Blindfolded, my wrists and ankles bound with duct tape, I was lead to the car and driven out into the dessert, were I was left by the side of the road.

EXERCISE **2.7**

1. Weather at work or at home, people should no it's best to avoid using course language.

2. All employees, without acception, will be fined $20.00 a day until moral on the job cite improves.

3. The advise given to us by the personnel firm we hired was to chose a women who's principle qualifications were a huge ego and shoes that complimented her outfits.

4. Emily is the supervisor whose responsible for monitoring the affects of automation on assembly-line personal.

EXERCISE **2.8**

Find and correct the 10 errors in the following paragraph.

I had a hard time chosing between two colleges, both of which offered the coarses I wanted. Both had good placement records, and I just couldn't make up my mind. I asked my friends for advise, but they were no help. Several were surprised that any college would even except me! Their negative view of my academic ability did nothing to improve my moral; in fact, it lead me to re-evaluate my selection of friends. My school counsellor, a women who's opinion I respect, didn't think one college was better then the other, so she suggested that I choose the school that was located were I preferred to live. I followed her advice, and I haven't regretted it.

EXERCISE **2.9**

Find and correct the 15 errors in the following paragraph.

Many people today are chosing a quieter way of life. They hope to live longer and more happily by following the "slower is better" principal. Some, on the advise of they're doctors, have been forced to slow down. One heart surgeon, for example, tells his patients to drive only in the slow lane rather then use the passing lane. They may arrive a few minutes later, but their blood pressure will not be effected. Others don't need to be prompted by their doctors. They except that living at a slower pace doesn't mean loosing out in any way. In fact, the opposite is true: chosing a healthy lifestyle benefits everyone. Piece and quite in one's personnel life lead to increased productivity, higher moral, and greater job satisfaction. Sometimes the improvements are miner, but as anyone who has consciencely tried to slow the pace of life can tell you, the slow lane is the fast lane to longevity.

Go to Web Exercises 2.3, 2.4

EXERCISE **2.10**

Below is a list of word pairs that are often confused. Use each word in a sentence that clearly differentiates it from the word or words that have a similar sound. Use your dictionary to help you. When you are finished, exchange papers with another student and check each other's work. No answers are given for this exercise.

1. altar, alter
2. breath, breathe

3. capital, capitol
4. stake, steak

5. waist, waste   8. emigrate, immigrate
6. chord, cord   9. hoard, horde
7. cloths, clothes   10. precede, proceed

EXERCISE **2.11**

This exercise is more challenging. All the words in the following passage are correctly spelled. The problem is that 20 of them are the wrong words—they don't mean what the writer intended. Can you solve the puzzle by supplying the right words?

Between 1946 and 1964, about 90 million people were born in North America. Known as "baby boomers," this group, which now constitutes one-third of Canada's population, has had a greater affect on society then any previous generation. As anyone in marketing or retail knows, boomers have been big consumers, thanks to there parents, who tasted wealth for the first time after the Depression and World War II. They're buying power made corporate giants of Coca-Cola, McDonald's, Levi Strauss, and Bell; latter, IBM would join the club. Whatever products and services were knew, weather related to fitness, health, beauty, or home decorating, boomers bought them and made millionaires of inventors of everything from Clearasil to Frisbees. Of course, they were buying only the allusion of beauty or fitness, but theirs was a supremely image-conscience era.

The baby boomers profoundly effected popular music, to, embracing rock and roll in all it's forms and making stars of performers as diverse as Elvis Presley, Tiny Tim, Diana Ross, Stevie Wonder, and the Beatles. Their sometimes fickle enthusiasms lead to short-lived celebrity status for other musicians who's music made a brief impact and than disappeared.

The boomers themselves where shaped by the assassination of President John F. Kennedy, the Vietnam War, the moon landing, Woodstock, and Canada's Centennial. However, the most profound influence on the men and woman of the generation was not an event but the gradual introduction of television into every home. This was the first generation to experience television as the dominant mass medium, and it's influence on everything from fashion to career goals, from family dinning to family dynamics, cannot be overestimated. Like it or not (and many resent the huge influence of the boomer generation), we still are living in a world largely shaped by their interests, values, morales, and whims.

3 The Apostrophe

What, you may ask, is a chapter on apostrophes doing in a unit on words? Why isn't it in Unit 4 with the other punctuation marks? Here's the reason: while all other punctuation marks show the intended relationship among parts of a sentence, apostrophes show the relationship between two words (in a possessive construction) or two parts of one word (in a contraction). Misused apostrophes change the meaning of words, and that is why we are discussing them here.

Can you spot how this sentence from a letter of application revealed the applicant's poor writing skills?

> I would like to contribute to you're companies success as it enters it's second decade of outstanding service to customer's.

Misused apostrophes can confuse, amuse, and sometimes annoy readers. Using them correctly is an indication that the writer is competent and careful. The example above contains four apostrophe errors, which irritated the reader so much that the applicant didn't even make it to the interview stage.

- Sometimes you need an apostrophe so that your reader can understand what you mean. For example, there's a world of difference between these two sentences:

  The instructor began class by calling the students' names.
  The instructor began class by calling the students names.

- In most cases, however, misused apostrophes just amuse or annoy an alert reader:

  The movie had it's moments.
  He does a days work every week.
  The Conservative's thank you for your contribution.

It isn't difficult to avoid such mistakes. Correctly used, the apostrophe indicates either **contraction** or **possession**. It never makes a singular word plural. These three sentences show you where to use—and not use—apostrophes:

1. The dog's chasing cars again. (Contraction: *dog's = dog is*)
2. The dog's bark is more reliable than the doorbell. (Possessive: the bark belongs to the dog)
3. The dogs bark incessantly. (Plural: no apostrophe)

Learn the rules that govern these uses, and you'll have no trouble with apostrophes.

CONTRACTION

Contraction is the combining of two words into one, as in *they're* or *can't*. Contractions are common in conversation and in informal written English. You should, however, avoid overusing contractions in the writing you do for college or work.

> When two words are combined into one, and one or more letters are left out, the apostrophe goes in the place of the missing letter(s).

Here are some examples.

I am	→ I'm	they are	→ they're
we will	→ we'll	it is	→ it's
she is	→ she's	it has	→ it's
do not	→ don't	who has	→ who's

Harmon Silas, calculating the thousand words his picture is worth, wonders what to do with contractions.

EXERCISE **3.1**

Place apostrophes correctly in these words, which are intended to be contractions. Notice that when the apostrophe is missing, the word often has a different meaning. Answers for exercises in this chapter begin on page 505.

1. cant   *Can't*
2. shed   *She'd*
3. hell   *he'll*
4. wed   *wed*
5. whos   *whos*

6. shell   *she'll*
7. wont   *won't*
8. well   *we'll*
9. lets   *let's*
10. Im   *I'm*

EXERCISE **3.2**

Make these sets of words into contractions.

1. they are   *they're*
2. I will   *I'll*
3. it has   *It's*
4. cannot   *can't*
5. everyone is   *everyone's*

6. could not   *Could't* *Couldn't*
7. who has   *Who's*
8. you are   *You're*
9. we would   *we'd*
10. will not   *will'n* *won't*

Go to Web Exercises 3.1, 3.2

EXERCISE **3.3**

Correct these sentences by placing apostrophes where they are needed.

1. Its almost certain that hell be late.

2. There wont be a problem if youre on time.

3. Im sure that contractions shouldnt be used in formal writing.

4. They're acceptable in conversation and in informal writing.

5. Well help you with your essay, but youll have to get started right away.

6. Its not that Im afraid to die; I just dont want to be there when it happens. (Woody Allen)

7. We havent yet decided whom to hire, but well let you know as soon as possible.

8. In my culture, a birthdays the most important day of the year, and anyone whos celebrating is the centre of attention.

9. Its just too much of a coincidence that youre leaving for a two-week holiday the day before your great-aunt Deena arrives for her annual visit.

10. If you cant be a good example, maybe youll be a horrible warning.

EXERCISE **3.4**

In some formal kinds of writing—academic, legal, and technical, for example—contractions are not acceptable. A good writer is able not only to contract two words into one but also to expand any contraction into its original two-word phrase. In the following paragraph, find and expand the contractions into their original form.

I'm writing to apply for the position of webmaster for BrilloVision.com that you've advertised in the *Daily News*. I've got the talent and background you're looking for. Currently, I work as a web designer for an online publication, Vexed.com, where they're very pleased with my work. If you click on their website, I think you'll like what you see. There's little in the way of web design and application that I haven't been involved in during the past two years. But it's time for me to move on to a new challenge, and BrilloVision.com promises the kind of opportunity I'm looking for. I guarantee you won't be disappointed if I join your team!

POSSESSION

The apostrophe is also used to show ownership or possession. Here's the rule that applies in most cases.

> If the owner word is singular, add 's to indicate possession.
> If the owner word is plural and ends in *s*, add only an apostrophe.

Here are some examples that illustrate the rule.

singer + 's = singer's voice   women + 's = women's voices
band + 's = band's instruments   James + 's = James's attitude
players + 's = players'$ uniforms   students + 's = students'$ report cards
ships + 's = ships'$ sails   colleges + 's = colleges'$ teams

To form a possessive, first find the word in the sentence that identifies the owner. Then decide if the owner is singular or plural. For example, "the supervisors duties" can have two meanings, depending on where you put the apostrophe:

the supervisor's duties (the duties belong to one *supervisor*)
the supervisors' duties (the duties belong to two or more *supervisors*)

> To solve an apostrophe problem, follow this two-step process:
> 1. Find the owner word.
> 2. Apply the possession rule.

Problem: Marias hair is a mess.
Solution: 1. The owner word is *Maria* (singular).
               2. Add 's to *Maria*.

   Maria's hair is a mess.

Problem: The technicians strike stopped our production.
Solution: 1. The owner word is *technicians* (plural).
               2. Add an apostrophe to *technicians*.

The *technicians'* strike stopped our production.

Sometimes the meaning of your sentence is determined by where you put the apostrophe.

Problem: The writer was delighted by the critics response to her book.

You have two possibilities to choose from, depending on your meaning.

Solution A: 1. The owner word is *critic* (singular).
           2. Add *'s* to *critic.*

The writer was delighted by the *critic's* response to her book.

Solution B: 1. The owner word is *critics* (plural).
           2. Add an apostrophe to *critics.*

The writer was delighted by the *critics'* response to her book.

Both solutions are correct, depending on whether the book was reviewed by one critic (Solution A) or by more than one critic (Solution B).

   Possession does not have to be literal. It can be used to express the notion of "belonging to" or "associated with." That is, the owner word need not refer to a person or group of people. Ideas or concepts (abstract nouns) can be "owners" too.

today's news = the news of today
a month's vacation = a vacation of one month
a year's salary = the salary of one year

EXERCISE **3.5**

In each of the following phrases, make the owner word possessive. Check your answers against ours on page 506.

1. woman beauty

2. witness testimony

3. families budgets

4. children school

5. the soldiers' uniforms

6. the book title

7. everyone choice

8. the Khans daughters

9. the oldest child responsibility

10. our country flag

Go to Web Exercises 3.3, 3.4

A few words, called **possessive pronouns**, are already possessive in form, so they don't have apostrophes.[2]

yours   ours
hers, his, its   theirs
                         whose

The decision is *hers*, not *ours*.
Whose cellphone is ringing, *yours* or *his*?
The puppy has lost *its* bone.

Four possessive words (*its, their, whose,* and *your*) are often confused with the contractions that sound like them. When deciding which spelling to use, expand the contraction into its original two words and try those words in your sentence. If the sentence still makes sense, use the contraction. If it doesn't, use the possessive.

Possessive	**Contraction**
its = *it* owns something	it's = it is/it has
their = *they* own something	they're = they are
whose = *who* owns something	who's = who is/who has
your = *you* own something	you're = you are

Error: They're (they are) going to sing they're (~~they are~~) latest song.
Revision: They're going to sing *their* latest song.

Error: It's (it is) you're (~~you are~~) favourite song.
Revision: It's *your* favourite song.

Error: Who's (~~who is~~) CD are you listening to?
Revision: *Whose* CD are you listening to?

Error: That car has a hole in it's (~~it is~~) muffler.
Revision: That car has a hole in *its* muffler.

---

[2] If you add an apostrophe to any of these words, you create an error. There are no such words as *your's, her's, their's,* or *our's.*

Words

EXERCISE **3.6**

Make the words in parentheses possessive. This exercise will help you discover how well you understand the difference between possessive pronouns and their sound-alike contractions. Check your answers against ours on page 506.

1. (Shahn) greatest fear is his (mother) disapproval.

2. (Students) supplies can be expensive, so I buy mine at (Devi) Dollar Store.

3. My parents would like to know (who) *whose* yogurt has been in (they) *their* fridge for months.

4. After only a (month) wear, my (son) jacket had holes in both sleeves.

5. Unfortunately, the (book) cover was much more interesting than (it) contents.

6. Our (team) *'s* biggest win came at the same time as our (league) other teams all lost.

7. This (month) *Fashion* magazine has two pages on (men) spring clothing and twenty pages on (women).'

8. This year, our (family) Thanksgiving celebration will be a quiet one as we think of other (families) poverty.

9. Our (country) healthcare system, one of (it) greatest assets, needs an overhaul if it is to remain affordable.

10. One way of overcoming writer's block is to disconnect (you) computer from (it) monitor so you can't see (you) draft as you type.

In the two exercises that follow, correct the sentences by placing apostrophes where they are needed in contractions and possessive constructions. Delete any misused apostrophes. Work with a partner in Exercise 3.7, but do Exercise 3.8 on your own. There are 10 errors in each exercise.

EXERCISE **3.7**

1. I've heard that your going to quit smoking.

2. It's true. My family doctors concerns about my health finally convinced me to quit.

3. Whos perfect? I am, at least in my mothers opinion.

4. Its a fact that most mothers' opinions of their children are unrealistically positive.

5. Most fathers' opinions of their daughters boyfriends are negative.

EXERCISE **3.8**

1. Todays' styles and tomorrows trends are featured in this months issue of *Flare* magazine.

2. To find bargains on sale or to sell you're own unwanted items, try eBays Internet site.

3. Hockeys playoff schedule puts the final's into the middle of June.

4. Doctors' stress levels are high, but secretaries' and police officers' stress levels are even higher.

Go to Web Exercise 3.5

PLURALS

The third apostrophe rule is very simple. Memorize it, apply it, and you will instantly correct many of your apostrophe errors.

Never use an apostrophe to make a word plural.

I'm sorry, but shouldn't there be an apostrophe in that?

The plural of most English words is formed by adding *s* to the root word (not *'s*). The *s* alone tells the reader that the word is plural: for example, *memos, letters, files, broadcasts, tweets, newspapers.* If you add an apostrophe + *s*, you are telling your reader that the word is either a contraction or a possessive.

Incorrect: Never use apostrophe's to make word's plural.
Correct: Never use apostrophes to make words plural.

EXERCISE **3.9**

Correct the misused and missing apostrophes in the following sentences. There are 10 errors in this exercise. Check your answers against ours on page 507.

1. When you feel like having a snack, you can choose between apples and Timbit's.

2. Yolandas career took off when she discovered its easy to sell childrens toys.

3. The Olympic Game's are held every two years.

4. Poker's an easy game to play if you are dealt ace's more often than your opponent's are.

5. Nobodies perfect, but if you consistently make apostrophe mistakes, you demonstrate that you don't understand possession and contraction's.

Go to Web Exercises 3.6, 3.7

Correct the misused and missing apostrophes in the three exercises that follow. There are 10 errors in each exercise.

EXERCISE **3.10**

1. Ive posted a sign on my front lawn: "Salesperson's welcome. Dog foods is expensive."

2. The leader's of the European Union country's meet in Brussels.

3. Three months work was wasted by a few minutes carelessness.

4. In Canada, when it's warm enough to expose you're skin to the sun, the insects feeding season is at it's height.

EXERCISE **3.11**

Our well-educated citizen's are one of our countries greatest natural resources. Canada can claim the highest percentage of university- and college-educated people of any country. According to the Organization for

Economic Co-operation and Development, at 48 percent, Canada topped
Japan and New Zealand, who's 41 percent tied for second. Its interesting to
note that the United States (40 percent) and the United Kingdom (32 percent)
placed fourth and tenth respectively, well behind our nations number. Canada
owes its high ranking to our immigrant's level of education. More than half of
our recent immigrants (those who arrived after 2001) came here with a university degree. Thats more than twice the proportion of degree holder's among
the countrys native-born population.

EXERCISE **3.12**

An American guard stopped a Canadian who was crossing the border near
Drummondville, Quebec, on his bicycle and carrying two heavy sack's. The
American demanded to know what was in the sacks, and the Canadians reply
was "Sand." The guards response was to search through the bags thoroughly,
but all he and his colleague's found was sand. On the next days shift, the
border guard saw the cyclist with his sacks again and went through the same
procedure, with the same result. For several week's, the Canadian carrying
sand appeared regularly at the border crossing, and each time the wary guard's
searched the sacks, but they never found anything suspicious. Then the cyclist
did not appear for a couple of weeks, and the guard forgot about the mystery
until one day, when he was off-duty and visiting Drummondville, he saw the
man on the street. He introduced himself and told the man that the guards
were convinced he had been smuggling something, but they couldnt figure
out what it was. Now that the border crossing's had stopped, he begged the
man to tell him what he had been smuggling. The man smiled and replied,
"Bicycle's."

Before you do the mastery test for this chapter, carefully review the information in the Summary box below.

SUMMARY

APOSTROPHE RULES

- When contracting two words into one, put an apostrophe in the place of the missing letter(s).
- Watch for owner words: they need apostrophes.
- To indicate possession, add *'s* to the owner word. (If the owner word is plural and already ends in *s*, just add the apostrophe.)
- Possessive pronouns (e.g., *theirs, its, ours*) do not take apostrophes.
- Never use an apostrophe to form the plural of a word.

EXERCISE **3.13**

This exercise will test your mastery of the apostrophe. There are 15 errors in the following sentences. Find and correct them.

1. If those bag's are your's, then where are our's?

2. Here at Canada College, we aim to meet our students'social need's as well as their academic goal's.

3. In just one week's time, childrens' fashion's will go on sale in our downtown store.

4. We offer a child-care program that let's you drop off your little one's in a professional daycare for only $5.00 an hour.

5. If your husbands the problem, you can drop him off at the Mens' Lounge on the fifth floor, where he can spend the time playing dart's and pinball while you shop until your patience or your money run's out.

4 | Capital Letters

Capital letters belong in a few specific places and nowhere else. Some writers suffer from "capitalitis." They put capital letters on words without thinking about their function in a sentence.

Not many people have this problem. If you are in the majority who generally use capitals correctly, skip this chapter and go on to something else. If you are puzzled about capital letters, though, or have readers who are puzzled by your use of them, read on.

Capitalize the first letter of any word that fits into one of the six categories highlighted below.

> 1. Capitalize the first word of a sentence, a direct quotation, or a sentence from a quoted source.

Are you illiterate? Write to us today for free help.

The novel began, "It was a dark and stormy night."

Lister Sinclair once said, "The only thing Canadians have in common is that we all hate Toronto."

EXERCISE 4.1

Add the seven missing capital letters to the following sentences. Answers for exercises in this chapter begin on page 508.

1. the pen is mightier than the sword.

2. Ping hurried back inside and said, "it's too cold to go to school today."

3. taped to the door was a sign that read, "not to be used as an exit or entrance."

4. in conclusion, I want you to think about the words of Wendell Johnson: "*always* and *never* are two words you should always remember never to use."

5. Our English teacher told us, "learning standard written English is, for most people, like learning another language."

---

2. Capitalize the names of specific people, places, and things.

Names of people (and their titles):

> Shania Twain, Governor General David Johnston, the Reverend Henry Jones, Professor Sandra Chin, Senator Anne Cools, Sergeant Preston, Ms. Akila Hashemi

Names of places, regions, and astronomical bodies (but not general geographic directions):

> Stanley Park, Lake Superior, Cape Breton Island; Nunavut, the Prairies, the Badlands; Saturn, Earth, the planet Mercury, the Asteroid Belt; south, north, east, west

Names of buildings, institutions, organizations, companies, departments, and products:

> the Fairmont Queen Elizabeth Hotel; McGill University, Seneca College; the Liberal Party, the Kiwanis Club; Petro-Canada, Rogers; the Department of English, the Human Resources Department; Kleenex, Volvo, Labatt Blue

EXERCISE **4.2**

Add the 20 capital letters that are missing in the following sentences. Check your answers against ours on page 508.

1. Do you find that visa is more popular than american express when you travel to faraway places such as Mexico, france, or Jupiter?

2. At loblaws, we argued over the cornflakes. Should we buy Kellogg, post, quaker, or president's choice?

3. Our stay at the Seaview hotel, overlooking the pacific ocean, was far better than our last vacation at the bates motel, where we faced west, overlooking the city dump.

4. As a member of the Waterloo alumni association, I am working to raise funds from companies such as disney, toyota, microsoft, and the cbc, where our graduates have been hired.

> 3. Capitalize the names of major historical events, historical periods, religions, holy texts, and holy days.

World War II, the Depression, the Renaissance; Islam, Judaism, Christianity, Buddhism, Hinduism; the Torah, the Koran, the Bible, the Upanishads; Ramadan, Yom Kippur, Easter

EXERCISE **4.3**

Add the 20 capital letters that are missing from the following sentences.

1. The crusades, which were religious wars between muslims and christians, raged through the middle ages.

2. The hindu religion recognizes and honours many gods; islam recognizes one god, allah; buddhism recognizes none.

3. The koran, the bible, and the torah agree on many principles.

4. The jewish festival of hanukkah often occurs near the same time that christians are celebrating christmas.

5. After world war I, many jews began to immigrate to Palestine, where they and the muslim population soon came into conflict.

Go to Web Exercise 4.1

4. Capitalize the days of the week, months of the year, and specific holidays—but not the seasons.

Wednesday; January; Remembrance Day, Canada Day; spring, autumn, winter

EXERCISE **4.4**

The following sentences contain both missing and unnecessary capitals. Find and correct the 15 errors, and then check your answers against ours on page 509.

1. My favourite months are january and february because I love all Winter sports.

2. This monday is valentine's day, when people exchange messages of love.

3. In the summer, big meals seem too much trouble; however, after thanksgiving, we need lots of food to survive the winter cold.

4. A National Holiday named flag day was once proposed, but it was never officially approved.

5. Thursday is canada day and also the official beginning of my Summer Vacation.

5. Capitalize major words in titles (books, magazines, films; essays, poems, songs; works of art; names of websites). Do not capitalize minor words (articles, prepositions, coordinating conjunctions) unless the word is the first or last word in the title.

How Not to Write (book)   *The Thinker* (sculpture)
Of Mice and Men (book, film)   "An Immigrant's Split Personality" (essay)
Maclean's (magazine)   "In Flanders Fields" (poem)
A Room with a View (book, film) *Facebook* (Internet site)

EXERCISE **4.5**

Add the 20 capital letters that are missing from the following sentences, and then check your answers against ours on page 509.

1. Don't you think that the authors of this book could have come up with a more imaginative title for this chapter? Why not "conquering capitals," for example?

2. Joseph Conrad's short novel *heart of darkness* became the blockbuster movie *apocalypse now*.

3. Botticelli's famous painting *birth of venus* inspired my poem "woman on the half shell."

4. The review of my book, *A happy vegan*, published in *the globe and mail*, was not favourable.

5. Clint Eastwood fans will be delighted that one of the early movies that made him internationally famous, *a fistful of dollars*, is now available on dvd.

Pay special attention to this next category. It is one that causes every writer trouble.

> 6. Capitalize the names of specific school courses

Marketing 101, Psychology 100, Mathematics 220, English 110

> but not the names of subject areas

marketing, sociology, mathematics, history, literature, poetry

> unless the subjects are languages or pertain to specific geographical areas.

English, Greek; the study of Chinese history, modern Caribbean literature, Latin American poetry

(Names of languages, countries, and geographical regions are always capitalized.)

EXERCISE **4.6**

Add or remove capital letters where necessary in the following sentences. There are 15 errors in this exercise. Check your answers against ours on page 509.

1. I want to take introductory french this term, but it is not offered until Winter.

2. Although my favourite subject is Math, I'm not doing very well in Professor Truman's course, business finance 101.

3. We began our study of sociology with the concept of relationships.

4. Laurie is studying to be a chef and is taking courses called food preparation, restaurant management, and english.

5. The prerequisite for Theology 210 is introduction to world religions, taught by professor Singh.

Go to Web Exercise 4.2

In the two exercises that follow, correct the spelling by adding or deleting capital letters as necessary.

EXERCISE **4.7**

1. Our youth group meets in the ottawa mosque every second thursday.

2. You must take some Science courses, or you'll never get into the college program you want in the Fall.

3. Gore Vidal, author of *the best man*, once said, "it is not enough to succeed; others must fail."

4. After the game, we went to the burger palace for a late snack and then went home to watch *this Hour Has 22 minutes* on television.

5. In our english course at caribou college, we studied *the englishman's boy*, a novel about life among the settlers of the canadian west.

EXERCISE **4.8**

Sherlock Holmes and his friend dr. watson were on a camping trip in british

columbia's rocky mountains. During the night, Holmes awakened his friend

and said, "Watson, look up. What do you see?"

Watson replied, "I see millions and millions of stars."

"And what does that tell you?" enquired Holmes.

"If I recall correctly, my astronomy 200 course taught me that there are

countless stars, Galaxies and planets. From my knowledge of Astrology, I

observe that taurus is in scorpio. From the position of the planets, I deduce it

is about 3:30 in the morning, and according to my understanding of

Meteorology, it will be a lovely Summer day tomorrow."

Holmes was silent for a moment and then said, "you Idiot, Watson,

someone has stolen our tent!"

EXERCISE **4.9**

This next exercise is the mastery test and contains 25 errors. Before you begin, we suggest you review the six capitalization rules that are highlighted on pages 52–56.

1. Dana loved her Accounting program, but she failed finance 440 in her
   second year and had to attend Summer School.

2. I plan to travel on air Canada to asia next summer to visit sri lanka, india,
   and Pakistan, where I have many relatives.

3. In cambridge, there is a small restaurant near the university where students like to gather. On the wall is a sign that reads, "in case of fire, pay
   bill promptly."

4. During the war of 1812, most of the combatants on both sides were americans since canada at the time was largely settled with immigrants from

the united states. This is why Alan Taylor has called his new book *the 1812 civil war*.

5. One of Canada's most famous painters was Tom Thomson, whose painting *the jack pine* is widely known. He died under mysterious circumstances when his canoe overturned in Algonquin park in 1917. The movie *The far shore* tells his story.

RAPID REVIEW

As a final test of your mastery of the skills you have worked on in Unit 1, correct the 15 errors in the following passage. Check the answers on page 510 to see if you need to review any of the material in Unit 1.

[1]In 1908, travellers in the Nova Scotia wilderness reported being blown away by the cite of a beaver dam because beavers were almost extinct at that time. [2]What a change 100 years has brought! [3]Now, the beaver is so common and so prolific that its being hunted and trapped as a nuisance across Canada. [4]In fact, Canadian trappers are issued a quota for the number of beaver's they are aloud to trap in their territory, and they must reach that quota or loose their trapping licence.

[5]Were not alone in our struggle to control these humongous, pesky rodents. [6]A *Canadian Geographic* film called *The super beaver* documents the creatures introduction to Tierra del Fuego, at the tip of South America, which has led to the complete and total devastation of the ecosystem. [7]The film tells us that only coral and humans have had a greater impact on Earths environment than beavers! [8]They have migrated to the mainland of South America, where without rigorous and expensive government intervention, they threaten to destroy millions of hectares of Argentinas land as they expand their territory northward. [9]It's difficult to except the fact that only 100 years ago, travellers in Canadas wilderness longed for a glimpse of what was then a rare and exotic animal.

UNIT 2

Sentences

QUICK QUIZ

This Quick Quiz will show you which chapters of Unit 2 you need to focus on. The passage below contains a total of 15 errors in sentence structure. You will find one or more examples of sentence fragments, run-ons, misplaced and dangling modifiers, and unparallel constructions. When you've made your corrections, turn to page 511 and compare your revisions with ours. For each error you miss, the Answer Key directs you to the chapter you need to work on.

[1]My heart goes out to anyone struggling to make sense of English idioms. [2]Students are frequently puzzled, often confused, and sometimes find amusement by the thousands of idiomatic expressions. [3]That give flavour and power to our language. [4]An idiom being a phrase whose meaning is difficult to figure out from the meanings of its individual words. [5]For example, the many idioms involving the word *heart*. [6]We describe a kind, generous person as having a "heart of gold," and a cold, unfeeling person as having a "heart of stone," these are relatively simple idioms to understand. [7]But how can we explain the difference between "heartache," which means sorrow or anguish, and "heartburn," which is a term for indigestion? [8]Some "heart" idioms have positive connotations, negative connotations cling to others, and some are neutral, many have to do with love. [9]When falling in love, the expression "lost my heart" is often used. [10]Or loving "from the bottom of my heart." [11]But when the relationship ends, we "cry our hearts out" we are "heartbroken" and our former lover is "heartless."

[12]"Heart" idioms apply to many aspects of life other than love. [13]For example, learning something "by heart." [14]This phrase means you memorize it. [15]If you want something very badly, you have "your heart set on it," to describe someone as "young at heart" means she is youthful in spirit if not in years. [16]To ask someone to "have a heart" meaning to ask for sympathy. [17]Frightened by a scene in a horror movie, the expression "heart-stopping" comes to mind, and you might have "your heart in your mouth" at the terrifying climax.

[18]English idioms using the word *heart* have a bewildering number of meanings that we only discover through experience. [19]People who know the language well understand these phrases automatically. [20]However, if you are still learning English, I advise you to "take heart" and do your best not to "lose heart" when frustrated by our illogical language.

5 Cracking the Sentence Code

A baby's first word is a big step, one that all parents mark as a significant stage of development. Not all parents recognize that an even more significant step in a baby's progress is the first time she puts together the two elements of a complete sentence: a subject and a verb. *Words* enable us to communicate images; *sentences* are the tools with which we communicate ideas.

There is nothing mysterious or difficult about sentences. You've been speaking them successfully since you were a toddler. The difficulty occurs when you try to write—not sentences, oddly enough, but paragraphs. Most college students, if asked to write 10 sentences on 10 different topics, could do so without error. But when those same students write paragraphs, errors such as fragments and run-ons appear. Sometimes these errors cause a communication failure; at other times, they cause the reader to think poorly of the writer.

The solution to sentence-structure problems has two parts.

Be sure every sentence you write
- has both a subject and a verb and
- expresses a complete thought

If English is your first language, test your sentences by reading them aloud. You may be able to tell by the sound whether they are complete and clear. Sometimes, however, your ear may mislead you, so this chapter will show you, step by step, how to decode your sentences to find their subjects and verbs. When you know how to decode sentences, you can make sure that every sentence you write is complete.

Read the following sentences aloud.

Yak skiing is one of Asia's newest sports.
Although yak skiing is still a young sport.

The second "sentence" doesn't sound right, does it? It does not make sense on its own and is in fact a sentence fragment.

Testing your sentences by reading them aloud won't work if you read your paragraphs straight through from beginning to end. The trick is to read from end to beginning. That is, read your last sentence aloud and *listen* to it. If it sounds all right, then read aloud the next-to-last sentence, and so on, until you have worked your way back to the first sentence you wrote.

Now, what do you do with the ones that don't sound correct? Before you can fix them, you need to decode each sentence to find out if it has both a subject and a verb. The subject and the verb are the bare essentials of a sentence. Every sentence you write must contain both. There is one exception:

In a **command**, the subject is suggested rather than stated.

Consider these examples:

Sign here. = [You] sign here. (The subject <u>you</u> is implied or understood.)
Charge it. = [You] charge it.
Play ball! = [You] play ball!

"MY INVENTION IS EVEN MORE REMARKABLE THAN YOURS. IT IS THE SIMPLE DECLARATIVE SENTENCE."

FINDING SUBJECTS AND VERBS[1]

A sentence is about *someone* or *something*. That someone or something is the **subject**. The word (or words) that tells what the subject *is* or *does* is the **verb**. In the following sentences, the subject is underlined once and the verb twice.

> Snow falls.
> Toshiki dislikes winter.
> We love snowboarding.
> Mt. Washington offers excellent opportunities for winter sports.
> In Canada, winter is six months long.
> Some people feel the cold severely.

The subject of a sentence is always a **noun** (the name of a person, place, thing, or concept) or a **pronoun** (a word such as *I, you, he, she, it, we,* or *they* used in place of a noun). In the examples above, the subjects include persons (*Toshiki, we, people*); a place (*Mt. Washington*); a thing (*snow*); and a concept (*winter*). In one sentence, a pronoun (*we*) is the subject.

> Find the verb first.

One way to find the verb in a sentence is to ask what the sentence says about the subject. There are two kinds of verbs:

- **Action verbs** tell you what the subject is doing. In the examples above, *falls, dislikes, love,* and *offers* are action verbs.
- **Linking verbs** link or connect a subject to a noun or adjective describing that subject. In the examples above, *is* and *feel* are linking verbs. Linking verbs tell you the subject's condition or state of being. (For example, "Tadpoles *become* frogs," "Frogs *feel* slimy.") The most common linking verbs are forms of *to be* (*am, is, are, was, were, have been,* etc.) and verbs such as *look, taste, feel, sound, appear, remain, seem,* and *become*.

Another way to find the verb in a sentence is to put a pronoun (*I, you, he, she, it, we,* or *they*) in front of the word you think is the verb. If the result makes sense, it is a verb. For example, you could put *it* in front of *falls* in the first sentence listed above: "It falls" makes sense, so you know *falls* is the verb in this sentence. Try this test with the other five sample sentences.

---

[1] If you have forgotten (or have never learned) the parts of speech and the basic sentence patterns, you will find this information in Appendix A (pages 478–85).

Keep these guidelines in mind as you work through the exercises below:

To find the subject, ask <u>who</u> or <u>what</u> the sentence is about.
To find the verb, ask what the subject <u>is</u> or <u>is doing</u>.

In each of the following sentences, underline the <u>subject</u> with one line and the <u>verb</u> with two. If you make even one mistake, go to the website and do the exercises listed under the Web icon that follows this exercise. Be sure you understand this material thoroughly before you go on. Answers for exercises in this chapter begin on page 512.

EXERCISE **5.1**

1. Canadians love doughnuts.

2. They eat more doughnuts than people in any other nation.

3. Most malls contain a doughnut shop.

4. Doughnuts taste sweet.

5. Glazed doughnuts are my favourite.

6. Hot chocolate is good with doughnuts.

7. Try a bran doughnut for breakfast.

8. It is good for your health.

9. Doughnut jokes are common on television.

10. Dentists like doughnuts too, but for different reasons.

Go to Web Exercises 5.1, 5.2

EXERCISE **5.2**

1. I bought a hybrid car.

2. Hybrids use both electric and gas motors.

3. They normally consume far less gas than other cars.

4. My neighbour drives an SUV.

5. Every day, she takes her children to school.

6. In her SUV, she feels safe in all weather.

7. Last Thursday, it snowed all day long.

8. My neighbour plowed her car into a snowdrift.

9. It became firmly stuck.

10. I drove her children home from school in my little hybrid.

Go to Web Exercise 5.3

Usually, but not always, the subject comes before the verb in a sentence.

Occasionally, we find the subject after the verb:

- in sentences beginning with *Here* + some form of *to be* or with *There* + some form of *to be* (*Here* and *there* are never the subject of a sentence.)

Here are the test results. (Who or what are? Results.)

There is a fly in my soup. (Who or what is? A fly.)

- in sentences that are deliberately inverted for emphasis

Finally, at the end of the long, boring joke came the pathetic punch line.

Out of the stadium and into the rain marched the demonstrators.

- in questions

Are we there yet?

Is she the one?

But notice that in questions beginning with *who, whose, what,* or *which,* the subject and verb are in "normal" order: subject followed by verb.

Who ate my sandwich?   Whose horse came first?

What caused the accident?   Which car uses less gas?

EXERCISE **5.3**

Underline the subject with one line and the verb with two. Watch out for inverted-order sentences. Check your answers against ours on page 512. If you made even one mistake, do the Web exercises that follow this exercise.

1. Is Tomas still on the team?

2. Consider it done.

3. Here are the answers to yesterday's quiz.

4. Is it your birthday today?

5. Into the pool leaped the terrified cat.

6. Where are the children?

7. There were only two students in class today.

8. Which elective is easier?

9. Are you happy with your choice?

10. Who let the dogs out?

Go to Web Exercises 5.4, 5.5

MORE ABOUT VERBS

The verb in a sentence may be a single word, as in the exercises you've just done, or it may be a group of words. When you are considering whether or not a word group is a verb, there are two points you should remember:

1. No verb form preceded by *to* is ever the verb of a sentence.[2]
2. **Helping verbs**[3] are often added to main verbs.

The list below contains the most common helping verbs.

be (all forms, including *am, are, is, was, were, will be, have/had been*)	can do/did may/may have must/must have shall/shall have will/will have	could/could have have/had might/might have ought should/should have would/would have

The complete verb in a sentence consists of the **main verb** + any helping verbs.

Below are a few of the forms of the verb *to take*. Study this list carefully, and note that when the sentence is in question form, the subject comes between the helping verb and the main verb.

We <u>are taking</u> a required
  English course.
You <u>can take</u> it with you.
<u>Could</u> Ravi <u>have taken</u> it?
<u>Did</u> you <u>take</u> your turn?
The money <u>has been taken</u>.
We <u>have taken</u> too much time.
You <u>may take</u> a break now.

We <u>might have taken</u> your advice.
You <u>must take</u> the bus.
Tania <u>ought to have taken</u> a course
  in stress management.
<u>Shall</u> we <u>take</u> his offer?
I <u>should take</u> more time.
We <u>will take</u> the championship.
We <u>should have taken</u> the gold medal.

---

[2] The form *to* + verb (e.g., *to speak, to write, to help*) is an infinitive. Infinitives can act as subjects or objects, but they are never verbs.

[3] If you are familiar with technical grammatical terms, you will know these verbs as **auxiliary verbs**. They also include modal auxiliaries and conditional forms (see Chapter 29).

One verb form ALWAYS requires a helping verb. Here's the rule:

> **A verb ending in *-ing* must have a helping verb (or verbs) before it.**

Here are a few of the forms a verb ending in *-ing* can take.

Mira <u>is taking</u> the test.
<u>Am</u> I <u>taking</u> your place?
You <u>are taking</u> an awfully long time.
Sami <u>will be taking</u> over your duties.
<u>Have</u> you <u>been taking</u> French lessons?

Sentences

EXERCISE **5.4**

Underline the complete verb with a double line. Check your answers against ours on page 513.

1. Your sister <u>is calling</u> from Mexico.

2. Tia <u>will arrive</u> from Finland tomorrow.

3. <u>Have</u> you <u>arranged</u> accommodation for our guests?

4. The restaurant <u>could have prepared</u> a vegetarian meal.

5. They <u>might have moved</u> away from the city.

6. Xue <u>should have completed</u> her diploma by now.

7. <u>Do</u> you <u>know</u> anything about them?

8. They <u>have visited</u> Venezuela twice.

9. We <u>must have practised</u> enough by now.

10. I <u>will be looking</u> for verbs in my sleep.

Go to Web Exercises 5.6, 5.7

Beware of certain words that are often confused with helping verbs:

> Words such as *always, ever, just, never, not, often, only,* and *sometimes* are
> NOT part of the verb.

These words usually appear in the middle of a verb phrase, but they are modifiers, not verbs. Do not underline them.

Sofia is always chosen first.
They have just been married.
That question has never before
  been asked.

Do you ever have doubts about
  your ability?
Will you never learn?
I have often wondered about that.

In the following two exercises, underline the subject with one line and the verb
with two. Check your answers to the first set (see page 513) before going on
to the next.

EXERCISE 5.5

1. I am making a nutritious breakfast.

2. It does not include Coca-Cola.

3. You can add fresh fruit to the cereal.

4. The toast should be almost ready now.

5. My doctor has often recommended yogurt for breakfast.

6. I could never eat yogurt without fruit.

7. With breakfast, I will drink at least two cups of coffee.

8. I don't like tea.

9. I simply cannot begin my day without coffee.

10. I should probably switch to decaf.

EXERCISE 5.6

1. I had never repaired water pipes before.

2. We now get our drinking water by courier.

3. Could you possibly be on time?

4. Have those jeans ever been washed?

5. Money has never come easily to me.

6. Your jokes are not always appreciated.

7. I have sometimes been seen in the library.

8. The librarians have often asked for my ID.

9. There should not be any more delays.

10. Has any turtle ever outlived the shaker of turtle food? (Jerry Seinfeld)

Go to Web Exercises 5.8, 5.9

MORE ABOUT SUBJECTS

Groups of words called **prepositional phrases** often come before the subject in a sentence or between the subject and the verb. When you're looking for the subject, prepositional phrases can trip you up unless you know the following rule:

The subject of a sentence is never in a prepositional phrase.

You must be able to identify prepositional phrases so that you will know where *not* to look for the subject.

A prepositional phrase is a group of words that begins with a **preposition** and ends with a noun or pronoun.

This noun or pronoun is called the **object** of the preposition. It is this word that, if you're not careful, you might think is the subject of the sentence.

Below is a list of prepositional phrases. The highlighted words are prepositions; the words in regular type are their objects.

about your message	**between** them	**near** the wall
above the door	**by** the way	**of** the memo
according to the book	**concerning** your request	**on** the desk
after the meeting	**despite** the shortfall	**onto** the floor
against the wall	**down** the corridor	**over** the page
along the hall	**except** the contract	**through** the window
among the staff	workers	**to** the staff
around the office	**for** the manager	**under** the table
before lunch	**from** the office	**until** the meeting
behind my back	**in** the filing cabinet	**up** the corridor
below the window	**inside** the office	**with** permission
beside my computer	**into** the elevator	**without** the software

Before you look for the subject in a sentence, lightly cross out all prepositional phrases.

A bird ~~in the hand~~ is messy.   (What is messy? The bird, not the hand.)

This deck ~~of cards~~ is unlucky.   (What is unlucky? The deck, not the cards.)

Many houses ~~in our neighbourhood~~ need painting.   (What needs painting? The houses, not the neighbourhood.)

In the following exercises, first cross out the prepositional phrase(s) in each sentence. Then underline the subject with one line and the verb with two. Check your answers for Exercise 5.7 on page 513, and if you made even one error, do Web exercises 5.10 and 5.11 before going on to Exercise 5.8.

EXERCISE **5.7**

1. Many people ~~in the crowd~~ were confused.

2. Fifty ~~of her~~ friends gave her a surprise party.

3. The official opening ~~of the new city hall~~ will be held tomorrow.

4. In the movies, the collision of two cars always results in a fire.

5. A couple of burgers should be enough for each of us.

6. Please decide on dessert before dinnertime.

7. Only a few of us have finished our homework.

8. After class, the people in my car pool meet in the cafeteria.

9. There is a show about laser surgery on television tonight.

10. In the land of the blind, the one-eyed man is king. (Erasmus)

Go to Web Exercises 5.10, 5.11

EXERCISE **5.8**

1. A party in our neighbours' apartment kept us awake until dawn.

2. The meeting of all students in our class solved nothing.

3. From the hallway came the sound of a loud argument.

4. According to the news, the temperature in Yellowknife fell 20°C overnight.

5. My naps in the afternoon are necessary because of my late-night activities.

6. Nothing in this world travels faster than a bad cheque.

7. For many students, lack of money is probably their most serious problem.

8. The plural of *choose* should be *cheese*.

9. After my acceptance to this college, I became interested in learning about the city.

10. My guarantee of an A in this course is valid only under certain conditions.

EXERCISE **5.9**

A recent study by Statistics Canada reveals some disturbing facts about the fitness of Canadians. According to the study, young Canadians spend more than nine hours a day on their backsides. Much of this time, of course, is spent in front of the television. As a result of their lack of exercise, their physical health is suffering. An example of the influence of television occurred in my son's arithmetic class. The teacher was frustrated by the children's lack of attention. Finally, in desperation, she presented a problem to the class in the hope of stimulating them. "What are 2 and 6 and 42 and 31?" One little boy showed enthusiasm by waving his hand in the air. With relief for the sudden interest, the teacher asked the boy for his answer. "NBC, CTV, HBO, and the Sports Network!"

Go to Web Exercises 5.12, 5.13

MULTIPLE SUBJECTS AND VERBS

So far, you have been decoding sentences containing a single subject and a single verb, even though the verb may have consisted of more than one word (a verb phrase). Sentences can, however, have more than one subject and one verb. Multiple subjects are called **compound subjects**; multiple verbs are **compound verbs**.

Here is a sentence with a multiple subject:

French fries and onion rings are Brian's idea of a balanced diet.

This sentence has a multiple verb:

Sherene walks and dresses like a supermodel.

And this sentence contains both a multiple subject and a multiple verb.

Alan and Carlos drove to the mall and shopped for hours.

The parts of a multiple subject are usually joined by *and* or *or*, sometimes by *but* or *nor*. Compound subjects and verbs may contain more than two elements. Look at the following examples.

Clarity, brevity, and simplicity are the basic qualities of good writing.

Raj deleted his work, shut down the computer, unplugged it, and dropped it out the window.

Identify the subjects and verbs in the three exercises that follow. First, cross out any prepositional phrases. Then underline the subjects with one line and the verbs with two. Be sure to underline all elements of a compound (or multiple) subject or verb (there may be more than two). Check your answers to each set (see pages 514–15), and if you've made any errors, do Web exercises 5.14 and 5.15 before you go on to the next exercise.

EXERCISE **5.10**

1. The Flames and the Stampeders call Calgary home.

2. My computer freezes and crashes with regularity.

3. Books can take you anywhere in the world and have more legroom than airplanes.

4. Poutine, tourtière, Nanaimo bars, and butter tarts constitute Canada's contribution to world cuisine.

5. According to some sources, hockey, football, lacrosse, and basketball are also Canadian inventions.

6. Measure the ingredients carefully and mix them thoroughly.

7. Many tobacco farmers, cod fishers, and coal miners are retraining for new careers.

8. The coyote stopped, stared at the small child, and then turned and loped away.

9. You may study my notes and my research results but may not copy my work.

10. Students with good time-management skills can research, organize, draft, and revise a first-class paper by the deadline.

Go to Web Exercises 5.14, 5.15

EXERCISE **5.11**

1. Verbs and subjects are sometimes hard to find.

2. Farmers, loggers, and fishers need and deserve the support of consumers.

3. Open the bottle, pour carefully, taste, and enjoy.

4. Where do you and your roommates get the energy for school, work, and fun?

5. Werner, Italo, and Pierre discussed and debated recipes all night.

6. During the following week, each one chose and prepared a meal for the other two.

7. Werner's sauerbraten and Black Forest cake amazed and delighted his friends.

8. Italo chopped, sliced, simmered, and baked a magnificent Italian meal.

9. Pierre and his sister worked in the kitchen for two days and prepared a delicious cassoulet.

10. By the end of the week, Pierre, Italo, and Werner were ready for a diet.

Go to Web Exercise 5.16

EXERCISE **5.12**

1. A fool and his money are soon parted.

2. I dream of success and worry about failure.

3. Nur and Aman paddled and portaged for 10 days.

4. From the back seat of the tiny car emerged a basketball player and a Newfoundland dog.

5. In the mist of early morning, a brontosaurus and a tyrannosaurus sniffed the moist air and hunted for food.

6. Pack your suitcases and prepare for a magical journey.

7. Why are goalies in hockey and kickers in football so superstitious?

8. In my dreams, the maid, butler, housekeeper, and chef wash the dishes, vacuum the floors, do the laundry, and make the meals.

9. According to the official course outline, students in this English course must take notes during every class and submit their notes to their instructor for evaluation.

10. In the opinion of many Canadians, the word *politician* is a synonym for "crook."

Go to Web Exercise 5.17

Here's a summary of what you've learned in this chapter. Keep it in front of you as you write the Mastery Test.

SUMMARY

SUBJECTS AND VERBS

- The subject is *who* or *what* the sentence is about.
- The verb tells what the subject *is* or *does*.
- The subject normally comes before the verb. (Exceptions are questions, sentences that begin with *here* or *there*, and sentences that begin with one or more prepositional phrases and are inverted for effect.)
- An infinitive (a phrase consisting of *to* + verb) is never the verb of a sentence.
- The complete verb consists of a main verb + any helping verbs.
- By itself, a word ending in *-ing* is not a verb.
- The subject of a sentence is never in a prepositional phrase.
- A sentence can have more than one subject and verb.

EXERCISE **5.13**

This exercise will test your ability to identify subjects and verbs in different kinds of sentences. First, cross out any prepositional phrases. Next, underline the subject(s) with one line and the verb(s) with two. Be sure to underline all elements in a compound subject or verb.

1. Turn the corner, put the past behind you, and get on with life.

2. Of all character traits, sincerity is the most difficult to fake.

3. We bought bread, tomatoes, and lettuce and made sandwiches for the group.

4. Old age may be difficult, but it is better than the alternative.

5. Provide a passport photo and self-addressed return envelope.

6. Many early immigrants to Canada arrived in Halifax and took the train west.

7. For most of the 20th century, they arrived by ship, were cleared through Customs at Pier 21 in Halifax, and were welcomed by hard-working volunteers.

8. Among the hopeful signs in our city are increased overall prosperity, less violent crime, and higher levels of employment.

9. Her lawyer, my lawyer, our accountant, and the mediator picked up the pen in turn, signed the document, and shook our hands.

10. The floors are cold, the windows are drafty, and the roof leaks in my newly purchased dream home.

Sentences

6 Solving Sentence-Fragment Problems

Every complete sentence has two characteristics. It contains a subject and a verb, and it expresses a complete thought. Any group of words that is punctuated as a sentence but lacks one of these characteristics is a **sentence fragment**. Fragments are appropriate in conversation and in some kinds of writing, but normally they are not acceptable in college, technical, or business writing.

There are two kinds of fragments you should watch out for: the "missing piece" fragment and the dependent clause fragment.

"MISSING PIECE" FRAGMENTS

Sometimes a group of words is punctuated as a sentence but is missing one or more of its essential parts: a subject or a verb. Consider the following examples:

1. Found it under the pile of clothes on your floor.
   (<u>Who</u> or <u>what</u> found it? The sentence doesn't tell you. The subject is missing.)

2. Their arguments about housework.
   (The sentence doesn't tell you what the arguments <u>were</u> or <u>did</u>. The verb is missing.)

3. During my favourite TV show.
   (<u>Who</u> or <u>what</u> <u>was</u> or <u>did</u> what? Both the subject and the verb are missing.)

4. The programmers working around the clock to trace the hacker.
   (Part of the verb is missing. Remember that a verb ending in *-ing* needs a helping verb to be complete.)

Finding fragments like these in your work is the hard part. Fixing them is easy. There are two ways to correct sentence fragments. Here's the first one.

> To change a "missing piece" fragment into a complete sentence, add whatever is missing: a subject, a verb, or both.

1. You may need to add a subject:

   Your <u>sister</u> found it under the pile of clothes on your floor.

2. You may need to add a verb:

   Their arguments <u>were</u> about housework. (linking verb)
   Their arguments about housework <u>destroyed</u> their relationship. (action verb)

3. You may need to add both a subject and a verb:

   My <u>mother</u> always <u>calls</u> during my favourite TV show.

4. Or you may need to add a helping verb:

   The programmers <u>are</u> working around the clock to trace the hacker.

Don't let the length of a fragment fool you. Students sometimes think that if a string of words is long, it must be a sentence. Not so. No matter how long the string of words, if it doesn't contain both a subject and a verb, it is not a sentence. For example, here's a description of a woman paddling a canoe on a lake in summertime:

> The paddle dipping into the lake, sliding beneath the surface, and emerging at the end of the stroke, the face of the paddle glistening in the sun and droplets from its edge making a trail in the water as she reaches forward to dip again just as before, repeating the movement hundreds of times, thousands of times, in a hypnotic rhythm that becomes as natural as breathing, as calming as meditation.

At 71 words, this "sentence" is long, but it is a fragment. It lacks both a subject and a verb. If you add "<u>She</u> <u>watches</u>" at the beginning of the fragment, you would have a complete sentence.

THE FIRST SENTENCE FRAGMENT

EXERCISE **6.1**

In the following exercise, decide whether each group of words is a complete sentence or a "missing piece" fragment. Write *S* in the space before each complete sentence and *F* before each fragment. Make each fragment into a complete sentence by adding whatever is missing: a subject, a verb, or both. Then compare your answers with our suggestions. Answers for exercises in this chapter begin on page 515.

1. __X__ One type of sentence-fragment error.

2. __F__ Glad to be able to help you.

3. __X__ Hoping to hear from you soon.

4. __X__ Saved by the bell.

5. __F__ To prevent a similar tragedy from happening again.

6. __F__ Not a good idea.

7. __F__ Attaching a DVD player to the television.

8. __S__ Close the door quietly on your way out.

9. __X__ No choice but to get up early.

10. __S__ Working as a server, for example, can be exhausting.

Go to Web Exercises 6.1, 6.2

Most of us have little difficulty identifying a fragment when it stands alone. But when we write, of course, we write in paragraphs, not in single sentences. Fragments are harder to identify when they occur in a context, as you'll see in the next exercise.

EXERCISE **6.2**

Read the following selections carefully. Decide whether each item contains only complete sentences or if it contains one or more sentence fragments. Write *S* in the space preceding items that contain only sentences. Put *F* beside items that contain fragments. Then check your answers.

1. __S__ This apartment suits me in every way. Except for the price. I can't afford it.

2. _____ In track and field, our college is well respected. Our team won the championship last year. Setting three new provincial records.

3. __S__ Whenever I go fishing, the fish aren't biting, but the mosquitoes are. Maybe I should give up fishing. And start collecting insects instead.

4. __S__ My son is a genius. On his last birthday, he was given a toy that was guaranteed to be unbreakable. Used it to break all his other toys.

5. __F__ We weren't lost, but we were certainly confused. I realized this when we passed City Hall. For the third time.

6. _____ We decided to walk downtown to the coffee shop. Where we both ordered tea, just to be different.

7. _____ My husband and I often go to the hockey arena. Not to watch sports but to hear the concerts of our favourite local bands. These concerts give new meaning to the word *cool*.

8. _____ According to the weather reporter at our local radio station, a storm with high winds and heavy rains is approaching our region. Yesterday, when the temperature hit 0°C, she predicted light snow.

9. _____ I enjoy reading travel books. About faraway, exotic places that I have never visited and will probably never get to see. The fun is in the dreaming, not the doing.

10. _____ Spending my days skiing and the nights dining and dancing. That's how I picture my retirement. Unfortunately, by then I'll be too old to enjoy it.

Once you have learned to identify fragments that occur within a paragraph, it's time to consider the best way to correct them. You could fix all of them the way we've identified above, by adding the missing piece or pieces to each fragment, and in some cases, that is your only choice. However, there is another, shorter, way that can often be used to correct fragments in context. You need to be familiar with this "fragment fixer":

> You can sometimes correct a "missing piece" fragment by attaching it to a complete sentence that comes before or after it—whichever makes better sense.

 Sometimes you need to put a comma between a "missing piece" fragment and the complete sentence to which you attach it. (See Chapter 17, "The Comma," Rule 3, page 217, and Rule 4, page 218.)

EXERCISE **6.3**

Now go back to the sentences in Exercise 6.2 and correct the fragments. As you go through the exercise, try to use both techniques we've identified for fixing fragments:

- Add the missing piece(s).
- Join the fragment to a complete sentence next to it.

When you've finished, compare your answers with ours on pages 515–16.

EXERCISE **6.4**

Read through the following paragraph, and put *S* before each complete sentence and *F* before each fragment. Then check your answers.

(1) _S_ David came home from his visit to the doctor. (2) _F_ Looking very worried. (3) _F_ His wife, noticing his worried expression. (4) _F_ Asked him what was troubling him. (5) _F_ Replying that the doctor told him he must take a pill every day for the rest of his life. (6) _F_ His wife puzzled by his concern. (7) _S_ Lots of people must take a pill a day. (8) _F_ Why worried? (9) _S_ David showed her the pill bottle. (10) _F_ Which contained only four pills.

EXERCISE **6.5**

Now correct the fragments you identified in the paragraph above. Use both fragment-fixing techniques that are highlighted on pages 83 and 86. Then compare your answers with ours on page 516.

DEPENDENT CLAUSE FRAGMENTS

Any group of words containing a subject and a verb is a **clause**. There are two kinds of clauses. An **independent clause** is one that can stand alone as a sentence. A **dependent clause**, as its name suggests, cannot stand alone as a sentence. It must depend on (be attached to) another clause to make sense.

Dependent clauses (also known as *subordinate clauses*) begin with dependent clause cues (technically known as **subordinating conjunctions**):

Dependent Clause Cues

after	that
although	though
as, as if	unless
as long as	until
as soon as	what, whatever
because	when, whenever
before	where, wherever
even if, even though	whether
if	which, whichever
since	while
so (that)	who, whose

Whenever a clause begins with one of these words or phrases, it is dependent.

A dependent clause must be attached to an independent clause. If it stands alone, it is a sentence fragment.

Here is an independent clause:

I am a not a good writer.

If we put one of the dependent clause cues in front of it, it can no longer stand alone:

Because I am not a good writer

We can correct this kind of fragment by attaching it to an independent clause:

Because I am not a good writer, I need to revise each paper three times.

Let's start with an easy exercise. Put an *S* before each clause that is independent and therefore a sentence. Put an *F* before each clause that is dependent and therefore a sentence fragment. Circle the dependent clause cue in each fragment. Then compare your answers with those on page 516.

1. __F__ (After) class is over.

2. __F__ (Until) I hear from the hiring committee.

3. __S__ Since yesterday, I have been on time.

4. __F__ Once the batteries are charged.

5. __SX__ Who encouraged us to keep trying.

6. __S__ Take a picture.

7. __F__ Even if there is an earthquake.

8. __F__ If your form has been filled out correctly.

9. __F__ Where you left your keys?

10. __F__ Although he was weak from hunger and exhausted from lack of sleep.

Most sentence fragments are dependent clauses punctuated as sentences. Fortunately, this is the easiest kind of fragment to fix.

> To correct a dependent clause fragment, join it either to the sentence that comes before it or to the one that comes after it—whichever link makes the most sense.

Problem: We want to move into our new apartment. As soon as the current tenants leave. It's perfect for our family.

The second "sentence" is incomplete; the dependent clause cue *as soon as* is the clue you need to identify it as a sentence fragment. You could join the fragment to the sentence that follows it, but then you would get "We want to move into our new apartment. As soon as the new tenants leave, it's perfect for our family," which doesn't make sense. The fragment should be linked to the sentence before it.

> Revision: We want to move into our new apartment as soon as the current tenants leave. It's perfect for our family.

If, as in the example above, your revised sentence ends with the dependent clause, do not put a comma before it. If, however, your revised sentence begins with the dependent clause, put a comma between it and the independent clause that follows.

> As soon as the current tenants leave, we want to move into our new apartment. It's perfect for our family. (See Chapter 17, "The Comma," Rule 3, on page 217.)

EXERCISE **6.7**

Correct the fragments in Exercise 6.6 by attaching each one to an independent clause that you have made up. Then compare your answers with our suggestions on pages 516–17. Be sure to put a comma after a dependent clause that comes at the beginning of a sentence.

Check your fragment-finding skills by trying the following exercises. The items in these exercises each contain three clauses, one of which is dependent, and therefore a fragment. Highlight the dependent clause fragment in each item.

EXERCISE **6.8**

1. Rain doesn't bother me. I like to stay inside and read. When the weather is miserable.

2. Walking is probably the best form of exercise there is. Unless you're in the water. Then swimming is preferable.

3. Whenever Kiki gets the opportunity. She loves to dance. But her boyfriend hates dancing, so she seldom gets the chance to show off her moves.

4. Please try this curry. After you've tasted it. I am sure you'll be able to tell me what's missing.

5. The report identifies a serious problem that we need to consider. Whenever our website is revised or updated. It is vulnerable to hackers.

Go to Web Exercise 6.3

EXERCISE **6.9**

1. I keep the temperature in my apartment very low. In order to save money. My friends have to wear sweaters when they visit.

2. Your idea that we should ask for directions was a good one. We would still be lost now. If we had relied on the map.

3. Home decoration isn't difficult. When you don't have enough money for furniture, carpets, or curtains. You have no choice but to be creative.

4. I believe that honesty is the best policy. If I found a million dollars in the street and discovered that it belonged to a poor, homeless person. I'd give it right back.

5. The names of many Canadian landmarks have been changed over the years. The Oldman River, for example, which runs through Lethbridge, was called the Belly River. Until local residents petitioned for a change to a more dignified name.

Go to Web Exercise 6.4

Sentences

EXERCISE **6.10**

Correct the sentence fragments you highlighted in Exercises 6.8 and 6.9. Make each fragment into a complete sentence by attaching it to the independent clause that precedes or follows it, whichever makes better sense. Remember to punctuate correctly: if a dependent clause comes at the beginning of your sentence, put a comma after it. Check your answers after each exercise.

EXERCISE **6.11**

Find and fix the 10 fragment errors in this passage. Check your punctuation carefully.

Some basic truths about the differences between men and women. While a woman marries a man expecting he will change. He won't. While a man marries a woman expecting that she will not change. She will. A woman worries about the future, Until she gets a husband. A man never worries about the future, Until he gets a wife. A woman will dress up, do her hair, and apply makeup to go shopping, get the mail, put out the garbage, water the plants, or go to the gym. While a man gets dressed up only for weddings and funerals. When it comes to her children, A woman knows all about them. Remembers their dental appointments and secret fears, best friends and romances, favourite foods, and hopes and dreams. A man, on the other hand, is vaguely aware of some short people living in the house. And finally, the matter of arguments. A woman has the last word in any argument. If a man says anything after the woman has the last word. He starts a new argument.

Go to Web Exercises 6.5, 6.6

EXERCISE **6.12**

The following paragraph contains both "missing piece" fragments and dependent clause fragments. There are 10 fragments in all. Revise the fragments any way you choose: either by adding the missing piece(s) or by joining fragments to appropriate independent clauses. Check your punctuation carefully.

People say that dogs and their owners grow to resemble each other. After several years of living together, I can think of many look-alike examples of pets and owners. Some of whom are practically clones. Take Boris, for example. A long-nosed, aristocratic Afghan hound. And my music teacher, Mr. Grabowski. Whose perfect posture, long, silky hair, and slightly cross-eyed appearance perfectly match those of his pet. Then there is my neighbour, Dave Maxwell. Whose Rottweiler is as loud, overweight, and undisciplined as his owner. Another example, Sweetums, Dave's wife's Pekinese. High-strung, fussy, spoiled, and yappy. The mirror image of Mrs. Maxwell. Especially when they return home after their regular appointment at the Dogs 'N' Dames spa, sporting pink ribbons in their freshly trimmed and tinted hair.

7 Solving Run-On Sentence Problems

Some sentences lack essential elements and thus are fragments. Other sentences contain two or more independent clauses that are incorrectly linked together. A sentence with inadequate punctuation between clauses is a **run-on**. Run-ons tend to occur when you write in a hurry, without taking time to organize your thoughts first. If you think about what you want to say and punctuate carefully, you shouldn't have any problems with run-ons.

There are two kinds of run-on sentence to watch out for: comma splices and fused sentences.

COMMA SPLICES

As its name suggests, the **comma splice** occurs when two complete sentences (independent clauses) are joined (or spliced) by a comma. Consider these examples:

Yogurt is good for you, poutine is not.

This film is boring, it has no plot.

FUSED SENTENCES

A **fused sentence** occurs when two complete sentences are joined together with no punctuation between them. For example:

Yogurt is good for you poutine is not.

This film is boring it has no plot.

There are four ways you can fix comma splices or fused sentences.

1. Make the independent clauses separate sentences.

Yogurt is good for you. Poutine is not.

This film is boring. It has no plot.

This solution works well if you do not use it too often. Writing that consists of nothing but single-clause sentences lacks smoothness and sounds choppy. (See Chapter 10.)

2. Separate the independent clauses with a comma and one of these words: *and, but, or, nor, for, so,* or *yet.*[1]

Yogurt is good for you, but poutine is not.

This film is boring, for it has no plot.

3. Make one clause dependent on the other by adding one of the dependent clause cues listed on page 88.

Yogurt is good for you although poutine is not.

This film is boring because it has no plot.

4. Use a semicolon, either by itself or with a transitional expression, to separate the independent clauses.[2]

Yogurt is good for you; poutine is not.

This film is boring; for one thing, it has no plot.

Note: All four solutions to comma splices and fused sentences require you to use a word or punctuation mark strong enough to come between two independent clauses. A comma by itself is too weak, and so is a dash.

The sentences in the following exercises will give you practice in correcting comma splices and fused sentences. Correct the sentences with errors (note that there is one correct sentence in each set), and then check your answers. Since there are several ways to fix each incorrect sentence, your answers may differ from our suggestions. If you are confused about when to use a semicolon and when to use a period, be sure to read Chapter 18 before going on. Answers for exercises in this chapter begin on page 518.

---

[1] These words are called **coordinating conjunctions** because they are used to join equal (or coordinating) clauses. See Appendix A, page 484, for an explanation and illustration of the different kinds of conjunctions and how to use them.

[2] If you are not sure when or why to use a semicolon, see Chapter 18, pages 227–32.

EXERCISE **7.1**

1. Press on the wound that will stop the bleeding.

2. Don't let your worries kill you, let the church help. (Sign outside a church)

3. I can't read it the print is too small. *because*

4. Here is my number, give me a call.

5. I'm busy right now, so you'll have to wait.

6. You'll love our new bikinis, they are simply the tops! (Sign in lingerie shop window)

7. Eat sensibly, exercise regularly, die anyway. *but have to*

8. That was a great dive, you get a perfect 10.

9. Listen to this man play, he's a jazz–blues musician, who calls himself Dr. John.

10. While you were out, you received one phone call, it was from a telemarketer.

EXERCISE **7.2**

1. I hate computers, they're always making mistakes.

2. I'm trying to stop playing computer games, they take up too much of my time.

3. My watch has stopped, I don't know what time it is. *so*

4. I'm innocent, this is a case of mistaken identity.

5. I'm going to stay up all night, I don't want to miss my 8:30 class. *because*

6. The microwave oven is the most important appliance in my home, without it, I'd starve.

7. Money may not be everything, it is far ahead of whatever is in second place.

8. There are two kinds of people in the world: those who are at their best early in the morning, and those who are at their best late at night.

9. Teachers are coming across more and more students who went from printing straight to a keyboard, they have never learned cursive script.

10. These students are at a huge disadvantage during exams, it takes far longer to print block capitals than it does to write cursive script.

Go to Web Exercise 7.1

EXERCISE **7.3**

1. My favourite music is the blues, it complements my usual mood.

2. This restaurant is terribly slow, it will be suppertime when we finally get our lunch.

3. I am pushing 60 that's enough exercise for me. (Mark Twain)

4. Smile when you speak, you can get away with saying almost anything.

5. Parking your car facing the wrong way on a city street is illegal and could cost you a fine.

6. That's the dumbest joke I've ever heard, it makes no sense.

7. The fine art of hitting an electronic device to get it to work again is called "percussive maintenance," nine times out of ten, it works.

8. The English language makes no sense, why do people recite at a play and play at a recital?

9. I write in my journal every day when I'm 90, I want to read about all the important events in my life.

10. We have not inherited the Earth from our ancestors we are borrowing it from our children.

Go to Web Exercise 7.2

EXERCISE **7.4**

In the paragraph that follows, correct the 10 run-on errors any way you choose. This would be a good time to review the four solutions to run-ons highlighted on pages 94–95. Your goal is to produce a paragraph in which the sentences are both correct and effective. Compare your revision to our suggestions on page 519.

Last year, an exchange student from the south of France came to live with us, her name was Simone, she came to Canada to practise her English and learn something about our culture. Simone was amazed by ice hockey, she had never seen the game before, and thought it was very exciting. In her first months here, Simone was surprised by what she perceived as Canadians' devotion to everything American, from television shows, to sports events, to music, to fast food, she confessed that she couldn't see much that was uniquely Canadian, she was disappointed by our lack of a distinct culture, after she made a week-long trip to Chicago, she began to understand some of the differences between the two countries; the relative cleanliness of Canada's cities, our support of multiculturalism, and our respect for law and order impressed her, the vastness of our country, with its huge expanses of untouched wilderness, intimidated her a little. Although she was homesick, especially in the first few weeks, Simone enjoyed her year in Canada when she was packing up to return to Provence; she was already planning her next visit, she wants to go camping on Prince Edward Island.

EXERCISE **7.5**

In the following exercise, correct the 10 run-on errors using a variety of the methods listed on pages 94–95. Our answers, on pages 519–20, are only suggestions.

Patience is a rare virtue in our "instant gratification" society, even in our written communication, we're so impatient that now we use short forms and initials instead of writing out words. Half a century ago, we might have written a letter (in ink on paper), put it in an envelope, and taken it to the nearest post office, eventually our letter would arrive at its destination, and if a reply was necessary, we might receive it within two weeks. Now the same communication takes seconds, so it is no wonder that our attention spans have shrunk to nanoseconds this explains the popularity of short-form communications like those used on Twitter, instant social media make it almost impossible for teachers to hold the attention of students who are used to receiving information in tiny, seconds-long bursts.

Patience, however, is a useful virtue, when we are impatient, we might remember the story of the snail that entered a bar and asked for a beer. The bartender, without a word, picked up the snail and threw it out of the bar, it rolled across the street into a ditch. Ten years passed, people were born and people died, countries appeared and disappeared, economies rose and fell, war followed peace, and peace followed war. The snail entered a bar and said, "Why did you do that?"

EXERCISE **7.6**

The following exercise will provide you with a double challenge of your sentence-structure expertise. In this exercise, you will find both fragments and run-ons. Work through it slowly and carefully, and then compare your results with our suggestions on page 520.

1. The snow continues to fall, hasn't let up for three days.

2. Eagles may soar, weasels don't get sucked into jet engines.

3. Computers are not intelligent, if they were, they wouldn't allow humans to touch their keyboards.

4. Going through the interview process a valuable experience. Even if you don't get the job.

5. A cup of coffee in the morning gets me started another at midday helps keep me alert after lunch.

6. CRNC is the home of the million-dollar guarantee, you give us a million dollars we guarantee to play any song you want.

7. Television is a mass medium, there is an old saying that it is called a medium because it rarely does anything well.

8. After studying the menu in my favourite vegetarian restaurant, my carnivorous husband observed, "This isn't food this is what food eats."

9. The first sign of adulthood is the discovery that the volume knob also turns to the left, for some people, this realization takes years.

10. The newspaper tells us that the weekend set records. Both for high temperatures and for traffic accidents, the two records are probably connected.

Go to Web Exercise 7.3

EXERCISE **7.7**

The following exercise contains 10 run-on errors. We suggest you review the four ways to correct these errors (pages 94–95) before you tackle this exercise. Your goal is to produce paragraphs in which all sentences are correct and effective.

An acquaintance of mine recently became a Canadian citizen, when she told me about her citizenship hearing, I couldn't bring myself to offer the congratulations she expected. Before her hearing, she was given a small book containing basic facts about Canada, she was told that the judge who interviewed her would question her on the information in that book, she didn't study the book, she never even opened it.

At the hearing, the judge asked her a few simple questions, such as the name of the governor general, some advantages of being a Canadian citizen, and whether healthcare was a federal or a provincial responsibility. But since she couldn't answer any of these questions, my friend just shrugged and waited for the judge to give her the answers, she expected to be told to come back when she had learned more about her adopted country, she was astonished when the judge congratulated her for successfully completing the interview and set a date to confirm her citizenship.

I find the judge's decision appalling for several reasons first, my friend's refusal to read the book suggests she doesn't have much respect for Canadian citizenship, second, her low opinion of our country's citizenship process was confirmed when the judge approved her application. Third, I suspect she was passed because she is an attractive blonde teacher who speaks with a slight English accent, if she had been a man or a woman of colour, or spoken little or no English, I can't help but think her application would have been rejected, it deserved to be.

8 Solving Modifier Problems

Having been underwater for more than 150 years, Dr. Philbrick found the warship in excellent condition.

Both students were expelled as a result of cheating by the college registrar.

Peng visited his family, who live in China during the summer.

How could Dr. Philbrick stay underwater for 150 years? Was the college registrar cheating? Does Peng's family live in China during the summer, or did Peng visit them during the summer? As you can see, the meaning in these examples is not clear. The confusion comes from incorrect placement of modifiers.

A **modifier** is a word or phrase that adds information about another word in a sentence. In the examples above, the highlighted words are modifiers. Used correctly, modifiers describe, explain, or limit another word, making its meaning more precise. Used carelessly, modifiers cause confusion or, even worse, amusement.

You need to be able to recognize and solve two kinds of modifier problems: **misplaced modifiers and dangling modifiers**.

MISPLACED MODIFIERS

Modifiers must be as close as possible to the words they apply to. Readers usually assume that a modifier modifies whatever it's next to. It's important to remember this because, as the following examples show, changing the position of a modifier can change the meaning of your sentence.

Only I love you. (No one else loves you.)

I only love you. (I have no other feelings for you.)

I love only you. (You are the only one I love.)

> To make sure a modifier is in the right place, ask yourself "What does it apply to?" and put it beside that word or phrase.

When a modifier is not close enough to the word it refers to, it is said to be misplaced.

> • A **misplaced modifier** can be a single word in the wrong place.

My supervisor told me that the payroll department needs someone who can use accounting software badly.

Is some company really hiring people to do poor work? Or does the company urgently need someone familiar with accounting software? The modifier *badly* belongs next to the word it applies to, *needs*:

My supervisor told me that the payroll department badly needs someone who can use accounting software.

> Be especially careful with these words: *almost, nearly,* just, *only, even, hardly, merely, scarcely.* Put them right before the words they modify.

Misplaced: I nearly passed every course I took in college.

Correct: I passed nearly every course I took in college.

Misplaced: Clive almost lost 5 kg while studying for exams.

Correct: Clive lost almost 5 kg while studying for exams.

Misplaced: Emilia only writes with her left hand.

Correct: Emilia writes only with her left hand.

- A misplaced modifier can also be a group of words in the wrong place.

(Babbling contentedly), the new mother watched her baby.

The modifier, *babbling contentedly*, is too far away from the word it applies to: *baby*. It seems to modify *mother*, making the sentence ridiculous. We need to revise the sentence.

The new mother watched her baby (babbling contentedly).

Now look at this example:

I worked for my aunt, who owns a variety store (during the summer).

During the summer applies to *worked* and should be closer to it:

(During the summer), I worked for my aunt, who owns a variety store.

Notice that a modifier need not always go right next to what it modifies. It should, however, be as close as possible to it.

Occasionally, as in the examples above, the modifier is obviously out of place. The writer's intention is clear, and the sentence is easy to correct. Sometimes, however, modifiers are misplaced in such a way that the meaning is not clear, as in this example:

My boss told me (on Friday) I was being let go.

Did the boss speak to the employee on Friday? Or did she tell the employee that Friday would be his last day? To avoid confusion, we must move the modifier and, depending on the meaning we want, write

(On Friday), my boss told me I was being let go.

or

My boss told me I was being let go (on Friday).

In the following exercises, rewrite the sentences, placing the modifiers correctly. Check your answers to each set before going on. Answers for exercises in this chapter begin on page 520.

Answers for exercises in this chapter begin on page 520.

EXERCISE **8.1**

1. They just closed before five.

2. We were almost splashed with mud by every car that passed.

3. She was exhausted after only walking 300 metres.

4. The French nearly drink wine with every meal, including lunch.

5. The suspect scarcely gave the police any information.

6. He was nearly underwater for two minutes before surfacing.

7. We went camping in a national park with lots of wildlife in August.

8. We will sell gas to anyone for cash in an approved container.

9. Minnie shampooed and groomed her dog wearing her bikini.

10. After the fire, she took her clothes to the cleaners with the most smoke damage.

EXERCISE **8.2**

1. The manager only fired those who had not met their sales quotas.

2. I have been fired nearly every week that I have worked here.

3. I had scarcely answered 12 of the 25 questions when time was up.

4. This is a book for serious readers with real depth.

5. We provide computers to all our staff that are constantly crashing.

6. Canadians practically enjoy the highest standard of living in the world.

7. We bought toys for the children with batteries included.

8. Loudly braying, Matti couldn't force the donkey to take a single step.

9. Tell me what you have read with your book closed.

10. Daisy crouched in the long grass and watched the lioness with her binoculars.

Go to Web Exercises 8.1, 8.2

DANGLING MODIFIERS

A **dangling modifier** occurs when there is no specific word or phrase in the sentence to which the modifier can sensibly refer. With no appropriate word to refer to, the modifier seems to apply to whatever it's next to, often with ridiculous results:

(After a good night's sleep), my teachers were impressed by my alertness.

(This sentence seems to say that the teachers had a good night's sleep.)

(While paying for our purchases), a security guard watched closely.

(The security guard paid for our purchases?)

Dangling modifiers are harder to fix than misplaced ones. You can't simply move danglers to another spot in the sentence. There are two ways to correct them. One way requires that you remember the following guideline:

> When a modifier comes at the beginning of the sentence, it modifies the subject of the sentence.

This rule means that you can avoid dangling modifiers by choosing the subjects of your sentences carefully.

1. Make sure that the subject is an appropriate one for the modifier to apply to.

Using this method, we can correct our two examples by changing the subjects.

(After a good night's sleep), I impressed my teachers with my alertness.

(While paying for our purchases), we were closely watched by a security guard.

> 2. Another way to correct a dangling modifier is to change it into a dependent clause.

After I had a good night's sleep, my teachers were impressed by my alertness.

While we paid for our purchases, a security guard watched us closely.

Sometimes a dangling modifier comes at the end of a sentence.

A Smart is the car for me, looking for efficiency and affordability.

Can you correct this sentence? Try it; then look at our suggestions at the bottom of the page.[1]

SUMMARY

AVOIDING MODIFIER PROBLEMS

1. Ask "What does the modifier refer to?"
2. Be sure there is a word or phrase in the sentence for the modifier to apply to.
3. Put the modifier as close as possible to the word or phrase it refers to.

---

[1] Here are two possible corrections for the Smart car sentence:

a. **Add an appropriate subject:** (Looking for efficiency and affordability), I decided a Smart was the car for me.
b. **Change the dangler to a dependent clause:** A Smart is the car for me since I am looking for efficiency and affordability.

The sentences in Exercises 8.3 and 8.4 contain dangling modifiers. Correct them by changing the subject of each sentence to one the modifier can appropriately apply to or by changing the dangler into a dependent clause. Then compare your answers with our suggestions on page 521.

EXERCISE **8.3**

1. Travelling in Quebec, knowing even a little French is useful.

2. Her saddle firmly cinched, Marie led the mare out of the barn.

3. After being seasick for two days, the ocean became calm.

4. Standing in the water for more than an hour, the cold numbed him to the bone.

5. Being very weak in math, the job was out of my reach.

6. Looking for a job, a good resumé is essential.

7. After spending two weeks constantly quarrelling, their relationship was over.

8. In less than a minute after applying the ointment, the pain began to ease.

9. Coming home on the bus, my wallet was stolen.

10. Having had the same roommate for three years, my parents suggested that I look for another.

EXERCISE **8.4**

1. As a college teacher, dangling modifiers are annoying.

2. Leaving the movie theatre, the sky was dark and a storm threatened.

3. Hoping to miss the rush-hour traffic, the alarm was set for 5:00 a.m.

4. After being an hour late, dinner was both overcooked and cold.

5. Driving recklessly, the police stopped André at a roadblock.

6. Dressed in a new miniskirt, her boyfriend thought Ping looked terrific.

7. After waiting for 20 minutes, the server finally came to our table.

8. Having been convicted of breaking and entering, the judge sentenced Bambi to two years in prison.

9. After revising her resumé, filling out the application, and going through the interview, the position was given to someone else.

10. Scoring the winning goal in overtime, the fans began chanting my name and wouldn't stop, even during the trophy presentation.

Correct the misplaced and dangling modifiers in Exercises 8.5 and 8.6. By now, you will have figured out at least one way to fix modifier problems. Now it's time for you to experiment with other "fixes." The more you experiment with moving sentence pieces around, the closer you will get to mastering sentence structure. Writing English sentences is like constructing jigsaw puzzles: pieces (words, phrases, clauses) fit in some places but not in others. Only experimentation and practice can teach you how to put the pieces into places where they work to clarify rather than cloud your message.

EXERCISE **8.5**

1. The sign said that students were only admitted to the pub.

2. As a responsible pet owner, my dog gets walked at least twice a day.

3. The lion was recaptured before anyone was mauled or bitten by the trainer.

4. Swimming isn't a good idea if polluted.

5. Suddenly slamming on the brakes, several passengers were thrown to the floor.

6. Employees who are late often are dismissed without notice.

7. After waiting for you for over an hour, the evening was ruined.

8. Munching on chicken wings during the game, our appetites for dinner were ruined.

9. We hired the first designer who applied because of her experience.

10. The president spoke glowingly of the retiring workers who had worked long and loyally for 20 minutes.

EXERCISE **8.6**

1. Just before leaving home, my cellphone rang.

2. The mosquitoes became increasingly annoying while relaxing on the back porch.

3. Startled by a loud knock on the door, Daniel's chin was nicked by his razor.

4. At the age of five, my mother taught me how to drive a tractor.

5. Sitting on the patio outside the restaurant, my brother drove by in my car and waved.

6. As a college student constantly faced with new assignments, the pressure is sometimes intolerable.

7. Having been to Cuba twice and Spain once, Jaime, who has never been outside the province, was fascinated by our travel stories.

8. When diving away from the inside pitch, the ball hit her on the elbow.

9. We bought fish and chips from a street vendor on the beach wrapped in newspaper and smelling deliciously of malt vinegar.

10. Wearing as little as the law allowed, they soon forgot the Winnipeg winter they had left behind under the Greek sun.

Go to Web Exercises 8.3, 8.4

This exercise will test your mastery of modifiers. Carefully read each item below before you revise it. Some sentences may contain more than one error.

1. As a computer programmer, the days are long and tiring.

2. Though drunk daily, many residents don't trust city water.

3. Being a music lover, an MP3 player is always in my pocket.

4. When roasted, you will be surprised by how delicious beets can be.

5. I heard about the team's star player being hurt on a sports phone-in show.

6. Listening to the rumours, the newlyweds are already on the road to separation.

7. Before buying a used car, the police recommend checking the ownership records.

8. Pierced with a stick and roasted over an open fire, you won't taste anything better than a vegetarian hot dog.

9. My jeans almost fit as well now as they nearly did 15 years ago when I wore them to class every day.

10. It's annoying when teachers hand out notes to students without first punching holes in them.

9 The Parallelism Principle

Brevity, clarity, and force: these are three characteristics of good writing style. **Parallelism** will reinforce these characteristics every time you write.

When your sentence contains a series of two or more items, they must be grammatically parallel. That is, they must be written in the same grammatical form. Consider this example:

> College requires us to manage our time, to work independently, and critical thinking.

The three items in this series are not parallel. Two are infinitive phrases (*to manage, to work*), but the third ends in *-ing* and is a noun phrase. To correct the sentence, you must put all items in the same grammatical form. You have two choices. You can write

> College requires us *to manage* our time, *to work* independently, and *to think critically*. (all infinitive phrases)

Or you can write

> College requires time management, independent work, and
> critical thinking. (all noun phrases)

Now look at an example with two non-parallel elements:

> Most people seek happiness in long-term relationships and work that provides them with satisfaction.

Again, you could correct this sentence in two ways. You could write "Most people seek happiness *in relationships that are long term* and *in work that provides them with satisfaction*," but that solution produces a long and clumsy sentence. The shorter version works better: "Most people seek happiness in *long-term relationships* and *satisfying work*." This version is concise, clear, and forceful.

Correct faulty parallelism by writing all items in a series in the same grammatical form: all words, all phrases, or all clauses.

One way to tell whether the items in a series are parallel is to write them out in list form, one below the other. That way, you can see at a glance if all the elements "match," that is, are in the same grammatical form.

Not Parallel	**Parallel**
My supervisor is *demanding, short-tempered,* and *an obnoxious person.*	My supervisor is *demanding, short-tempered,* and *obnoxious.*
(This list has two adjectives and a noun phrase.)	(This list has three adjectives.)
I support myself by *delivering pizza, poker,* and *shooting pool.*	I support myself by *delivering pizza, playing poker,* and *shooting pool.*
(This list has two phrases and one single word as objects of the preposition *by*.)	(This list has three phrases as objects of the preposition *by*.)
Jules wants a job that *will interest him, will challenge him,* and *pays well.*	Jules wants a job that *will interest him,* (will) *challenge him,* and (will) *pay him well.*
(This series of clauses contains two future tense verbs and one present tense verb.)	(All three subordinate clauses contain future tense verbs.)

As you can see, achieving parallelism is partly a matter of developing an ear for the sound of a correct list. A parallel sentence has a smooth, unbroken rhythm. Practice and the exercises in this chapter will help. Once you have mastered parallelism in your sentences, you will be ready to develop ideas in parallel sequence—in thesis statements, for example—and thus to write clear, well-organized prose. Far from being a frill, parallelism is a fundamental characteristic of good writing.

Sentences

Working with a partner, make any necessary corrections in the following exercises. As you work through these sentences, read them aloud, trying to spot parallelism errors from the change in rhythm that the faulty element produces. Then revise each sentence to bring the faulty element into line with the other element(s) in the series. Check your answers to each set of 10 before going on. Answers for exercises in this chapter begin on page 522.

EXERCISE **9.1**

1. This is a book to read, enjoy, and keep in your memory.

2. The new brochure on career opportunities is attractive and contains lots of information.

3. Gracefully but with care, Bonita descended the stairs in her floor-length gown and five-inch heels.

4. He ate his supper, did the dishes, watched television, and bedtime.

5. Barking dogs and children who never stop screaming keep me from enjoying the park.

6. Ali was discouraged by the low pay, being forced to work long hours, and the office politics.

7. In this clinic, we care for the sick, the injured, and homeless people.

8. If she wasn't constantly eating chips, playing bingo, and cigarette smoking, she'd have plenty of money for groceries.

9. If I can't be an RCMP officer, I want to be a chef, an architect, or in stand-up comedy.

10. So far, the countries I have enjoyed most are China for its people, France for its food, and the beaches of Brazil.

Go to Web Exercises 9.1, 9.2

EXERCISE **9.2**

1. Being unable to speak the language, I was confused, frustrated, and it's embarrassing.

2. Trying your best and success are not always the same thing.

3. I hold a baseball bat right-handed but play hockey left-handed.

4. A good student attends all classes and projects are always finished on time.

5. A good teacher motivates with enthusiasm, informs with sensitivity, and is a compassionate counsellor.

6. A good college president has the judgment of Solomon, Plato's wisdom, and the wit of Rick Mercer.

7. Licking one's fingers and to pick one's teeth in a restaurant are one way to get attention.

8. To succeed in this economy, small businesses must be creative and show flexibility.

9. Canadians must register the cars they drive, the businesses they own, the contracts they make, the houses they buy, and gun possession.

10. This course requires you to complete three major assignments: write a research paper on a Canadian author, to read three contemporary Canadian novels, and seeing two Canadian plays.

Go to Web Exercises 9.3, 9.4

EXERCISE **9.3**

Revise the following lists to make all three items parallel. You may choose any item as the basis for your parallel structure. Then check your answers before proceeding. We've provided an example below:

Incorrect:	health	happiness	wise
Correct:	health	happiness	wisdom

1. read	learn	have understanding
2. brushing	to rinse	floss
3. tighten	adjust	make looser
4. broadcasting	nursing	being an engineer
5. insight	intelligence	being knowledgeable
6. highly motivated	fully trained	having lots of education
7. information	education	entertaining
8. evaluating carefully	waiting patiently	fully exploring
9. efficient	always on time	being organized
10. without value	meaningless	uninteresting

EXERCISE **9.4**

Create a sentence for each of the parallel lists you developed in Exercise 9.3.
Example:

One who has health, happiness, and wisdom is truly rich.

EXERCISE **9.5**

As a test of your mastery of parallel structure, correct the six errors in the following paragraph.

The dictionary is a useful educational resource. Everyone knows that its three chief functions are to check the spelling, for finding out the meanings of words, and what the correct pronunciation is. Few people, however, use the dictionary for discovery as well as learning. There are several ways to use the dictionary as an aid to discovery. One is randomly looking at words, another is to read a page or two thoroughly, and still another is to skim the text looking for unfamiliar words. By this last method I discovered the word *steatopygous*, a term I now try to use at least once a day. You can increase your vocabulary significantly by using the dictionary, and, of course, a large and varied vocabulary can be used to baffle your colleagues, employers will be impressed, and your English teacher will be surprised.

EXERCISE **9.6**

Many errors in parallelism occur in the lists of bulleted points that are commonly featured in reports and presentations. The following exercise tests your ability to correct errors in lists. Make the bulleted points in each set parallel. (Your answers may vary from our suggestions on pages 523–24, depending on which of the items in the list you choose as the model for the others to parallel.)

1. A coach has four responsibilities:

   - To encourage and motivate

   - Teaching skills and techniques

   - Developing teamwork and cooperation

   - To build physical and mental strength

2. The college will undertake the following steps to conserve energy:

   - Building temperatures will be lowered by two degrees in winter

   - Lights in all rooms will be put on motion sensors

   - Raising the temperature in buildings by two degrees in summer

   - All windows will be replaced with high-efficiency glass

3. In selecting a location for the new college residence, we must be mindful of transportation factors:

   - Convenient access to mass transit

   - Making sure there is ample parking for all residents with cars

   - Ensuring easy connections to major highways

   - Immediate access to the bicycle-path network

   - On-site availability of pedestrian walkways

4. New programming guidelines for the college radio station prescribe the following:

- Alternate and independent music to be played exclusively
- No advertising between 6 p.m. and midnight
- Newscasts to include only local and college material
- Show hosts keeping their talk between songs to less than 30 seconds
- Strict observance of station regulations regarding obscenity and swearing
- Hourly station identification

5. The following regulations regarding the use of communication devices such as cellphones, personal digital assistants, iPads and tablets, smartphones, and netbooks will apply from 1 April 2013:

- No communication devices will be permitted in any exam rooms
- Ring tones, alarms, and audio turned off in all lectures, seminars, and labs
- Students may use communication devices only in designated areas of the college
- Only specified classwork is permitted in lectures, seminars, and labs

EXERCISE **9.7**

As a test of your ability to correct faulty parallelism, revise the following sentences.

1. Travel teaches us to be tolerant, resourceful, patience, and independence.

2. The Vancouver Canucks are a good team: hard-hitting, fast-skating, and thinking quickly.

3. They are an odd couple: Suniti is calm and placid, while Sunir shows tension and nervousness.

4. After studying the explanations and all the exercises have been completed, you'll be a better writer.

5. In our community, two related crimes are rapidly increasing: drug abuse and theft of property.

6. She is talkative and aggressive but also has enthusiasm and works hard.

7. The fear of losing is forgotten in the winning joyfulness.

8. A good nurse is knowledgeable, kind, and has sensitivity and skill.

9. The most common excuses people give for being late for work are bad traffic, they didn't sleep well, weather, and problems related to transporting their children.

10. According to a survey conducted last year, some unusual excuses for lateness included a man who said he'd be late because his car was infested with bees; a woman claiming her karma was out of sync; and a worker insisted he was on time, but the company clock was wrong.

Sentences

10 Refining by Combining

SENTENCE COMBINING

If you have worked carefully through Unit 2 to this chapter, you should now be writing complete sentences—a solid achievement, but one that does not yet meet the requirements of academic and professional prose. Your paragraphs may consist of sentences that are repetitious and monotonous; that is, your writing may be lacking in style. Now is the time to try your hand at **sentence combining**, a technique that enables you to produce correct and pleasing sentences. Sentence combining accomplishes three things: it reinforces your meaning; it refines and polishes your writing; and it results in a style that will keep your reader alert and interested in what you have to say.

Let's look at two short, technically correct sentences that could be combined:

Our office manager is highly efficient.
She will be promoted soon.

There are four ways of combining these two statements into a single sentence. Note that the meanings of the resulting sentences are slightly different. These differences are important when you're deciding which method to use in a particular situation.

1. You can connect them with an appropriate linking word, such as *and, but, or, nor, for, so,* and *yet.*

Our office manager is highly efficient, so she will be promoted soon.
Our office manager will be promoted soon, for she is highly efficient.

2. You can change one of the sentences into a subordinate clause.

Our office manager, who is highly efficient, will be promoted soon.
Because our office manager is highly efficient, she will be promoted soon.

3. You can change one of the sentences into a modifying phrase.

Being highly efficient , our office manager will be promoted soon.
Our office manager, a highly efficient woman , will be promoted soon.

4. Sometimes you can reduce one of your sentences to a single-word modifier.

Our efficient office manager will be promoted soon.

In sentence combining, you are free to move parts of the sentence around, change words, add or delete words, or make whatever other changes you choose. Anything goes, as long as you don't drastically alter the meaning of the base sentences. Remember that your aim in combining sentences is to create effective sentences, not long ones.

COORDINATION OR SUBORDINATION?

When you join two or more short independent clauses, you need to think about their logical relationship. Are the ideas equally significant? If so, link them with an appropriate coordinating construction: a linking word such as *and, but, so, for, or, nor,* or *yet.* Is one idea more significant than the other? Put it in the main clause and put the less important idea in a subordinate construction: a clause, phrase, or word.

The most common way of linking ideas is with **conjunctions**. Every conjunction has a distinct meaning and purpose. If you choose your conjunctions carefully, you will reinforce the meaning you wish to convey to your reader. If you choose them carelessly, you will not say what you mean and may confuse your reader.

COORDINATION

To join two ideas that are equal in content or importance, use either
- a **coordinating conjunction** (*and, but, so, for, or, nor, yet*) or
- **correlative conjunctions**: *either ... or, neither ... nor, not only ... but also, both ... and*

Consider these examples:

1. Illogical relation:

   Water is vital to life, for it must be protected.

   Logical relation:

   Water is vital to life, so it must be protected. (coordinating conjunction)

   Logical relation:

   Water must be protected, for it is vital to life. (coordinating conjunction)

2. Illogical relation:

   I reread the text and reviewed my notes, so I failed the test anyway.

   Logical relation:

   I reread the text and reviewed my notes, but I failed the test anyway.
   (coordinating conjunction)

3. Poor logical relation:

   Mr. Benson teaches school, and he is a writer too.

   Logical relation:

   Mr. Benson is both a teacher and a writer. (correlative conjunctions)

4. Poor logical relation:

   I am not young, and I am not inexperienced either.

   Logical relation:

   I am neither young nor inexperienced. (correlative conjunctions)

EXERCISE **10.1**

Combine the following sentences by using a coordinating conjunction or a pair of correlative conjunctions, as appropriate. Make your combined sentence as concise as possible by eliminating unnecessary words. Answers for exercises in this chapter begin on page 524.

1. Our town may be small. Our town is not backward.

2. Our final exam will be held on Friday afternoon. Or it will be held on Monday morning.

3. This book promises to help me manage my money. I will buy it.

4. I have completed all the exercises. My sentence skills are gradually improving.

5. This man is not my father. He is not my husband either.

SUBORDINATION

> To connect ideas of unequal importance, put the dominant idea in a main clause and the less significant idea in a subordinate clause beginning with either
> - a **relative pronoun** (*who, whom, whose, which,* or *that*) or
> - a **subordinating conjunction** such as *although, because, if, when, where,* or *after* (see list on page 88)

Consider these examples:

1. Illogical relation:

   Karin did well on all her tests, and she began working with a tutor.

   Logical relation:

   After she began working with a tutor, Karin did well on all her tests. (subordinating conjunction)

   Logical relation:

   Karin did well on all her tests after she began working with a tutor. (subordinating conjunction)

2. Illogical relation:

   No day is depressing to my English teacher, and she is an incurable optimist.

Logical relation:

No day is depressing to my English teacher, who is an incurable optimist. (relative pronoun)

Logical relation:

Because she is an incurable optimist, no day is depressing to my English teacher. (subordinating conjunction)

EXERCISE **10.2**

For each item below, consider the two sentences and the conjunctions (provided in parentheses). Decide which conjunction more logically expresses the relationship between the sentences and write the combined sentence in the space provided. Check your answers against ours on page 524.

1. My favourite team is the Vancouver Canucks. My father prefers the Montreal Canadiens. (so/although)

_____

_____

2. We will take a picnic to the ballgame today. The rain stays away. (and/if)

_____

_____

3. Our vacation this year will be in October. We will visit Nova Scotia to see the autumn colours. (and/when)

_____

_____

4. My Facebook page says I am a good dancer. My favourite type of music is opera. (for/even though)

_____

_____

5. Art is long. Life is short. (where/but)

_____

_____

"GOT IDEA. TALK BETTER. COMBINE WORDS. MAKE SENTENCES."

TIPS ON USING CONJUNCTIONS AND RELATIVE PRONOUNS

A. Using Conjunctions to Combine Clauses

Use only one connecting word to join two clauses.

This rule applies whether you intend to create a sentence consisting of two coordinating independent clauses or a sentence consisting of a main clause and a subordinate clause. For example, let's suppose you want to combine "I enjoy school" with "I also like my part-time job."

Incorrect: *Although* I enjoy school, *and* I also like my part-time job.

Correct: I enjoy school, *and* I also like my part-time job.

Also correct: *Although* I enjoy school, I also like my part-time job.

Now test your understanding of this important point by doing the following exercise. Answers to exercises in this section begin on page 524.

EXERCISE **10.A**

Read through the sentences below and decide whether each one is correct or incorrect. In the incorrect sentences, cross out the unnecessary conjunction. Be sure your revised sentences are correctly capitalized and punctuated. Check your answers on pages 524–25.

1. Although the test was difficult, but I passed it.

2. After eating our lunch, then we went back to work on our project.

3. When December is over, winter continues for two or three months.

4. Since our essay is due tomorrow, so we must stay up late tonight.

5. Even though the pictures are good, yet I hate seeing myself.

6. Before the party, she cooked food for 12 people.

7. Though having a car would be convenient, but I need the money for other things.

8. If this book will help me, so I will buy it.

9. When you find a mistake, so you must correct it.

10. Although that program frequently crashes, but this program is stable.

Go to Web Exercise 10.1

B. Using Relative Pronouns to Combine Clauses

You can often combine two clauses by using a relative pronoun (*who, whom, whose, that, which*) to join them. (If you are not sure when to use *that/which* or *who/whom*, see Chapter 15, pages 197–98). On the next page are some examples of the different ways you can use a relative pronoun to join two clauses.

Separate Sentences	Combined Sentence
The man is waiting in the car. He is my father.	The man *who* is waiting in the car is my father. (NOT "The man who is waiting in the car he is my father.")
Yesterday Gina met Raffi. His family lives in Beirut.	Yesterday, Gina met Raffi *whose* family lives in Beirut.
I need a copy of *Frankenstein*. Ms. Lee assigned this book last week.	I need a copy of *Frankenstein, which* Ms. Lee assigned last week.
Frankenstein is a novel. It was written in 1818 by Mary Shelley.	*Frankenstein* is a novel *that* was written in 1818 by Mary Shelley.

EXERCISE **10.B**

Combine the following sentences using the relative pronoun given in parentheses as the link. Then check your answers on page 525.

1. I have a teacher. The teacher is always losing his glasses. (who)

2. Here is the computer. This computer is always crashing. (that)

3. I am enrolled in an art class. The class meets Wednesday evenings. (that)

4. That singer just won a Grammy. I always forget her name. (whose)

5. The cellphone is broken. It is the cellphone you gave me. (that)

6. My plant is dead. You forgot to water it. (which)

7. The parcel finally arrived. I was waiting for it. (that)

8. Lisa babysits for a man. The man's wife speaks only Japanese. (whose)

9. The taxi driver took me to the airport. He drove 20 kilometres over the speed limit all the way. (who)

10. My roommate is finally moving out. His snoring keeps me awake. (whose)

Go to Web Exercise 10.2

In the following exercises, combine the pairs of sentences. We have provided two possible conjunctions to join each pair. First, decide if the ideas in the sentences are equal or unequal in significance. If the ideas are of equal logical weight, use the coordinating conjunction to join them. If one idea is less important, express it in a dependent clause beginning with a subordinating conjunction. Subordinate clauses can come before or after the main clause, so some of your answers may differ from ours. After you finish each exercise, check your answers against ours on page 525.

EXERCISE **10.3**

1. The tortoise is slow but steady. It will win the race. (for/because)

   _____

   _____

2. The calendar says it is April. It feels like February. (but/since)

   _____

   _____

3. Nicole used the wi-fi from her neighbour's apartment. He changed the password. (yet/until)

   _____

   _____

4. I sometimes have bad dreams. They don't usually bother me unless I eat pepperoni pizza as a late-night snack. (but/even if)

   _____

   _____

5. Gregor procrastinates by playing video games. His essay remains unfinished. (for/while)

   _____

   _____

EXERCISE **10.4**

1. The Nissan Juke is a small SUV. It has received excellent reviews. (which/and)

_____

_____

2. The iPad is on my wish list. I'm hoping I get it as a birthday present. (that/so)

_____

_____

3. Parking downtown is impossible. We are moving to the suburbs. (because/and)

_____

_____

4. I don't mind doing this exercise. I'll be glad when it's finished. (although/for)

_____

_____

5. Carson blogs incessantly. He thinks all his thoughts are interesting. (who/so)

_____

_____

In the following exercises, try your solutions aloud before you write them. You may also want to refer to Chapter 17 for advice on using the comma.

EXERCISE **10.5**

1. Our apartment is large and comfortable.
   Our apartment is reasonably priced. (yet)

   _____

   _____

2. Alien spacecraft are observing Earth.
   Some people believe this. (that)

   _____

   _____

3. Our company will sponsor a marathon runner.
   One of the employees must enter the race. (but)

   _____

   _____

4. Hybrid cars are becoming more popular.
   Hybrid cars cost more than comparable gas-powered models. (even though)

   _____

   _____

5. Heidi's grades improved.
   She followed her study schedule. (when)

   _____

   _____

6. Your outfit is not appropriate for the office.
   Your outfit would look just right in an after-hours club. (but)

   _____

   _____

7. Strong coffee keeps me awake.
   I love the taste of strong coffee.
   I like my coffee black. (although)

   _____

   _____

8. The chef wrote this book.
   He owns a restaurant just down the street. (who)

   _____

   _____

9. You have the freedom to do all the things you wanted.
   You are too old to enjoy them. (just when)

   _____

   _____

10. I don't eat meat.
    I don't eat poultry, either. (Combine these two different ways.)

    (a) _____

    (b) _____

In exercises 10.6 and 10.7, use a variety of sentence-combining techniques to join each set of statements into longer, more interesting units.

(*Hint:* Read through each set of statements before you begin to combine them. Try several variations aloud or in your head before writing down your preferred solution.) There are many ways to combine these short statements to make smooth, effective sentences. Our answers are only suggestions.

Sentences

EXERCISE **10.6**

1. The village is very small.
   I grew up in the village.

   _____

   _____

   _____

2. My car is in the repair shop.
   It needs a new alternator.

   _____

   _____

   _____

3. The gates are down.
   The lights are flashing.
   A train is not coming.

   _____

   _____

   _____

4. I read this book from cover to cover.
   I completed all the exercises in this book.
   My writing skills improved.

   _____

   _____

   _____

5. You are a polite person.
   You are considerate of the feelings of others.
   You should be more assertive.

   _____

_____

_____

6. My wife enjoys watching hockey.
   I prefer watching soccer.
   Soccer is the world's most popular spectator sport.

_____

_____

_____

7. Meiling shot this movie on her cellphone.
   She edited it on her iPad.
   She posted it on YouTube.
   It is not very good.

_____

_____

_____

8. My ex-girlfriend is a cruel person.
   She broke up with me on Twitter.
   She deleted me from her friends list.

_____

_____

_____

9. My vacation in Florida was disappointing.
   The weather was cold.
   I don't like shopping malls.
   Shopping malls are everywhere in Florida.

_____

_____

_____

10. This restaurant is very expensive.
The food is good.
The service is excellent.
I don't mind paying the price.

_____

_____

_____

EXERCISE **10.7**

1. Weyburn, Saskatchewan, is a small town.
I was born in Weyburn.
I have not lived there since I was a baby.

_____

_____

_____

2. Hanna is very good at reading a road map.
She can find her way anywhere.
She cannot fold it properly.

_____

_____

_____

3. Justin Bieber is a pop phenomenon.
Most talented musicians never make it.
It is safer to go to college and work toward a career.

_____

_____

_____

Sentences

4. I should have backed up my files.
   I should have unplugged the computer.
   I lost all my files.
   My hard drive was destroyed by a lightning strike.

   _____

   _____

   _____

5. Ying decided not to buy the car.
   The car had many of the features she was looking for.
   It was the right price.
   It was the wrong colour.

   _____

   _____

   _____

6. Vijay's father bought a new car.
   He is a surgeon.
   Vijay is allowed to wash the car.
   Vijay is not allowed to drive it.

   _____

   _____

   _____

7. Tina is a Canadian citizen.
   She was born in Halifax.
   Her mother was born in Chicago.
   She has American citizenship too.

   _____

   _____

   _____

8. I lost weight.
My clothes don't fit.
I need to buy a new wardrobe.
I don't have the money to buy the clothes I like.

_____

_____

_____

9. Jenn hates winter weather.
She is fit and athletic.
She vacations every Spring Break in Mexico.
She likes to run on the beach.

_____

_____

_____

10. In most of the Middle East, young people are in the majority.
There is high unemployment.
There is little opportunity.
These situations lead to unrest and rebellion.

_____

_____

_____

EXERCISE **10.8**

Study the sets of statements below and decide if the statements are equally significant or if one statement in each set is more important than the other(s). Then combine the statements into a single sentence that reflects your decision. That is, use a coordinating conjunction to join statements of equal importance; use a subordinating conjunction to join a less important statement to the main clause.

1. Dominoes is my favourite game.
My friends prefer cards.
We play their games on weekdays.
We play dominoes on weekends.

_____

_____

_____

2. I should be working on my essay.
   I don't know what to write about.
   I am playing solitaire on my computer.
   I am feeling guilty.

   _____

   _____

   _____

3. Irina is studying Italian.
   She is very good with languages.
   She already speaks Greek, French, and English.

   _____

   _____

   _____

4. To talk to my friends in China, I use Skype.
   It is a software program.
   It allows us to talk free.
   We can see each other on our monitors.

   _____

   _____

   _____

5. Woody Allen is a witty writer.
   He said that life is full of loneliness, suffering, and misery.
   He said that life is over far too soon.

   _____

   _____

   _____

After you have practised sentence combining, you can evaluate your work. Read your sentences out loud. How they *sound* is important. Test your work against these six characteristics of successful sentences.

SUMMARY

CHARACTERISTICS OF SUCCESSFUL SENTENCES

1. **Meaning:** Have you said what you mean?
2. **Clarity:** Is each sentence clear? Can it be understood on the first reading?
3. **Coherence:** Do the parts of your sentences fit together logically and smoothly?
4. **Emphasis:** Is the most important idea in a main clause? Does it appear either at the beginning or at the end of the sentence?
5. **Conciseness:** Is every sentence direct and to the point? Have you cut out all redundant or repetitious words?
6. **Rhythm:** Do your sentences flow smoothly? Are there any interruptions in the development of the key idea(s)? If so, do the interruptions help to emphasize important points, or do they distract the reader?

If your sentences pass all six tests of successful sentence style, you can be confident that they are both technically correct and pleasing to the ear. No reader could ask for more.

RAPID REVIEW

As a final test of your ability to use correct sentence structure, read the following passage carefully. It contains a total of 15 errors, including one or more sentence fragments, run-ons, misplaced and dangling modifiers, and unparallel constructions. *Tip:* Read each paragraph all the way through before you begin revising. For each error you miss, the Answer Key on pages 527–28 directs you to the chapter(s) you should review.

[1]Last year, while driving through rural Alberta, a sign at the end of a farmer's lane: "For Sale: Talking Dog. $15." [2]Curious, my car had hardly stopped before rushing out to ask the farmer about the dog. [3]He directed me to a kennel behind the house, there was a beautiful golden retriever dozing in the warm sun. [4]Kneeling down beside him and making sure no one was looking. [5]I quietly asked him if he could really talk. [6]He opened one eye and yawning and said, "Of course."

[7]I must have fainted from the shock, the dog was licking my face when I regained consciousness. [8]When I recovered my composure, I asked him how he had come to be here in a farmyard in Alberta. [9]His tale was both complicated and full of interest. [10]He told me that when he discovered he could talk, he volunteered to help the RCMP in their canine unit, the police quickly discovered he was too valuable for that task and assigned him to undercover work. [11]He would curl up near a suspect and eavesdrop, thus catching many criminals, earning the admiration of his police comrades, and won many

medals. [12]He was reassigned to Canada's spy agency, CSIS, the stress of constant travelling and spying on world leaders and suspected enemies tired him out soon. [13]At only eight years old, a military veterinarian told him that the stress of his undercover life had weakened his heart and retirement should be his choice. [14]The veterinarian had a brother in Alberta who would give the dog a comfortable home where he could enjoy a peaceful retirement. [15]"So here I am," the dog concluded.

[16]I couldn't wait to return to the farmer and offer to buy this heroic dog I couldn't resist asking why he only wanted $15 for such an amazing animal. [17]The farmer shrugged and replied, "Because he's a liar, that's why. He never did any of those things."

UNIT 3

Grammar

Grammar

QUICK QUIZ

This Quick Quiz will show you which chapters of Unit 3 you need to pay special attention to. The paragraph below contains 15 errors in grammar: verb forms, subject–verb agreement, verb tense consistency, pronoun form, pronoun–antecedent agreement, and pronoun consistency.

When you have made your corrections, turn to page 528 and compare your revisions with ours. For each error you miss, the Answer Key directs you to the chapter you need to work on.

[1]Every generation have one or two defining moments which are so significant that everyone remembers precisely where they were, when the event occurred. [2]Most of the events that have became part of our consciousness are tragic, but there's exceptions. [3]Nobody that was alive when the Allied victory that ended World War II was declared are likely to forget the mingled joy and relief of that occasion. [4]Every Canadian hockey fan, even if they were not watching the game at the time, remember The Goal: Paul Henderson's winner in the 1972 series against the Soviet Union. [5]Neither of these glorious moments are going to fade from the memories of those who experienced them. [6]Memorable tragic moments, however, are more common than joyful ones, and somehow they seemed more important to us as we look back. [7]My contemporaries and me all remember exactly where we were, when President John F. Kennedy was shot, while them who were born after 1980 will never

forget the destruction of the World Trade Center in New York City in 2001.

[8]No one that saw the televised images of the twin towers as they collapsed and

crumbled are ever likely to forget the horror of those moments.

11 Choosing the Correct Verb Form

Errors in grammar are like flies in soup. Most of the time, they don't affect meaning any more than flies affect flavour, but they are distracting and irritating. You must eliminate grammar errors from your writing if you want your readers to pay attention to what you say rather than to how you say it.

The verb is the most complex and essential part of a sentence. In fact, a verb is to a sentence what an engine is to a car: the source of power and a frequent cause of trouble.[1]

This chapter looks at two verb problems that occur in many people's writing: incorrect use of irregular verbs and difficulties with the passive voice.

THE PRINCIPAL PARTS OF VERBS

All verb formations are based on a verb's **principal parts**. Technically, the principal parts are not the **tenses** (time indicators) of the verb; they are the elements that we use to construct the various tenses.

Every verb has four forms, called its principal parts:
1. the **infinitive** form—the form used with *to*
2. the **simple past** (also called the **past tense**)
3. the **present participle**: the *-ing* form
4. the **past participle**: the form used with *has* or *have*

Here are some examples:

Infinitive	Simple Past	Present Participle	Past Participle
A. (to) call	called	calling	(has) called
(to) dance	danced	dancing	(has) danced
(to) work	worked	working	(has) worked

[1] Verb tenses are reviewed in Chapter 28. Negatives, modals, conditionals, and participial adjectives (e.g., *confused* and *confusing*) are reviewed in Chapter 29.

Infinitive	Simple Past	Present Participle	Past Participle
B. (to) do	did	doing	(has) done
(to) eat	ate	eating	(has) eaten
(to) say	said	saying	(has) said

If you study the list above, you will notice an important feature of principal parts. In the first group of three verbs (A), the simple past and the past participle are identical: they are both formed by adding -*ed* (or simply -*d* if the verb ends in -*e*, as *dance* does). When both the simple past and the past participle of a verb are formed with -*ed*, the verb is called a **regular verb**. Fortunately, most of the many thousands of English verbs are regular.

In the second group (B), the verbs are called **irregular verbs** because the simple past and past participle are not formed by adding -*ed*. With *do* and *eat*, the simple past and the past participle are different words: *did/done, ate/eaten*. The simple past and past participle of *say* are the same, *said*, but they are not formed with the regular -*ed* ending.

Unfortunately, although there are only a few hundred irregular verbs in English, these verbs are among the most common in the language; for example, *begin, come, do, go, see,* and *write* are all irregular. Their simple past tenses and past participles are formed in unpredictable ways. Consider the following sentences, all of which are grammatically incorrect:

I begun classes yesterday.

He come to see me last week.

I done it before.

She has went away on vacation.

He seen his girlfriend with another man.

I have wrote you an email answering your questions.

Depending on your experience with English, these sentences may or may not sound wrong to you, but if you look at the irregular verbs listed on pages 147–49, you will understand why they are incorrect. What are the correct forms of the verbs in the sentences above? Write them in above the incorrect forms.

If you are not sure of the principal parts of a verb, check your dictionary. If the verb is irregular, you will find the principal parts listed after the entry for the infinitive (base) form. For instance, if you look up *sing* in your dictionary, you will find *sang* (simple past), *sung* (past participle), and *singing* (present participle).

Grammar

If no principal parts are listed after the verb you are checking, it is regular; you form its simple past and past participle by adding *-ed*.

The verbs in the list on pages 147–49 are used so frequently you should take the time to learn their principal parts. We have not included the present participle (the *-ing* form) because it rarely causes difficulty. The good news is that not every verb on this list will cause you trouble.

To identify the verbs that cause you problems, cover the middle and right-hand columns of the list with a blank piece of paper. Begin with the infinitive form of the first verb, *be*. Say the past tense and past participle of *be*. Move the paper down one line to check your responses. If your answers are correct, go to the next verb in the left-hand column, *bear*. Again, say the past tense and the past participle, check your responses, and move on to the next verb, *beat*. Continue this exercise until you reach the end of the list.

Whenever you come to a verb whose past tense or past participle you aren't sure of or misidentify, highlight that verb across all three columns (infinitive, simple past, past participle). After you've gone through the list once, you'll have a quick and easy reference to the correct forms of verbs you need to watch out for.

GRAMMARIAN

THE PRINCIPAL PARTS OF IRREGULAR VERBS

Infinitive	Simple Past	Past Participle
(Use with *to* and with helping/auxiliary verbs)		(Use with *has, have had*)
be (am, is)	was/were	been
bear	bore	borne
beat	beat	beaten
become	became	become
begin	began	begun
bend	bent	bent
bind	bound	bound
bite	bit	bitten
bleed	bled	bled
blow	blew	blown
break	broke	broken
bring	brought (*not* brang)	brought (*not* brung)
broadcast	broadcast	broadcast
build	built	built
burst	burst	burst
buy	bought	bought
catch	caught	caught
choose	chose	chosen
cling	clung	clung
come	came	come
cost	cost	cost
cut	cut	cut
deal	dealt	dealt
dig	dug	dug
dive	dived/dove	dived
do	did (*not* done)	done
draw	drew	drawn
dream	dreamed/dreamt	dreamed/dreamt
drink	drank (*not* drunk)	drunk
eat	ate	eaten
fall	fell	fallen
feed	fed	fed
feel	felt	felt
fight	fought	fought
find	found	found

Grammar

Infinitive	Simple Past	Past Participle
(Use with *to* and with helping/auxiliary verbs)		(Use with *has, have had*)
flee	fled	fled
fling	flung	flung
fly	flew	flown
forbid	forbade	forbidden
forget	forgot	forgotten/forgot
forgive	forgave	forgiven
freeze	froze	frozen
get	got	got/gotten
give	gave	given
go	went	gone (*not* went)
grow	grew	grown
have	had	had
hear	heard	heard
hide	hid	hidden
hit	hit	hit
hold	held	held
hurt	hurt	hurt
keep	kept	kept
know	knew	known
lay (to put or place)	laid	laid
lead	led	led
leave	left	left
lie (to recline)	lay	lain (*not* layed *or* laid)
light	lit/lighted	lit/lighted
lose	lost	lost
make	made	made
mean	meant	meant
meet	met	met
mistake	mistook	mistaken
pay	paid	paid
raise	raised	raised
ride	rode	ridden
ring	rang	rung
rise	rose	risen
run	ran	run
say	said	said
see	saw (*not* seen)	seen
seek	sought	sought

Infinitive (Use with *to* and with helping/auxiliary verbs)	**Simple Past**	**Past Participle** (Use with *has, have had*)
sell	sold	sold
set	set	set
shake	shook	shaken (*not* shook)
shine	shone	shone
shoot	shot	shot
show	showed	shown
shrink	shrank	shrunk
sing	sang	sung
sink	sank	sunk
sit	sat	sat
sleep	slept	slept
slide	slid	slid
speak	spoke	spoken
speed	sped	sped
spend	spent	spent
spin	spun	spun
stand	stood	stood
steal	stole	stolen
stick	stuck	stuck
sting	stung	stung
strike (hit)	struck	struck
strike (affect)	struck	stricken
strive	strove	striven
swear	swore	sworn
swim	swam	swum
swing	swung (*not* swang)	swung
take	took	taken
teach	taught	taught
tear	tore	torn
tell	told	told
think	thought	thought
throw	threw	thrown
understand	understood	understood
wear	wore	worn
weave	wove	woven
win	won	won
wind	wound	wound
withdraw	withdrew	withdrawn
write	wrote	written

Grammar

The sentences in the exercises below require both the simple past and the past participle of the verb shown at the left. Working with a partner, write the required form in each blank. Do not add or remove helping verbs. Check your answers after each exercise. Answers for exercises in this chapter begin on page 529.

EXERCISE **11.1**

1. wear — You _were_ your good hiking boots only once, but after you have _worn_ them several times, you won't want to take them off.

2. give — The tourists _gave_ Tania a tip after she had _given_ them directions to the hotel.

3. begin — After the project had _begun_, the members of the team soon _began_ to disagree on the procedure to follow.

4. eat — I _ate_ as though I had not _eaten_ in a month.

5. cost — The vacation in Cuba _cost_ less than last year's trip to Jamaica had _cost_ and was much more fun.

6. bring — If you have _brought_ your children with you, I hope you also _bring_ enough toys and movies to keep them occupied during your stay.

7. grow — The noise from the party next door _grew_ louder by the hour, but by midnight I had _grown_ used to it, and went to sleep.

8. sit — Marc _sat_ in front of the TV all morning; by evening he will have _seated / sit_ there for eight hours—a full workday!

9. write — After she had _written_ the essay that was due last week, she _wrote_ emails to all her friends.

10. pay — I _paid_ off my credit cards, so I have not _paid_ this month's rent.

EXERCISE **11.2**

1. ride   I had never _ridden_ in a stretch limo until I _rode_ in one to Xue's wedding.

2. sing   She _sang_ a little song that her mother had _sung_ to her when she was a baby.

3. teach   Harold had been _taught_ to play poker by his father, and he _taught_ his daughter the same way.

4. find   He _found_ the solution that hundreds of mathematicians over three centuries had not _found_.

5. fly   Suzhu had once _flown_ to Whitehorse, so when she _flew_ north to Tuktoyaktuk, she knew what to expect.

6. feel   At first, they had _felt_ silly in their new pink uniforms, but after winning three games in a row, they _felt_ much better.

7. lie   The cat _lay_ right where the dog had _lain_ all morning.

8. go   We _went_ to our new home to find that the movers had _gone_ to the wrong address to deliver our furniture.

9. lose   The reason you _lost_ those customers is that you have _lost_ confidence in your ability to sell our product.

10. steal   I _stole_ two customers away from the sales representative who earlier had _stolen_ my best account.

Go to Web Exercise 11.1

EXERCISE **11.3**

1. think

I had _thought_ that you were right, but when I _thought_ more about your answer, I realized you were wrong.

2. buy

If we had _bought_ this stock 20 years ago, the shares we _bought_ would now be worth a fortune.

3. do

They _did._ what was asked, but their competitors, who had _done._ a better job, got the contract.

4. show

Today our agent _showed_ us a house that was much better suited to our needs than anything she had _shown_ us previously.

5. hurt

Budget cuts had _hurt_ the project, but today's decision to lay off two of our workers _hurt_ it even more.

6. throw

The rope had not been _thrown_ far enough to reach those in the water, so Mia pulled it in and _threwed_ it again.

7. lay

Elzbieta _laid_ her passport on the official's desk where the other tourists had _laid._ theirs.

8. put

I have _put_ your notebook in the mail, but your pen and glasses I will _put_ away until I see you again.

9. fight

My parents _fought_ again today, the way they have _fought_ almost every day for the past 20 years.

10. break

She _broke._ the Canadian record only six months after she had _broken_ her arm in training.

Go to Web Exercise 11.2

EXERCISE **11.4**

Correct the 20 verb errors in the following sentences.

1. I have not forgave Mohsin for copying the essay that had took me three

   weeks to write.

   brought

2. We brung a suitcase full of souvenirs when we come home from Taiwan.
                                                              threw
3. Our cans of pop had froze solid, but once they thawed, we drunk them

   anyway.
                                    laid
4. Sneaking into class late, Viktor lay his essay on the desk with the others;
         written
   he had wrote it during his lunch break.
      swam
5. First we swum out to the wreck and then we doved to look for the

   treasure.
                              eaten
6. Too late, after they had ate all the salad and pasta they could hold, they
   saw
   seen the dessert table.
                                                          gone
7. Television is nature's way of telling us we should have went out and did

   something enjoyable this evening.
         sang   *forbade*
8. After I swang the bat and hit my little sister, my parents forbid me to play

   baseball in the backyard.
                                                    did
9. My husband gave the contractor a bonus because he done the job on time,

   forgetting that I had already paid the man and that he hadn't filled the

   huge hole he digged in our basement.

10. Capital punishment is no longer practise in Canada, but in some U.S.

    states, you can be executed if you have broke certain laws.

Grammar

CHOOSING BETWEEN ACTIVE AND PASSIVE VOICE

Verbs have another quality besides tense (or time). Verbs also have what is called **voice**, which refers to the quality of being either active or passive. In sentences with **active-voice** verbs, the "doer" of the action is the grammatical subject of the sentence.

Active voice: Good <u>parents</u> <u>support</u> their children.
A <u>car</u> <u>crushed</u> the cat.
<u>Someone</u> <u>will show</u> a movie in class.

In sentences with **passive-voice** verbs, the grammatical subject of the sentence is the "receiver" of the action (that is, the subject is "passively" acted upon), and the "doer" becomes an object of the preposition *by* or is absent from the sentence entirely, as in the third example below.

Passive voice: <u>Children</u> <u>are supported</u> by good parents.
The <u>cat</u> <u>was crushed</u> by a car.
A <u>movie</u> <u>will be shown</u> in class.

Notice that active and passive verbs can be in any tense. Present, past, and future tense verbs are used in both sets of examples above. Can you tell which is which?

Passive-voice verbs are formed by using a form of *be* + the past participle form of the verb. This is another reason you need to know the past participle form of irregular verbs; for instance, in the third example above, the correct passive construction is *will be shown*, not *will be showed*. In the examples below, note the different tenses and pay special attention to the passive-voice verb forms.

	Active	**Passive**
present	The owner signs the cheques.	The cheques are signed by the owner.
past	The owner signed the cheques.	The cheques were signed by the owner.
future	The owner will sign the cheques.	The cheques will be signed by the owner.
present progressive	The owner is signing the cheques.	The cheques are being signed by the owner.
past progressive	The owner was signing the cheques.	The cheques were being signed by the owner.

EXERCISE **11.5**

Use two lines to underline the verbs in the sentences below. Then identify the verbs as either active (A) or passive (P). The first one is done for you. The answers to this exercise begin on page 530.

1. __A__ Our professor <u>checks</u> our homework every day.

2. __P__ The report is being prepared by the marketing department.

3. __P__ The limousine was driven by a chauffeur.

4. __A__ Eva will invite Tariq to the party.

5. __P__ The CN Tower is visited by hundreds of people every day.

6. __A__ Sula designed and made this jewellery.

7. __A__ *The English Patient* was written by Canadian author Michael Ondaatje.

8. __A__ Hollywood made the book into a successful movie.

9. __P__ The song was performed by Eminem.

10. __P__ Two metres of snow had to be shovelled off the driveway.

EXERCISE **11.6**

Now rewrite the sentences in Exercise 11.5, changing active-voice verbs to passive and passive-voice verbs to active. Use two lines to underline the verbs. We've done the first sentence for you as an example.

1. Our homework <u>is checked</u> by our professor every day.

2. The market department is preparing the report.

3. A chauffeur ~~was~~ drove the limousine.

4. Tariq will be invited for party by Eva.

5. Hundreds of people visits CN tower. every day

6. Jewellery were made and designed by Sula.

7. Canadian author Michael Ondaatje wrote The English Patient

8. Successfull movie were made book by Hollywood

9. Eminem performed the song.

10. The driveway shovelled off 2 metres of snow.

Active-voice verbs are more direct and emphatic than passive verbs. Good writers use the active voice unless there is a specific reason to use the passive. There are three situations in which the passive voice is preferable:

1. The person or agent that performed the action is not known.

The computer had been left unplugged for two days.
Primate Road is the name that has been given to our street.
This workstation is not ergonomically designed.

2. You want to place the emphasis on the person, place, or object that was affected by an action rather than on the subject that performed the action.

The computer lab was broken into by a group of angry students.

This sentence focuses the reader's attention on the computer lab rather than on the students. If we reconstruct the sentence in the active voice, we produce a quite different effect.

A group of angry students broke into the computer lab.

3. You are writing a technical report, a scientific report, or a legal document.

Passive verbs are the appropriate choice when the focus is on the facts, methods, or procedures involved in an experiment, situation, or event rather than on the person(s) who discovered or performed them. Passive verbs establish an impersonal tone that is appropriate to these kinds of writing. Contrast the emphasis and tone of these sentence pairs:

Passive: The heat was increased to 150°C and was maintained at that temperature.
Active: My lab partner and I increased the heat to 150°C and maintained it at that temperature.

Passive: Our annual report was approved by the board on February 15.
Active: The board approved our annual report on February 15.

In general, because active verbs are more concise and forceful than passive verbs, they add focus and strength to your writing. When you find a passive verb in your writing, think about *who* is doing *what* to *whom*. Ask yourself why the *who* is not the subject of your sentence. If there is a good reason, then use the passive voice. Otherwise, change the verb.

EXERCISE **11.7**

Rewrite the sentences below, changing the verbs from passive to active voice. You may need to add a word or phrase to identify the doer of the action expressed by the verb.

1. Our hungry stomachs were filled by the delicious curry.

2. The gas for the trip was bought by Lisa.

3. The dishes were washed by our houseguests.

4. His business card was given to me by the sales representative.

5. An error in your bill was made by our computer.

6. This essay has not been formatted in APA style, as required.

7. On our first anniversary, our portrait was taken by a professional photographer.

8. American election practices are not always understood by Canadians.

9. In today's class, your research papers will be worked on by all of you.

10. All the information you need to become a competent writer is contained in this book.

EXERCISE **11.8**

Rewrite the sentences below, changing the verbs from passive to active voice. Then compare your revision to the original and, keeping in mind the three reasons for choosing the passive voice (page 156), decide which sentence is more effective.

1. The professor was told by Lola that she was finding the course too difficult.

2. A master chef prepared this meal.

3. The burning building was carefully entered by three firefighters.

4. The lights had been left on the whole time we were away.

5. In the final ceremony, the Olympic flag was carried by a biathlete.

6. The last thing ever done by my kids to earn money was lose their baby teeth. (Phyllis Diller)

7. His bookcase is used by my brother to hold his bowling trophies and empty fast-food containers.

8. A state of emergency has been declared and a special fund to aid the flood victims has been set up by the provincial government.

9. The project was delayed because of poor communication among the members of the team.

10. There are two reasons newspapers will never be replaced by electronic devices: a birdcage can't be lined with a TV, and fish and chips can't be served in a smartphone.

Go to Web Exercises 11.3, 11.4

EXERCISE **11.9**

Rewrite the following paragraph, changing verbs from passive voice to active voice where appropriate. Ten changes are required.

Photography is a hobby that is enjoyed by many people, from novices to experts. A very expensive camera is not needed, though to get the most enjoyment from taking quality pictures, a single-lens reflex (SLR) camera is preferred by most serious photographers over the "point and click" variety. But excellent snapshots suitable for uploading to an online album can be taken by a simple, inexpensive "point and shoot" camera. No matter what level of expertise you have, or how expensive your camera, improvements in the quality of your pictures can be made. Many courses are available where everything from basic photography to complex artistic effects can be learned. Once the capabilities of the camera have been mastered, the artistry of photography comes into play. Whether sports photography is preferred or close-up nature shots, portraits, or landscapes, many outlets for the creative eye are presented by this hobby. Furthermore, once the perfect picture has been taken, the result is a work of art that friends and family and even people far beyond your immediate circle can enjoy for many years.

Grammar

12 Mastering Subject–Verb Agreement

SINGULAR AND PLURAL

One of the most common writing errors is lack of **agreement** between subject and verb. Both must be singular, or both must be plural. If one is singular and the other plural, you have an agreement problem. You have another kind of agreement problem if your subject and verb are not both in the same "person" (see Chapter 16).

Let's clarify some terms. First, it's important to distinguish between **singular** and **plural**:

- *Singular* means one person or thing.
- *Plural* means more than one person or thing.

Second, it's important to know what we mean when we refer to the concept of **person**:

- *First person* is the person(s) speaking or writing: *I, me; we, us.*
- *Second person* is the person(s) being addressed: *you.*
- *Third person* is the person(s) being spoken or written about: *he, him, she, her, it; they, them.*

Here's an example of the singular and plural forms of a regular verb in the present tense:

	Singular	Plural
First person	I win	we win
Second person	you win	you win
Third person	she wins (*or* he, it, the horse wins)	they win (*or* the horses win)

The third-person singular form often causes trouble because the endings of the verb and its subject do not match. Third-person singular present tense verbs end in *-s,* but their singular subjects do not. Third-person plural verbs never end in *-s,* while their subjects normally do. Look at these examples:

A <u>fire</u> <u>burns</u>.
The <u>car</u> <u>skids</u>.
A <u>neighbour</u> <u>cares</u> for our children.

The three singular verbs, all of which end in *-s* (*burns, skids, cares*), agree with their singular subjects (*fire, car, neighbour*), none of which ends in *-s*. When the subjects become plural, the verbs change form too.

Four <u>fires</u> <u>burn</u>.
The <u>cars</u> <u>skid</u>.
The <u>neighbours</u> <u>care</u> for our children.

Now all of the subjects end in *-s,* and none of the verbs do.

To ensure subject–verb agreement, follow this basic rule:

> Subjects and verbs must both be either singular or plural.

This rule causes difficulty only when the writer doesn't know which word in the sentence is the subject and so makes the verb agree with the wrong word. As long as you decode the sentence correctly (see Chapter 5), you'll have no problem making every subject agree with its verb.

If you have not already done so, now is the time to memorize this next rule:

> The subject of a clause or sentence is NEVER in a prepositional phrase.

Here's an example of how errors occur:

Only one of the 2,000 ticket buyers are going to win.

What is the subject of this sentence? It's not *buyers,* but *one.* The verb must agree with *one,* which is clearly singular. The verb *are* does not agree with *one,* so the sentence is incorrect. It should read

Only <u>one</u> ~~of the 2,000 ticket buyers~~ <u>is</u> going to win.

If you are careful about identifying the subject of your sentence, even when it is separated from the verb by other words or phrases, you'll have no difficulty with subject–verb agreement. Before you try the exercises in this chapter, reinforce what you've learned by studying these examples.

Incorrect:	One of my sisters speak five languages.
Correct:	One ~~of my sisters~~ <u>speaks</u> five languages.
Incorrect:	Serena, one of the few girls on the team, keep trying for a perfect score.
Correct:	Serena, ~~one of the few girls on the team~~, <u>keeps</u> trying for a perfect score.
Incorrect:	One of the journalism students keep writing graffiti on the walls of the computer lab.
Correct:	One ~~of the journalism students~~ <u>keeps</u> writing graffiti ~~on the walls of the computer lab~~.

EXERCISE **12.1**

Underline the subject in each sentence. Answers for exercises in this chapter begin on page 531.

1. The <u>key</u> to power is knowledge.
2. Here are the <u>invoices</u> for this shipment of software.
3. In the <u>future</u>, instead of live animals, <u>people</u> may choose intelligent machines as pets.
4. At the front of the line stood <u>Professor Kersey</u>, waiting to see Santa.
5. <u>Jupiter and Saturn</u>, the solar system's largest planets, appear close together in the western sky.

Pay special attention to words that end in *-one, -thing,* or *-body*. They cause problems for nearly every writer.

> Words ending in *-one*, *-thing*, or *-body* are always singular.

When used as subjects, these pronouns require singular verbs:

anyone	anything	anybody
everyone	everything	everybody
no one	nothing	nobody
someone	something	somebody

The last part of the pronoun subject is the tip-off here: every*one*, any*thing*, no*body*. If you focus on this last part, you'll remember to use a singular verb with these subjects.

These words tend to cause trouble when modifiers come between them and their verbs. For example, you would never write "Everyone are here." But when you insert a word or phrase between the subject and the verb, you might, if you weren't careful, write this: "<u>Everyone</u> involved in implementing the company's new policies and procedures <u>are</u> here." The meaning is plural: several people are present. But the subject (*everyone*) is singular, so the verb must be *is*.

Most subject–verb agreement errors are caused by violations of this rule. Be sure you understand it. Memorize it, and then test your understanding by doing the following exercise before you go any further.

EXERCISE **12.2**

Circle the correct verb for each of the following sentences. Check your answers against ours on page 532.

1. Somebody with a taste for Reese's Pieces (has/have) found my hidden stash of candy.
2. Nothing (succeed/succeeds) like success.
3. Nobody on the team (show/shows) much respect for the coach.
4. Why is it that everybody we meet (talk/talks) to you instead of me?
5. Anyone with three cars (has/have) huge insurance payments.

Go to Web Exercise 12.1

EXERCISE **12.3**

Change the subject and verb in each sentence from plural to singular. Underline the subject once and the verb twice. Then check your answers.

1. Our papers are due on Tuesday.

2. Skiers love cold weather and heavy snowfalls.

3. Snow shovellers do not.

Has

4. Have the lucky winners collected the lottery money?

5. The articles in this journal give you the background information you need.

6. Why do teenagers fall in love?

has

7. Only recently have our track coaches become interested in chemistry.

is

8. So far, only two of your answers have been incorrect.

has

9. The pressures of schoolwork and part-time work have caused ~~many~~ students to drop out.

family of

10. Under our back porch live two skunks and their four babies.

Go to Web Exercise 12.2

EXERCISE **12.4**

Rewrite each sentence, switching the positions of the main elements (the subject and the object or complement) and revising the verb accordingly. For example,

Peanuts are my favourite snack.
My favourite snack is peanuts.

1. Hockey players are a good example.

2. A healthy type of oily fish is sardines.

3. Trees are an important supplier of oxygen to the Earth.

4. What irritates us on our quiet lake is noisy speedboats.

5. Fresh fruits and vegetables are an important part of a balanced diet.

EXERCISE **12.5**

This exercise will challenge your ability to make subjects and verbs agree. Rewrite the following paragraph, changing its nouns and verbs from plural to singular. Your first sentence will be "A **dog seems** to understand the **mood** of **its owner**."

Dogs seem to understand the moods of their owners. They are tuned in to any shifts in emotion or changes in health of the humans they live with. Doctors will often suggest adding pets to households where there are people suffering from depression or emotional problems. Dogs are sympathetic companions. The moods of people in retirement homes or even hospital wards can be brightened by visits from pet owners and their dogs. Dogs never tire of hearing about the "good old days," and they are uncritical and unselfish in giving affection. Doctors will often encourage epilepsy sufferers to adopt specially trained dogs. Such dogs are so attuned to the health of their owners that they can sense when seizures are about to occur long before the owners can. The dogs then warn the owners of the coming attack, so the owners are able to take safety precautions.

So far, so good. You can find the subject, even when it's hiding on the far side of the verb or separated from the verb by one or more prepositional phrases. You can match up singular subjects with singular verbs and plural subjects with plural verbs. Now let's take a look at a few of the complications that make subject–verb agreement such a disagreeable problem.

FOUR SPECIAL CASES

Some subjects are tricky. They look singular but are plural, or they look plural when they're really singular. There are four kinds of these slippery subjects, all of them common and all of them likely to trip up the unwary writer:

1. multiple subjects joined by *or, either … or, neither … nor*, or *not … but*

Most multiple subjects we've dealt with so far have been joined by *and* and have required plural verbs, so agreement hasn't been a problem. But watch

Grammar

out when the two or more elements of a compound subject are joined by *or*, *either ... or, neither ... nor*, or *not ... but*. In these cases, the verb agrees in number with the nearest subject. That is, if the subject closest to the verb is singular, the verb will be singular; if the subject closest to the verb is plural, the verb must be plural too.

> Neither the <u>federal government</u> nor the <u>provinces</u> effectively <u>control</u> pollution.

> Neither the <u>provinces</u> nor the <u>federal government</u> effectively <u>controls</u> pollution.

EXERCISE **12.6**

Circle the correct verb for each of the following sentences. Then check your answers against ours on page 532.

1. For a liberal arts program, either of the schools you are considering (is/are) fine.
2. Not longer prison sentences but the likelihood of getting caught (deters/deter) criminal behaviour.
3. Fast cars, powerful boats, or any video about them (fascinate/fascinates) five-year-old Joshua.
4. Neither bribery nor threats (influences/influence) my opinion of violence in hockey.
5. Either the professor or one of the lab assistants (sign/signs) the after-hours pass for the lab.

Go to Web Exercise 12.3

> **2. subjects that look multiple but really aren't**

Don't be fooled by phrases beginning with words such as *with, like, as well as, together with, in addition to*, and *including*. These prepositional phrases are NOT part of the subject of the sentence. Since they do not affect the verb, you can mentally cross them out.

My math professor, ~~as well as my counsellor,~~ has advised me to change my major.

Two people were involved in the advising; nevertheless, the subject (math professor) is singular, so the verb must be singular (has advised).

All my courses, ~~including English,~~ seem easier this term.

If you mentally cross out the phrase "including English," you can easily see that the verb (seem) must be plural to agree with the plural subject (courses).

EXERCISE **12.7**

Circle the correct verb for each of the following sentences. Then check your answers against ours on page 532.

1. Anar, like her sisters, (want/wants) to be a nurse.
2. One hot dog with ketchup, mustard, and pickles (has/have) more calories than you can imagine.
3. Our itinerary, including a Vieux Québec tour and a ferry ride to Lévis, (promise/promises) to be fascinating.
4. Eddie, together with his band, (is/are) performing tonight in the student pub.
5. "People skills," such as a sense of humour, (doesn't/don't) usually appear on a resumé although they are essential in the workplace.

Go to Web Exercise 12.4

3. collective nouns

A collective noun is a word naming a group. Some examples are *audience, band, class, committee, company, crowd, family, gang, group,* and *majority*. When you are referring to the group acting all together, as a unit, use a singular verb. When you are referring to the members of the group acting individually, use a plural verb.

The <u>team</u> <u>is</u> sure to win tomorrow's game.	(Here *team* refers to the group acting as one unit.)
The <u>team</u> <u>are</u> getting into their uniforms now.	(The members of the team are acting individually.)

EXERCISE **12.8**

Circle the correct verb in each case, and then check your answers against ours on page 532.

1. The public (love/<u>loves</u>) any political scandal involving adultery, blackmail, or bribery.
2. Our audience (<u>thinks</u>/think) we are better than Broken Social Scene!
3. The committee (<u>recommends</u>/recommend) stricter rules for parking.
4. The jury (<u>wants</u>/want) to spend the long weekend with their families.
5. The crowd (<u>was</u>/were) mostly dressed in jeans and T-shirts.

4. units of money, time, mass, length, and distance

These expressions require singular verbs.

<u>Fifteen dollars</u> <u>is</u> too much to pay for a hamburger.

<u>Two hours</u> <u>seems</u> like four in our sociology class.

<u>Eighty kilograms</u> <u>is</u> the mass of an average man.

<u>Ten kilometres</u> <u>is</u> too far to walk for groceries.

EXERCISE **12.9**

Circle the correct verb for each of the following sentences, and then check your answers against ours on page 533.

1. Seven metres of cable (hold/<u>holds</u>) the pole upright.
2. A 12-kilogram turkey (<u>is</u>/are) far too large for 10 people.
3. If you have good equipment and move at a steady speed, the 19 kilometres of the ski trail (go/<u>goes</u>) by very quickly.

4. Five hundred grams of grapes (was/were) more than I could eat.

5. When you're waiting for a plane, 10 minutes (seem/seems) like two hours.

Go to Web Exercise 12.5

The next three exercises review all of the troublesome aspects of subject–verb agreement. Correct the errors in each exercise, and then check your answers before going on. Answers for this section of the chapter begin on page 533.

EXERCISE **12.10**

1. The amount of government money directed toward job creation are enormous.

2. Not the weekly quizzes but the final exam are what I'm worried about.

3. Everyone within four blocks of the crime scene were interviewed by the detectives.

4. Either the tires or the alignment are causing the steering vibration.

5. There's no good reasons for skipping lunch.

6. This province, along with six others, have voted in favour of a federally supported drug program.

7. When Yusuf emptied his pockets, he found that $2.00 were all he had left to buy lunch.

8. The band, together with the backup players, the roadies, and the producers, are staying in a motel near the concert site.

9. We'd better fill up with gas: 400 kilometres of mountain roads lie ahead.

10. It seems that in every group project, one of the team members get stuck with most of the work.

EXERCISE **12.11**

1. Each day that passes brings us closer to the end of term.

2. Members of the Quechua tribe, who live in the Andes Mountains, has two or three more litres of blood than people living at lower elevations.

3. The swim team has been billeted with host families during their stay in Seattle.

4. Neither fame nor riches is my goal in life.

5. The original model for the king in a standard deck of playing cards are thought to be King Charles I of England.

6. A large planet together with two small stars are visible on the eastern horizon.

7. The lack of things to write about are my problem.

8. One faculty member in addition to a group of students have volunteered to help us clean out the lab.

9. Not only cat hairs but also ragweed make me sneeze.

10. Everyone who successfully completed these exercises deserve high praise.

Go to Web Exercises 12.6, 12.7

EXERCISE **12.12**

There are 10 errors in this paragraph. Can you find and correct them?

Most jobs now require computer skills, but the digital revolution has not improved our quality of life. Since a desktop computer, complete with head-phones for sound-based functions, exist in every office, work should be simpler. However, neither increased efficiency nor improved employee morale have resulted from our switch from paper to computers. Indeed, each worker's tasks has become more complex. In the past, for example, one invoice or two purchase orders was needed to complete a request for supplies. The process, including online confirmation, now require five separate documents. The result of this unnecessary complication, not surprisingly, are frustration and curses. Everyone, including the supervisors, are fed up with the extra work. When our division implement a new computer system next month, I expect at least two of my co-workers to quit. Fifteen hours of training are needed to learn the new system, and that is more time than any of us have to waste.

Go to Web Exercise 12.8

EXERCISE **12.13**

Complete the sentences using present tense verbs. After you complete this exercise, check the answer section to see whether your verbs should be singular or plural.

1. Neither my supervisor nor my colleagues

2. Everybody with two or more pets

3. Not the lead singer but the musicians

4. Anyone with red hair

5. Every one of his employees

6. Ten dollars

7. The whole family, including the children and grandparents

8. Not the instructor but the students

9. Either a Big Mac or a Whopper

10. No one among the hundreds present

EXERCISE **12.14**

Write your own sentences, choosing your subjects as indicated and using present tense verbs.

1. Use a unit of time as your subject (e.g., your age).

2. Use a multiple subject.

3. Use *no one* as your subject.

4. Use *everything* as your subject.

5. Use *neither … nor*.

6. Use *either … or*.

7. Use a singular subject + *together with*.

8. Use a plural subject + *in addition to*.

9. Use your own height as your subject.

10. Use a multiple subject joined by *or*.

The box at the top of the next page contains a summary of the rules governing subject–verb agreement. Review these rules carefully before you do the Mastery Test for this chapter.

SUMMARY

RULES GOVERNING SUBJECT–VERB AGREEMENT

- Subjects and verbs must agree: both must be singular, or both must be plural.
- The subject of a sentence is never in a prepositional phrase.
- Pronouns ending in *-one*, *-thing*, or *-body* are singular and require singular verbs.
- Subjects joined by *and* are always plural.
- When subjects are joined by *or*, *either… or*, *neither … nor*, or *not … but*, the verb agrees with the subject that is closest to it.
- When looking for the subject in a sentence, ignore phrases beginning with *as well as*, *including*, *in addition to*, *like*, *together with*, and so on. They are prepositional phrases.
- Collective nouns are usually singular.
- Units of money, time, mass, length, and distance are always singular.

Grammar

EXERCISE **12.15**

As a final check of your mastery of subject–verb agreement, correct the 15 errors in the following exercise.

Travel Advisory

Anyone from North America who wants to travel abroad, either alone or

with friends, are advised to remember that other countries are not like home.

Caution with respect to food, language, and customs are advisable, and the insecure traveller might want to consider visiting someplace safe such as Banff, Blaine, or Beaver Creek. The traveller who insists on crossing an ocean can expect to encounter situations, customs, and especially foods that will be a challenge. The French, for example, for reasons known only to them, consumes vast quantities of butter and garlic with their beloved *escargots*; however, no amount of butter and garlic piled on snails disguise the fact that they are slugs in a shell. And although croissants, the delectable breakfast of choice in much of Europe, is available everywhere, no foreigner attempting to pronounce the word *croissant* in a French bakery or Italian supermarket are likely to be understood. Cautious travellers will avoid the certain embarrassment and potential stomach upset that results from eating strange foods. Look instead for a local Pizza Hut, KFC, or McDonald's that provide familiar food in a familiar setting.

Another problem for the overseas traveller is that foreigners insist on speaking languages with which no one other than the natives are familiar. Neither shouting nor speaking very slowly and clearly seem to have any effect on their ability to understand simple English.

As for foreign customs, every country in the world celebrate traditions that those of us who prefers our adventures on television find bizarre and dangerous. Even a few days in foreign lands is enough to spell disaster. Spanish bulls, Italian drivers, German beer drinkers, Japanese subways, Brazilian beaches: all should be avoided by the traveller who want to return safe and sound to loved ones at home. In fact, anyone who are likely to be made uncomfortable by unfamiliar, exotic, or even new experiences, are advised either to stay home or vacation in the West Edmonton Mall.

Grammar

13 Keeping Your Tenses Consistent

Verbs are time markers. Changes in tense express changes in time: past, present, or future.

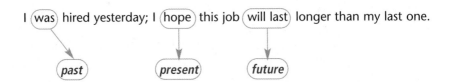

I (was) hired yesterday; I (hope) this job (will last) longer than my last one.

past   *present*   *future*

Sometimes, as in the sentence above, it is necessary to use several different tenses in a single sentence to get the meaning across. But most of the time, whether you're writing a sentence or a paragraph, you use one tense throughout. Normally, you choose either the past or the present tense, depending on the nature of your topic. (Few paragraphs are written completely in the future tense.) Here is the rule to follow:

Don't change tense unless meaning requires it.

Readers like and expect consistency. If you begin a sentence with "I argued, protested, and even appealed to his masculine pride," the reader will tune in to the past tense verbs and expect any other verbs in the sentence to be in the past tense, too. So, if you finish the sentence with "... but he looks at me with those big brown eyes and gets me to pay for dinner," your readers will be yanked out of one time frame into another. This sort of jolting is uncomfortable, and readers don't like it.

Shifting tenses is like shifting gears: it should be done smoothly and when necessary—never abruptly, out of carelessness, or on a whim. Avoid causing verbal whiplash; keep your tenses consistent. Consider these two examples, both of which mix tenses inappropriately.

Problem: I*'m standing* right behind Caro when she suddenly *screamed.*
Solution 1: I *was standing* right behind Caro when she suddenly *screamed.*
Solution 2: I*'m standing* right behind Caro when she suddenly *screams.*

Problem: Luca *procrastinated* until the last minute and then *begins* to write his paper. When he *gets* halfway through, he *decided* to change his topic.

Solution 1:   Luca *procrastinated* until the last minute and then *began* to write his paper. When he *got* halfway through, he *decided* to change his topic.

Solution 2:   Luca *procrastinates* until the last minute and then *begins* to write his paper. When he *gets* halfway through, he *decides* to change his topic.

Now look at the following example, which expresses a more complex idea.

Problem: I *handed* my paper in just before the deadline, but when I *see* the professor the next day, she *says* it was late, so I *will lose* marks.

This sentence is a hopeless muddle. It begins with the past tense, shifts to the present for no reason, and ends with the future.

Solution: I *handed* my paper in just before the deadline, but when I *saw* the professor the next day, she *said* it was late, so I *will lose* marks.

Here the past tense is used consistently until the last clause, where the shift to future tense is appropriate to the meaning.

In the following exercises, most—but not all—of the sentences contain unnecessary tense shifts. Use the first verb in each sentence as your time marker and change the tense(s) of the other verb(s) to agree with it. Answers for exercises in this chapter begin on page 534.

Go to Web Exercise 13.1

Grammar

EXERCISE **13.1**

1. Your professor is in a meeting until 4 p.m., so you had to wait to see her.

2. Giles tried to laugh, but he is too upset even to speak.

3. After his fiancée broke up with him, she refuses to return his ring.

4. Some people believe that, in the future, humans will live for 200 years.

5. The rebellion failed because the people do not support it.

6. I enjoy my work, but I was not going to let it take over my life.

7. Prejudice is learned and will be hard to outgrow.

8. A Canadian is someone who thinks that an income tax refund was a gift from the government.

9. Piers went to Laval for his vacation every summer and stays with his aunt and uncle on a farm.

10. Shahn likes to play cricket with his Canadian friends even though most of them didn't understand the rules.

Go to Web Exercise 13.2

EXERCISE **13.2**

Correct the 15 faulty time shifts in the following passage. Use the italicized verb as your time marker. Then check your answers.

A young businesswoman *decides* that the best way to ensure success in her new business is to rent impressive office space. She looked around at what is available and eventually selected a corner suite in a new downtown office tower. She then will decide to install fine furniture: a walnut desk, leather chairs, and brushed-steel fixtures. Last, she finished the office decor with expensive carpets and fine art.

On her first day in her beautiful new office, she saw a man come into the reception area, and, wanting to make a good impression, picked up the phone and pretended to speak to a customer. She saw that her visitor was looking at her with interest, so she began to talk to her imaginary customer as though she will negotiate a huge deal. She mentioned enormous sales numbers and huge sums of money, and finally concluded the "conversation" and hangs up the phone. She then turned to her visitor and asked how she could help him. The man replies, "I am here to install the phone."

Grammar

EXERCISE **13.3**

Correct the 15 faulty time shifts in the following passage. Use the italicized verb as your time marker. Then check your answers.

A large, scruffy-looking man *walked* into a Cadillac dealership on Bay Street in Toronto and proceeds to stroll around the showroom, studying the cars on display. The salesman, taking note of the battered black cowboy hat, scuffed western boots, and weathered leather vest, decides to ignore him. The man spends 10 minutes or so looking at each model, frequently checking to see if the salesman would help him. The salesman doesn't move from his desk at the back of the showroom, but he watches the big man carefully.

Finally, obviously annoyed, the man gives an exaggerated tip of his weather-beaten hat in the direction of the salesman and walks out of the dealership. About an hour later, a sleek Mercedes-Benz sedan pulls up to the Cadillac dealership, and the driver honks the horn until the salesman looks over. It's the same scruffy man, now driving a car worth more than any of the Cadillacs in the showroom. The man blows a kiss at the salesman and drives away. The bearded man in the shabby clothes is Ronnie Hawkins, the great blues/rockabilly/country singer who has just made a fortune from his latest hit album.

EXERCISE **13.4**

Correct the 15 faulty time shifts in the following paragraph. Use the italicized verb as your time marker.

I sometimes think that life *was* much simpler 40 or 50 years ago. Food, for example, is a lot less complicated. There were simply not as many nutritional concerns for us to worry about. We just drink our milk and eat our vegetables; we don't bother with low-fat cookbooks or calorie counting. Eating meat is not a political statement, and dessert was a treat to be enjoyed, not a substance we have to analyze for its fat and sugar content. Because we know nothing about mad cow disease, we cooked our burgers medium-rare and gobbled them down happily. We don't worry about pesticides and bought plenty of farm-fresh produce when it is in season. Because genetically modified foods were developed much later, we thought that Frankenfood is the stuff of science fiction, not

standard grocery fare. We never imagined that even basic foods, such as milk,

would become controversial. Neither do we realize that scientists would one

day be growing new varieties of grain in test tubes. Certainly, we cannot have

predicted the mammoth health food industry that would develop by the end of

the 20th century. When I was a youngster, I thought granola is an exotic food,

wheat germ is a contagious disease, and the word *organic* applies to a branch of

chemistry. I am better informed today, but I'm not sure I am better off.

14 Choosing the Correct Pronoun Form

"Pronoun? That's just a noun used by a professional!" When a character in a television sitcom spoke this line, the audience cracked up. His TV wife corrected him, bossily pointing out that a pronoun is a word that stands in for a noun, replacing it in a sentence so the noun doesn't have to be repeated. His response: "Both answers are acceptable."

Of course, he's wrong, and his wife is right. (In sitcoms, the wife is always right.) Generally, pronouns are not well understood. In this chapter and the two following, we will look at the three aspects of pronoun usage that can trip you up if you're not careful: **pronoun form**, **agreement**, and **consistency**. We will also consider the special problem of using pronouns in a way that avoids sexist language.

Three kinds of pronouns can cause difficulty for writers:

Personal pronouns	Examples: I, we, she, they
Relative pronouns	Examples: who, which, that
Indefinite pronouns	Examples: any, somebody, none, each

(See pages 480–82 for a complete list of these pronouns.)

The first thing you need to do is be sure you are using the correct pronoun form. Look at these examples of incorrect pronoun usage:

Her and me offered to pick up the car.
Between you and I, I think Ted's mother does his homework.

How do you know which form of a pronoun to use? The answer depends on the pronoun's place and function in your sentence.

SUBJECT AND OBJECT PRONOUNS

There are two forms of personal pronouns. One is used for subjects, and one is used for objects. Pronoun errors occur when you confuse the two. In Chapter 5, you learned to identify the subject of a sentence. Keep that information in mind as you learn the following basic rule.

When the subject of a sentence is (or is referred to by) a pronoun, that pronoun must be in **subject** form; otherwise, use the **object** form.

Subject Pronouns

Singular	Plural
I	we
you	you
he, she, it, one	they

She and *I* offered to pick up the car.
(The pronouns are the subject of the sentence.)

The lucky winners of the free tickets to the World Wrestling Championships are *they*.
(The pronoun refers to the subject of the sentence, *winners*.)

The only person who got an A in the course was *she*.
(The pronoun refers to the subject of the sentence, *person*.)

We serious bikers prefer Harleys to Hondas.
(The pronoun refers to the subject of the sentence, *bikers*.)

Object Pronouns

Singular	Plural
me	us
you	you
him, her, it, one	them

Between you and *me*, I think Ted's mother does his homework.
(*Me* is not the subject of the sentence; it is one of the objects of the preposition *between*.)

Sasha saw *him* and *me* having coffee at Tim Hortons.
(*Him* and *me* are not the subject of the verb *saw*; Sasha is, so the pronouns must be in the object form.)

The police are always suspicious of *us* bikers.
(*Us* does not refer to the subject of the sentence, *police*; it refers to *bikers*, the object of the preposition *of*.)

Grammar

Be especially careful with pronouns that occur in multiple subjects or after prepositions. If you remember the following two rules, you'll be able to eliminate most potential errors in pronoun form.

1. All pronouns in a compound (multiple) subject are always in subject form.
2. Pronouns that follow a preposition are always in object form.

She and *I* have season's tickets.
(The pronouns are used as a compound subject.)

We are delighted for *you* and *her*.
(The pronouns follow the preposition *for*.)

When you're dealing with a pair of pronouns and can't decide which form to use, try this test.[1] Mentally cross out one pronoun at a time, then read aloud the sentence you've created. Applying this technique to the first example above, you get "*She* has season's tickets" and "*I* have season's tickets," both of which sound right and are correct. In the second sentence, if you try the pronouns separately, you get "We are delighted for *you*" and "We are delighted for *her*." Again, you know by the sound that these are the correct forms. You would never say "*Her* had tickets" or "*Me* had tickets," or "We are delighted for *she*." If you deal with paired pronouns one at a time, you are unlikely to choose the wrong form.

Note, too, that when a pair of pronouns includes *I* or *me*, that pronoun comes last. For example, we write "*She* and *I*" (not "*I* and *she*") and "between *you* and *me*" (not "between *me* and *you*"). There is no grammatical reason for this rule. It's based on courtesy. Good manners require that you speak of others first and yourself last.

EXERCISE **14.1**

Choose the correct pronouns from the words given in parentheses. Answers for exercises in this chapter begin on page 535.

1. There's nobody in the building but (us/we).

2. My mother and (her/she) cannot agree on anything.

---

[1] This test is reliable only for those who are fluent in English. Until they become fluent, unfortunately, English language learners must rely on memorizing the rules.

3. Except for Vikram and (her/she), no one knows how to enter the data manually.

4. (Me and Anton/Anton and I) are best friends.

5. The work will go much faster if (he/him) and Roland do it by themselves.

6. Sami and (he/him) wrote, shot, and edited the entire film.

7. It will be difficult to choose between (she/her) and (I/me).

8. Every year, my grandmother knits sweaters for my brother and (I/me).

9. Surely your sister wasn't serious when she said (they/them) and their children were coming to stay with us for three weeks?

10. (Him and me/He and I/I and he) have completely different tastes in music.

EXERCISE **14.2**

Correct the 15 errors in pronoun form in the following sentences.

1. Have you and her ever tried rock climbing?

2. Him and Alex take the same math class.

3. It is not up to you or I to discipline your sister's children.

4. Living with our parents isn't easy, either for we or they.

5. Him and his mother get along fine, but him and his father are constantly arguing.

6. Was it him who served you? Or was it her?

7. Him and Marie finished on time; except for they and their staff, no one else met the deadline.

8. Susana and me are going to be your trainers for the next month.

9. In terms of career potential, I don't think there's much difference between we and they.

10. For once, there was no one ahead of Trina and I in the lineup outside the registrar's office.

Grammar

Go to Web Exercises 14.1, 14.2

USING PRONOUNS IN CONTRAST CONSTRUCTIONS

Choosing the correct pronoun form is more than just a matter of not wanting to appear ignorant or careless. Sometimes the form you use determines the meaning of your sentence. Consider these two sentences:

Gina treats her dog better than *I*.
Gina treats her dog better than *me*.

There's a world of difference between the meaning of the subject form ("Gina treats her dog better than *I* [do]") and the object form ("Gina treats her dog better than [she treats] *me*").

When using a pronoun after *than, as well as,* or *as,* decide whether you mean to contrast the pronoun with the subject of the sentence. If you do, use the subject form of the pronoun. If not, use the object form.

Meiling would rather listen to an iPod than I.
(*I* is contrasted with *Meiling*.)

Meiling would rather listen to an iPod than me.
(*Me* is contrasted with *iPod*.)

Here's a quick way to check that you've used the correct pronoun form. If you've used a subject form, mentally insert a verb after it. If you've used an object form, mentally insert a preposition before it. If your sentences make sense, you have chosen correctly. For example,

Meiling would rather listen to an iPod than I [would].
Meiling would rather listen to an iPod than [to] me.

Some writers prefer to leave the clarifying verb or preposition in place, a practice that eliminates any possibility of confusion.

Grammar

EXERCISE **14.3**

Correct the errors in the following sentences. Check your answers against ours on pages 535–36.

1. The prize is sure to go to Omar and she.

2. No one likes our cooking class more than me.

3. In fact, nobody in the class eats as much as me.

4. It's not surprising that I am much bigger than them.

5. My mother would rather cook for my brother than I because he never complains when dinner is burned or raw.

6. At last I have met someone who loves barbecued eel as much as me!

7. More than me, Yuxiang uses the computer to draft and revise his papers.

8. He doesn't write as well as me, but he does write faster.

9. Only a few Mexican food fanatics can eat as many jalapeno peppers as him.

10. I think you have as much trouble with English as me.

Go to Web Exercise 14.3

EXERCISE **14.4**

Revise the following paragraphs to correct the 10 errors in pronoun form.

Us Canadians take pride in being "multicultural" and sharing in one another's traditions, and we are all far richer for this diversity. This wealth of cultural tradition is perhaps best recognized in the amazing choice of cuisines from every corner of the world that are available to we food lovers. Newcomers and visitors are often astounded by the variety of dishes and ingredients available to they and their families in Canada's restaurants and markets. Older immigrants, however, sometimes find it difficult to adjust. For example, my grandfather came here from England as an adult and to he and his sisters, pasta was "foreign muck"; anything cooked with garlic was "offensive"; and curry was "inedible." My siblings and me, having been brought up in a multicultural environment, often think of our grandfather's generation when we sit down to a delicious meal of spaghetti in garlic sauce or spicy curried lamb! When my grandparents were growing up, their daily menu was very plain and narrowly traditional; they had no concept of the food varieties available to my friends and I.

I imagine that future generations will be even more fortunate. Canada now trains and attracts great chefs who are accustomed to cooking in a multicultural environment; it is them who are combining some of the surprising elements found in delicious "fusion" dishes. Thai–Polynesian and

Caribbean–Indian fusions are examples of some of the imaginative creations now available to we adventurous restaurant diners. The enormously varied and delicious cuisines of the regions of Africa are also now becoming widely available to those of we who delight in trying food outside our normal experience. Our children and grandchildren can look forward to ever more varied and interesting foods, prepared by creative chefs and served in authentic style. They and us are truly fortunate to be living in a nation that values multiculturalism and celebrates our differences as well as our common bonds.

Grammar

15 Mastering Pronoun– Antecedent Agreement

"I am writing in response to your ad for a server and bartender, male or female. Being both, I am applying for the position."

Pronoun confusion can take several forms, and some of the resulting sentences can be unintentionally hilarious. In this chapter, we'll look at how to use pronouns consistently throughout a sentence or paragraph to avoid confusing (and embarrassing) mistakes.

PRONOUN–ANTECEDENT AGREEMENT

The name of this pronoun problem may sound difficult, but the idea is simple. Pronouns are words that substitute for or refer to a person, place, or thing mentioned elsewhere in your sentence or paragraph. The word(s) that a pronoun substitutes for or refers to is called the **antecedent**.

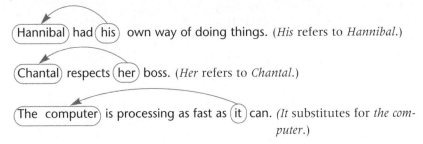

Hannibal had his own way of doing things. (*His* refers to *Hannibal*.)

Chantal respects her boss. (*Her* refers to *Chantal*.)

The computer is processing as fast as it can. (*It* substitutes for *the computer*.)

Usually, as in these three examples, the antecedent comes before the pronoun[1] that refers to it. Here is the rule to remember:

A pronoun must agree with its antecedent in
- number (singular or plural)
- person (first, second, or third)
- gender (masculine, feminine, or neuter)

---

[1] Strictly speaking, possessive words such as *my, his, her, our,* and *their* are pronominal adjectives rather than pronouns. We are dealing with them in this chapter, however, because they follow the same agreement rule that governs pronouns.

Most of the time, you follow this rule without even realizing that you know it. For example, you would never write

Hannibal had *your* own way of doing things.

Chantal respects *its* boss.

The computer is processing as fast as *she* can.

You know these sentences are incorrect even if you may not know exactly why.

There are three kinds of pronoun–antecedent agreement that you need to learn. Unlike the examples above, they are not obvious, and you need to know them so you can watch out for them. The rules you need to learn involve **indefinite pronouns ending in** *-one*, *-body*, **or** *-thing*; **vague references**; and **relative pronouns**.

1. PRONOUNS ENDING IN *-ONE*, *-BODY*, *-THING*

The most common pronoun–antecedent agreement problem involves the following **indefinite pronouns**:

anyone	anybody	anything
everyone	everybody	everything
no one	nobody	nothing
someone	somebody	something
each (one)		

In Chapter 12, you learned that when these words are used as subjects, they are singular and require singular verbs. So it makes sense that the pronouns that stand for or refer to them must also be singular.

> Antecedents ending in *-one*, *-body*, and *-thing* are singular.
> They must be referred to by singular pronouns: he, she, it; his, her, its.

Everything has *its* place and should be in it.

Everyone deserves a break from *her* children now and then.

Everybody is expected to do *his* share of the work.

No one had the courage to express *his* anger.

Now take another look at the last three sentences. Until the latter half of the 20th century, the pronouns *he, him,* and *his* were used with singular antecedents to refer to both men and women. Modern readers are sensitive to gender bias in writing, and most think it inappropriate to use the masculine pronoun to refer to both sexes. As a writer, you should be aware of this sensitivity. If you want to appeal to the broadest possible audience, you should avoid what readers may consider sexist language.

In informal usage, it has become acceptable to use plural pronouns with *one, body,* and *thing* antecedents. Although they are grammatically singular, they are often plural in meaning, and in conversation we tend to say

Everybody is expected to do *their* share of the work.

No one had the courage to express *their* anger.

This usage is acceptable in speech, but it is not acceptable in academic or professional writing.

Writers sometimes make errors in pronoun–antecedent agreement because they are trying not to identify the gender of the person(s) referred to. "Everybody is expected to do *their* share of the work" is grammatically incorrect, as we have seen; however, it does avoid making "everybody" male or "everybody" female. The writer could replace the plural *their* with the singular and non-sexist *his or her*—"Everybody is expected to do *his or her* share of the work"—but *his or her* sounds clumsy if it is used frequently. There are two better ways to solve the problem:

1. Revise the sentence to leave out the pronoun.

Everybody is expected to share the work.

No one had the courage to protest.

Such creative avoidance of gender-specific language or incorrect constructions can be an interesting intellectual challenge. The resulting sentence sometimes sound a little artificial, however. The second solution is easier to accomplish.

2. Revise the sentence to make both the antecedent and the pronoun plural.

We are all expected to do *our* share of the work.

Staff members did not have the courage to express *their* anger.

Here are a couple of examples for you to study:

Problem:	*Everybody* has been given *his* assignment.
Solution 1:	*Everybody* has been given *an* assignment.
Solution 2:	*All* of the students have been given *their* assignments.

Problem:	*No one* likes to have *his* writing corrected.
Solution 1:	*No one* likes to have written work corrected.
Solution 2:	Most *people* dislike having *their* writing corrected.

If you are writing on a word processor, you may be able to use the grammar checker to ensure agreement between indefinite pronouns and their antecedents. Some grammar checkers will catch this type of error. The revisions offered by the checker may not be elegant, but they usually are technically correct. This step takes less time than you might think and is well worth it, especially if your instructor has asked for a formal paper or report.

EXERCISE **15.1**

Identify the most appropriate word(s) from the choices given in parentheses. Check your answers carefully before continuing. Answers for exercises in this chapter begin on page 536.

1. The caller refused to leave (his/her/a) message.
2. Can anyone bring (his/her/a) car?
3. Each player on the team has (her/their) strengths.
4. The men's hockey team lost 11 to 1; every team member played below (his/their) ability.
5. It seemed that everyone in the mall was talking on (his/her/their/a) cellphone.
6. Would someone kindly lend (his/her/their/a) copy of the textbook to Lisa?
7. A bandleader is someone who is not afraid to face (his/her/their/the) music.
8. Everyone is expected to pay (his or her/their/a) share of the expenses.
9. We will try to return to (its/their) owner anything we find in the locker room.
10. Anyone who wants a high mark for (his/their/this) essay should see me after class and write (his/their/a) cheque payable to me.

EXERCISE **15.2**

Correct the errors in the following sentences, being careful to avoid awkward repetition and sexist language. Because there is more than one way to correct these errors, your answers may differ from our suggestions.

1. Everyone is a product of their environment as well as heredity.

2. No one as capable as you needs to have help with their assignment.

3. Each car in all categories will be judged on their bodywork, engine, and interior.

4. Every movie-, theatre-, and concertgoer knows how annoying it is to have their evening's enjoyment spoiled by a ringing cellphone.

5. Put the sign at the curb so anyone looking for our yard sale won't have to waste their time driving around the neighbourhood.

6. Everyone who pays their membership fee in advance will receive a free session with a personal trainer.

7. A smart husband knows enough to think twice before they say anything.

8. Ultimate is a game in which everyone enjoys themselves, whether their team finishes first or last.

9. No one on the football team has been able to convince their parents to donate his or her house for the party.

10. Every child wants to grow up as fast as possible, but once they reach adulthood, they wish they could go back.

Go to Web Exercise 15.1

2. VAGUE REFERENCES

Avoiding the second potential difficulty with pronoun–antecedent agreement requires common sense and the ability to put yourself in your reader's place. If you read your writing from your reader's point of view, it is unlikely that you will break the following rule.

Every pronoun must have a clearly identifiable antecedent.

The mistake that occurs when you fail to follow this rule is called **vague reference**.

Luc pointed to his brother and said that he had saved his life.

Who saved whom? Here's another:

Danielle wrote a song about her sister when she was five years old.

Is the song about a five-year-old sister, or was Danielle a musically talented child?

In sentences like these, you can only guess the meaning because you don't know who the pronouns refer to. The antecedents are not clear. You can make such sentences less confusing either by using proper names (Luc, Danielle) more frequently or by changing the sentences around. These solutions aren't difficult; they just take a little time and some imagination. Try them on our examples above.

Another type of vague reference occurs when there is no antecedent for the pronoun to refer to.

Zoe loves dog shows and is going to enter hers when *it's* old enough. (Enter what? The dog or the show?)

Snowboarding is Clara's favourite sport, and she's hoping to get *one* for her birthday. (One what?)

My roommate smokes constantly, *which* I hate. (There is no noun or pronoun for *which* to refer to.)

My sister's work schedule overlaps with her husband's. *This* creates child-care problems. (What does *this* refer to?)

Grammar

How would you revise these sentences? Try it, and then see our suggestions below.

Suggestions: Zoe loves dog shows and is going to enter her *puppy* when it's old enough.

Snowboarding is Clara's favourite sport, and she's hoping to get *a board* for her birthday.

My roommate has a habit of constantly smoking, *which* I hate.

My sister's work schedule overlaps with her husband's. *This* conflict creates child-care problems.

Make sure that every pronoun has a clear antecedent and that every pronoun agrees with its antecedent. Both must be singular, or both must be plural. Once you have mastered this principle, you'll have no trouble with pronoun–antecedent agreement.

EXERCISE **15.3**

Correct the following sentences as necessary. There are several ways to fix each one. In some cases, the antecedent is missing, and you need to supply one. In other cases, the antecedent is so vague that the meaning of the sentence can be interpreted in more than one way; you need to rewrite these sentences to make the meaning clear. Check your answers against ours on pages 536–37.

1. Every time Hassan looked at the dog, he barked.

2. What did Mei say to her mother before she hung up the phone?

3. Karla didn't hear my question, which was because she was eavesdropping on the couple in the next booth.

4. I lost my temper and slammed my fist on the table, breaking it.

5. Some of our friends are already parents, but we're not in a hurry to have one.

6. My wife was annoyed when I didn't notice she had fallen overboard; this was because I was concentrating on landing my fish.

7. When I learned that smoking was the cause of my asthma, I gave them up for good.

8. Kevin told Yu to leave the books on the table beside his computer.

9. At our college, they strictly enforce the "no smoking" policy.

10. Being on time is a challenge for my girlfriend, so I'm getting her one for her birthday.

Go to Web Exercise 15.2

3. RELATIVE PRONOUNS

The third potential difficulty with pronoun–antecedent agreement is how to use relative pronouns—*who, whom, whose, which,* and *that*—correctly. Relative pronouns must refer to someone or something already mentioned in the sentence. Here is the guideline to follow:

> Use *who* and *whom* to refer to people.
> Use *that* and *which* to refer to everything else.

The chef *who* prepared this meal deserves a medal.

The servers *who* presented it deserve to be fired.

The appetizer *that* I ordered was covered with limp cilantro.

My soup, *which* was cold, arrived at the same time as my main course.

My father's meal, *which* was delicious, demonstrated the talent *that* the chef is famous for.

Whether you need *who* or *whom*[2] depends on the pronoun's place and function in your sentence. Apply the basic pronoun rule:

---

[2] The distinction between *who* and *whom* has all but disappeared in spoken English and is becoming rarer in written English. Ask your instructor for guidance.

If the pronoun is, or refers to, the subject of the sentence, or if the pronoun is followed by a verb, use *who*. Otherwise, use *whom*. Or you can revise the sentence to eliminate the pronoun.

Lilia is the lucky woman *who* drew the winning ticket for a week's holiday in Moose Factory. (The pronoun refers to the subject of the sentence, *Lilia*.)

The trip's promoters were willing to settle for *whom* they could get. (The pronoun does not refer to the subject, *promoters*; it is the object of the preposition *for*.)

A better solution is to solve the problem by rewriting the sentence so you don't need either *who* or *whom*.

Lilia drew the winning ticket for a week's holiday in Moose Factory.

The trip's promoters were willing to settle for anyone they could get.

That is required more often than *which*. You should use *which* only in a clause that is separated from the rest of the sentence by commas. (See Comma Rule 4, page 218.)

The moose *that* I met looked hostile.

The moose, *which* was standing right in front of my car, looked hostile.

EXERCISE **15.4**

Correct the pronoun errors in the following sentences. Remember: use *who* or *whom* to refer to people; use *that* or *which* to refer to everything else. Check your answers against ours on page 537.

1. Chi Keung is the technician that can fix your problem.

2. I would have won, except for one judge that placed me fourth.

3. A grouch is a person which knows himself and isn't happy about what he

   knows.

4. The sales clerk that sold me my DVD player didn't know what he was talking about.

5. Everyone that was at the party had a good time, though a few had more punch than was good for them.

6. The open-office concept sounds good to anyone that has worked in a stuffy little cubicle all day.

7. I wish I could find someone in our class that could help me with my homework.

8. I regularly order supplies from companies who are located in cities all across the country.

9. The tests which we wrote today were designed to discourage anyone that didn't have the knowledge, preparation, and stamina to endure them.

10. My roommate has just started on the term paper, that was assigned a month ago, for her political science course.

Go to Web Exercise 15.3

EXERCISE **15.5**

Revise the following paragraphs, which contain 10 pronoun–antecedent agreement errors. If you change a subject from singular to plural, don't forget to change the verb to agree. Some of your answers may differ from our suggestions and still be correct.

Everyone in North America seems obsessed with showing their grasp of useless information. Trivia games have been hugely popular for decades, and they continue to attract large audiences. The trivia player is expected to have at their fingertips all sorts of obscure information, from sports statistics to popular music, from world geography to the film industry. Team trivia contests have become important fundraising events for charity. Teams of eight to ten players answer trivia questions in competition with other teams. Each member of a team is expected to have their own particular area of expertise and to help their team gain points by answering the questions in that area. At the end of the contest, the winning team will usually have answered correctly more than 80 percent of the questions called out by the quizmaster.

Another forum for trivia is the television shows in which the contestant must demonstrate their knowledge individually in a high-pressure, game-show format. Alone, each contestant faces the show's host, who may give them assistance if they ask for it. In other games, one contestant plays against another and must demonstrate superior knowledge if they want to win. Playing trivia at home is also popular, and many households have one.

Whether you play alone, with friends, on a team, or on television, they should keep the game in perspective. After all, the object of any trivia game is to reward the players who demonstrate that they know more about unimportant and irrelevant facts than anyone else in the game!

SUMMARY

PRONOUNS AND ANTECEDENTS

- Every pronoun must agree with its antecedent (a word or phrase mentioned, usually earlier, in the sentence or paragraph). Both must be singular, or both must be plural.
- Antecedents ending in *-one*, *-body*, and *-thing* are singular and must be referred to by singular pronouns: *he, she, it; his, her, its.*
- A pronoun must clearly refer to a specific antecedent.
- Use *who* and *whom* to refer to people; use *that* and *which* to refer to animals, objects, and ideas.
- As a courtesy to your reader, try to make your writing gender neutral.

EXERCISE **15.6**

Correct the 15 errors in the following paragraphs. Part of the challenge in this Mastery Test is to make the paragraphs not only grammatically correct but also free of sexist language. Before you try the test, we suggest that you review the rules for pronoun–antecedent agreement in the Summary box above.

Barbecuing season is upon us, but since mine is quite old and actually starting to rust, I am looking at new, shiny ones in the hardware stores. For some reason that is probably buried in our genetic makeup, it seems to be men, many of which otherwise are incapable of boiling water, that are the cooking experts outside of the kitchen. Every one of them that enjoys outdoor cooking knows that the more expensive their equipment, the better the food they prepare will taste. For this reason, the barbecue has evolved from a simple grill with a fire underneath it into an enormous, stainless-steel contraption that would not seem out of place in a science fiction movie. The barbecue chef can now command enough heat in their gas-fired monster to incinerate bricks. They have side burners, warming trays, pizza ovens, built-in refrigerators, and even TVs at their disposal.

Does all this technology make better hamburgers or steaks? Well, they certainly do make it easier to produce good results in the hands of a capable cook that uses their equipment with confidence and knowledge. However, the best barbecue in the world can't prevent inept cooks from using them to produce hamburgers that resemble burnt offerings or steaks that taste like shoe leather.

As I survey the various barbecues for sale, I think of a friend that asked a salesman if he would show him his favourite model. The salesman took him to a barbecue that cost almost as much as a compact car and said that it was the best model for impressing the neighbours, but "You wouldn't want to cook anything on it!"

Maintaining Person Agreement

So far, we have focused on using pronouns correctly and clearly within a sentence. Now let's turn to the problem of **person agreement**, which means using pronouns consistently throughout a sentence or a paragraph. There are three categories of person that we use when we write or speak:

	Singular	**Plural**
First person	I; me	we; us
Second person	you	you
Third person	she, he, it, one; her, him *and all pronouns ending in* -one, -body, -thing	they; them

Here is the rule for person agreement:

> Do not mix "persons" unless the meaning requires it.

In other words, be consistent. If you begin a sentence using a second-person pronoun, you should use the second person all the way through. Look at this sentence:

If *you* want to succeed, *one* must work hard.

Mixing second-person *you* with third-person *one* is the most common error. Here's another example:

At 35, just when *you* have *your* head together, *one's* body begins to fall apart.

We can correct this error by using the second person throughout:

At 35, just when *you* have *your* head together, *your* body begins to fall apart.

We can also correct it by using the third person throughout:

> At 35, just when *one* has *one's* head together, *one's* body begins to fall apart.

or

> At 35, just when *one* has *his* or *her* head together, *one's* body begins to fall apart.

These last two sentences raise two points of style that you should consider:

1. Don't overuse *one*.

All three revised sentences are grammatically correct, but they make different impressions on the reader, and impressions are an important part of communication.

- The first sentence, in the second person, sounds the most informal—like something you would speak. It's a bit casual for general writing purposes.
- The second sentence, which uses *one* three times, sounds the most formal—even a little stuffy.
- The third sentence falls between the other two in formality. It is the one you'd be most likely to use in writing for school or business.

Although it is grammatically correct and non-sexist, this third sentence raises another problem. Frequent use of *he or she* in a continuous prose passage, whether that passage is as short as a paragraph or as long as a paper, is guaranteed to irritate your reader.

2. Don't overuse *he or she*.

He or she is inclusive, but it is a wordy construction. If it is used too frequently, the reader cannot help shifting focus from what you're saying to how you're saying it. The best writing is transparent—that is, it doesn't call attention to itself. If your reader becomes distracted by your style, your meaning is lost. Consider this sentence:

> A student can easily pass this course if he or she applies himself or herself to his or her studies.

Readers deserve better. There are two better solutions to this problem that are already familiar to you because they are the same as those for making pronouns ending in *-one*, *body*, or *thing* agree with their antecedents:

1. You can change the whole sentence to the plural.

   Students can easily pass this course if they apply themselves to their studies.

2. You can rewrite the sentence without using pronouns.

   A student can easily pass this course by applying good study habits.

EXERCISE **16.1**

Select the most appropriate word(s) from the choices given in parentheses. Answers for exercises in this chapter begin on page 538.

1. If you want to be a rock star (one/you) should start developing a stage personality early.
2. A person can succeed at almost anything if (you have/they have/he or she has) talent and determination.
3. When we laugh, the world laughs with (you/one/us).
4. You can save a great deal of time if (one fills/you fill/we fill) out the forms before going to the passport office.
5. Clarify the question before beginning to write, or (one/you) may lose your focus.
6. Our opinions will never be heard unless (one tries/we try/you try) to communicate them in logical order.
7. I wish that (one/we) had a few more options to choose from.
8. (One/You) should not question Professor Snape in class because he loses his temper, and you don't want that to happen.
9. Anyone with a telephone can get (his or her/one's/their/your) voice heard on the radio.
10. Call-in programs give everyone the opportunity to make sure the whole world knows (one's/our/your) ignorance of the issues.

Go to Web Exercise 16.1

EXERCISE **16.2**

Correct the errors in pronoun consistency in the following sentences.

1. The faster one goes, the more you need good brakes.

2. One is never too old to learn, but you are never too young to know every-thing.

3. One always removes your shoes when entering a mosque.

4. The speed limit is the speed one goes as soon as you see a police car.

5. When one visits Beijing, you must see the Great Wall, the Forbidden City, and the Temple of Heaven.

6. Experience is that marvellous thing that enables us to recognize a mistake when you make it again. (F.P. Jones)

7. If you can't cope with the pressure, one must expect to be replaced by someone who can.

8. We all believed his story because you couldn't believe he would lie.

9. Diaries are places to record our private thoughts, and you ought to be bru-tally honest when making your entries.

10. Most people enjoy eating when you are with good friends in relaxed sur-roundings.

Go to Web Exercise 16.2

EXERCISE **16.3**

Correct the five consistency errors in the following paragraph. Look for errors in number agreement (singular versus plural) as well as person agreement.

Those of us who enjoy baseball find it difficult to explain one's enthusiasm to non-fans. We baseball enthusiasts can watch a game of three hours or more as one follows each play with rapt attention. We true fans get excited by a no-hitter—a game in which, by definition, nothing happens. They claim that the game is about much more than mere action, but non-fans must be forgiven if you don't get the point. To them, watching a baseball game is about as exciting as watching paint dry.

EXERCISE **16.4**

Rewrite the following paragraph in the first-person plural, using *we, our,* and *us* as your base pronouns. As you revise, correct the 10 errors in agreement of person and number. Be sure to change verbs, where necessary, to agree with their revised subjects. (The quotation from Robert Frost has been altered to suit the purpose of this exercise.)

When one is at the beginning of our careers, it seems impossible that you may one day wish to work less. The drive to get ahead leads many of us to sacrifice one's leisure, one's community responsibilities, even one's family life for the sake of one's careers. Normally, as you age, one's priorities begin to change, and career success becomes less important than quality of life. Not everyone, however, experiences this shift in priorities. Indeed, some people work themselves to death, while others are so committed to their work throughout their lives that they die within months of retirement—presumably from stress caused by lack of work. The poet Robert Frost once observed, "By working faithfully eight hours a day, you may eventually get to be a boss. Then one can work twelve hours a day." Those of you who are living and working in the early years of the 21st century would be wise to take Frost's words to heart.

EXERCISE **16.5**

Find and correct the 10 errors in pronoun agreement (person and number) in the following passage.

If a Canadian has ever travelled by train, then you know what a pleasure it is to be whisked to one's destination without effort while enjoying a relaxed and even productive trip. Train travel is neither as luxurious nor as convenient as it once was, when we could travel to virtually any destination across Canada while you enjoyed fine dining, relaxed in one's own stateroom, and slept comfortably in your well-appointed bedroom. However, even today, the train offers travellers a convenient, relatively efficient, and comfortable option for travel to many destinations while enabling you to work or relax on the journey.

If one considers the duration of train travel versus air travel, it first appears that the airplane is much faster for short to medium distances, but if we take into account the time required to get to the airport (which is usually far outside the city), factor in that we must allow at least two hours to go through identity and security checks, and include the time it takes to get from the airport of arrival to your hotel or other final destination, the actual time from departure to arrival is highly comparable. Furthermore, train travel allows us to relax in comfortable seats, use computers and cellphones to work or communicate, or just watch the landscape pass by one's picture window. Train travel is far from perfect, but as more and more Canadians recognize its benefits, we may see Canadian passenger trains approach the level of convenience and efficiency now enjoyed by European rail travellers.

RAPID REVIEW

The passage below contains a total of 15 errors in verb form, subject–verb agreement, pronoun form, pronoun–antecedent agreement, and tense and pronoun consistency. When you've made your corrections, turn to pages 539–40 and compare your answers with ours. For each error you miss, the Answer Key directs you to the chapter you need to review.

[1]A professor at our college begun the last week of term by giving a demonstration to her business administration students. [2]For 15 weeks, she had spoke about the need for balance in life, but she felt that she had not yet gotten her message across. [3]She suspected that most of the students that sat before her was still primarily focused on money and career advancement. [4]"People in business," she began, "sometimes have a hard time remembering one's true priorities." [5]She placed a large glass jar on the desk and fills it with golf balls and asked the students if the jar was full. [6]Each of the students nodded their heads. [7]She then pours pebbles into the jar, which filled up the spaces around the golf balls. [8]"Is it full now?" she asked. [9]Everyone laughed and said that they thought it was full. [10]Then sand was poured into the jar by the professor, filling it to the brim. [11]Everyone that was watching agreed that the jar was now full. [12]Then the professor poured two cups of coffee into the jar. [13]She brought the demonstration to a close with this explanation: [14]"The golf balls represents the important things in your life: health, family, and relationships.

[15]The pebbles are the less important things such as jobs, hobbies, cars, and houses. [16]And the sand is the small, unimportant stuff. [17]If I had filled the jar with sand, there wouldn't have been room for anything else. [18]The same thing is true in life: if you fill your life with small stuff, will have no room for the important things. [19]Take care of the important things first; there is always room for the small stuff."

[20]One student asked what the coffee represents. [21]"No matter how full your life may seem," the professor replied with a smile, "there's always room for a cup of coffee with a friend!"

UNIT 4

Punctuation

Punctuation

QUICK QUIZ

The following quick quiz will let you see at a glance which chapters of Unit 4 you need to concentrate on. The passage below contains 15 errors in punctuation: missing or misused commas, semicolons, colons, quotation marks, question marks, and exclamation marks. (*Note:* Each pair of quotation marks counts as one punctuation mark.) When you've finished your corrections, turn to page 540 and compare your answers with ours. For each error you make, the Answer Key directs you to the chapter(s) you need to work on.

[1]When we go to a movie most of us like to sit back, munch away on a bucket of popcorn, and get lost in a good story. [2]Some people however delight in examining each frame to see if the producers of the film have made mistakes called "bloopers." [3]One kind of blooper is an anachronism. [4]An anachronism is something that is inconsistent with the time period in which the movie is set. [5]For example in *Pirates of the Caribbean: Curse of the Black Pearl* when Jack is shouting at his men a film-crew member in a white T-shirt and tan cowboy hat is clearly visible over his shoulder. [6]In *Gladiator*, Russell Crowe walks past a field marked with tractor-tire tracks. [7]Filter-tipped cigarettes in *Titanic* a Volkswagen Beetle in *The Godfather*, and white, canvas sneakers in *The Ten Commandments* are other glaring examples of anachronisms. [8]Whoops.

[9]Another kind of blooper is: the continuity mistake. [10]This kind of slip-up involves inconsistencies from one film sequence to the next. [11]For example, if a character drinks from a glass in one shot, the glass must contain less liquid,

not more, in the next. [12]Continuity problems abound; cigarettes get longer instead of shorter or appear and disappear from an actor's hand, hair changes style or length, and jewellery changes location. [13]Did you notice any of these bloopers when you watched the following films. [14]In *The Aviator*, the canopy on Leonardo DiCaprio's airplane pops on and off from sequence to sequence. [15]In *Lord of the Rings: Return of the King*, Frodo's scar moves several times from the right side of his face to the left and back again. [16]In *Harry Potter and the Order of the Phoenix*, while Harry is having a nightmare in bed his shirt changes from short-sleeved to long-sleeved.

[17]When we encounter a work of art, we want to experience what the poet Coleridge called the willing suspension of disbelief. [18]We need to believe because getting lost in the story is the essence of a great movie. [19]Bloopers can interfere with this belief but so can looking too hard for mistakes!

Punctuation

17 The Comma

Many writers-in-training tend to sprinkle punctuation like pepper over their prose. Please do not use punctuation to spice up or decorate your writing. Punctuation marks are functional: they indicate to the reader how the various parts of a sentence relate to one another. By changing the punctuation, you can change the meaning of a sentence. Here are two examples to prove the point.

1. An instructor wrote the following sentence on the board and asked the class to punctuate it appropriately: "woman without her man is nothing."

   The men wrote, "Woman, without her man, is nothing."
   The women wrote, "Woman: without her, man is nothing."

2. Now it's your turn. Punctuate this sentence: "I think there is only one person to blame myself."

   If you wrote, "I think there is only one person to blame, myself," the reader will understand that you believe only one person—who may or may not be known to you—is to blame.

   If you wrote, "I think there is only one person to blame: myself," the reader will understand that you are personally accepting the blame.

The comma is the most frequently used—and misused—punctuation mark in English. Perhaps nothing is so sure a sign of a competent writer as the correct use of commas. This chapter presents five comma rules that cover most situations in which commas are required. If you apply these five rules faithfully, your reader will not be confused by missing or misplaced commas in your writing. And if, as occasionally happens, the sentence you are writing is not covered by one of our five rules, remember the first commandment of comma usage: WHEN IN DOUBT, LEAVE IT OUT.

FIVE COMMA RULES

> **RULE 1**
> Use commas to separate three or more items in a series. The items may be expressed in words, phrases, or clauses.

Words	The required subjects in this program are math, physics, and English.
Phrases	Punctuation marks are the traffic signals of prose: they tell us to slow down, notice this, take a detour, and stop. (Lynne Truss)
Clauses	Wing-Kee went to the movies, Jan and Yasmin went to play pool, and I went to bed.

The comma before the *and* at the end of the list is optional, but we advise you to use it. Misunderstandings can occur if it is left out.

EXERCISE **17.1**

Insert commas where necessary in the following sentences. Answers for exercises in this chapter begin on page 541.

1. My favourite philosophers are Rick Mercer, Tina Fey, and Don Cherry.

2. If you ignore my terrible accent, poor grammar, and limited vocabulary, my French is excellent.

3. Wei held two aces, a King, a Queen, and a Jack in his hand.

4. Cambodian food is spicy, colourful, nourishing, and delicious.

5. In Canada, the seasons are spring, summer, fall, winter, winter, and winter.

6. We'll have a hamburger and French fries to begin with.

7. The successful applicant will have excellent communication and computer skills, a friendly disposition and a willingness to work hard.

8. Sleeping through my alarm dozing during sociology napping in the library, after lunch and snoozing in front of the TV, are all symptoms of my overactive nightlife.

9. Of Paris Moscow Sydney Madrid and Beijing, which is not a national capital?

10. Both, my doctor and my nutritionist agree that I should eat better, exercise more, and stop smoking.

The second comma rule is already familiar to you. You encountered it in Chapter 7, "Solving Run-On Sentence Problems."

RULE 2
Put a comma between independent clauses when they are joined by

for	but	so
and	or	
nor	yet	

(You can remember these words easily if you notice that their first letters spell "fanboys.")

I hope I do well in the interview, for I really want this job.

I like Elvis Costello, but I prefer Diana Krall.

We shape our tools, and our tools shape us. (Marshall McLuhan)

I knew I was going to be late, so I went back to sleep.

Be sure that the sentence you are punctuating contains two independent clauses rather than one clause with a single subject and a multiple verb.

We loved the book but hated the movie.
(*We* is the subject, and there are two verbs, *loved* and *hated*. Do not put a comma between two or more verbs that share a single subject.)

We both loved the book, but Kim hated the movie.
(This sentence contains two independent clauses—*We loved* and *Kim hated*—joined by *but*. The comma is required here.)

EXERCISE **17.2**

Insert commas where they are needed in the following sentences. Then check your answers against ours on page 541.

1. Rudi and I are good friends, yet we often disagree.

2. I wonder why the sun lightens our hair but darkens our skin.

3. Please pay attention, for the topic of today's lesson will be on the exam.

4. Money can't buy happiness, but it makes misery easier to live with.

5. Honesty may be the best policy, but it is not the cheapest.

6. Canadians are proud of their country, but don't approve of too much flag-waving.

7. The power went out at work today, so we packed up early and went home.

8. Pack an extra jacket, or sweater, for evenings in September can be cold.

9. This is my first full-time job, and I don't want to mess it up.

10. Noah had the last two of every creature on his ark, so why didn't he swat those mosquitoes?

RULE 3

Put a comma after an introductory word, phrase, or dependent clause that comes BEFORE an independent clause.

Word	Rob, you aren't paying attention.
Phrase	Exhausted and cranky from staying up all night, I staggered into class.
Clause	If that's their idea of a large pizza, we'd better order two.
Clause	Until she got her promotion, she was quite friendly.

But note that if a subordinate clause FOLLOWS a main clause, no comma is needed (e.g., She was quite friendly until she got her promotion).

EXERCISE **17.3**

Insert commas where they are needed in the following sentences. Then check your answers against ours on pages 541–42.

1. First, do no harm.

2. Before we begin, we need to understand what an independent clause is.

3. According to my stomach, lunchtime came and went about an hour ago.

4. In the end, we will be judged by how much happiness we have given others.

5. If you live by the calendar, your days are numbered.

6. No matter how much I practise my singing, never improves.

7. When you are right about something, it's considered polite not to gloat.

8. When everything is coming your way, you are in the wrong lane.

9. Until I went to France, I didn't think I could remember a word of my high school French.

10. I didn't think I could remember a word of my high school French until I went to France.

RULE 4

Use commas to set off any word, phrase, or dependent clause that is NOT ESSENTIAL to the main idea of the sentence.

Following this rule can make the difference between your readers' understanding and misunderstanding what you write. For example, the following two sentences are identical, except for a pair of commas. But notice what a difference those two tiny marks make to meaning:

The students who haven't done their homework will lose one full grade.
(Only the students who failed to do their homework will be penalized.)

The students, who haven't done their homework, will lose one full grade.
(All the students failed to do their homework, and all will be penalized one grade.)

To test whether a word, phrase, or clause is essential to the meaning of your sentence, mentally put parentheses around it. If the sentence still makes complete sense (i.e., the main idea is unchanged; the sentence just delivers less information), the material in parentheses is *not essential* and should be set off from the rest of the sentence by a comma or commas.

Non-essential information can appear at the beginning of a sentence,[1] in the middle, or at the end of a sentence. Study the following examples.

> Alice Munro ⟨ one of Canada's best-known novelists ⟩ spends the summer in Clinton and the winter in Comox.

Most readers would be puzzled the first time they read this sentence if it had no punctuation. They would assume all of the information is equally important. In fact, the material in broken parentheses is extra information, a supplementary detail. It can be deleted without changing the sentence's meaning, and so it should be separated from the rest of the sentence by commas:

> Alice Munro, one of Canada's best-known novelists, spends the summer in Clinton and the winter in Comox.

Here's another example to consider:

> The Queen ⟨ who has twice as many birthdays as anyone else ⟩ officially celebrates her birthday on May 24.

Again, the sentence is hard to read. You can't count on your readers to go back and reread every sentence they don't understand at first glance. As a writer, your responsibility is to give readers the clues they need as to what is crucial information and what isn't. In the example above, the information in broken parentheses is not essential to the meaning of the sentence, so it should be set off by commas:

> The Queen, who has twice as many birthdays as anyone else, officially celebrates her birthday on May 24.

In this next sentence, the non-essential information comes at the end.

> Although born on April 21, the Queen officially celebrates her birthday on May 24 ⟨ the anniversary of Queen Victoria's birth ⟩ .

---

[1] Rule 3 covers non-essential information at the beginning of a sentence.

The phrase "the anniversary of Queen Victoria's birth" is not essential to the main idea, so it should be separated from the rest of the sentence by a comma:

> Although born on April 21, the Queen officially celebrates her birthday on May 24, the anniversary of Queen Victoria's birth.

And finally, consider this sentence:

> Writing a letter of application ⟨ that is clear, complete, and concise ⟩ is a challenge.

If you take out "that is clear, complete, and concise," you change the meaning of the sentence. Not all letters of application are a challenge to write. Writing vague and wordy letters is easy; anyone can do it. The words "that is clear, complete, and concise" are essential to the meaning of the sentence, and so they are not set off by commas:

> Writing a letter of application that is clear, complete, and concise is a challenge.

EXERCISE **17.4**

Insert commas where they are missing in the following sentences. Check your answers against ours on page 542.

1. Commas like capitals, are clues, to meaning.

2. Our hope, of course, is that the terrorists will be caught and punished.

3. Our family doctor like, our family dog never comes, when we call.

4. Our adventure began in Barcelona, which is the site of a famous unfinished cathedral, designed by Gaudi.

5. Gaudi who in his 50s, was killed by a bus, began the cathedral as atonement for the sins of mankind.

6. An opportunist is someone, who goes ahead and does what the rest of us wish, we had the courage to do.

7. Our car made it all the way from Thunder Bay to Saskatoon, a piece of good luck that surprised us all.

8. Anyone who arrives during July or August, will have to adjust to the overwhelming heat and humidity, before trying to do any work.

9. My bike despite its age and rust gets me around town efficiently and cheaply.

10. A compliment like a good perfume should be pleasing but not overpowering.

RULE 5

Use commas to separate coordinate adjectives but not cumulative adjectives.

Coordinate adjectives are adjectives that
- can be arranged in any order and
- can be separated by the word *and*

without changing the meaning of the sentence.

Our company is looking for energetic, courteous salespeople.

The adjectives *energetic* and *courteous* could appear in reverse order, and you could put *and* between them:

Our company is looking for courteous and energetic salespeople.

In a series of **cumulative adjectives**, however, each adjective modifies the word that follows it. You cannot change their order, nor can you insert *and* between them.

The bride wore a pale pink silk dress, and the groom wore a navy wool suit.

You wouldn't say "The bride wore a silk pink pale dress" or "The groom wore a navy and wool suit." Commas are not used between cumulative adjectives.

EXERCISE **17.5**

Insert commas where they are needed in the following sentences. Check your answers against ours on page 542 before continuing.

1. The pen you gave me leaked dark blue ink onto my white shirt.

2. Do you want your portrait in a glossy finish or a matte finish?

3. Bright yellow fabric that repels stains is ideal for rain gear.

4. Toronto in the summer is hot smoggy and humid.

5. This month's *Road and Track* features a car made of lightweight durable aluminum.

6. Our new uniforms are surprisingly contemporary comfortable and flattering.

7. This ergonomic efficient full-function tablet comes in a variety of eye-popping colours.

8. We ordered a nutritious low-calorie salad for lunch and then indulged in apple pie topped with vanilla ice cream for dessert.

9. When she retired, my mother bought herself a large comfortable leather reclining chair, which is almost exclusively used by my father.

10. We survived the long high-velocity descent but almost didn't survive the jarring unexpected crash landing.

The rest of the exercises in this chapter require you to apply all five comma rules. Before you start, write out the five rules and keep them in front of you as you work through the exercises. Refer to the rules frequently as you punctuate the sentences. After you've finished each exercise, check your answers (see pages 542–43) and make sure you understand any mistakes you've made.

EXERCISE **17.6**

1. No words in the English language rhyme with *month orange silver* or *purple*.

2. I call my salary "take-home pay" for home is the only place I can afford to go on what I make.

3. Unless the union intervenes tomorrow will be my last day on the job.

4. James went to the bank to withdraw enough money to pay for his tuition his books and the student activity fee.

5. In a moment of foolish optimism I invested my life savings in a software development company.

6. The happiest years of my life in my opinion were the years I spent in college.

7. Sabina dances all night in the clubs and she sleeps all day in bed.

8. Doing punctuation exercises is not very exciting but it's cleaner than tuning your car.

9. This year instead of the traditional gold watch we will be giving retiring employees a framed photograph of our company's president.

10. Iqaluit which was called Frobisher Bay until 1987 is a major centre on Baffin Island in Canada's eastern Arctic region.

Go to Web Exercises 17.1, 17.2

EXERCISE **17.7**

Insert the 15 commas that are missing from the following paragraphs.

One of Canada's former prime ministers was John Diefenbaker. According to John Robert Colombo, author of many books about Canada, this was Diefenbaker's favourite story:

Two English ladies were travelling across Canada by train. They admired the Maritime provinces loved Quebec and Ontario and were fascinated by the Prairies. As they travelled across the Prairie provinces they were amazed by the vast openness of the landscape. The bright red sunsets and endless hectares of golden wheat impressed and moved them. Eventually however they began to wonder where they were. One of them decided to ask the conductor so she left the compartment to find him. Having checked the bar car the baggage car and the observation car she finally found him in the dining car and asked for the name of the nearest town. He replied "Saskatoon Saskatchewan." When she returned to her compartment her companion asked her if she had learned where they were. She replied, "No I still don't know where we are but wherever it is they don't speak English!"

Go to Web Exercises 17.3, 17.4

SUMMARY

THE FIVE COMMA RULES

1. Use commas to separate three or more items in a series. The items may be expressed as words, phrases, or clauses.
2. Put a comma between independent clauses when they are joined by *for*, *and*, *nor*, *but*, *or*, *yet*, or *so*.
3. Put a comma after an introductory word, phrase, or dependent clause that comes BEFORE an independent clause.
4. Use commas to set off any word, phrase, or dependent clause that is NOT ESSENTIAL to the main idea of the sentence.
5. Use commas to separate coordinate adjectives but not cumulative adjectives.

EXERCISE **17.8**

Insert the 15 commas that are missing in the following passage.

As long as you are prepared and confident you'll find that an employment interview need not be a terrifying experience. Some people actually enjoy employment interviews and attend them with enthusiasm. Most of us however are intimidated by the prospect of being interrogated by an interviewer or (even worse) a team of interviewers.

To prepare for an interview the first thing you should do is to find out as much as you can about the company. Among the things you need to know are the title of the job you are applying for approximately how much it pays the name of the person who will conduct the interview the address of the company and the location of the washrooms. Employment consultants usually recommend that you make an advance visit to confirm how long it takes to get there and where the interview room is. While on your scouting mission you can learn valuable information about the company's working conditions employee attitudes and even dress code.

Punctuation

On the day of the interview be sure to show up 10 or 15 minutes before your scheduled appointment. When the interviewer greets you you should do three things: memorize his or her name identify yourself and extend your hand. Your handshake should be brief and firm, not limply passive or bone-crushingly aggressive. Practise! Now all you have to do is relax and enjoy the interview.

"I typed it that way because I thought that punctuation would just slow it down."

The Semicolon

18

The semicolon and the colon are often confused and used as if they were interchangeable. They have distinct purposes, however, and their correct use can dramatically improve a reader's understanding of your writing. The semicolon has three functions.

> 1. A semicolon can replace a period; that is, it can appear between two independent clauses.

You should use a semicolon when the two clauses (sentences) you are joining are closely connected in meaning or when there is a cause-and-effect relationship between them.

I'm too tired; I can't stay awake any longer.

Montréal is not the city's original name; it was once called Ville-Marie.

A period could have been used instead of a semicolon in either of these sentences, but the close connection between the clauses makes a semicolon more effective in communicating the writer's meaning.

> 2. Certain transitional words or phrases can be put between independent clauses to show a cause-and-effect relationship or the continuation of an idea.

Words or phrases used in this way are usually preceded by a semicolon and followed by a comma:

; also,	; furthermore,	; nevertheless,
; as a result,	; however,	; on the other hand,
; besides,	; in addition,	; otherwise,
; consequently,	; in fact,	; then,
; finally,	; instead,	; therefore,
; for example,	; moreover,	; thus,
		; unfortunately,

The forecast called for sun; instead, we got snow.

My monitor went blank; nevertheless, I kept on typing.

I'm not offended by all the dumb blond jokes because I know I'm not dumb; besides, I also know I'm not blond. (Dolly Parton)

In other words, A SEMICOLON + A TRANSITIONAL WORD/PHRASE + A COMMA = a link strong enough to come between two related independent clauses.

Note, however, that, when these transitional words and phrases are used as non-essential expressions rather than as connecting words, they are separated from the rest of the sentence by commas (Chapter 17, Rule 4, page 218).

Your application form, unfortunately, was not completed correctly.

The emissions test, moreover, will ensure that your car is running well.

> 3. To make a complex list easier to read and understand, use semicolons between the items instead of commas.

A complex list is one in which at least one component part already contains commas. Here are two examples:

I grew up in a series of small towns: Cumberland, British Columbia; Red Deer, Alberta; and Timmins, Ontario.

When we opened the refrigerator, we found a limp, brown head of lettuce; two small containers of yogurt, whose "best before" dates had long since passed; and a hard, dried-up piece of cheddar cheese.

EXERCISE 18.1

Put a check mark (✓) before the sentences that are correctly punctuated. Answers for exercises in this chapter begin on page 543.

1. _____ We'll have to go soon; for it's getting late.

2. _____ It's been raining steadily for a month; if it doesn't stop soon, I'm building an ark.

3. _____ I don't remember if my childhood was happy or not; I was only a kid at the time.

4. ___✓___ Here's a book you should read; it's about improving your manners.

5. ___✗___ My brother and I have not spoken in almost three years; which is how long we have had text messaging.

6. ___✗___ If a tree falls in the woods, where no one can hear it; does it make a noise?

7. ___✓___ Cooking tasty food is easy; anything with enough garlic in it will be delicious.

8. ___✓___ Invented by a Canadian in the late 19th century; basketball is one of the world's most popular sports.

9. ___✓___ My neighbour works for a high-tech company; but he can't program his own VCR.

10. ___✓___ I think; therefore, I'm single. (Lizz Winstead)

EXERCISE **18.2**

Correct the faulty punctuation in Exercise 18.1.

EXERCISE **18.3**

Insert or delete commas and semicolons where necessary in these sentences.

1. We're late again, this is the third time this week.

2. My boyfriend always buys me jewellery, that I don't like; however, Harold the Gold Buyer is always happy to see me.

3. I need to replace my computer; because it continually freezes.

4. When life hands you lemons; make lemonade.

5. If you ever need a loan or a helping hand; just call Michel.

6. Travelling in Italy broadens the mind, eating Italian food broadens the behind.

7. North America's oldest continuously run horse race; the Queen's Plate, predates the Kentucky Derby by 15 years.

Punctuation

8. We can't afford dinner at an expensive restaurant; so let's have spaghetti and salad at home.

9. I am a marvellous housekeeper, every time I leave a man I keep his house.

10. A man has to do what a man has to do, a woman must do what he can't.

Go to Web Exercise 18.1

EXERCISE **18.4**

Correct the punctuation in these sentences by deleting or inserting commas and semicolons where necessary. Check your answers carefully before continuing.

1. Concluding that we weren't really welcome; we left and went to Tim Hortons for coffee.

2. Horton was a native of Cochrane, Ontario; there's a very popular Tim Hortons shop in his hometown.

3. He played hockey for the Toronto Maple Leafs at a time when they were league champions, he was a key player on their defensive line.

4. Horton was killed in a car accident near St. Catharines, Ontario, while commuting from Toronto to Buffalo.

5. Horton ended his career playing for the Buffalo Sabres; nevertheless, it is as a member of the Toronto Maple Leafs that he is best remembered.

6. The doughnut chain that he started has made his name a household word in Canada, and even in parts of the United States.

7. The word *doughnut* is an abbreviated form of the original *dough nought*, which means a zero made from dough.

8. Deep-fried in fat and made from starch and sugar, doughnuts tend to pack on the pounds, some Tim Hortons outlets have been obliged to install reinforced seating for their customers.

9. When Tim Hortons became smoke-free, long-time patrons fumed since cigarettes and coffee were thought to go together as naturally as Don Cherry and bad suits; however, the concept actually increased the chain's popularity.

10. It's sad but true that this icon of the Canadian way of life, named for one of Canada's hockey heroes, is no longer a Canadian corporation, Wendy's bought it in 1995.

Go to Web Exercise 18.2

EXERCISE **18.5**

Have you mastered the semicolon? Try this exercise and find out. To sort out the punctuation of the following passage, you will need to insert semicolons and change commas to semicolons or semicolons to commas where necessary. There are 10 errors to correct.

Just when we thought university research had grown completely out of touch with the real world; we discovered that the University of Hertfordshire in England had spent many months and much money to identify the favourite jokes of each nationality. We congratulate the scholars of Hertfordshire for their dedication to improving the minds of their students with this important research; and we thank them for sharing the results with the rest of the world. We all gain by knowing which jokes are found funniest by which nationalities.

In Australia, for example, the favourite joke is about a woman in a panic about her appearance, she visited her doctor. She complained that her hair had suddenly become thin and frizzy, her eyes were puffy, dull, and bloodshot, and her skin was wrinkled, blotchy, and grey. She demanded to know what was wrong with her. The doctor replied, "I'm not sure, I'll have to conduct some tests. But the good news is that there is nothing wrong with your eyesight."

Not surprisingly, the Hertfordshire researchers found that the English liked pub jokes, the Germans enjoyed military jokes, and the Americans preferred golf jokes, however, Canadians were perhaps the most predictable. They chose a joke that belittled their American neighbours while simultaneously implying admiration and envy: When NASA first started sending astronauts into orbit, scientists quickly discovered that ballpoint pens don't write in space, zero gravity prevented the ink from flowing. To solve this problem, American scientists spent more than $12 billion and a decade of experimentation to develop a super pen, it would write underwater, in zero gravity, upside down, on glass; even in temperatures below minus 300° Fahrenheit. The Russians used a pencil.

The Colon

19

The colon functions as an introducer. When a statement is followed by a list, one or more examples, or a quotation, the colon alerts the reader that some sort of explanatory detail is coming up.

> When I travel, I am never without three things: sturdy shoes, a money belt, and my laptop.

> There is only one enemy we cannot defeat: time.

> We have two choices: to study or to fail.

> Early in his career, Robert Fulford did not think very highly of intellectual life in Canada: "My generation of Canadians grew up believing that, if we were very good or very smart, or both, we would someday *graduate* from Canada."

The statement that precedes the colon must be a complete sentence (independent clause).

A colon should never come immediately after *is, are, was,* or *were.* Here's an example of what *not* to write:

> The only things I am violently allergic to are: cats, ragweed, and country music.

This construction is incorrect because the statement before the colon is not a complete sentence.

There are three different situations in which you need to use a colon.

> 1. Use a colon between an independent clause and a LIST or one or more EXAMPLES that define, explain, summarize, or illustrate the independent clause.

The information after the colon often answers the question "what?" or "who?"

> I am violently allergic to three things: (what?) cats, ragweed, and country music.

Business and industry face a new challenge: (what?) the rising value of the Canadian dollar.

The president has found the ideal candidate for the position: (who?) her brother.

2. Use a colon after a complete sentence introducing a quotation.

Maude Barlow of the Council of Canadians encouraged young people to vote: "If you want to know who is going to change this country, go home and look in the mirror."

3. Use a colon to separate the title of a book, film, or television show from a subtitle.

The Voice of Knowledge: A Practical Guide to Inner Peace

The Chronicles of Narnia: The Voyage of the Dawn Treader

Seinfeld: The Wizard

 If you remember this summary, you'll have no more trouble with colons: the colon follows an independent clause and introduces an example, a list, or a quotation that amplifies the meaning of that clause.

EXERCISE **19.1**

Put a check mark (✓) next to those sentences that are correctly punctuated. Answers for exercises in this chapter begin on page 544.

1. _____ The best way to concentrate on what you are reading is to turn off the TV.

2. _____ Here is a good example of what I mean, Starbucks.

3. _____ I read only one kind of book: technical manuals.

4. _____ We agree on the most important things in life: food and music.

5. _____ My car is so badly built that, instead of a warranty, it came with: an apology.

6. _____ There are many species of fish in this lake, including: pike, bass, and walleye.

7. _____ Two common causes of failure are: poor time management and inadequate preparation.

8. _____ Although the results are not yet conclusive, the experiment proved one thing: we're on the right track.

9. _____ This apartment would be perfect if it had more storage, there aren't enough closets, bookshelves, or even drawers.

10. _____ The difference between Canadians and Americans is that: Canadians know there is a difference.

EXERCISE **19.2**

Correct the faulty punctuation in Exercise 19.1.

Go to Web Exercise 19.1

EXERCISE **19.3**

Correct the following sentences as necessary.

1. Our dog knows only one trick, pretending to be deaf.

2. Let me give you an example of a female role model, Adrienne Clarkson.

3. If at first you don't succeed: become a consultant and teach someone else.

4. There is nothing we can do about our incompetent manager, she's the owner's daughter.

5. Leila spends too much time: shopping at the malls, talking on the phone, and watching TV.

6. Your research paper lacks three important features; a title page, a references page, and some content in between.

7. The shortstop on our baseball team caught only one thing all season, a cold.

8. My mother always wanted a successful son, so I did my part, I urged her to have more children.

9. Looking forward to a good horror story, I was disappointed in Margaret Atwood's book *Negotiating with the Dead; A Writer on Writing.*

10. Of course, I have no one to blame but myself I should have read the subtitle before buying the book.

Go to Web Exercise 19.2

EXERCISE **19.4**

The following paragraph will test all you have learned in the past three chapters. Insert commas, semicolons, and colons where appropriate in this passage. There are 15 errors.

A class of Grade 4 students was studying Laura Secord, one of Canada's heroes. They learned how she lived in the village of Queenston a community that had been taken over by the Americans during their invasion in 1813. American officers were billeted at her house, this is how she found out that the invaders were about to launch an attack against a small force led by Lieutenant Fitzgibbon in nearby Beaver Dams. Without regard for her own safety Secord set out on a 30-kilometre trek through mosquito-infested bush and swamp across enemy lines over the Niagara Escarpment to warn the British officer and his Aboriginal allies. After 18 hours of hard travel she stumbled across her rescuers a band of Aboriginals who agreed to take her to Fitzgibbon. Having been warned by Secord Fitzgibbon and his 50 soldiers and their 400 Aboriginal allies were able to prepare for a fight that would go down in history; the Battle of Beaver Dams. The American column was destroyed, of 500 men, 100 were killed and the rest were taken prisoner. Thanks to her heroism the American invasion was stopped Fitzgibbon and his men were safe and Secord's name would become famous.

At the end of the lesson, the teacher asked what would have happened if Laura Secord had not showed such courage. Robbie the class clown, had a ready reply "We'd be eating Martha Washington chocolates instead of Laura Secords!"

EXERCISE **19.5**

Now test your ability to use colons correctly. Correct the punctuation in the following sentences.

1. There is only one thing worse than getting old; the alternative.

2. The pioneers made their own: candles, soap, butter, and beer.

3. There are three kinds of people, those who can count and those who can't.

4. In Chapter 19, I learned that colons follow independent clauses and introduce: examples, lists, or quotations.

5. My lawyer defines a will as: a dead giveaway.

6. There are two sides to every divorce, yours and the idiot's.

7. My roommate, who loves horror movies, persuaded me to go with her to see *Nosferatu, The Vampire*.

8. Our program is one of the most difficult at college, but when we graduate, we can expect: interesting employment, a good salary, and many opportunities to travel.

9. There is a secret to taking good notes, take them from someone who goes to class.

10. A palindrome is a word or sentence that reads the same backward as it does forward, such as: *level, noon, madam, Laval,* and *don't nod.*

20 Quotation Marks

USING QUOTATION MARKS CORRECTLY

A quotation is a group of words originally spoken or written by another person that you want to include in your paper. Quotations can enhance meaning and add interest to your writing—as long as they are used sparingly, like spice. If you insert a quotation into every other sentence, your own ideas will be buried under the weight of other people's words. Your reader wants to hear what YOU think about your topic. Use the words of others to support your ideas, not as substitutes for them.

When you quote, you need to provide a signal to your reader that these words are not your own; they have been borrowed from another writer or speaker. Quotation marks (" ") are used to set off short passages of quoted material and some titles. Long passages of quoted material are treated differently, as you'll see later.

Quotation marks come in pairs. There must be a set to show where the quotation or title begins and a set to show where it ends. The words in between must be *exactly* what you heard or read. If you wish to omit or change a word or words and can do so without changing the meaning of the original, you may do so, but again you must alert your reader that you have altered the original. To find how to add, delete, or alter an original source so that it fits smoothly into your paragraph, go to the documented essay in Unit 7 on page 463 (formatted in MLA style) or on page 468 (APA style). Note how the author modifies her source quotation in the last sentence of the third paragraph. She indicates that word(s) have been omitted by using three spaced dots called ellipses (. . .). Words that have been added or changed are enclosed in square brackets [. . .].

The only other thing you need to know about quotations is how to introduce and punctuate them.

PUNCTUATING DIALOGUE

When you quote direct speech, start with a double quotation mark (") and use normal sentence punctuation. If you include the speaker's name in your sentence, set it off with commas. Put a comma or an end punctuation mark—whichever is appropriate—inside the final set of quotation marks.

"Yes, officer," said the young man, "that's her. That's the lady I stole the purse from."

Put quotation marks around the speaker's exact words. Do not use quotation marks with indirect speech (a paraphrase or summary of someone's words).

The young man confessed that the woman the officer pointed to was the woman from whom he had stolen the purse.

EXERCISE **20.1**

In the following sentences, place quotation marks where they are needed and insert any necessary punctuation before and after each quotation. Answers for exercises in this chapter begin on page 546.

1. The most famous quotation in the history of Canadian sports is "Foster Hewitt's He shoots! He scores! "

2. Michael Kesterton describes Canada's national animal, the beaver, as a distant relative of the sewer rat.

3. "All we want," said Yvon Deschamps, is an independent Québec within a strong and united Canada.

4. In the opinion of writer Barry Callaghan We Canadians have raised being boring to an art form.

5. Will and Ian Ferguson sum up Canadian cuisine as follows If you let a Canadian anywhere near a piece of food, [he or she is] sure to fling it into a deep fryer. Or cover it with sugar. Or fling it into a deep fryer and *then* cover it with sugar.

FORMATTING AND PUNCTUATING QUOTATIONS

Inserting quotations from print and electronic sources into your own writing smoothly and seamlessly is not easy. It takes practice. Quotations cannot simply be dropped (splash!) into your paragraphs. Every quotation MUST be introduced, usually in a phrase or clause that identifies the source.

When you quote a *short passage* (three lines of print or less), you should work it into your own sentence using appropriate punctuation.

1. Normally, you use a short phrase and a comma to mark off a quotation of one or more sentences. Put your quotation marks at the beginning and end of the passage you are quoting, including the end punctuation mark.

   According to Margaret Atwood, "If you like men, you can like Americans. Cautiously. Selectively. Beginning with the feet. One at a time."

   "As you grow old," wrote Richard Needham, "you lose your interest in sex, your friends drift away, and your children often ignore you. There are other advantages, of course, but these would seem to me the outstanding ones."

   "My idea of long-range planning is lunch," confesses Frank Ogden, one of Canada's foremost futurists.

2. If your own introductory words form a complete sentence, use a colon to introduce the quotation.

   Frank Ogden, one of Canada's foremost futurists, confesses that he has little respect for traditional business-planning cycles: "My idea of long-range planning is lunch."

3. If the passage you are quoting is a couple of words, a phrase, or anything less than a complete sentence, do not use any punctuation to introduce it.

   Woody Allen's one regret in life is that he is "not someone else."

   Neil Bissoondath argues that racism is based on "willful ignorance and an acceptance of—and comfort with—stereotype."

4. A quotation *within* a quotation is punctuated by single quotation marks.

   According to John Robert Colombo, "The most widely quoted Canadian aphorism of all time is Marshall McLuhan's 'The medium is the message.'"

EXERCISE **20.2**

In the following sentences, place quotation marks where they are needed and insert any necessary punctuation before and after each quotation. Then check your answers against ours on page 546.

1. Oscar Wilde had witty observations about almost everything, including age The old believe everything; the middle-aged suspect everything; the young know everything.

2. I've been on a constant diet for the past two decades, complains Erma Bombeck. I've lost a total of 789 pounds. By all accounts, I should be hanging from a charm bracelet.

3. The only reason I wear glasses, said Woody Allen, is so that I can drive my car—or find it.

4. Roseanne Barr thinks job titles are important I don't like to be called "housewife." I prefer "domestic goddess."

5. Historian and journalist Pierre Berton summed up the difference between Canadians and Americans as follows You ask an American how he's feeling, and he cries Great! You ask a Canadian, and he answers Not bad, or Pas mal.

All of the lines of a *long quotation* (more than three lines of print) should be indented 2.5 cm from the left margin. Do not use quotation marks around a long quotation that is set off from the text.

A block indentation, as described above, indicates to the reader that the words set off in this way are not yours but some other writer's. Here is an example:

> In "An Immigrant's Split Personality," Sun-Kyung Yi describes the painful dilemma faced by the children of immigrants, who often feel torn between two worlds. She cites her own case as an example. Neither Korean nor Canadian, she
>
>> remain[s] slightly distant from both cultures, accepted fully by neither. The hyphenated Canadian personifies the ideal of multiculturalism, but unless the host culture and the immigrant cultures can find ways to merge their distinct identities, sharing the best of both, this cultural schizophrenia will continue. (454)

Yi, Sun-Kyung. "An Immigrant's Split Personality." *Globe and Mail* 12 April 1992. Print.

College writing normally requires that you indicate the source of any material you quote. In the example on page 241, since the author's name and the article title are included in the introduction to the quotation, the full reference (which is given in parentheses at the bottom on page 241) would appear in a "Works Cited" or "References" list at the end of your paper or, if your instructor prefers, in a footnote or as an endnote.

The following examples illustrate the two basic ways to incorporate a short quotation into your own writing and credit your source. The first example identifies the author in the sentence introducing the quotation; the second does not. Both examples include the page number where the quotation appears in the publication.

> American humorist Mark Twain once observed, "I never let schooling interfere with my education" (97).

> An American humorist once noted, "I never let schooling interfere with my education" (Twain 97).

These source identifications are called *parenthetical citations* and refer to entries in the "Works Cited" or "References" list. For further information on format and documentation, see our website at **www.bareplus4e.nelson.com**.

Find out what format your instructor requires and follow it. Some institutions are very particular about documentation, so you would be wise to ask your instructor which style to use. As a general rule, if you are writing a paper for a humanities course and need more details than we provide on this text's website, we suggest you consult the *MLA Handbook for Writers of Research Papers*, 7th ed. (New York: MLA, 2009) or access the MLA website at **www.mla.org**. These Modern Language Association resources provide information on citing all types of sources, including material obtained from Internet sites.

For papers in the social sciences, the standard reference is the *Publication Manual of the American Psychological Association*, 6th ed. (Washington, DC: APA, 2010). Check **www.apastyle.org** for specific details on using APA style, including instruction on citing online information.

The information and exercises that follow are based on the MLA format.

FORMATTING AND PUNCTUATING TITLES

- *Italicize* the titles of books and other works made up of parts.

- Use quotation marks around the titles of parts of books and the titles of parts of other works.

The title of anything that is published or produced as a separate entity (e.g., books, magazines, newspapers, pamphlets, plays, movies, TV shows, CDs) should be italicized. The title of anything that has been published or produced as *part* of a separate entity (e.g., articles, essays, stories, poems, a single episode of a TV series, songs) should be placed in quotation marks. As you can see from the following examples, this rule is very simple, and it applies to all types of sources, both print and electronic.

Book:	*The Bare Essentials Plus*
Chapter in a book:	"Quotation Marks"
Magazine:	*Maclean's*
Article in a magazine:	"Yesterday's Canadian"
Newspaper:	*Calgary Herald*
Article in a newspaper:	"The Ramallah Miracle"
TV program:	*The Nature of Things*
TV episode:	"The Hobbit Enigma"
Music CD:	*So Beautiful or So What*
Song on CD:	"The Afterlife"
Website sponsor:	*National Film Board of Canada*
Website page:	"The Facebook Challenge"

Why the difference? The way you format and punctuate a title gives your reader some indication as to what sort of document you are quoting from or referring to: it may be a complete work that the reader can find listed by title, author, or subject in a library, or it may be an excerpt that the reader can find only by looking up the name of the work in which it was published.

EXERCISE **20.3**

Insert the necessary quotation marks or italics in the following sentences. Check your answers against ours on pages 546–47 before continuing.

1. You can find my article, "What's Wrong with the Entire World, in the April

edition of my blog, The Ghastly Truth."

Punctuation

2. The cooking column of England's Daily Mail newspaper had rather startling advice: One can peel tomatoes easily by plunging in boiling water for a minute.

3. Last night, we rented the hit Québec-produced movie C.R.A.Z.Y., in which Patsy Cline's classic song Crazy is a recurring theme.

4. Two books have influenced my life recently: Jonathan Safran Foer's Eating Animals has changed what I eat, and Richard Carlson's Don't Sweat the Small Stuff has helped me put things in perspective.

5. Canada's national anthem is derived from a French song, Chant national, which was first performed in Québec City in 1880.

6. O Canada, the English version of Chant national, was written by R. Stanley Weir, a Montréal judge and poet, and was first performed in 1908.

7. When I read the review of Daybreakers, a vampire movie with a twist, I wanted to go right out and see it, but then I decided to wait to get it on Netflix so I could dress in my vampire clothes and eat ketchup sandwiches while I watched it.

8. Britney Spears, who is at least as famous for her behaviour as she is for songs like Toxic and Till the World Ends, revealed in an interview that she might have been a geography major: I like travelling to overseas places, like Canada.

9. When asked what the best thing he had read all year was, Justin Timberlake, writer/singer of Girlfriend, Gone, Like I Love You, and others, replied, You mean, like a book?

10. Eric Deggans, the critic for the St. Petersburg Times, comments on the phenomenon of game show reruns such as Jeopardy and Wheel of Fortune in his blog, The Feed.

Go to Web Exercises 20.1, 20.2

EXERCISE **20.4**

This exercise is designed to test your understanding of how to punctuate short quotations and titles in your writing. Do you know when and where to use quotation marks and italics (or underlining)? Do you know what punctuation marks to use to introduce and conclude a short quotation? Try this exercise to find out.

1. We are all immigrants to this place wrote Margaret Atwood even if we were born here.

2. In their book How to Be a Canadian, Will and Ian Ferguson have a chapter entitled How the Canadian Government Works. The chapter consists of two words It doesn't.

3. One of Pierre Trudeau's lesser-known statements defines the Liberal Party as follows We are the extreme centre, the radical middle. That is our position.

4. Mark Twain, the author of the classic American novels Tom Sawyer and Huckleberry Finn, wrote my favourite quote on anger: Anger is an acid that can do more harm to the vessel in which it is stored than to anything on which it is poured.

5. The great American poet Robert Frost, who wrote such memorable poems as Fire and Ice and The Road Not Taken, was famous for pointed political observations such as this one A jury consists of 12 persons chosen to decide who has the better lawyer.

6. An article called The University Crunch, on overcrowding in Canada's colleges and universities, can be found on the Maclean's magazine website: **www.macleans.ca**.

Punctuation

7. A few years ago, on CBC Television's program Hockey Night in Canada, Don Cherry informed his audience Most guys that wear visors are Europeans and French guys.

8. Time magazine's annual award for the year's best blogs went to Talking Points Memo and The Huffington Post.

9. The last word on growing up goes to American humorist Mark Twain, in this famous observation When I was a boy of 14, my father was so ignorant. When I got to be 21, I was amazed to see how much he'd learned in seven years.

10. The line Fools rush in where angels fear to tread was written not by a pop singer but by the English poet Alexander Pope, author of such classic books as Essay on Man and Essay on Criticism, as well as the famous observation A little learning is a dangerous thing.

Question Marks, Exclamation Marks, and Punctuation Review

21

THE QUESTION MARK

Everyone knows that a question mark follows an interrogative, or asking, sentence, but we all sometimes forget to include it. Let this chapter serve as a reminder not to forget!

> Put a question mark at the end of every interrogative sentence.

The question mark gives your readers an important clue to the meaning of your sentence. "There's more?" (interrogative) means something quite different from "There's more!" (exclamatory), and both are different from "There's more." (declarative). When you speak, your tone of voice conveys the meaning you intend; when you write, your punctuation tells your reader what you mean.

The only time you don't end a question with a question mark is when the question is part of a statement.

Question	Statement
Are you going?	I asked if you were going.
Do you know them?	I wonder if you know them.
Is there enough evidence to convict him?	The jury deliberated whether there was enough evidence to convict him.

EXERCISE **21.1**

Insert the correct end punctuation for the following sentences, and then check your answers. Answers for exercises in this chapter begin on page 547.

1. If the game ends in a tie, who will win the series?

2. Can you explain what a rhetorical question is?

3. I want to know what's going on here?

4. Why do they bother to report power outages on TV ?

5. Are you aware that half the population is below average ?

6. If olive oil comes from olives, and corn oil comes from corn, I wonder where baby oil comes from ?

7. I read your report carefully, and I question your conclusions .

8. I'm curious about the human being who first decided that eating snails was a good idea.

9. I also wonder if that person would have found snails edible, let alone delectable, if they hadn't been buried under quantities of butter and garlic .

10. Do you know another word for *thesaurus* ?

Go to Web Exercise 21.1

THE EXCLAMATION MARK

Consider the difference in tone between these two sentences:

There's a man behind you.
There's a man behind you!

In the first sentence, information is being supplied, perhaps about the line of people waiting their turn at a grocery store checkout counter. The second sentence might be a shouted warning about a mugger.

Use an exclamation mark as end punctuation only in sentences requiring extreme emphasis or dramatic effect.

Note that the exclamation mark will have "punch" or dramatic effect only if you use it sparingly. If you use an exclamation mark after every other sentence, how will your readers know when you really mean to indicate excitement? Overuse of exclamation marks is a technique used by comic book writers to heighten the impact of their characters' words. Ironically, the effect is to neutralize the impact: when all conversation is at top volume, top volume becomes the norm, and the writer is left with no way to indicate emphasis— other than by adding two, three, or more exclamation marks to punctuate each statement. This is why you seldom find exclamation marks in academic or business writing.

Almost any sentence could end with an exclamation mark, but remember that the punctuation changes the emotional force of the sentence. Read the following sentences with and without an exclamation mark, and picture the situation that would call for each reading.

They've moved	Don't touch that button
The file was empty	Listen to that noise

EXERCISE **21.2**

Add the appropriate end punctuation in the following sentences. Then compare your answers with our suggestions on page 547. (Answers will vary, depending on the tone and impact the writer wants to convey.)

1. I quit
2. Stop, thief
3. This salsa is scorching
4. He's on the stairway, right behind you
5. We won I can't believe it
6. The crowd chanted triumphantly, "Go, Habs, go "
7. Waving her new credit card, Tessa raced through the mall shouting, "Charge it "
8. Take the money and run
9. Help My brain is overloaded with punctuation and is about to explode
10. This music is horrible I'm going home

EXERCISE **21.3**

Supply the missing punctuation for the 15 sentences in the following paragraph. Check your answers before continuing.

[1]What a day [2]My daughter was scheduled to make a presentation to her Grade 3 class, and the entire family was stressed. [3]She and her mother had come up with a topic but hadn't shared it with me. [4]Why, I don't know [5]Aren't

fathers supposed to be supportive and encouraging, even if they don't have a clue, what the female portion of the household is doing. [6]Anyway, my wife took our daughter off to school to do the big demonstration, and when they left, I discovered some celery, raisins, and peanut butter on the kitchen counter. [7]What was I supposed to do. [8]I smeared the peanut butter on the celery and put the raisins in the peanut butter. [9]Was it ever a good breakfast. [10]Just as I finished eating, the car zoomed up the driveway and screeched to a stop; mother and daughter dashed into the house and ran into the kitchen. [11]"Where are the raisins and celery and peanut butter?" they screamed. [12]I told them I had eaten it and asked, what the fuss was about. [13]There was more screaming. [14]I had eaten my daughter's demonstration. [15]The teacher told them later that was the first time she had heard the excuse, "My daddy ate my homework."

EXERCISE **21.4**

Supply appropriate punctuation for the 15 sentences in the following paragraph.

[1]I wonder why it is that I cannot dance. [2]My girlfriend would go out dancing every night of the week if she didn't have morning classes. [3]And can she ever dance. [4]When she is really into the music, I've seen her receive applause from an entire club as she leaves the dance floor. [5]They applaud me, too, but it's because they're glad to see me sit down. [6]Why is it that every part of my body moves to a different rhythm. [7]When my hips find the beat, my feet are half a beat behind, and my shoulders move around on their own as if I had some horrible nervous disorder. [8]Is it because I'm tall, and nerve impulses have to travel a long way to get from one part of my frame to another. [9]I've been told that, when dancing, I look like a stork with an uncontrollable itch in a vital part of its anatomy. [10]Talk about embarrassing. [11]"What can I do?" I ask myself.

[12]Should I subject myself to weeks of torture and take dancing lessons when I suspect they wouldn't help in the least?[13]Is there no medical cure for my condition.[14]I must have been born without a rhythm gene[15]I wonder if it's too late to get a transplant.

PUNCTUATION REVIEW

The exercises that follow will test your knowledge of the punctuation marks you have studied in Unit 4. All of the sentences below contain errors: punctuation or italics are either missing or misused. Work through the exercises slowly and carefully. Check your answers before continuing. If you make a mistake, go back to the chapter that deals with the punctuation mark you missed, and review the explanation and examples.

Snapshots

"Do you always have to shout?
Well? Do you? Huh?"

EXERCISE **21.5**

There are 30 errors in this exercise. (Each incorrect punctuation mark counts as one error; each incomplete set of quotation marks also counts as one error.)

1. If you want to make your living as a comedian, you must: remember the punch line.

2. Good health, according to my doctor, should be defined as: the slowest possible rate at which one can die.

3. The fast pace of life doesn't bother me, it's the sudden stop at the end that has me worried.

4. This new fad diet can be summed up in a single sentence If it tastes good, don't eat it."

5. Being a news junkie I rely on the radio to keep me informed, however I also read a national newspaper, subscribe to Maclean's and watch The National on CBC each night.

6. Don't worry about avoiding temptation, advised Winston Churchill. As you grow older, it will avoid you.

7. The directions are simple: preheat the oven to 350° Fahrenheit take the lasagna out of the box remove the foil from the top put the lasagna in the oven and ignore it for 45 minutes.

8. In spite of what my partner says I'm really quite an elegant dresser On formal occasions for example I insist that the trouser cuffs of my formal pants just brush the tops of my sandals.

9. Columbus first encountered turkeys, which were unknown in Europe in his time, on an island off the coast of Honduras, he was served roast turkey by the Aboriginal peoples. According to Margaret Visser, author of The Rituals of Dinner At ceremonial feasts, the Spaniards were served huge tamales containing a whole turkey each.

10. George Bernard Shaw sent an invitation to his new play, Major Barbara, to Winston Churchill, along with a note saying Here are two tickets to opening night. Bring a friend ... if you have one. Churchill replied I cannot attend the first night but will come on the second ... if there is one.

Go to Web Exercise 21.1

EXERCISE **21.6**

Insert the 15 punctuation marks that are missing in the following passage. You will need to use at least one colon, semicolon, question mark, and exclamation mark, in addition to quotation marks and commas.

Another round of job-hunting, said Joe as he contemplated the day ahead of him. He had woken up to his alarm clock (made in India) set his coffee maker (made in Hong Kong) shaved with his electric razor (made in Indonesia) and made toast in his pop-up toaster (made in Taiwan). Then he put on his cotton shirt (made in Sri Lanka) and his designer jeans (made in Singapore) finally, he slipped into his running shoes (made in Pakistan), and he was ready to face the day. First he checked the news on his computer (made in China) to see if there was anything of interest nothing except more bad economic news. After a quick check of his cellphone (made in Germany) to see if anyone had texted him with a job offer he got into his car (made in Korea) and drove off on his daily search for a decent job.

Does this sound at all familiar. We shop at Walmart and congratulate ourselves on how much we have saved by buying products made in every country of the world but one Canada. Then we wonder why our economy can't produce jobs for young graduates. Duh. We are a trading nation so goods must be imported but we can make a conscious decision to assist our own economy when confronted with a choice between a Canadian-made product and one made offshore. We may end up buying less but we help ourselves when we buy Canadian.

Snapshots

"Yes, I'm very punctual. I always use commas and periods."

RAPID REVIEW

Supply the 15 punctuation marks that are missing in the following passage. (*Note:* Each pair of quotation marks counts as one punctuation mark.) Then turn to page 549 to compare your revision with our answer. The Answer Key will direct you to the chapter(s) you need to review.

[1]A Member of Parliament was asked to give a major speech to the executives of Canada's banks and investment companies. [2]Since his staff included a professional speechwriter he called her into his office and explained the importance of his audience the government policies he wanted to talk about and the tone and approach he thought would be appropriate for the occasion. [3]The speechwriter asked only one question she wanted to know how long the speech should be. [4]The MP told her the speech should be no longer than 20 minutes. [5]Knowing how important this address would be for her boss the writer went right to work she stayed late to draft what she thought was a masterpiece.

[6]On the day after the big speech the writer was at her desk early she was eager to learn how her speech had been received. [7]When her boss called she could tell from the tone of his voice that he was angry. [8]The speech was a disaster he bellowed. [9]I asked for a 20-minute speech, not a 60-minute speech! [10]Before I was finished, half the audience had left the hall and most of the others were asleep. [11]The writer thought for a minute before replying that she had given him exactly what he had asked for notes for a 20-minute speech and two copies.

UNIT 5

Paragraphs and Essays

Paragraphs and Essays

22 Finding Something to Write About

Every writer knows that content is important. Not so many seem to know that form is just as important. In fact, you can't really separate the two: *what you say is how you say it*. Writing a paper (or an essay or a report or a letter or anything else) is like doing a chemistry experiment or baking a cake: you need the right amount of the right ingredients put together in the right proportions and in the right order. There are five steps to follow:

1. Choose a satisfactory subject.
2. Discover your thesis and main points.
3. Write a thesis statement and/or an outline.
4. Write the paragraphs.
5. Revise the paper.

If you follow these steps faithfully, in order, we guarantee that you will write clear, organized papers.

Note that, when you get to step 3, you have a choice. You can choose to plan your paper with a thesis statement, with an outline, or with both. The thesis statement approach works well for short papers—about 500 words or less. An outline is necessary for longer papers. Ideally, you should learn to use both methods of organizing your writing. In fact, your teacher may require that you do so.

Steps 1, 2, and 3 make up the planning stage of the writing process. Be warned: done properly, these three steps will take you about as long as steps 4 and 5, which involve the actual writing. The longer you spend on planning, the less time you'll spend on drafting and revising, and the better your paper will be.

CHOOSING A SATISFACTORY SUBJECT

Unless you are assigned a specific subject by a teacher or supervisor, choosing your subject can be the most difficult part of writing a paper. Apply the following guidelines carefully, because no amount of instruction can help you write a good paper on something you don't know anything about or on something that is inappropriate for your audience or purpose. Your subject should satisfy the *4-S TEST*.

> A satisfactory subject is SIGNIFICANT, SINGLE, SPECIFIC, and SUPPORTABLE.

1. Your subject should be SIGNIFICANT. Write about something that your reader needs or might want to know. Consider your audience and choose a subject that they will find significant. This doesn't mean that you can't ever be humorous, but, unless you're another Stephen Leacock, an essay on "How I deposit money in my bank" will probably be of little interest to your readers. The subject you choose must be worthy of the time and attention you expect your readers to give to your paper.

2. Your subject should be SINGLE. Don't try to cover too much in your paper. A thorough discussion of one topic is more satisfying to a reader than a skimpy, superficial treatment of several topics. A subject such as "The challenge of government funding cutbacks to colleges and universities" includes too much to deal with in one paper. Limit yourself to a single topic, such as "How private-sector donations are helping our college meet the challenge of funding cutbacks."

3. Your subject should be SPECIFIC. This requirement is closely tied to the "single" requirement. Given a choice between a general topic and a specific one, you should choose the latter. In a short paper, you can't hope to say anything new or significant about a large topic: "Employment opportunities in Canada," for example. But you could write an interesting, detailed discussion on a more specific topic, such as "Employment opportunities in Nova Scotia's hospitality industry."

   You can narrow a broad subject by applying one or more limiting factors to it. Try thinking of your subject in terms of a specific *kind*, *time*, *place*, *number*, or *person* associated with it. To come up with the hospitality topic, for example, we limited the subject of employment opportunities in Canada in terms of both place and kind.

4. Your subject must be SUPPORTABLE. You must know something about the subject (preferably, more than your reader does), or you must be able to find out about it. Your discussion of your subject will be clear and convincing only if you can include examples, facts, quotations, descriptions, anecdotes, and other details. Supporting evidence can be taken from your

Paragraphs and Essays

own experience or from the experience of other people. In other words, your topic may require you to do some research.[1]

EXERCISE 22.1

Imagine that you have been asked to write a 500-word paper and given this list of subjects to choose from. Test each subject against the 4-S guidelines and identify what's wrong with it. Answers for exercises in this chapter begin on page 550.

1. The computer industry
2. The five senses
3. Recharging your iPod
4. The dangers of obesity and anorexia
5. How to insert a European-back earring
6. Characteristics of baby boomers, Generation Xers, and the millennials
7. The Olympics in 2020
8. Problems our children will face as parents
9. How to parasail or bungee-jump safely
10. Canada's parliamentary system

EXERCISE 22.2

Apply the 4-S guidelines to the following subjects. Some are possibilities for short papers but fail to satisfy one or more of the guidelines. Others are hopeless. Revise the "possible" subjects to make them significant, single, specific, and supportable.

1. Bottled water
2. Some people are very attractive.
3. How to curl your hair
4. The Canadian Shield

---

[1] Many colleges and most universities require students to write formal research papers in their first year. The five steps to essay writing that we outline in this unit apply to research papers as well as to informal and in-class essays. In addition to finding and incorporating information from sources in your essay, a research paper requires that you format and document your paper according to specific guidelines. On our website—**www.bareplus4e.nelson.com**—you will find links to MLA and APA style guidelines, the two styles most frequently required in courses at the undergraduate level.

5. Insects that are helpful to farmers
6. How to mix paint
7. Predicting the future
8. Canadian war heroes
9. Global positioning systems
10. Internet piracy

EXERCISE **22.3**

List three subjects that you might choose to write about. Make sure each subject is *significant*, *single*, *specific*, and *supportable*.

DISCOVERING YOUR THESIS AND MAIN POINTS

Once you've chosen a suitable subject for your paper, you need to decide what you want to say about it. There are many possible ways of thinking and writing about any subject. In a short paper, you can deal effectively with only a few aspects of your topic. How do you decide what approach to take?

The approach to your subject that you choose is your thesis: a **thesis** is an idea about a limited subject. It is an opinion or point of view that needs to be explained or proved so your reader can understand it. A thesis is not a statement of fact. Compare the examples that follow.

Fact	Thesis
Most people experience some anxiety when they begin a first job.	The stress I experienced in my first job was caused by my employer, my co-workers, and—surprisingly—myself. (Needs to be explained.)
For several years, Canada ranked first on the United Nations' list of the world's best countries to live in.	Canadians don't know how lucky they are. (Needs to be explained.)
Some universities do not require students to demonstrate writing competence before graduation.	All universities should require students to demonstrate writing competence before graduation. (Needs to be proved.)

Paragraphs and Essays

A thesis can be discovered in several ways. Brainstorming, freewriting, listing, and clustering are strategies that many college students are familiar with from high school. You should continue to use any technique you've learned that produces good results. However, if these approaches haven't worked well for you, you may need a more structured approach to discovering what it is you can and want to say about a subject.

Try questioning—asking lead-in questions about your subject. A lead-in question is one that guides you into your subject by pointing to an angle or viewpoint—a thesis—that you can explore in your paper. The answers to your lead-in question become the main points your paper will explain.

SIX QUESTIONS TO ASK ABOUT YOUR SUBJECT

1. How can my subject be defined or explained? What are its significant features or characteristics? Examples: Tumblr, alcoholism, the Canadian personality
2. How is my subject made or done? How does it work? Examples: how to protect yourself from identity theft, how to make a short film, the rules of cricket (or any other game)
3. What are the main kinds, components, features, or functions of my subject? Examples: Facebook addicts, smartphones, a floor manager's duties
4. What are the main similarities and/or differences between my subject and something it is often compared to? Examples: iPhone and BlackBerry, soccer and hockey, Canadians and _____
5. What are the causes or effects of my subject? Examples: causes (or effects) of bullying, some effects of single-sex classrooms, causes of first-year dropout
6. What are the advantages or disadvantages of my subject? What are the reasons for or against it? Examples: public transit, wind power, smartphones in classrooms

These questions suggest some familiar ways of looking at or thinking about a subject. Some questions will yield better results than others, and most subjects will produce answers to more than one of the questions. Choose as your subject the question that produces the answers you can or want to explain.

Here's an example of how the process works. Let's assume you've been asked to write a paper on the topic "A satisfying career."[2] If you apply each question to your subject and make notes of the answers, you might end up with a list like this one:

1. "What is a satisfying career? What are its significant features or characteristics?"

   This question produces useful answers. Answers might include a career that is interesting, pays well, is respected, and provides opportunities for advancement.

2. "How is a satisfying career made or chosen?"

   This question would also work. Some answers might include self-analysis, career counselling, experience (perhaps through part-time or volunteer work), research, or aptitude tests.

3. "What are the main parts or components of a satisfying career?"

   We could use this question, too. The components of a satisfying career might include challenging work, good pay, compatible co-workers, and respect in the community.

4. "How is a satisfying career different from something it is often compared to?"

   This question has limited possibilities. We could develop a contrast between a satisfying career and an unsatisfying one, but there isn't much new to say. The main points are obvious and could be explained more easily in response to question 1 than to question 4.

---

[2] If your instructor has assigned the topic of your essay, don't grumble—be grateful. The way your instructor words the assignment may contain information that will help you decide how to approach it. Assignment instructions usually contain "direction words," which are reliable clues to the kind of paper your instructor is looking for. For example, Define means you should apply question 1; Describe points you to questions 1 and 2; Discuss and Explain tell you to apply questions 3, 4, 5, and possibly 6; and Evaluate points you to question 6.

Paragraphs and Essays

5. "Does a satisfying career have causes or effects?"

It has both:

- What causes a satisfying career?

Self-analysis, planning, preparation

- What are the effects of a satisfying career?

Confidence, stability, recognition, happiness

6. "What are the advantages or disadvantages of a satisfying career?"

Unless you can think of some unusual advantages (i.e., ones that are not covered by the answers to question 3 above), this question doesn't produce answers that are worth the time you and your readers would have to spend on it. We've already discovered the advantages in the answers to question 3, and there aren't many disadvantages to a satisfying career!

Asking these six questions about your subject will help you decide on the best way to approach it. The best approach is the one that you can answer fully and convincingly and that will appeal to your readers as original and persuasive.

The questioning strategy we've outlined above will give you two advantages:

- It will help you define your thesis by identifying the point of view you can best explain or defend.
- It will help you develop your paper by providing some solid main points to work with.

 Don't rush this process! The more time you spend exploring your subject in the planning stage, the easier the drafting of the paper will be.

Below you will find eight sample subjects, together with main points that were discovered by applying the questions on page 262. Study these examples carefully. Figure out the logic that leads from subject to question to main points in each case. When you're finished, you should have a good understanding of how the questioning process can work for you.

Subject	Selected Question	Main Points
A good teacher	(1) What are the characteristics of a good teacher?	• knowledge of subject • ability to communicate • respect for students

Subject	Selected Question	Main Points
A successful party	(2) How do you give a successful party?	• invite the right mix of people • plan the entertainment • prepare the food in advance • provide a relaxed, friendly atmosphere
Ending a relationship	(2) How can one break off a relationship?	• in person • by phone or voice mail • by text or email message • through friends • by "un-friending" on Facebook
Smartphones	(3) What are the features of smartphones?	• high-definition video recording and playback • text and voice communication with upload and download capability • access to Internet and email
Communication	(4) Differences between spoken and written language	• speech is spontaneous; writing isn't • speech is transitory; writing is permanent • speech can't be revised; writing can
Refugees in Canada	(5) What are the main causes of refugees coming to Canada?	• persecution in homeland • war in homeland • poverty in homeland
Ending a relationship	(5) What are the causes of breakups?	• failure to communicate • unrealistic expectations • financial incompatibility • friendships with others

Paragraphs and Essays

Subject	Selected Question	Main Points
Minority government	(6) What are the advantages of a minority government?	• forces compromise from extreme positions • is more responsive to and reflective of the wishes of the entire electorate • engages interest in meaningful debate and discussion of issues

As a general rule, you should try to identify between *two* (the absolute minimum) and *five* (the manageable maximum) main ideas to support your subject. If you have only one main idea, your subject is suitable for a paragraph or two, not for an essay. If you have discovered more than five main ideas that require discussion, you have too much material for a short paper. Either select the most important aspects of the subject or take another look at it to see how you can focus it more specifically.

EXERCISE **22.4**

Working with a partner, select a question from the highlighted list on page 262 and generate good main points for each subject.

Subject	Selected Question	Main Points
1. My chosen career	•	• • •
2. Owning a car versus using public transit	•	• • •
3. My family's (or my ancestors') immigration to Canada	•	• • •

Subject	Selected Question	Main Points
4. Leaving home	•	•
		•
		•
5. Blues (or another kind of music)	•	•
		•
		•
6. Social networks (choose one)	•	•
		•
		•
7. Time management	•	•
		•
		•
8. Blogs	•	•
		•
		•
9. Travelling alone	•	•
		•
		•
10. Achieving a balanced life	•	•
		•
		•

Paragraphs and Essays

EXERCISE **22.5**

For each of the three subjects you chose in Exercise 22.3, list two to five main points. To discover suitable main points, use a technique that has worked for you in the past, such as brainstorming, or apply to your subject the six questions highlighted on page 262 until you find a question that yields answers you could write about. The answers to that question are your main points.

Go to Web Exercise 22.1

TESTING YOUR MAIN POINTS

Now take a close look at the main points you've chosen for each subject in Exercise 22.5. It may be necessary to revise some of them before going any further. Are some points too trivial to bother with? Do any of the points overlap in meaning? Are there any points that are not directly related to your subject?

Main points must be SIGNIFICANT, DISTINCT, and RELEVANT.

To be satisfactory, the main points you have chosen to write about must all be SIGNIFICANT: they must require at least one paragraph of explanation. If you have any trivial ideas on your list, now is the time to discard them.

Each of the main points you've chosen must also be DISTINCT. That is, each must be different from all the others. There must be no overlap in meaning. Check to be sure you haven't given two different labels to what is really one aspect of your subject.

Finally, each point must be RELEVANT; it must be *clearly related* to your subject; that is, it must be an aspect of the subject you are writing about, not some other subject. For example, if you're writing about the advantages of a subject, cross out any disadvantages that may have appeared on your list. (Doing this may sound obvious, but trust us: irrelevant points show up in essays more often than you might think.)

EXERCISE **22.6**

Each of the following subjects is followed by some possible main points. Working with a partner, identify the unsatisfactory point(s) in each group.

1. Advantages of physical fitness
   - improved muscle tone
   - weight loss
   - improved appearance
   - improved stamina
   - better looks

2. Reasons for drug abuse among adolescents
   - peer pressure
   - school/parental pressure
   - alcohol
   - boredom
   - depression

3. Problems faced by new immigrants in Canada
   - finding suitable work
   - learning a new language
   - finding a suitable place to live
   - buying a wardrobe for summer and winter
   - adjusting to the climate

4. The main kinds of daytime television shows
   - talk shows
   - quiz shows
   - reality shows
   - the Oprah Winfrey Network
   - game shows

5. Characteristics of depression
   - fatigue and insomnia
   - rapid weight gain or weight loss
   - loss of sex drive
   - poor sleep
   - low self-esteem

6. Advantages of e-books
- can be read on a variety of electronic devices
- can download and erase
- often less expensive than print editions
- may include links to Web information
- can cause eye strain from video screens

7. Reasons to buy Canadian
- keep Canadians employed
- pay taxes to our government rather than a foreign one
- get high-quality goods
- sometimes have to pay more
- get product protection (warranty)

8. Alternative energy sources
- wind
- tides
- geothermal
- solar
- coal

9. Reasons to quit smoking
- financial savings
- threat of lung cancer
- threat of heart disease
- high cost of cigarettes
- socially unacceptable

10. How to save money
- keep a record of all purchases
- establish a budget
- eat and entertain at home
- always shop with a list
- reuse rather than replace
- keep track of income and spending

Go to Web Exercise 22.2

Study the main points you chose in Exercise 22.5 on page 268. Cross out any that are not significant, unique, or related to your subject. If necessary, add new main points so that you end up with at least three main points for each subject.

ORGANIZING YOUR MAIN POINTS

Now that you've identified three or four main points to discuss, you need to decide on the order in which to present them in your paper. Choose the order that is most appropriate for your specific subject.

There are four ways to arrange main points in an essay: CHRONOLOGICAL, CLIMACTIC, LOGICALLY LINKED, and RANDOM order.

1. **Chronological order** means in order of time sequence, from first to last. Here's an example:

Subject	**Main Points**
The development of a relationship	• attraction
	• meeting
	• discovery
	• intimacy

2. In **climactic order**, you present your strongest or most important point last. Generally, you would discuss your second-strongest point first and the others in between like this:

Subject	**Main Points**
Reasons for the federal government to legislate lower carbon emissions	• Airborne pollutants endanger the health of individual Canadians.
	• Damage to trees hurts the economy.
	• Our emissions affect other countries as well as Canada.
	• Global warming caused by carbon emissions threatens our very existence.

Paragraphs and Essays

3. **Logically linked order** means that the main points are connected in such a way that one point must be explained before the next can be understood. Consider this example:

Subject

Main causes of gang involvement

Main Points

- lack of opportunity for work
- lack of recreational facilities
- boredom
- need for an accepting peer group

The logical link here is this: because of unemployment, recreational facilities are needed, and because of both unemployment and inadequate recreational facilities, boredom becomes a problem. Bored by having nothing to do and nowhere to go, young people need an accepting peer group to bolster their self-esteem. The first three points must be explained before the reader can fully understand the fourth.

4. **Random order** means the main points of your paper could be satisfactorily explained in any order. A random arrangement of points is acceptable only if the main points are *equally significant* and *not chronologically or causally linked*, as in this example:

Subject

Reasons to cycle to school

Main Points

- fitness
- economy
- enjoyment

These three points are independent and equally important. They could be effectively explained in any order.

EXERCISE **22.8**

Below, we have identified 10 subjects, together with several main points that could be used to develop each one. For each subject, number the points so that they are arranged in the suggested order. Other arrangements are possible for some of the subjects below.

Subject	**Order**	**Main Points**
1. How to prepare for a job interview	Chronological	___ Visit the company's website. ___ Dress appropriately. ___ Prepare answers to standard interview questions. ___ Ask a friend to role-play the interview with you.

Subject	**Order**	**Main Points**
2. Reasons for student financial struggles	Climactic	___ They lack family assistance. ___ They lack government assistance. ___ They can't manage money effectively. ___ They can't find part-time work.
3. How to write a research paper	Chronological	___ Read and take notes on selected research sources. ___ Draft the paper. ___ Compile a working bibliography of research sources. ___ Define the subject. ___ Type and proofread the final draft. ___ Insert source citations and reference list. ___ Revise the paper.
4. Effects of malnutrition	Logical	___ Malnutrition affects the productivity and prosperity of nations as a whole. ___ Malnutrition impedes the mental and physical development of children. ___ Undernourished children become sickly adults unable to participate fully in their society.
5. Why pornography should be banned	Chronological	___ It degrades those who make it. ___ It brutalizes society as a whole. ___ It desensitizes those who view it.

Subject	Order	Main Points
6. Why young people don't vote	Climactic	____ The voting process is intimidating. ____ The politicians and politics seem corrupt or irrelevant. ____ They lack interest in political issues.
7. How to vote	Chronological	____ Make sure you are on the voting list. ____ Present your voter card. ____ Go to the specified polling station on election day. ____ Take your ballot to the private voting station. ____ Put your ballot through the slot in the ballot box. ____ Mark an X in the circle next to your candidate of choice. ____ Fold the ballot and return to the election officer's table. ____ Follow the results on TV or radio.
8. How public transit benefits society as a whole	Climactic	____ It allows city planners to develop commercial corridors. ____ It frees up core space for parks and development. ____ It moves people to and from city centres quickly. ____ It reduces pollution by taking cars off the roads.

Subject	Order	Main Points
9. Stock market cycles	Logical	____ Prices stabilize and begin to rise. ____ Overeager investors create "bubbles." ____ Investors realize that bubbles do not reflect worth and begin selling. ____ The sell-off becomes widespread and can create panic, causing prices to fall.
10. How technology benefits humankind	Climactic	____ Knowledge: virtually all of human knowledge is accessible on a computer. ____ Entertainment: a vast array of programming and gaming opportunities are available. ____ Democracy: technology enables everyone to express opinions, acquire information, and communicate with others around the world. ____ Communication: technology enables us to be instantly in touch with one another, at any time, in any place.

EXERCISE **22.9**

The main points in items 2, 5, 8, and 10 in Exercise 22.8 could be arranged differently, depending on your view of their significance. Discuss alternative arrangements with your partner, and provide an alternative order for each item. Be prepared to explain why the order you've chosen is preferable to the one we suggested.

EXERCISE **22.10**

Using your list of subjects and main points from Exercise 22.7, arrange the main points for each subject in the most appropriate order. (*Note:* Keep your answer sheet. You will need it for some of the next chapter's exercises.)

In this chapter, you've learned how to choose a satisfactory subject; how to discover a thesis; and how to find, test, and arrange main points that support your thesis. Now it's time to think about how to plan your paper: by the thesis statement method (Chapter 23) or by the outline method (Chapter 24). We think the former generally works best for short papers and the latter for long papers, but this distinction isn't hard and fast. Your wisest choice is to learn both ways to organize and develop a paper. Often, you will get the best results when you use them together.

The Thesis Statement

23

In Chapter 22, you chose a topic and selected some aspects of it to discuss. Your next task is to plan your paper. There are several methods to choose from, ranging from a sentence or two (a thesis statement) to a formal outline. For short papers, we recommend that you use the method presented in this chapter. For longer papers, or if your instructor requires a more detailed outline, refer to the instructions in Chapter 24, "The Outline."

The key to a well-organized essay is a **thesis statement**—a statement near the beginning of your paper that announces its subject and scope. The thesis statement helps both you and your readers because it previews the plan of your paper. It tells your readers what they are going to read about.

In fiction, telling readers in advance what they are going to find would never do. But for practical, everyday kinds of writing, advance notice works well. Term papers, technical reports, research papers, office memoranda, and business letters are no place for suspense or surprises. In these kinds of writing, you're more likely to get and keep your readers' attention if you indicate the subject and scope of your paper at the outset. A thesis statement acts like a table of contents. It's a kind of map of the territory covered in your paper: it keeps your reader (and you) on the right track.

> A thesis statement clearly and concisely indicates the SUBJECT of your paper, the MAIN POINTS you will discuss, and the ORDER in which you will discuss them.[1]

To write a thesis statement, you join your *subject* to your *main points*, which you have arranged in an appropriate order. To join the two parts of a thesis statement, you use a *link*. Your link can be a word or a phrase such as *are, include, consist of, because,* or *since,* or it can be a colon.[2] Here is a simple formula for constructing a thesis statement. (*S* stands for your subject.)

---

[1] Not all thesis statements retain the preview portion (i.e., the identification of main points in order of discussion) in the final draft. Nevertheless, we recommend that you begin the drafting process with a full thesis statement. You can always omit the preview of main points in your final copy if it seems redundant.

[2] Remember that a colon can be used only after an independent clause. See Chapter 19 if you need a review.

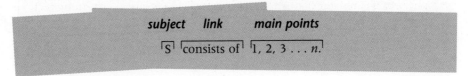

subject   *link*   *main points*

$\lceil S \rceil$ $\lceil$ consists of $\rceil$ $\lceil$ 1, 2, 3 . . . *n*. $\rceil$

Here's an example:

subject   *link*   *main points*

Three types of dangerous drivers (are) speeders, tailgaters, and multitaskers.

EXERCISE **23.1**

In each of the following thesis statements, highlight the subject, circle the link, and underline the main points. Answers for exercises in this chapter begin on page 553.

1. Three essential components of a strong and lasting relationship are good communication, sexual compatibility, and mutual respect.

2. If I were you, I would avoid eating in the cafeteria because the food is expensive, tasteless, and unhealthy.

3. Behavioural psychologists classify parents into four different types: indulgent, authoritarian, indifferent, and authoritative.

4. Fad diets are not the quick and easy fixes to weight problems that they may seem to be; in fact, they are often costly, ineffective, and even dangerous.

5. Aerobic exercise, strength and endurance training, and flexibility exercises are the essential components of a total fitness program.

6. The responsibilities of a modern union include protecting the jobs of current employees, seeking to improve their working conditions and compensation, and protecting the pensions and benefits of pensioners.

7. Because they lack basic skills, study skills, or motivation, some students run the risk of failure in college.

8. Hollywood is in financial trouble. Even well-known stars, stunning technical effects, and a hugely expensive advertising campaign no longer guarantee a blockbuster movie.

9. *The Simpsons* amuses and provokes viewers with its depiction of a smart-alecky, underachieving son; a talented, overachieving daughter; and a hopeless, blundering father.

10. In order to prosper in the decades to come, Canada must lessen its dependence on a resource-based economy, cultivate a spirit of entrepreneurship, increase productivity, and encourage immigration.

When you combine your subject with your main points to form a thesis statement, there is an important rule to remember:

Main points must be stated in GRAMMATICALLY PARALLEL FORM.

This rule means that if main point 1 is a word, then main points 2 and 3 and so on must be words, too. If main point 1 is a phrase, then the rest must be phrases. If your first main point is a dependent clause, then the rest must be dependent clauses. Take another look at the model thesis statements in Exercise 23.1. In every example, the main points are worded in grammatically parallel form. For each of those thesis statements, decide whether words, phrases, or dependent clauses were used. If you think your understanding of parallelism is a bit wobbly, review Chapter 9 and do Web Exercise 23.1 before continuing.

Go to Web Exercise 23.1

Paragraphs and Essays

EXERCISE **23.2**

Put a check mark (✓) before the sentences that are grammatically parallel. When you have completed the exercise, check your answers against ours on page 553.

1. _____ A good counsellor must have knowledge, insight, patience, and compassion.

2. _____ Good writing involves applying the principles of organization, sentence structure, spelling, and you have to punctuate correctly.

3. _____ Our company requires employees to be knowledgeable, totally honest, disciplined, and we have to be able to rely on them.

4. _____ Hobbies are important because they provide us with recreational activities, stimulation, and they are relaxing.

5. _____ Some of the negative effects of caffeine are heart palpitations, nervousness, and you have difficulty sleeping.

EXERCISE **23.3**

Now revise the incorrect sentences in Exercise 23.2.

Go to Web Exercise 23.2

EXERCISE **23.4**

Revise the following draft thesis statements. Be sure that the main points of each statement are significant, distinct, relevant, and grammatically parallel. Some sentences contain more than one kind of error. Identify the error(s) and make corrections as needed; then compare your revisions with our suggested answers on page 554.

1. The four kinds of essay writing are description, narrative, expository, and argumentation.

2. Intramural sports offer students a way to get involved in their school, an opportunity to meet friends, uniforms, and they can keep fit.

3. Increasingly, scientists are finding links between the weather and diseases such as colds, arthritic ailments, cancer, and aging.

4. The most prolific producers of pretentious language are politicians, teachers and administrators, those who write advertising copy, educators, and sportswriters.

5. There are three categories of students whom teachers find difficult: those who skip class, sleeping in class, and those who disrupt class.

EXERCISE **23.5**

Do this exercise with a partner. For each of the following potential thesis statements, assess the main points we've provided to see if they form appropriate support for the thesis. Then, using the points that pass the test, write a grammatically parallel thesis statement. Highlight the subject, circle the link, and underline the main points with straight lines. We've done part of the first question for you as an example. (*Tip:* Read each question all the way through before you decide which main points can be kept, which should be revised, and which should be discarded.)

1. Thesis: To succeed in college, a student requires several essential qualities.

   From the list below, choose the main points that support the subject:

   • motivation *Yes, a student must really want to succeed.*

   • choosing a major *No, that's part of the process of going to college, but not a quality required to succeed.*

   • organizational skills *Yes, good college students are able to set priorities and manage their time to achieve their priorities.*

   • academic skills *Yes, a good student must have solid academic skills to achieve success.*

   • writing ability *Good writing ability is one of the academic skills that students require, so it wouldn't be mentioned separately in the thesis statement.*

- time-management skills *Time management is an organizational skill, so it would be dealt with in that paragraph.*
- achieving a higher income *No. It's true that, over a lifetime, college graduates generally earn more than high-school graduates, but higher earnings isn't a quality. It's a result.*
- living in residence *No. Why?*

A. **Thesis statement:** To succeed in college, a student requires three essential qualities(:) *good academic skills, organizational skills,* and *motivation.*

Now rewrite the thesis statement using *are* as a link.

B. _____

_____

_____

2. **Thesis:** Some forms of electronic communication can improve a student's social life.

- instant messaging
- iPods
- blogging
- expensive gadgets
- Internet dating

A. **Thesis statement:** Some forms of electronic communication can improve a student's social life; for example, _____

_____

_____

Rewrite the thesis statement using *are* as a link.

B. _____

_____

_____

3. **Thesis:** Living in Canada has some advantages over living in the United States.

- universal medical care
- pleasant climate
- less crime
- tundra
- more affordable post-secondary education
- multicultural environment

A. **Thesis statement:** There are at least three advantages to living in Canada rather than in the United States _____

_____

_____

Rewrite the thesis statement using *because* as a link.

B. _____

_____

_____

4. **Thesis:** Immigration benefits Canada.

- Immigrants supply talents and skills our country lacks.
- We need immigrant labourers to maintain our workforce numbers.
- Immigrants must often learn a new language.
- Immigrants enrich Canadian cultural life.
- Immigrants may find it difficult to adjust to life in Canada.

A. **Thesis statement:** Immigration benefits Canada because _____

_____

_____

Paragraphs and Essays

Rewrite the thesis statement using *such as* as a link.

B. _____

_____

_____

In the last question of this exercise, you need first to create a thesis out of the subject we've provided. (Remember: a thesis is a statement that must be argued or explained.) Two satisfactory main points are identified below. Choose a third point and write two different versions of a thesis statement on this subject. Thesis statement A should put the main points first.

5. Subject: Maintaining a healthy lifestyle

   • balanced diet

   • adequate exercise

   • your choice

A. (Main points first) _____

_____

_____

B. Maintaining a healthy lifestyle involves _____

_____

_____

EXERCISE **23.6**

 Exchange with another pair of students the thesis statements you created for Exercise 23.5. Check each thesis statement for completeness and grammatical parallelism. Suggest revisions if they are needed. When you are all satisfied with the thesis statements you've checked and revised, decide which one you prefer and why.

For each of the topics below, provide main points and write a thesis statement. Then exchange papers with a partner and check each other's work.

1. Learning a new language

   •

   •

   •

Thesis statement: _____

_____

_____

_____

2. What I've learned from my family since I became an adult

   •

   •

   •

Thesis statement: _____

_____

_____

_____

3. What a college education means to me

   •

   •

   •

Thesis statement: _____

_____

_____

_____

Paragraphs and Essays

4. What makes me laugh

- _____
- _____
- _____

Thesis statement: _____

_____

_____

_____

5. My financial priorities after graduation

- _____
- _____
- _____

Thesis statement: _____

_____

_____

_____

EXERCISE **23.8**

Find the subjects and main points you produced for Exercise 22.10 in Chapter 22. Combine each subject with its main points to make a thesis statement. Be sure the main points are expressed in parallel form. Then trade papers with another student and check each other's work. Discuss any revisions you think are necessary.

We said at the beginning of this chapter that a thesis statement outlines your paper for you. Before we turn to the actual writing of the paper, you should have a general idea of what the finished product will look like.

In a short paper, each main point can be explained in a single paragraph. The main points of your subject become the _topics_ of the paragraphs, as shown on page 287 in the model format for a paper with three main points.[3] Once

---

[3] Chapter 25 will show you how to develop your paragraphs fully and convincingly.

you've mastered this basic structure, you can modify, expand, and develop it to suit papers of any length or kind.

Please note that the model format depicted below is a basic guideline for anyone who is learning to write English prose. Not all essays are—or should be—five paragraphs long. As you will see in the readings in Unit 7, unified, coherent essays can be shorter or longer, depending on their subject and purpose. As you gain writing experience, you will learn how to adapt the basic format to suit your needs. A competent and confident writer always adapts form to content, never the other way around. But learners must start somewhere, and the five-paragraph format is an excellent structure with which to begin.

Title

Paragraph 1:
Contains your
introduction
and thesis
statement

Subject consists of main points 1, 2, and 3.
Topic sentence introducing main point 1.

Paragraph 2:
Explains your
first main point

Topic sentence introducing main point 2.

Paragraph 3:
Explains your
second main
point

Topic sentence introducing main point 3.

Paragraph 4:
Explains your
third main point

Paragraph 5:
Summarizes your
main points and
states your
conclusion

Paragraphs and Essays

Notice the proportions of the paragraphs. This model is for a paper whose main points are approximately equal in significance, so the body paragraphs are approximately equal in length. In a paper in which the last main point is most significant, the paragraph that explains it will probably be longer than the others.

Notice, too, that the introductory and concluding paragraphs are shorter than the ones that explain the main points. Your introduction should not ramble on, and your conclusion should not trail off. Get to your main points as quickly as you can, and "end with a bang, not a whimper" (T.S. Eliot).

EXERCISE **23.9**

An example of a paper that follows the model format exactly is Brian Green's "Career Consciousness" on pages 436–37 in Unit 7, Readings. Read it through, and then go back and underline the thesis statement and the **topic sentences**.

The Outline

24

For longer compositions—business and technical reports, research papers, and the like—an outline is often necessary. A good outline maps out your paper from beginning to end. It shows what you have to say about your main points before you begin drafting. Outlining spares you the pain of discovering too late that you have too much information about one point and little or nothing to say about another.

Once you've chosen a satisfactory subject and main points, the next step is to expand this material into an organized plan for your paper. At this point, you may need to do some more thinking or reading to gather additional information. *Evidence*, the term used for supporting information, consists of data, facts, and statements that have been tested and validated by scholars through research or by writers through personal experience. (For the kinds of evidence you can choose from, see "Developing Your Paragraphs" in Chapter 25.) After you've assembled the information you need, prepare the outline.[1]

There are as many different approaches to outlining as there are writers. The outline you prepare will vary depending on your approach to the topic, the amount of time before the due date, and your instructor's preference (or requirement). Here are a few of the strategies you can choose from:

1. Writers who like to begin with brainstorming, freewriting, or another inductive technique often choose to postpone outlining until after they see what their creative juices produce.
2. Some writers prefer to start with a "scratch" outline, which consists of one- or two-word points that act as a bare-bones guide.
3. Other writers like an informal outline that sketches out the parts of the paper in more detail, showing major headings and a few supporting points.
4. Some writers do best with a full, formal outline with main points, subheadings, and various levels of evidence (up to nine in Word), which are identified by changes in indentation and font size.

---

[1] The four ways to arrange main ideas in a paper, which we explained in Chapter 23, also apply to the arrangement of evidence within a paragraph. Choose whichever order best suits the nature of your topic and the needs of your audience.

Whatever approach is right for you, your topic, and your instructor, the time you spend on outlining is invested, not wasted. Your investment will pay off in time saved during drafting and revising.

SCRATCH OUTLINE

As we've seen in Chapters 22 and 23, writing an essay requires you to select a thesis and main points, which you arrange in an order that will make sense to your reader. A thesis and main points form the beginnings of a scratch outline. Key these into your word processor, together with a few of the ideas you will elaborate on as you develop the main points. Now you have a bare-bones outline to guide you as you draft the body of your paper. Here's an example:

Thesis: A satisfying career—interesting, rewarding, productive
- interesting
  1. enjoyable
  2. comparable to hobbies
  3. Clive Beddoe
- rewarding
  1. money
  2. emotional rewards
- productive
  1. need to contribute
  2. unproductive jobs

While this outline means nothing to anyone other than its author, this is the skeleton of a paper. Once the writer puts some meat on the bones, adds an introduction and a conclusion, he or she will have a good first draft.

INFORMAL OUTLINE

An informal outline carries the scratch outline a step further, adding ideas and examples that will form the content of each paragraph. If whole sentences occur to you, key them in, but generally, the informal outline is in point form.

Introduction
  What is a career?
  Thesis: A satisfying career should be interesting, rewarding, and productive.

- interesting
    1. look forward to going to work
    2. leisure activities are stimulating; why not your career?
        — examples: artists, Clive Beddoe
    3. important not to waste your life doing something you hate
- rewarding
    1. know yourself: what do you need?
        — are you ambitious? need status, high salary?
        — or a relaxed, low-stress environment?
    2. success is what it means to you
        — examples: technician, news director—which one is "successful"?
- productive
    1. human nature to want to contribute, to make a difference
    2. some jobs are easy but meaningless
        — examples: factory job, night shift

Conclusion

Understanding yourself is key.

Don't be swayed by opinions of others.

Strive to improve for your own sake, not your employer's.

FORMAL OUTLINE

A formal outline is more detailed than a scratch or informal outline. It may be drafted in point form, but even if it isn't, the finished outline usually consists of complete sentences. If you have access to a word-processing program with an outline feature, try it out. Most programs have a "document view" called "Outline," which can be invaluable: it will create a formal outline as fast as you can type. In Word, select the View tab and choose Outline. (In Apple's Pages, the "Template Chooser" has a variety of Outline options.)

Here's how to proceed:

1. Key in your main points, in the order you chose for your thesis statement, and hit Enter after each one.
2. Move the cursor to the end of your first main point, hit Enter, and select Level 2 from the window at the top of the screen. This will indent and reduce the font size of the next line you type, which should be a supporting point for the first main point.
3. Hit Enter again and select Level 3 to add examples or other evidence to develop this supporting point.

Paragraphs and Essays

By repeating this process for each of your main points, you will end up with a clear visual plan of your essay. The outline will look something like this:

+ Introduction
  – Attention-getter
  – Thesis statement or statement of subject

+ First main point
     + Supporting point
       – Evidence
     + Supporting point
       – Evidence

+ Second main point
     + Supporting point
       – Evidence
     + Supporting point
       – Evidence

+ Third main point
     + Supporting point
       – Evidence
     + Supporting point
       – Evidence
     + Supporting point
       – Evidence

+ Conclusion
  – Summary
  – Memorable statement

The outline stage is the time to decide how to present the supporting information under each main point and how much time to spend on a particular point. If, for example, you have six subheadings under your first main point and one under your second, you need to rebalance your paper. Main points should be supported by approximately equal amounts of information.

Creating a satisfactory outline takes time. Be prepared to spend time adding, deleting, and rearranging your main points and supporting details until you're completely satisfied with their arrangement and proportions.

Now you are ready to draft your paper. Make the main points into paragraph divisions, develop the supporting points, and add an introduction and a conclusion. (Chapter 25 explains how.)

To show you the relationship between an outline and the final product, we've re-created the outline that was used to write "Career Consciousness" on pages 436–37.

Introduction

Attention-getter: Choosing a life's vocation is not a decision to be taken lightly.

Thesis statement: A satisfying career is one that is stimulating, rewarding, and productive.

I. A satisfying career is stimulating.
   A. When you get up in the morning, you look forward to your day.
      1. While not the image most people have of work, it is achievable.
      2. Most people can enjoy work just as they enjoy leisure activities.
   B. Many successful people have turned their interests into careers.
      1. Career professionals in the arts get paid for what they love to do.
         a. write, compose, paint, sculpt, etc.
         b. act, dance, sing, etc.
      2. Clive Beddoe turned his love of flying into the development of WestJet.
   C. If you deny yourself the chance to do what you love, you will spend most of your life wishing you were doing something else.

II. A satisfying career is rewarding, both financially and emotionally.
   A. To choose the right career, you must know yourself.
      1. Do you seek power and status?
      2. Or would you prefer a lower-profile position with less stress?
   B. Success is a state of mind.
      1. Contrast the careers of a small-town TV tech and a big-city news director.
         a. TV tech loves his job, family, community, and volunteer activities.
         b. News director thrives on deadlines, big-city life, money, and recognition her job provides.
      2. Both feel they are successful in their careers.

III. A satisfying career is productive.
   A. People need meaningful work.
      1. People need to feel they make a difference.
      2. Friendly co-workers, a pleasant routine, and money do not make up for lack of appreciation.

Paragraphs and Essays

B. Many people go unnoticed in their working lives.
   1. Some boast about reading paperbacks on the job.
   2. Some sleep through the night shift and fish or golf during the day.
C. Knowing that you are doing something worthwhile is essential to your sense of well-being.

Conclusion

Summary: It's not easy to find a career that provides stimulating, enjoyable, and meaningful work.
A. You need to understand yourself.
B. Make career decisions consistent with your values and goals.
C. Once you have found a satisfying career, keep working at it.
   1. Seek challenges and opportunities that stimulate you.
   2. Enjoy the rewards of doing your job well.
   3. Strive for improvement for your own sake, not your employer's.
Memorable Statement: Your career will occupy three-quarters of your life, so make the most of it!

EXERCISE **24.1**

Turn to "Career Consciousness" on pages 436–37. Highlight the sentences that correspond to the headings and subheadings in the outline on pages 293–94.

EXERCISE **24.2**

1. Read "The Second-Language Struggle," which begins on page 462.
2. Working with a partner, create for this essay
   • a scratch outline
   • an informal outline
   • a formal outline
3. Exchange your work with another team and compare outlines. Are there significant differences between the two teams' outlines? If so, which set of outlines best captures the essence of Waldman's essay?

EXERCISE **24.3**

Turn to the subjects and main points you developed for Exercise 22.10 in Chapter 22 and create an informal or a formal outline for a paper on one of those subjects.

Paragraphs

25

With your thesis statement and outline in front of you, you are ready to turn your main points into paragraphs. Does that sound like a magician's trick? It isn't. All you need to know is what a paragraph looks like and how to put one together.

A paragraph looks like this:

<u>A sentence that introduces the **topic** (or main idea) of the paragraph goes here.</u>

Three or more sentences that specifically support or explain the topic go in here.

_____
_____
_____
_____
_____

<u>A sentence that concludes your explanation of the topic goes here.</u>

Sometimes you can explain a main point satisfactorily in a single paragraph. If the main point is complicated and requires lots of support, you will need two or more paragraphs. Nevertheless, whether it is explaining a main point or a supporting point, every paragraph must contain three things: a **topic sentence** (usually the first sentence in the paragraph), several sentences that develop the topic, and a conclusion or a transition to the next paragraph.

A clear statement of your main idea—usually a single sentence—is a good way to start a paragraph. The sentences that follow should support or expand on the topic. The key to making the paragraph *unified* (an important quality of paragraphs) is to make sure that each of your supporting sentences relates directly to the main idea introduced in the topic sentence.

EXERCISE 25.1

Read through the three paragraphs specified on the next page, and then, with a partner, identify the three basic paragraph components: the topic sentence(s), the supporting sentences, and the conclusion. When you've completed the exercise, compare your answers with our suggestions on pages 555–56.

1. Gabor Maté, "Embraced by the Needle," paragraph 9
2. Margaret Wente, "The New Heavyweight Champions," paragraph 1
3. Lawrence Hill, "Don't Call Me That Word," paragraph 7

DEVELOPING YOUR PARAGRAPHS

How do you put a paragraph together? First, write your topic sentence, telling your reader what topic (main point or key idea) you're going to discuss in the paragraph. Next, develop the topic. An adequately developed paragraph gives enough supporting information to make the topic completely clear to the reader. A body paragraph typically runs between 75 and 200 words (introductions and conclusions are shorter), so you will need lots of supporting information for each point.

Unless you are writing from a detailed outline and have all the supporting material you need in front of you, you have to do some more thinking at this point. Put yourself in your reader's place. What does your reader need to know in order to understand your point clearly? Ask yourself the six questions discussed below to determine what *kind(s) of development* to use to support a particular topic sentence. The kind of development you choose is up to you. Let your topic and your reader be your guides.

1. Is a DEFINITION necessary?

If you're using a term that may be unfamiliar to your reader, you should define it. Use your own words in the definition. Your reader needs to know what *you* mean by the term—and, besides, quoting from the dictionary is a boring way to develop a paragraph. In the following paragraph, Jeffrey Moussaieff Masson, author of "Dear Dad" (see pages 446–49), defines and describes a penguin *tortue*, a term with which few readers would be familiar.[1]

---

[1] The page numbers in parentheses at the end of each block quotation in this chapter indicate either the page number in the book or article from which the quotation was taken or the page number in Unit 7, "Readings," where you will find the quotation in its context.

[As] soon as the bad weather starts, generally in June, the males need some protection from the bitter cold, and nearly all of them find it by forming a *tortue*, which is a throng of very densely packed penguins. When the storms come they move in close to one another, shoulder to shoulder, and form a circle. The middle of the tortue is unusually warm and one would think that every penguin fights to be at the epicentre of warmth. But in fact what looks like an immobile mass is really a very slowly revolving spiral. The constantly shifting formation is such that every penguin, all the while balancing [a] single precious egg on his feet, eventually winds up in the middle of the tortue, only to find himself later at the periphery. (448)

Reprinted by permission of the author.

You should also include a definition if you're using a familiar term in a specific or unusual way. In the following paragraphs, Angela Long explains what she means by *religion*:

I stopped going to church at the age of 12 when my grandfather died, and up until that point, religion was waking up every Sunday morning to get ready for the 10 o'clock service.

Religion was my mother delivering a freshly ironed dress to my bedroom door, and the smell of shoe polish in the kitchen. It was something that interfered with watching cartoons. It was a dark, windowless room in a basement where preteens drew scenes from the life of Jesus with crayons on paper plates. I didn't know much about Jesus except that I could never get his beard right. (440)

Reprinted by permission of the author. First published in *Geez* magazine Summer 2008.

© Wilfred Hildonen. Reproduction rights obtainable from CartoonStock. www.cartoonstock.com

Paragraphs and Essays

EXERCISE **25.2**

Write a paragraph in which you define one of the following terms:

generosity (*or* stinginess)	karma (*or* qi)	racism
a good (*or* bad) friend	a good (*or* bad)	extrovert
a good (*or* bad)	place to live	(*or* introvert)
marriage	a good (*or* bad) parent	success (*or* failure)

2. Would EXAMPLES help to clarify the point?

Providing examples is probably the most common method of developing a topic. Readers who encounter unsupported generalizations or statements of opinion are not convinced. They know they've been left dangling. Certainly they will be confused; they may even become suspicious, thinking that the writer is trying to put one over on them. One of the most effective ways of getting your idea across to your readers is by providing clear, relevant examples. In the passage below, Richard Lederer lists examples that support his point that English is a confusing language:

English is a crazy language. Let's look at a number of familiar English words and phrases that turn out to mean the opposite or something very different from what we think they mean:

A non-stop flight. Never get on one of these. You'll never get down.

A near miss. *A near miss* is, in reality, a collision. A close call is actually a near hit.

A hot water heater. Who heats hot water? This is similar to garbage disposal. Actually, the stuff isn't garbage until after you dispose of it.

A hot cup of coffee. Here again the English language gets us in hot water. Who cares if the cup is hot? Surely we mean a *cup of hot coffee.*

Doughnut holes. Aren't those little treats really *doughnut balls?* The hole is what's left in the original doughnut. (And if a candy cane is shaped like a cane, why isn't a doughnut shaped like a nut?)

A one-night stand. So who's standing? Similarly, to sleep with someone. Who's sleeping? (444)

Reprinted by permission of the author. First published in *Crazy English* (Pocketbooks 1998).

Sometimes one or two examples developed in detail are enough to enable the reader to understand what you mean. In the following paragraph, Brian Green first defines what he means by *a rewarding career,* and then he provides two different examples to illustrate his definition.

If your career is stimulating, then chances are good that it can also be rewarding. A good career offers two kinds of rewards: financial and emotional. Rewarding work doesn't just happen; it's something you need to plan for. The first and most important step is to know yourself. Only if you know who you are and what you need to be happy can you consciously seek out career experiences that will bring you satisfaction and steer clear of those that will annoy or stress you. Are you genuinely ambitious, or is power something you seek because you think it is expected of you? The pursuit of status and a high salary brings some people pure pleasure. Many people, however, find leadership positions excruciatingly stressful. Career enjoyment depends to some extent on whether or not you are successful, and success is a state of mind. Consider two graduates from the same college program. One is a technician in a small-town television station who loves his work, takes pride in keeping the station on the air, and delights in raising his family in a community where he is involved in volunteer activities ranging from sports to firefighting. The other is a news director at one of Canada's major television networks. Her work is highly stressful, full of risks, and continually scrutinized by viewers, competitors, and her supervisors. She thrives on the adrenaline rush of nightly production, and loves the big-city life, the financial rewards of her position, and the national recognition she receives. Which graduate is "successful"? Certainly, both feel their careers are rewarding, according to their individual definitions of the term. (436–37)

EXERCISE **25.3**

Write a six- to ten-sentence paragraph based on one of the topic sentences below, using examples to develop it.

Facebook is (not) a waste of precious time.

Fast food is the new tobacco.

Internet dating sites are an advantage/harmful.

Adolescence/the 20s/middle age is the most difficult stage of life.

Outside its own borders, the United States is probably the world's most disliked country.

Paragraphs and Essays

3. Is a SERIES OF STEPS or STAGES involved?

Sometimes the most effective way to develop the main idea of your paragraph is by explaining how to do it—that is, by relating the process or series of steps involved. Make sure you break the process down into its component parts and explain the steps logically and precisely. Below, Jeffrey Masson explains the process of courtship among penguins:

> The emperors usually wait for good weather to copulate, any time between April 10 and June 6. They separate themselves somewhat from the rest of the colony and face each other, remaining still for a time. Then the male bends his head, contracts his abdomen, and shows the female the spot on his belly where he has a flap of skin that serves as a kind of pouch for the egg and baby chick. This stimulates the female to do the same. Their heads touch, and the male bends his head down to touch the female's pouch. Both begin to tremble visibly. Then the female lies face down on the ice, partially spreads her wings and opens her legs. The male climbs onto her back and they mate for 10 to 30 seconds. (446)

Reprinted by permission of the author.

EXERCISE 25.4

Write a paragraph developed as a series of steps telling your reader how to make or do something you are good at. (Choose a significant topic, not a trivial one.)

4. Would SPECIFIC DETAILS be useful?

Providing your reader with concrete, specific, descriptive details can be an effective way of developing your main point. In the following paragraph, highlight the specific details that bring to life Russell Wangersky's description of Newfoundland's outport communities:

> There's life yet in gritty, tightly knit outport communities. In Reefs Harbour on Newfoundland's Northern Peninsula, a handful of fishing sheds, their sides weathered to a uniform silver-grey, stand like forgotten teeth on a half-buried lower jaw. Lobster markers hang from coils of

yellow rope inside their dusty windows. A single boat curves in towards the harbour, its engine the only sound in the still air, a solitary fisherman at the stern. Every few seconds, a small wave breaks over the shoals in the harbour, loud enough to drown out the vessel's approach. You can't shake the feeling that Reefs Harbour is asleep, asleep like Rip Van Winkle, breathing slowly through a nap that could last for years. (438)

Reprinted by permission of the author.

In some paragraphs, numerical facts or statistics can be used to support your point effectively. Ever since Benjamin Disraeli's immortal comment that the media publish "lies, damned lies, and statistics," however, critical readers tend to be suspicious of statistics, so be very sure that your facts are correct and that your statistics are current.

[Mated penguins] stay together afterward constantly, leaning against one another when they are standing up, or if they lie down, the female will glide her head under that of her mate. About a month later, between May 1 and June 12, the female lays a single greenish-white egg. French researchers noted that the annual dates on which the colony's first egg was laid varied by only eight days in 16 years of observation. Weighing almost a pound, and measuring up to 131 millimetres long and 86 millimetres wide, this is one of the largest eggs of any bird. The male stays by the female's side, his eyes fixed on her pouch. As soon as he sees the egg, he sings a variation of what has been called the "ecstatic" display by early observers, and she too takes up the melody. (447)

Reprinted by permission of the author.

EXERCISE 25.5

Write an eight- to ten-sentence paragraph describing one of the following topics. Include details that involve several of the physical senses: sight, hearing, touch, smell, and taste. Be sure to begin with a clearly identifiable topic sentence.

Your favourite family meal
The best video game/movie ever
Your favourite club/coffee shop
An embarrassing incident
A locker room after a game
Your place of worship
Your favourite space in your favourite place

Paragraphs and Essays

5. Would a COMPARISON or CONTRAST help to clarify your point?

A **comparison** points out similarities between objects, people, or ideas; it shows how two different things are alike. A **contrast** points out dissimilarities between things; it shows how two objects, people, or ideas are different. A **comparison and contrast** identifies both similarities and differences. In the paragraph below, Sun-Kyung Yi contrasts the two sides of her "split personality."

> When I was younger, toying with the idea of entertaining two separate identities was a real treat, like a secret game for which no one knew the rules but me. I was known as Angela to the outside world, and as Sun-Kyung at home. I ate bologna sandwiches in the school lunchroom and rice and kimchee for dinner. I chatted about teen idols and giggled with my girlfriends during my classes, and ambitiously practiced piano and studied in the evenings, planning to become a doctor when I grew up. I waved hellos and goodbyes to my teachers, but bowed to my parents' friends visiting our home. I could also look straight in the eyes of my teachers and friends and talk frankly with them instead of staring at my feet with my mouth shut when Koreans talked to me. Going outside the home meant I was able to relax from the constraints of my cultural conditioning, until I walked back in the door and had to return to being an obedient and submissive daughter. (452–53)

EXERCISE **25.6**

Write a paragraph comparing or contrasting two cities (or perhaps countries, generations, musicians, writers/books, clothing brands, or sports teams). Begin your paragraph with a clearly identifiable topic sentence and support it with fresh, original points. The differences in size, climate, and world status between London, England, and London, Ontario, will not grab a reader's attention; the differences in the cities' ethnic mixes, employment possibilities, and cultural opportunities might interest a Canadian reader.

6. Would a PARAPHRASE or QUOTATION be appropriate?

A **paraphrase** is a summary of someone else's idea in your own words. It is fair to rewrite the idea, but you still must identify your source, as you do with a quotation. Use a quotation when you find that someone else—an expert in a particular field, a well-known author, or a respected public figure—has said what you want to say better or more convincingly than you could ever hope to say it. In these cases, quotations—as long as they are kept short and not used too frequently—are useful in developing your topic. In the following paragraph, Nell Waldman uses first a paraphrase and then a quotation from experts to explain one reason that it is so difficult for adults to learn a second language.

> An adult has intellectual and cognitive skills that a child lacks. An adult can think abstractly and is able to memorize and use dictionaries (Crystal 373). These skills might seem to make it easier to learn a new language. However, an adult already has a firmly established first language in his intellectual repertoire, and the native language actually interferes with mastering the second language. H. Douglas Brown describes the process whereby remnants of the native language collide with the new language: "The relatively permanent incorporation of incorrect linguistic forms into a person's second language competence . . . [is] referred to as *fossilization*" (217). The fossils of our native language tend to keep turning up as errors in the new language we are struggling to learn. (464)

College writing normally requires that you identify the source of any material you quote or paraphrase. The easiest way to do this is to give a page reference in parentheses at the end of your quotation and full publication details in the Works Cited or References list at the end of your paper. If you give the author's name in the sentence leading up to the quotation, you need give in parentheses only the page number(s) of the source in which you found it. If you do not give the author's name in your introduction to the quotation, you need to include it, together with the page number(s), in the parentheses at the end of the quotation. (For APA style, provide the year, as well as the page number(s).) If the quotation is short enough to be included in your own sentence, put the period *after* the source information. For example,

> In an analysis of contemporary labour trends in Canada, Margaret Wente observes that "in 2007 . . . [Canada] became the first country in the Western world where women outnumbered men in the work force . . . [and] all evidence suggests the gender shift is permanent" (460).

> A well-known Canadian journalist reports a surprising and puzzling change in Canada's workplace trends: "Back in 2007 . . . [we] became the first country in the Western world where women outnumbered men in the work force. . . . All evidence suggests the gender shift is permanent" (Wente 460).

Paragraphs and Essays

At the end of your paper, include a "Works Cited" or "References" list: a list in alphabetical order by authors' surnames of all the books, articles, and other publications from which you have quoted in your paper. Follow the instructions given in the style guide your instructor recommends, or go to More Information on the Student Resources page of our website at **www .bareplus4e.nelson.com** for details of MLA and APA style requirements.[2]

When you plan the paragraphs of your essay, remember that you will often need to use more than one method of development to explain each point. The six methods outlined in this chapter can be used in any combination. Choose whichever kinds of development will best help your reader understand what you want to say about your topic.

EXERCISE **25.7**

Working with a partner, identify the kinds of development used in the following paragraphs, which we have taken from essays in Unit 7. (More than one kind of development may be present in each.) Then turn to page 556 to check your answers.

1. "Clinging to the Rock," paragraph 4
2. "The Second-Language Struggle," paragraph 2
3. "I Believe in Deviled Eggs," paragraph 3
4. "Dear Dad," paragraph 12
5. "Career Consciousness," paragraph 4
6. "Dear Dad," paragraph 4
7. "The New Heavyweight Champions," paragraph 6
8. "Crazy English," paragraph 9
9. "The New Heavyweight Champions," paragraph 3
10. "An Immigrant's Split Personality," paragraph 10

EXERCISE **25.8**

Choose one of the following topic sentences (or make up one of your own) and write a paragraph of approximately six to ten sentences using one or more of the methods of paragraph development discussed in this chapter. When you've completed your paragraph, exchange your work with another student, read his or her paragraph carefully, and identify the method(s) of development your partner has chosen. Were you given enough information to understand the topic? If not, what additional information did you need?

---

[2] See pages 463–66 for examples of an essay written in MLA format and pages 467–71 for the same paper in APA format.

1. Life is like a game of _____.
2. You cannot trust information you find on the Net.
3. Failing in college requires careful planning.
4. How to "get away from it all."
5. _____ is a profession with a future.
6. Yesterday's music is (not) better than today's.
7. Taking the time to earn a post-secondary diploma/degree is definitely (not) worth it.
8. Canadians don't appreciate how lucky they are.
9. Few Canadians understand the experience of being a refugee.
10. A near miss.

WRITING INTRODUCTIONS AND CONCLUSIONS

Two paragraphs in your paper are not developed in the way we've just outlined: the *introduction* and the *conclusion*. All too often, these paragraphs are dull or clumsy and detract from a paper's effectiveness. But they needn't. Here's how to write good ones.

The introduction is worth special attention because that's where your reader either sits up and takes notice of your paper or sighs and pitches it into the wastebasket. Occasionally, for a short paper, you can begin by simply stating your thesis. More usually, though, an **attention-getter** comes before the **thesis statement**. An attention-getter is a sentence or two designed to get the reader interested in what you have to say.

There are several kinds of attention-getters to choose from:

1. a question (see "The Second-Language Struggle," page 463)
2. a definition (see "Career Consciousness," page 436)
3. a little-known or striking fact (see "An Immigrant's Split Personality," page 452)
4. a comparison or contrast that will intrigue your reader (see "Dear Dad," page 446)
5. an interesting incident or **anecdote** related to your subject (see "Embraced by the Needle," page 455)

Add your thesis statement to the attention-getter and your introduction is complete.

The closing paragraph, too, usually has two parts: a *summary* of the main points of your paper (phrased differently, please—not a word-for-word repetition of your thesis statement or topic sentences) and a *memorable statement*. Your memorable statement may take several forms. For example, it may

1. refer to the content of your opening paragraph (see "Career Consciousness," page 437)
2. include a relevant or thought-provoking quotation, statement, or question (see "The Second-Language Struggle," page 465)
3. emphasize the value or significance of your subject (see "Many Faiths, One Truth," page 452)
4. make a suggestion for change (see "An Immigrant's Split Personality," page 454)
5. offer a solution, make a prediction, or invite the reader to get involved (see "Clinging to the Rock," page 439, and "Career Consciousness," page 437)

EXERCISE **25.9**

Using as many of the different kinds as you can, write an attention-getter and a memorable statement for each of the following topics.

1. College professors should (not) be required to take courses in how to teach.
2. Honesty is (not) always the best policy.
3. *Facebook* is (not) a waste of precious time.
4. The experience of war changes one in unexpected ways.
5. Being a man (or woman) today is not easy.
6. The environment is the most important political issue facing us today.
7. We can learn much from our grandparents (or children).
8. On-demand video streaming providers (e.g., Netflix) will quickly destroy community movie theatres.
9. Bad storms and atypical floods and droughts suggest that global warming is causing destructive climate change.
10. Happiness is a function of who you are, not what you have.

KEEPING YOUR READER WITH YOU

As you write your paragraphs, keep in mind that you want to make it as easy as possible for your reader to follow your paper. Clear transitions and an appropriate tone can make the difference between an essay that confuses readers and one that enlightens them.

TRANSITIONS

Transitions are words and phrases that show the relationship between one point and the next, making a paragraph or a paper read smoothly. Like turn signals on a car, they tell the person following you where you're going. Following are some common transitions you can use to keep your reader on track.

1. to show a time relationship: first, second, third, next, before, during, after, now, then, finally, last
2. to add an idea or example: in addition, also, another, furthermore, similarly, for example, for instance
3. to show contrast: although, but, however, instead, nevertheless, on the other hand, in contrast, on the contrary
4. to show a cause–effect relationship: as a result, consequently, because, since, therefore, thus

Here is a paragraph that has adequate development but no transitions:

> There are several good reasons you should not smoke. Smoking is harmful to your lungs and heart. It is annoying and dangerous to those around you who do not smoke. Smoking is an unattractive and dirty habit. It is difficult to quit. Most worthwhile things in life are hard to achieve.

Not very easy to read, is it? Readers are jerked from point to point until, battered and bruised, they reach the end. This kind of writing is unfair to readers. It makes them do too much of the work—more work than many readers will

Paragraphs and Essays

be willing to do. The ideas may all be there, but the readers have to figure out for themselves how the points fit together. After a couple of paragraphs like this one, even a patient reader can become annoyed.

Now read the same paragraph with the transitions added:

> There are several good reasons you should not smoke. Among them, three stand out as the most persuasive. First, smoking is harmful to your lungs and heart. Second, it is both annoying and dangerous to those around you who do not smoke. In addition to these compelling facts, smoking is an unattractive and dirty habit. Furthermore, once you begin, it is difficult to quit; but then, most worthwhile things in life are hard to achieve.

In the revised paragraph, the highlighted transitions gently guide readers from one point to the next. By the time the readers arrive at the conclusion, they know not only what ideas the writer had in mind but also how they fit together. Transitions make a reader's job easier and more rewarding.

TONE

One final point: as you write the paragraphs of your paper, be conscious of your **tone**. Your audience, purpose, and subject will all influence the tone you choose, which must be appropriate to all three. The words you use, the examples, quotations, and other supporting materials you choose to help explain your main points all contribute to your tone.

When you are trying to explain something to someone, particularly if it's something you feel strongly about, you may be tempted to get highly emotional in your discussion. If you give in to this temptation, chances are you won't be convincing. What will be communicated is the strength of your feelings, not the depth of your understanding or the validity of your opinion. To be clear and credible, you need to restrain your enthusiasm or anger and present your points in a calm, reasonable way.

We have a few suggestions to help you find and maintain the right tone:

- Be tactful. Avoid phrases such as "Any idiot can see," "No sane person could believe," and "It is obvious that." What is obvious to you isn't necessarily obvious to someone who has a limited understanding of your subject or disagrees with your opinion.
- Don't address your readers as though they were children or ignorant. Never use sarcasm, profanity, or slang. (If you do, your readers will neither take you seriously nor respect you.)

- Don't apologize for your interpretation of your subject. Have confidence in yourself. You've thought long and hard about your subject, you've found good supporting material to help explain it, and you believe in its significance. State your thesis positively. If you hang back, using phrases such as "I may be wrong, but" or "I tend to feel that," your reader won't be inclined to give your points the consideration they deserve. If you present your argument with assurance and courtesy, your writing will be both clear and convincing.

The following paragraph is an example of inappropriate tone. The writer is enthusiastic about the topic, but the tone is arrogant, bossy, and tactless rather than persuasive.

> How dumb can people get? Here's this guy with a bumper sticker reading "Out of work yet? Keep buying foreign!" on his "North American" car parked in a Walmart parking lot. What can you buy in Walmart that's made in Canada? Zilch. And besides, the car this idiot is driving wasn't made in Canada or even the U.S. The engine was imported from Japan, and the transmission was made by Mexicans working for next to nothing. The plastic body moulding came from that model of capitalism and human rights, China, and the interior finishings were made in Taiwan. Not foreign? Give me a break. About the only part of this car that was made here is the bumper that holds his stupid sticker. Meanwhile, parked right next to him was a "Japanese" car that was manufactured in Canada by Ontario workers. Sticker Guy is obviously too ignorant to get the irony.

Now read the paragraph below, which argues the same point but in a more tactful way.

> As the driver pulled into the parking spot beside me, I could hardly help noticing his bumper sticker: "Out of work yet? Keep buying foreign!" It was attached to a car produced by one of North America's "Big Three" automakers, but the message lost much of its force because of where we were: in a Walmart parking lot. There is precious little to buy in Walmart that has been produced in Canada. However, even that fact is beside the point, given the current internationalization of the auto industry. The car with the sticker on it, while nominally North American in origin, had an engine produced in Japan, a transmission built in Mexico, plastic body moulding made in China, and interior finishings imported from Taiwan. One of the few parts actually made in Canada, ironically, was the bumper to which the sticker was attached. Meanwhile, the car next to it, a "Japanese" mid-size, had been built in Ontario.

Paragraphs and Essays

EXERCISE **25.10**

The following paragraph is a draft written for a general reader. The writer's purpose is to persuade his audience that fighting should be banned in professional hockey. Revise the paragraph to make it appropriate for its audience and purpose by deleting or rewording any lapses in tone. Then compare your answer with our suggestion on page 556.

We've all heard the arguments: "It's part of the game," "It's what the fans want," "It prevents dangerous, dirty play." What nonsense! Fighting has no place in hockey or any team sport, and people who think differently are Neanderthals. Anyone with half a brain knows that fighting is banned in every other sport. What makes hockey any different? If the fans wanted fighting, they wouldn't watch the Olympics or World Championships. Ever seen the ratings for those events? Through the roof! Meanwhile, NHL ratings are in decline, and the game is treated as a third-rate sport in most of the world. Hockey can be a beautiful, fast, skilful, creative game, but when goons who have no purpose other than to fight are sent out onto the ice, it is a joke.

EXERCISE **25.11**

Do either A or B.

A. Using one of the thesis statements you prepared in Chapter 23, Exercise 23.7, write an essay of 400–500 words.
B. Using the outline you prepared in Chapter 24, Exercise 24.3, write a paper of approximately 500 words.

Revising Your Paper

26

No one can write in a single draft an essay that is perfectly organized and developed, let alone one that is free of grammar, spelling, and punctuation errors. The purpose of the first draft is to get down on paper something you can work with until it meets your reader's needs and expectations. Planning and drafting should take about half the time you devote to writing a paper. The other half should be devoted to revision.

Revision is the process of refining your message until

- it says what you want it to say
- your reader(s) will understand it
- your reader(s) will receive it favourably

These three goals are the essentials of good communication. You can achieve them only if you keep your readers in mind as you revise. Because a first draft reflects the contents of the writer's mind, it usually seems fine to the writer. But in order to transfer an idea as clearly as possible from the mind of the writer to the mind of the reader, revision is necessary. The idea needs to be honed and refined until it is as clear to your reader as it is to you. By revising from your reader's point of view, you can avoid misunderstandings before they happen.

WHAT IS REVISION?

Revision means "re-seeing." It does *not* mean "re-copying." The aim of revision is to improve your writing's organization, accuracy, and style. Revising is a three-stage process. Each step requires that you read through your entire essay, painful though this may be. The goal of your first reading is to ensure that you've organized and developed your ideas in a way that your reader can follow. In your second reading, you focus on paragraphs and sentences—the building blocks of prose. Your third reading concentrates on correctness. Here are the steps to follow in revising a paper.

1. Improve the whole paper by revising its content and organization.
2. Refine paragraph and sentence structure, and correct any grammatical errors.
3. Edit and proofread to catch errors in word choice, spelling, and punctuation.

Inexperienced writers often skip the first two stages and concentrate on the third, thinking they will save time. They are making a mistake. They are wasting time—both theirs and their readers'—because the result is writing that doesn't communicate clearly and won't make a positive impression.

The best way to begin revising is to do nothing to the early version of your paper for several days. Let as much time as possible pass between completing your first draft and rereading it. Ten minutes, or even half a day, is not enough. The danger in rereading too soon is that you're likely to "read" what you *think* you've written—what exists in your head, not on the page.

If you haven't allowed enough time for this cooling-off period, don't despair. There are two other things you can do to help you get some distance from your draft. If your first draft is handwritten, type it out. Reading your essay in a different form helps you to "re-see" its content. Alternatively, read your paper aloud and listen to it from the point of view of your reader. Hear how your explanation unfolds, and mark every place your reader may find something unclear, irrelevant, inadequately developed, or out of order. To succeed as a writer—even if your message consists of a brief clinical record or an outline of a simple task—you must be able to get into the head of your reader and compose your message to complement the knowledge (and the lack of knowledge) that resides there.

STEP 1: REVISE CONTENT AND ORGANIZATION

As you read your paper aloud, keep in mind the three possible kinds of changes you can make at this stage:

1. You can REARRANGE information. This is the kind of revision that is most often needed but least often done. Consider the order in which you've arranged your paragraphs. From your reader's point of view, is this the most effective order in which to present your ideas? If you are not already using a word-processing program, now is the time to begin. With a good word processor, moving blocks of text around is as easy as dealing a deck of cards.

2. You can ADD information. Adding new main ideas or further development of the ideas already there is often necessary to make your message interesting, clear, and convincing. It's a good idea to ask a friend to read your draft and identify what you should expand on or clarify. (Be sure to return the favour. You can learn a great deal by critiquing other people's writing.)

3. You can DELETE information. Now is the time to cut out anything that is repetitious, insignificant, or irrelevant to your subject and reader.

"JUNIOR'S WRITING HAS IMPROVED. HIS LETTERS FROM COLLEGE, PLEADING FOR MORE MONEY, ARE FORCEFULLY AND FLAWLESSLY WRITTEN."

Use the checklist that follows to guide you as you review your paper's form and content.

CONTENT AND ORGANIZATION CHECKLIST

ACCURACY

Is everything you have said accurate?

- Is your information consistent with your own experience or observations and with what you have discovered through research?
- Are all your facts and evidence up to date?

Paragraphs and Essays

COMPLETENESS

Have you included enough main ideas and development to explain your subject and convince your reader? (Remember that "enough" means from the reader's point of view, not the writer's.)

- If your paper involved research, have you provided an appropriate source citation for every quotation and/or paraphrase?
- Have you attached a Works Cited or References list, if one is required?

SUBJECT

Is your subject

- significant? Does it avoid the trivial or the obvious?
- single? Does it avoid double or combined subjects?
- specific? Is it focused and precise?
- supportable? Have you provided enough evidence to make your meaning clear and convincing?

MAIN POINTS

Are your main points

- significant? Have you deleted any unimportant ones?
- distinct? Are they all different from one another, or is there an overlap in content?
- relevant? Do all points relate directly to your subject?
- arranged in the most appropriate order? Again, "appropriate" means from the reader's perspective. Choose chronological, climactic, logical, or random order, depending on which is most likely to help the reader make sense of your information.

INTRODUCTION

Does your introduction

- catch attention and make the reader want to read on?
- contain a clearly identifiable thesis statement?
- identify the main points that your paper will explain?

CONCLUSION

Does your conclusion

- contain a summary or reinforcement of your main points, rephrased to avoid word-for-word repetition?
- contain a statement that effectively clinches your argument and leaves the reader with something to think about?

TONE

Is your tone consistent, reasonable, courteous, and confident throughout your essay?

When you have carefully considered these questions, it's time to move on to the second stage of the revision process.

EXERCISE **26.1**

Go back to the essay you wrote for Exercise 25.11. That paper is a first draft. Use the Content and Organization Checklist on pages 313–14 to find and correct any errors or omissions in form and content.

STEP 2: REVISE PARAGRAPHS AND SENTENCES

For this step, too, you should allow time—at least a couple of days—between your first revision and your second. Enough time must elapse to allow you to tackle your paper as if you were seeing it for the first time. Once again, read your draft aloud, and use this list of questions to help you improve it.

PARAGRAPH AND SENTENCE CHECKLIST

PARAGRAPHS

Does each paragraph

- begin with a clear, identifiable topic sentence?
- develop one—and only one—main idea?
- present one or more kinds of development appropriate to the main idea?
- contain clear and effective transitions to signal the relationship between sentences? between paragraphs?

SENTENCES

Sentence Structure

1. Is each sentence clear and complete?
   - Are there any fragments or run-ons?
   - Are there any misplaced or dangling modifiers?
   - Are all lists (whether words, phrases, or clauses) expressed in parallel form?
2. Are your sentences varied in length? Could some be combined to improve the clarity and impact of your message?

Grammar

1. Have you used verbs correctly?
   - Are all verbs in the correct form?
   - Do all verbs agree with their subjects?
   - Are all verbs in the correct tense?
   - Are there any confusing shifts in verb tense within a paragraph?
2. Have you used pronouns correctly?
   - Are all pronouns in the correct form?
   - Do all pronouns agree with their antecedents?
   - Have all vague pronoun references been eliminated?

When you're sure you've answered these questions satisfactorily, go to the third and last stage of the revision process.

EXERCISE **26.2**

Now apply the Paragraph and Sentence Checklist to the version of the essay you created in Exercise 26.1, and revise any errors in paragraph structure, sentence structure, and grammar.

"Shall I rephrase this letter so it makes sense?"

STEP 3: EDIT AND PROOFREAD

By now you're probably so tired of refining your paper that you may be tempted to skip **editing**—correcting errors in grammar, word choice, spelling, punctuation, and formatting—and **proofreading**—correcting errors in typing or writing that appear in the final draft. But these final tasks are essential if you want your paper to make a positive impression.

Misspellings, faulty punctuation, and messiness don't always create misunderstandings, but they do cause the reader to form a lower opinion of you and your work. Not convinced? Go to **www.youtube.com/watch?v=p_rwB5_3PQc** and see for yourself.

Most word-processing programs include a grammar checker and a spell checker. It is worthwhile running your writing through these programs at the editing stage. The newer programs have some useful features. For example, they will question (but not correct) your use of apostrophes, they will sometimes catch errors in subject–verb agreement, and they will catch obvious misspellings and typos.

But don't make the mistake of assuming these programs will do all of your editing for you. Many errors slip past a computer's grammar database, no matter how comprehensive the salesperson told you it is. Only you or a knowledgeable and patient friend can find and correct all errors.

If spelling is a particular problem for you, you should first run your paper through a spell checker. After that, you're on your own. Read your paper backward, word-by-word, from the end to the beginning. Reading backward forces you to look at each word by itself and helps you to spot those that look suspicious. Whenever you're in doubt about the spelling of a word, look it up! If you find this task too tedious to bear, ask a good speller to read through your paper for you and identify any errors. (Then take this person out for dinner. If you get an A, add a show.)

The next checklist outlines the questions to ask yourself when you are editing.

EDITING CHECKLIST

WORDS

Usage

Have you used words to *mean* rather than *impress*?

- Have you eliminated any slang, pretentious language, or offensive language?
- Have you cut out any unnecessary words?
- Have you corrected any "abusages"?
- Have you looked up the meanings of words that you're not absolutely certain about?

Spelling

Are all words spelled correctly?

- Have you double-checked any homonyms? (See Chapter 2, and triple-check any words listed there that cause you trouble.)
- Have you used capital letters where they are needed?
- Have you used apostrophes correctly for possessives and omitted them from plurals?

PUNCTUATION

Within Sentences

- Have you eliminated any unnecessary commas and included commas where needed? (Refer to the five comma rules in Chapter 17 as you consider this question.)
- Have you used colons and semicolons where appropriate?
- Are all quotations appropriately marked?

Beginnings and Endings

- Does each sentence begin with a capital letter?
- Do all questions—and only questions—end with a question mark?
- Are all quotation marks correctly placed?

FORMATTING AND DOCUMENTATION (IF REQUIRED)

- Does your paper satisfy all details of the format specified by your instructor?
- Have you provided a reference for the source of every quotation and paraphrase?
- Have you attached a properly formatted Works Cited or References list?

EXERCISE **26.3**

Now scan or key into your word processor the revised draft of the essay you produced for Exercise 26.2.[1] This is your last chance to make this essay error-free. There are two parts to this exercise:

1. Using the Editing Checklist above, revise errors in word usage, spelling, and punctuation. Save your file as "Draft 3" and print it.

2. Follow the "Tips for Effective Proofreading" below to find and correct any errors or typos you may have missed. Save your file under a new name ("Draft 4" or "Final Draft") and print it.

---

[1] If you do not have access to a word processor, complete this exercise using a different colour of pen for each draft. In order to learn your strengths and weaknesses, you must be able to identify the changes you make at each stage of the revision process.

© John Morris. Reproduction rights obtainable from CartoonStock. www.cartoonstock.com

"Contrary to your belief Miss Tonks, spelling and punctuation is not a fad!"

TIPS FOR EFFECTIVE PROOFREADING

By the time you have finished editing, you will have gone over your paper so many times you may have practically memorized it. When you are very familiar with a piece of writing, it's hard to spot the small mistakes that may have crept in as you produced your final copy. Here are some tips to help you find those tiny, elusive errors:

1. Read through your essay line by line, using a ruler to guide you.
2. If you've been keeping a list of your most frequent errors in this course, scan your essay for the mistakes you are most likely to make.
3. Use the Quick Revision Guide on the inside front cover of this book to make a final check of all aspects of your paper.
4. Use the list of correction marks on the inside back cover to check for errors your instructor has identified in your writing.

Paragraphs and Essays

Your "last" draft may need further revision after your proofreading review. If so, take the time to revise the paper one last time so that the version you hand in is clean and easy to read. Computers make editing and proofreading almost painless since errors are so easy to correct.

EXERCISE **26.4**

Exchange with a partner the essays you each produced in Exercise 26.3. (This exercise works best if you choose a partner whose writing skills are better than your own.) Apply the three checklists to your partner's paper. Use a coloured pen, and note in the margins any problems you find in content and organization (Step 1), and correct on the paper errors you find in Steps 2 and 3. Be prepared to spend at least an hour on this exercise. Wise people know that the best way to learn a skill is to teach it. That's what this exercise requires you to do: teach your partner.

At long last, you're ready to submit your paper. If you've followed the three steps to revision conscientiously, you can hand in your paper with confidence that it says what you want it to say, both about your subject and about you. One last word of advice:

DON'T FORGET TO KEEP A COPY FOR YOUR FILES!

Go to Web Exercise 26.1

EXERCISE **26.5**

Revise the following passage in three stages: first, apply all of the questions in the Step 2 Paragraph and Sentence Checklist on pages 315–16, and then apply all of the questions in the Step 3 Editing Checklist on pages 317–18. Finally, review Tips for Effective Proofreading above. Then compare your final draft with ours on pages 556–57.

Do you find it a struggle to pay the bills every month. When living beyond your means, even a small shortfall at the end of each month can quickly add up to a humongous debt. To beat this problem you can basically choose to spend less or earning more. At first, the former may seem the more difficulty choice, cutting back on what you spend may mean giving up some of the things you "need" such as eating out, movies, or the latest fashions. Doing without such expensive pleasures, however, often produce significant savings, you may even save enough to balance the monthly books.

Earning more money than what you now bring in and continuing to spend at your present pace may seem like a more attractive way to go, but is it realistic. There is the challenge of finding another job that pays better. Or adding part-time work to the job you already have, either way your going to loose even more of your already scarce study and leisure time. There is the fact that most people continue to spend at the same rate, regardless of how much money we make so its likely that, even with additional income, you'll still be in the hole at the end of the month. The best solution to the end-of-month budget blues is likely a combination of cutting costs where practical and adding to income where possible.

Paragraphs and Essays

27 | Using Research Resources Responsibly

PARAPHRASE OR PLAGIARISM?

In our culture, using someone else's words or ideas in your writing without acknowledging their source is considered to be **plagiarism**, and it is a punishable offence. At its most serious, plagiarism is an attempt to deceive the reader into thinking you wrote the material. In the academic world, even if unintentional, plagiarism can lead to consequences ranging from a grade of zero on a paper to expulsion from the college or university. In the business world and in the media, a writer who plagiarizes can expect to be fired.

Many students think that it is all right to use information they've found if they change the wording of the material they want to "borrow." This is not so. *Any information or ideas that cannot be considered common knowledge must be acknowledged or credited.* Even if you put someone else's original idea into your own words, you must tell your reader the source of the information. Any material that is taken word for word from another writer must be put in quotation marks and its source given. (See Crediting Your Sources, below.)

When you want to express an idea from someone else's work, you have the options of paraphrasing, summarizing (a summary is a condensed paraphrase), or quoting the idea. Although quoting requires the least work on your part, it is the technique you should use least frequently. College and university instructors are looking for your ability to **paraphrase**. Paraphrasing is the inclusion of another writer's idea in your essay that is expressed in your own words. The ability to paraphrase well is an immensely useful skill, but it is not easy to learn. You will need much experience before you can produce effective paraphrases. One of the reasons you are assigned research papers in college or university is to give you practice in paraphrasing. Here are the guidelines to follow:

1. A paraphrase must be a clear and accurate rewording of the author's idea.
2. A paraphrase must express the author's idea in your own words and sentences.
3. The source of your paraphrase must be included in the documentation format that your instructor requires.

To see the differences between paraphrase and plagiarism, study the paragraphs that follow. We have taken as our example a paragraph from "Career Consciousness," which you will find on page 437.

Original

It is not easy to find a career that provides stimulating, enjoyable, and meaningful work. Understanding yourself—your interests, needs, values, and goals—is an essential first step. Making long-term decisions consistent with your values and goals is the difficult second step. Too many people spend their lives in careers that make them miserable because they allow themselves to be governed by parents, friends, or simple inertia. Finally, once you have launched your career, never rest. Actively seek challenges and opportunities that stimulate you. Relish the rewards of meeting those challenges, being productive, and doing your job well. Continually strive to improve, not for the sake of your employer, but for your own sake. Your career will occupy three-quarters of your life, so make the most of it!

Unacceptable paraphrase

In "Career Consciousness," Brian Green points out that it is not easy to find a career that is stimulating, enjoyable, and meaningful. The first step is to understand yourself, your interests, needs, values, and goals. The second step is making long-term decisions consistent with your values and goals. Too often, people devote their lives to careers that make them unhappy because they permit themselves to be influenced by family, friends, or plain laziness. Once you have decided on a career, look for challenges and opportunities that are stimulating, and keep striving to improve, not for the sake of the employer, but for your own sake. Make the most of your career because it will occupy three-quarters of your life.

Neither a quotation nor a true paraphrase, this paragraph is an example of plagiarism. Its phrasing is too close to that of the original. Even though the paragraph acknowledges the source of the ideas, it presents those ideas in the same order and often in the same words as the original. And when the words are not identical, the sentence structure is. For example, compare these two sentences and note the correspondence between the two sets of highlighted words:

Original

Too many people spend their lives in careers that make them miserable because they allow themselves to be governed by parents, friends, or simple inertia.

and

Unacceptable paraphrase

Too often, people devote their lives to careers that make them unhappy because they permit themselves to be influenced by family, friends, or plain laziness.

The second sentence is an example of what happens when an inexperienced writer tries to create a paraphrase by relying on a thesaurus to "translate" the original. The identical sentence structure is a dead giveaway—not only of what the writer was trying to do, but also of how he or she was trying to do it.

Better paraphrase

Two factors are essential to long-term career satisfaction. In "Career Consciousness," Brian Green says that the first is to know yourself and make a career choice that is consistent with your personal values and goals, rather than allow the decision to be made for you by others. The second, according to Green, is to continue to look for opportunities once you have begun your career. By continually seeking ways to improve your performance and meet new challenges, not only will you please your employer, but you will also make your job stimulating and satisfying.

USING ONLINE SOURCES

When using Internet sources for research, remember that the Internet is largely unregulated. Even seasoned researchers are sometimes fooled into thinking that a particular posting is factual when it is only someone's—and not necessarily an expert's—opinion. One of your responsibilities as a student researcher is to evaluate the sources of information you use to ensure that they are authoritative and creditable. Many websites try to give the appearance of being official and objective when in fact they have a distinct point of view that they are trying to promote. Unfortunately, there is no standard test or measure you can apply to distinguish between fact and propaganda.

One of the most popular sites for research material is Wikipedia, which is a gold mine of information. However, researchers must be aware that Wikipedia entries are written by subscribers. Can this information be trusted? Since entries are monitored by professional scholars and expert amateurs, as well as by Wikipedia employees, in many cases, it can. But there is no guarantee that a Wikipedia entry is accurate, up to date, or unbiased. If you cannot rely on

"Nice essay, Tom, your cut and paste skills are beyond reproach."

Wikipedia without question, imagine how careful you must be in using information from blogs and discussion forums!

Always check the reliability of an Internet source. One way to confirm the accuracy of information you want to use is by consulting several other sources to see if they agree. If you are unsure about a source, check with your instructor to confirm whether information from that source is reliable for the research project you are doing.

CREDITING YOUR SOURCES: MLA AND APA DOCUMENTATION

When you use material that you have found in your reading, you must tell the reader where that material came from. This process is called *documentation*, and it consists of two parts: parenthetical citations, which you insert into the text

Paragraphs and Essays

of your paper immediately after the quotations or paraphrases that you've used to support a point, and a list at the end of the paper of all of the sources you refer to in your paper.

There are two reasons you must use source citations: first, they protect you from the charge of plagiarism, and, second, they enable your readers to locate your sources if they want to read more about your subject. Unfortunately, you cannot just name the author and title of the work(s) you have borrowed from. The standard style for papers in the humanities (English, history, art, philosophy, etc.) differs from the standard style required for papers in the social sciences (economics, psychology, sociology, political science, etc.). Your instructors may have specific requirements for acknowledging sources; if so, follow them to the letter. And don't be surprised if different teachers have different requirements. Documentation styles are a kind of shorthand for experienced readers: scholars can look at a References or Works Cited entry and know immediately what kind of source it identifies and whether or not that source is current and reliable.

As a student researcher, you need to be familiar with at least two documentation systems: MLA and APA. The initials stand for the organizations (Modern Language Association and American Psychological Association) that developed these formats for writers submitting papers for publication in these organizations' journals.

In MLA and APA styles, basic information about sources (called an in-text citation) is given in parentheses immediately following the quoted or referenced material in the body of your paper. In MLA style, in-text citations provide the author's last name and the page number in the document where the material was found. APA style also requires the publication year in the in-text citation. At the end of the essay, a Works Cited (MLA) or References (APA) page gives detailed information about each source, including the author's name, title of the work, publisher, place of publication, and year of publication—not always in that order. The format of each reference depends on where you found the information: on the Internet, in a book, journal, magazine, interview, and so on. In Unit 7, you will find an essay that we have formatted both in APA style (pages 467–71) and in MLA style (pages 463–66). For specific instructions on how to credit various kinds of sources in both styles, go to the Student Resources page on this book's website at **www.bareplus4e.nelson.com**, click on More Information and then on Format and Documentation.

EXERCISE **27.1**

 We have provided three paragraphs (taken from readings in Unit 7), each of which is followed by a paragraph that is intended to be a paraphrase of the original. Work with a partner to compare each paraphrase to the original and determine if it is an acceptable paraphrase or if it is plagiarism. Check your answers against ours on page 557. Then work on your own to revise the plagiarized paragraphs to make them true paraphrases.

1. From "An Immigrant's Split Personality," pages 452–53:

Original:

   When I was younger, toying with the idea of entertaining two separate identities was a real treat, like a secret game for which no one knew the rules but me. I was known as Angela to the outside world, and as Sun-Kyung at home. I ate bologna sandwiches in the school lunchroom and rice and kimchee for dinner. I chatted about teen idols and giggled with my girlfriends during my classes, and ambitiously practiced piano and studied in the evenings, planning to become a doctor when I grew up. I waved hellos and goodbyes to my teachers, but bowed to my parents' friends visiting our home. I could also look straight into the eyes of my teachers and friends and talk frankly with them instead of staring at my feet with my mouth shut when Koreans talked to me. Going outside the home meant I was able to relax from the constraints of my cultural conditioning, until I walked back in the door and had to return to being an obedient and submissive daughter.

Paraphrase?

   First-generation immigrants sometimes adopt two personalities: one outside the home and a different one inside. In her essay "An Immigrant's Split Personality," Sun-Kyung Yi says that she thought of her two identities as a secret game for which no one knew the rules but her. She was Angela in the outside world and Sun-Kyung at home. She ate bologna sandwiches, gossiped about teen idols with girlfriends, and waved hello and goodbye when outside her home. But in her home, she ate rice and kimchee, practised the piano and studied in the evenings, and bowed to her parents' friends. She could look directly at her teachers and friends and talk openly with them, but when she was with Koreans, she stared at her feet with her mouth closed. Outside, she was free of cultural constraints, but at home she was expected to behave like an obedient and submissive daughter.

2. From "Embraced by the Needle," page 456:

Original:

   But what of families where there was not abuse, but love, where parents did their best to provide their children with a secure nurturing home?

Paragraphs and Essays

One also sees addictions arising in such families. The unseen factor here is the stress the parents themselves lived under even if they did not recognize it. That stress could come from relationship problems, or from outside circumstances such as economic pressure or political disruption. The most frequent source of hidden stress is the parents' own childhood histories that saddled them with emotional baggage they had never become conscious of. What we are not aware of in ourselves, we pass on to our children.

"Embraced by the Needle," Gabor Maté. Originally published in the *Globe and Mail* 27 August 2001. © Gabor Maté M.D.

Paraphrase?

Drug addicts do not always come from broken or dysfunctional homes, homes where the parents are themselves drug users or foster an atmosphere in which drug use is inevitable. Even children from secure, loving homes can fall prey to addiction if the conditions are right. Gabor Maté, in his essay entitled "Embraced by the Needle," observes that stress, even stress that is unrecognized or unconscious, can lead to addictive behaviour in the children of households where it is present. Such parental stress, Maté suggests, can come from many sources, including economic circumstances, personal conflicts, even unresolved childhood issues.

3. From "The New Heavyweight Champions," page 460:

Original:

Could this be the future? Very likely. At every age and income level, women are more likely than ever before to be the major or sole breadwinner in the family. The reason is not that more women are working, but that fewer men are. Three-quarters of the people who lost their jobs in the U.S. recession were men, and the hardest-hit sectors were the male worlds of construction, manufacturing and finance. Many of those jobs aren't coming back. In the city of Hamilton—once known as Steeltown—just 2 per cent of the population still works in steel. In Sudbury, the town that nickel built, Inco's unionized labour force has shrunk from 12,000 to around 3,300 souls, who are currently locked in a futile long-term strike with their foreign owner.

"The New Heavyweight Champions" by Margaret Wente. *Globe and Mail,* June 12, 2010 © The Globe and Mail Inc. All Rights Reserved.

Paraphrase?

Margaret Wente suggests in her essay "The New Heavyweight Champions" that in the future women will be the sole wage earners in the family. She points out that traditional men's jobs have been disappearing and illustrates her point with examples. Seventy-five percent of those who lost their jobs in the recent recession in the U.S. were men who held jobs especially in construction, manufacturing, and finance. In Canada, she uses Hamilton and Sudbury as examples, noting that the city once called Steeltown now employs only 2 percent of its workforce in the steel industry, and at Inco the unionized workforce has shrunk by almost 8,000.

UNIT 6

For ESL Learners: A Review of the Basics

For ESL Learners:
A Review

INTRODUCTION

As a college student, you are preparing for a meaningful and rewarding career. If you are preparing for this career in a language that is not native to you, English, we congratulate you on your achievement. Your hard work and your ability to use two (or more) languages suggest that you are able to achieve a high level of success.

However, you may feel that your communication skills in English are holding you back. Even if your command of spoken English is good, you may lack fluency with *standard written English (SWE)*, and poor writing skills can hinder your opportunities for academic and career success.

The ability to use SWE confidently helps you in three ways. First, it gives you the power to express your ideas clearly. Second, it helps you win the respect of your readers. And third, it increases the number of people with whom you can communicate. That's why employers look for people who can use SWE effectively.

This unit of *The Bare Essentials Plus* is designed specifically to help those who are learning *English as a second language (ESL)* master the conventions of SWE. It focuses on the most common problem areas for English language learners. These include verb tenses and verb formation, plural forms and quantity expressions, articles, and prepositions. Even highly sophisticated ESL writers occasionally make mistakes in these constructions, mistakes that are evident to native speakers. Working on these problem areas will develop and improve your ability to write in English.

These chapters provide concise explanation—likely less explanation than you have come to expect in advanced grammar texts. But there are many exercises and much opportunity for you to practise specific writing skills. Grammatical explanation can certainly help you to understand what constitutes correct English, but ultimately you must gain confidence in your ability to write correctly without constant reference to grammar rules. This confidence is what will make you a fluent writer of English.

You may also find Unit 6 useful as you work on your English speaking and pronunciation skills. If you are in a class with other students who have learned English as a second or additional language, you can do the exercises out loud in class as speaking practice. Hearing and saying the words will help you to remember the grammatical structures and to improve your pronunciation; in turn, you will become a more fluent speaker of English.

QUICK QUIZ

The following Quick Quiz will let you see at a glance which chapters of Unit 6 you need to focus on. The paragraphs below contain 15 errors in verb tense, negative verb formation, participial adjectives, modal auxiliaries, singular and plural forms, articles, and prepositions. Once you've made your corrections, turn to pages 557–58 and compare them with ours. For each error you miss, the Answer Key directs you to the chapter you need to work on. (*Speaking/listening tip:* This Quick Quiz is challenging. It may be helpful to listen to it as it is read aloud, perhaps by a native English speaker. Then you can practise your pronunciation by reading it aloud yourself, paying particular attention to the examples in paragraphs 2 and 3.)

[1]People learn their first language when they are very young. [2]Most of us understand spoken words and respond to them along the time we are two or three years old. [3]It takes another few years for us to learn how to read and write, but we acquire our first language easily. [4]By most of us, however, learning a second language is a slow and exasperating process. [5]Most people who study English as a second language are especially frustrating by three of its peculiarities: its disorderly pronunciation, its inconsistent spelling, and its enormous vocabulary.

[6]English is having sounds that are difficult for speakers of other languages. [7]The *th* sound is one of them. [8]Why is it pronounced differently in words such as *this* and *think*? [9]The consonant sounds *l*, *r*, and *w* also present problems. [10]Many new English speakers don't hear the differences between *light, right,*

and *white*, so they pronounce them as the same word. [11]There are also more vowel sounds in English than in most other language. [12]The *a* sound in the words *bat* and *mat* is peculiar to English, so second-language learners often pronounce *bet*, *bat*, and *but* identically. [13]To native speakers of English, these words are having quite distinct sounds that many second-language learners do not hear and so cannot pronounce. [14]Many English language learner find it difficult to pronounce the unusual vowel sounds that occur in the words *bird*, *word*, and *nurse*. [15]The fact that the same sound occurs in words with three different vowels—*i*, *o*, and *u*—is example of second major difficulty with English: its inconsistent spelling system.

[16]Most native speakers would agree that English spelling is difficult. [17]Why do *tough* and *stuff* rhyme when their spellings are so different? [18]Shouldn't *tough* rhyme with *cough*? [19]But *cough* rhymes with *off*. [20]Why does *clamour* rhyme with *hammer* while *worm* and *storm*, which should rhyme, don't rhyme? [21]There isn't no single answer. [22]Because English has absorbed many words, sounds, and spellings from other languages, it has some wacky spelling patterns. [23]Almost 75 percent of English words are spelled regularly. [24]Unfortunately, the 25 percent of English words spelled in unpredictable ways are the most commonly used word in the language: for example, *Wednesday, answer, knee*. [25]All of us, second-language learners and native speakers alike, simply have to learn to spell.

[26]English also has a huge vocabulary, in part because it borrows freely from other languages. [27]The roots of English are Germanic, but the Celts, Romans, French, and many others have contributed heavily to the language. [28]The gigantic *Oxford English Dictionary* lists about 500,000 words and does not include about another half-million technical and scientific word.

[29]English is difficult language for all of these reason, but it's a rich and sat-isfied one that is worth the effort to learn.

For ESL Learners: A Review

28 Choosing the Correct Verb Tense

In English, the tense of a verb signals the time of an action: present, past, or future.

> I *work* hard every day.
> I *worked* at the library yesterday.
> I *will work* at the library next summer.

Of course, as you know, there is more to the English tense system than this simple example suggests. English verbs change in complicated and subtle ways to describe complex time relations.

> I *am working* at the library now, but I *have worked* at a number of different jobs in the past. I *will be working* for most of my life, so it *is* important that I *learn* more things than I *have learned* so far.

Trying to sort out the tenses of the verbs in these sentences can be a real headache for English language learners. Another headache is the fact that some verb tenses have the same meaning, or close to the same meaning. Most native speakers will not hear a difference in meaning between "I am working at the library now" and "I work at the library now." However, native speakers will certainly pick up the mistake if you say or write "I am been working at the library now" or "I will work at a number of different jobs in the past." To write clearly, you require a thorough understanding of—and lots of practice with—the English verb tense system. This chapter will provide you with both.

To see at a glance how the English tense system expresses past, present, and future time, study the Time Line on pages 586–87. The symbol key below explains how to interpret the time line and also the graphic illustrations of tenses covered in this chapter.

- ▲ indicates *now*, the present moment.
- ● represents *a completed action* or *state of being*.
- ○ indicates *an event that occurred or will occur sometime after the action represented by* ● *took place.*

⁓⁓ represents *a continuing action or condition*, both of which are expressed by the progressive forms of a verb.

------- indicates that *the action or condition may continue into the future.*

Now that you have an overview of the six basic tenses and the "times" they represent, let's look at how the various tenses are formed. Then we will focus on how to use each one.

VERB TENSE FORMATION

The chart below shows how the different tenses are formed. It provides two examples, *work* (a regular verb) and *grow* (an irregular verb), to illustrate the changes. The principal parts of the verbs are presented first because all tenses are formed from them. As you will see from studying the examples below, most tenses are created by adding **auxiliary** or "helping" verbs formed from the verbs *be* (*am, is, are, was, were*) or *have* (*has, have, had*). Study the patterns below. See pages 144–49 for more information about principal parts of verbs.

Principal Parts

Base/ infinitive	Present participle	Past	Past participle
(to) work	working	worked	(have) worked
(to) grow	growing	grew	(have) grown

Tense	Example *(work)*	Example *(grow)*
Present Tenses		
Simple present (base; base + *s* for third-person singular)	work/works	grow/grows
Present progressive (*am/is/are* + present participle)	am/is/are working	am/is/are growing
Present perfect (*has/have* + past participle)	has/have worked	has/have grown
Present perfect progressive (*has/have* + *been* + present participle)	has/have been working	has/have been growing

Tense	Example *(work)*	Example *(grow)*
Past Tenses		
Simple past (past form)	worked	grew
Past progressive (was/were + present participle)	was/were working	was/were growing
Past perfect (*had* + past participle)	had worked	had grown
Past perfect progressive (*had* + *been* + present participle)	had been working	had been growing
Future Tenses **Simple future** (*will* + base) OR (*am/is/are going to* + base)	will work am/is/are going to work	will grow am/is/are going to grow
Future progressive (*will be* + present participle)	will be working	will be growing
Future perfect (*will have* + past participle)	will have worked	will have grown
Future perfect progressive (*will have* + *been* + present participle)	will have been working	will have been growing

The chart above shows how to form all the English tenses. Some tenses, however, such as the future perfect progressive, are rarely used because the same meaning can usually be expressed in a less complicated manner. So while this chapter will provide an overview of all tenses, we will concentrate on the ones most commonly used in order to make sure that you understand how to form them correctly and use them appropriately.

Fill in the "missing pieces" (either a principal part or an auxiliary verb) to form the required verb tense from the base verbs *go* and *see*. The first one has been done for you. (*Speaking/listening tip:* Try to do this exercise orally, on your own, in class, or with a small group, before you pick up your pencil. Many of the exercises in this chapter offer good opportunities for speaking practice.) Answers for exercises in this chapter begin on page 558.

	go	**see**
1. present perfect progressive:	He <u>has</u> been <u>going</u>.	He <u>has</u> been <u>seeing</u>.
2. past progressive:	I was _____.	I was _____.
3. simple present:	He _____. They _____.	He _____. They _____.
4. present progressive:	You _____ _____.	You _____ _____.
5. simple past:	We _____.	We _____.
6. future progressive:	She _____ be _____.	She _____ be _____.
7. present perfect:	It _____ _____.	It _____ _____.
8. past perfect:	We had _____.	We had _____.
9. simple future:	You _____ _____.	You _____ _____.
10. past perfect progressive:	Someone had ____ ____.	Someone had ____ ____.

This exercise requires you to practise with the "pieces" (principal parts and auxiliaries) that are used to form various verb tenses. Use only one word for each blank. The first verb form has been provided for you. After you have filled in each blank, identify the verb tense used.

1. He will <u>*be*</u> going with us. (Tense: _____)

2. The business _____ _____ doing very well this year. (Tense:

_____)

3. My parents _____ always _____ good to me. (Tense: _____)

4. I _____ leaving for Vancouver next week. (Tense: _____)

5. My friend _____ lived in Canada for two years, but he returned to Poland last week. (Tense: _____)

6. You _____ _____ working very hard, so why not take a break? (Tense: _____)

7. The movie _____ _____ playing for 30 minutes by the time we got there. (Tense: _____)

8. We _____ playing tennis yesterday when the rain began. (Tense: _____)

9. I _____ taking off my running shoes right now because they _____ killing my feet. (Tense: _____)

10. Linsey _____ eating dinner when the phone rang. (Tense: _____)

THE PRESENT TENSES

A. THE SIMPLE PRESENT TENSE

The simple present is used to express present time (especially with non-action verbs called **linking verbs**), general truths, and regular or habitual activity.

Gianni *is* a handsome man.
I *hope* that you *are* happy now.
People *need* food and water to survive.
Sarah *swims* every day.

B. THE PRESENT PROGRESSIVE TENSE

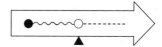

> The present progressive is used to express an activity that is in progress now or one that is ongoing. Sometimes the activity is taking place over a period of time such as this week, month, or even year.

I *am talking* to you on my cellphone.
They *are driving* home right now.
Everyone *is learning* verb tenses this week.

Some English verbs are not to be used in any of the progressive tenses. Such verbs describe conditions or states of being rather than actions in progress. Often, these "non-progressive" verbs express mental (cognitive) or emotional states, possession (ownership), or sense perception. Study the following list. (We will come back to the asterisked words later.)

States of being: appear,* be,* cost, exist, look, seem, weigh*

Mental (cognitive) or emotional states: appreciate, believe, care, dislike, doubt, envy, fear, feel, forget, hate, imagine, know, like, love, mean, mind, need, prefer, realize, recognize, remember, suppose, think,* understand, want

Possession: belong, have,* own, possess

Sense perception: appear,* be, feel,* hear, see,* smell,* taste*

To repeat, these state-of-being verbs are NOT used in the progressive tenses. You wouldn't say "I am liking her very much." You would use the simple present: "I like her very much." In the following sentences, replace the incorrect verb forms (in italics) with correct ones.

I *am hearing* that you *are owning* a laptop computer. I *am needing* to borrow one for today's class. I *am knowing* that you *are hating* to lend your things, but I *am promising* to return it this evening.

(The verbs in italics should be changed to *hear, own, need, know, hate,* and *promise,* all in the simple present tense.)

Note that 10 of the verbs on the list—the ones marked with an asterisk (*)—can be used to describe actions as well as states of being or conditions.

For ESL Learners: A Review

State of Being	Action
Solaya *weighs* 65 kilograms.	Solaya is *weighing* herself this morning to see how much she has gained.
Tom *appears* old and tired.	Tom *is appearing* on a reality TV show.
The food *tastes* good.	We *are tasting* the soup to see if it's good.

Often, you have to decide whether the verb is expressing a state of being or an action before you can decide whether or not to use a progressive tense.

Incorrect: He *is having* a car.
He *is smelling* of cigarette smoke.
I *am knowing* you for a long time.

Correct: He *has* a car.
She *smells* of cigarette smoke.
I *have known* you for a long time.

EXERCISE 28.3

Fill in each blank with the appropriate tense—simple present or present progressive—of the verb given in parentheses. Then check your answers against ours on page 559. (*Speaking/listening tip:* Try to do this exercise orally, on your own, in class, or with a small group, before you pick up your pencil.)

1. It (snow) _____ again today. In my country, it often (rain)

   _____, but it never (snow) _____.

2. My father usually (come) _____ to see my games, but tonight

   he (work) _____ a late shift.

3. I (study) _____ almost every night, but tonight I (go)

   _____ to visit some friends.

4. A ticket home (cost) _____ so much that I (doubt)

   _____ I can afford the trip.

5. I (know) _____ you can get a college degree if you (work) _____ hard.

6. My boyfriend usually (text) _____ me after work, but it is now 10 p.m., and I (wait, still) _____ for his message. I wonder what he (do) _____.

7. The baby (cry) _____ again. He always (cry) _____ when his mother (leave) _____.

8. What (do, she) _____ right now? She (appear) _____ in a Broadway play.

9. The little girl (look) _____ tired, but right now she (look) _____ at her favourite storybook.

10. Wanda (want) _____ to get a good job, but she (have) _____ to finish her college education first.

Go to Web Exercises 28.1, 28.2

C. THE PRESENT PERFECT TENSE

The present perfect tense is used to express three different meanings:

> 1. events that occurred (or didn't occur) at some unspecified time in the past, the consequences of which persist in the present

The rain *has stopped.*
I *haven't voted* yet.

2. events that were repeated several or many unspecified times in the
   past and are likely to occur again in the present and future

It *has rained* practically every day this month.
I *have* always *voted* for the best person.

3. events that began at some unspecified time in the past and continue
   into the present

Yu *has lived* in Canada for a long time.
The children *have been* good today.

Sentences requiring the present perfect tense frequently contain words or
phrases that suggest action beginning in the past and persisting into the
present, such as *for, since, for a long time, already, so far, always, often, during,
recently,* and *this year.*

 Note that *for* is used with a period of time and *since* is used with a specific
point in time.

I have lived in Canada *for* 13 years.
I have lived in Canada *since* 1999.

EXERCISE **28.4**

Answer the questions using the present perfect tense and completing the time
phrases correctly. Then check your answers against ours on pages 559–60.
(*Speaking/listening tip:* Try to do this exercise orally, on your own, in class, or
with a small group, before you pick up your pencil.)

1. Does Rahim like to travel?

   Yes, he does. He (go) _____ to many different places during his

   life. He (visit) _____ both Asia and Africa (since/for) 2002.

2. Are you taking an ESL course this semester?

   No, I (take, already) _____ it. I (study) _____

   English (since/for) 11 years.

3. Do you love me?

   Yes, I (love, always) _____ you. I (know) _____ you
   (since/for) I was young, and I (love, never) _____ anyone but
   you.

4. Does Amir like to cook?

   Yes, he loves to cook. He made us a delicious tajine last night. He (prepare)
   _____ a wonderful meal every night this week.

5. When did you move to Canada?

   I moved here in _____. I (be) _____ here (since/for)
   _____ years.

D. THE PRESENT PERFECT PROGRESSIVE TENSE

> The present perfect progressive is used
> - to express actions that began at some unspecified time in the past and
>   continue in the present or
> - to emphasize the duration of a single past-to-present action

Other than the emphasis on the duration of an action, this tense has almost
the same meaning as the present perfect tense. Time phrases such as *for*, *since*,
all afternoon, *all day*, and *all year* are often used with the present perfect progressive tense to emphasize the period of time over which the action has been
taking place.

The class *has been working* on verb tenses. (And they are still working on
them.)

I *have been sitting* here all day. (And I am still sitting here.)

Your husband *has been waiting* for you for over an hour. (And he is still
waiting.)

The present perfect progressive and present perfect tenses often express the same meaning, especially when the sentence contains *since* or *for*.

Juan *has been living* here since 1997.   Juan *has lived* here since 1997.

I *have been working* here for 20 years.   I *have worked* here for 20 years.

EXERCISE **28.5**

Fill in the blanks with the correct form of the present perfect progressive. Check your answers against ours on page 560.

1. (snow) It _____ all day.

2. (study) They _____ physics for three days straight.

3. (look) We _____ for a new house right now.

4. (answer) She _____ all of the email messages.

5. (ring) The phone _____ all morning.

EXERCISE **28.6**

Fill in the blanks in the sentences below with either the present perfect or the present perfect progressive form of the verb provided. In some sentences, either tense may be used.

1. It (rain) _____ all night, and the basement is flooded.

2. There (be) _____ four big rainstorms already this week.

3. I always (do) _____ my homework carefully, and for the

   past two months, I also (work) _____ with a tutor.

4. Lorenzo (see, not) _____ his father since 2006.

5. How long (you, live) _____ in Canada?

Go to Web Exercises 28.3, 28.4

THE PAST TENSES

A. THE SIMPLE PAST TENSE

The simple past tense indicates an action or a state that began and ended in the past. It can be used to refer to an event completed once in the past or to an event completed several times in the past.

I *ate* too much last night.
The weather *was* horrible last winter.
Binh *lived* in Hong Kong before he *moved* to Montréal.

B. THE PAST PROGRESSIVE TENSE

The past progressive tense is used to express an action or condition that began and ended sometime in the past. It emphasizes the duration—or ongoing quality—of an event that is now completed.

The boys *were watching* television all morning.
I *was flying* home from Halifax every month last year.
What *were* you *doing* in Halifax?
I *was studying* at Dalhousie University.

The past progressive is also used to indicate an action that was taking place when another occurred. It is often used with time words such as *for* or *since*, or with a clause that uses *when* or *while* to denote simultaneous occurrences.

Julieta *was driving* to school when the accident happened.
While they *were cooking* dinner, the power went off.

Sometimes there is little difference in meaning between the past and the past progressive: "It snowed last night" and "It was snowing last night" mean the same thing, and both are correct.

For ESL Learners: A Review

EXERCISE **28.7**

Fill in each blank with the appropriate tense—simple past or past progressive—of the verb given in parentheses. If you are not sure how to form verbs in the negative, see page 363 in Chapter 29 before completing this exercise. Then check your answers against ours on page 560. (*Speaking/listening tip:* Try to do this exercise orally, on your own, in class, or with a small group, before you pick up your pencil.)

1. Three of us (smoke) _____ in the upstairs washroom when the boss (walk) _____ in.

2. The cat (hide) _____ behind the fish tank when I (see) _____ his tail twitch and (catch) _____ him.

3. While their sister (prepare) _____ their lunch, the children (run) _____ into the house and (turn) _____ on the television.

4. When we (work) _____ outside in the yard last night, we (feel) _____ the jolt of a small earthquake.

5. Rick (try) _____ to do his homework when his girlfriend (come) _____ over. He never (finish) _____ his work.

6. While we (watch) _____ television, the telephone (ring) _____.

7. The professor (teach) _____ an important lesson when two men (come) _____ in late and (disturb) _____ the class.

8. I (hear, not) _____ you arrive last night because I (sleep) _____.

9. (eat) _____ you _____ breakfast this morning when I (phone) _____?

10. While I (look) _____ at my boyfriend's Facebook profile, I (notice) _____ that his relationship status said "Married."

C. THE PAST PERFECT TENSE

Sometimes two different actions or conditions that occurred in the past are included in the same sentence.

> The past perfect tense is used to depict an action that was completed before another event (or time) in the past. It is the "further in the past" tense.

In other words, the action that happened first chronologically is expressed by the past perfect; the action that occurred after it is expressed in the simple past.

I *had left* the building before the bomb *exploded.*

Obviously the leaving happened first (and so is in the past perfect tense)—before the explosion (in the simple past tense)—or the speaker wouldn't be around to tell the story.

> The past perfect tense is frequently used with time expressions, such as **after, before,** and **when.**

Kareem realized his mistake after he *had spoken.*

The class *had left* before the instructor found the room.

To be fair, however, we should acknowledge that if the time sequence is clear from other elements in the sentence, the past perfect is often not necessary. Most native English speakers would not hear an error in the following sentences:

I *left* the building before the bomb *exploded.*

Kareem *realized* his mistake after he *spoke.*

The class *left* before the instructor *found* the room.

However, in sentences with *just, already, scarcely, hardly,* and *no sooner than*, the past perfect is required.

My boyfriend *had* already *gone* home when I *arrived.*

We *had* hardly *unpacked* our suitcases when the fun *began.*

In these sentences, using the simple past (*already went* and *hardly unpacked*) would be incorrect.

EXERCISE **28.8**

Fill in the blanks with the appropriate tense—simple past or past perfect—of the verbs in parentheses. Then check your answers against ours on page 560. (*Speaking/listening tip:* Try to do this exercise orally, on your own, in class, or with a small group, before you pick up your pencil.)

1. Tyshawn was late for class. The professor (give, just) ___ a quiz when he (get) ___ there.

2. Yesterday my friend Ronit (see) ___ an old friend whom she (see, not) ___ in years.

3. I almost missed my flight. Everyone (board, already) ___ the plane by the time I (rush) ___ in.

4. They (eat, scarcely) ___ anything when the waiter (remove) _____ their plates.

5. The movie (start, hardly) ___ when the audience (walk) ___ out.

D. THE PAST PERFECT PROGRESSIVE TENSE

The past perfect progressive tense emphasizes the duration of a past event that took place before another event. Often it is used to refer to a past event that was in progress before being interrupted by another event.

He *had been waiting* in the doctor's office for an hour by the time she arrived.

They *had been talking* about Carol when she walked in.

The exercise below will help you with the time sequencing of English verbs by reminding you of the difference between the present perfect progressive (*has/have + been + present participle*) and the past perfect progressive (*had + been + present participle*).

EXERCISE **28.9**

Fill in the blanks in the sentences below with the present perfect progressive tense or the past perfect progressive tense as appropriate. Then check your answers against ours on page 560–61.

1. It is 6 p.m. I (work) _____ for 10 hours straight, so it is time to

   go home.

2. It was 6 p.m. I (work) _____ for 10 hours straight, so it was time

   to go home.

3. I woke up feeling strange this morning because I (dream) _____

   about dinosaurs all night.

4. Kyle (ride) _____ his bicycle for two hours by the time he (get)

   _____ home.

5. They (date) _____ for a year before they broke up.

EXERCISE **28.10**

Fill in each blank with the most appropriate tense—simple past, past perfect, or past perfect progressive—of the verb in parentheses. In some sentences, more than one answer is possible.

1. By the time I (realize) _____ that I needed an elective to grad-

   uate, I (drop, already) _____ my history course.

2. The child (play) _____ outside when her babysitter (arrive)

   _____ yesterday.

3. Karin's sister (arrive) _____ about 10 minutes after Karin (leave)

   _____.

4. I (listen, not) _____ when they (make) _____ the

   announcement.

For ESL Learners: A Review

5. By the time Kim (work) _____ the night shift for three months,

   she (think) _____ that she would never have a social life again.

6. We (look) _____ forward to our vacation for months

   when my wife (get) _____ a promotion, and we (have)

   _____ to cancel our plans.

7. If I (know) _____ how difficult this course (be) _____,

   I would have signed up for something easier.

8. Ana (live) _____ in California for three years when she

   (open) _____ her first business.

9. My parents (give) _____ me a thousand dollars when they

   (come) _____ to visit me last year.

10. Kim (think, never) _____ about her friend's feelings; she (be)

    _____ very selfish when she made the decision.

Go to Web Exercises 28.5, 28.6

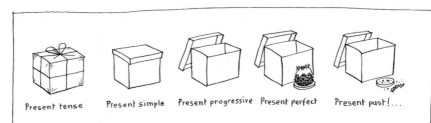

Present tense   Present simple   Present progressive   Present perfect   Present past!...

Review the present and past tenses by filling in the blanks using any of the tenses studied so far.

1. When I (get) _____ home last night, everyone (eat, already)

   _____ dinner.

2. We (go) _____ to sleep before the roof (collapse) _____.

3. Julia (work) _____ in this office for a year, and now she (get)

   _____ a raise and a promotion.

4. Hockey (be, always) _____ Canadians' favourite sport; we

   (play) _____ the game for more than 150 years.

5. Although Ali (live) _____ in Toronto since he was 10, he (visit,

   never) _____ the CN Tower.

6. While Igor (talk) _____ on the phone, the bathtub (overflow)

   _____.

7. They (wait) _____ for two years to adopt a child, and their

   baby (arrive/just) _____.

8. (you, finish) _____ your homework yet?

9. Yesterday my father (make) _____ me go to the barber who (cut)

   _____ his hair for the past 20 years.

10. While I (wait) _____ for my turn, I (notice) _____ that I

    (be) _____ the only person under 50 in the shop.

THE FUTURE TENSES

A. THE SIMPLE FUTURE TENSE

There are two ways to express the simple future tense:
1. *will* + base form:

I *will go* home.
They *will see* you tomorrow.

2. (*be*) + *going to* + base form:

I *am going to go* home.
They *are going to see* you tomorrow.

Both constructions have the same meaning. In informal English, especially speech, *will* is usually contracted to *'ll* in the future tense:

I'*ll go* home. They'*ll see* you tomorrow.
You'*ll go* home. We'*ll see* them tomorrow.

Won't is the contraction for *will not*: You *won't see* me tomorrow.

The (*be*) + *going to* + *base form* is usually used when the sentence expresses a prior plan or decision. The *will* + *base form* is used to express willingness or ability. The following examples illustrate the difference.

Prior plan: (*be*) + *going to* + base

Why did you buy these flippers?
I *am going to learn* how to snorkel. (NOT "I *will learn* how to snorkel.")

Willingness: *will* + base

Help me! I'm broke, and my rent is due today.
Ask Roderigo. Maybe he'*ll lend* you some money. (NOT "Ask Roderigo. Maybe he *is going to lend* you some money.")

Traditional grammar texts often describe different (and very subtle) changes in meanings expressed by the future tense—for example, promise, prediction, permission, volition, supposition, concession—and prescribe using a specific form for each purpose. However, these meanings are often difficult to separate from futurity, and native speakers rarely hear lapses in these distinctions as grammatical errors. Traditional grammar texts also teach that *shall* is used with first-person subjects (*I shall go home*) and *will* is used with second- and third-person subjects (*You/They will go home*). In North American English, this distinction is obsolete. In short, don't spend a lot of time worrying about the differences between *will* and *am/is/are going to* or between *shall* and *will*.

EXERCISE **28.12**

Fill in the blanks with the appropriate form of the future: *will* + *base form* or (*be*) + *going to* + *base form* of the verbs in parentheses. Then check your answers against ours on pages 561–62. (*Speaking/listening tip:* Try to do this exercise orally, on your own, in class, or with a small group, before you pick up your pencil.)

1. He (arrive) _____ tonight, but I (be, not) _____ here.

2. Tomorrow is his birthday, so he (have) _____ dinner with friends.

3. Since you (take) _____ an elective course next semester, I suggest you sign up for sociology. You (enjoy) _____ Professor Singh's sense of humour.

4. Our neighbours (build) _____ an addition onto their home next summer. I hope we (be) _____ on vacation when the construction begins.

5. Raoul (buy) _____ a computer because he hopes that his children (send) _____ him emails and pictures.

B. THE FUTURE PROGRESSIVE TENSE

> The future progressive tense expresses an action that will be in progress at a time in the future. There is often little difference in meaning between the future progressive and the simple future.

I *will be seeing* him later tonight.   I *will see* him later tonight.
Tomorrow you *will be dining* with us.   Tomorrow *you will dine* with us.

EXERCISE **28.13**

Use the appropriate verb form—future or future progressive—to fill in the blanks in these sentences. Check your answers against ours on page 562.

1. I have no idea where I (work) _____ next week, but I (let) _____ you know as soon as I find out.

2. This time tomorrow, we (sit) _____ on a beach with margaritas in our hands.

3. I (have, not) _____ time to talk on the phone this afternoon

  because I (cook) _____ a traditional dinner for 14 people.

4. Ravi says that he (teach) _____ in Tokyo next year.

5. We (stay, not) _____ at this hotel again.

C. THE FUTURE PERFECT TENSE

> The future perfect expresses an action that will be completed before another time or action in the future.

By next June, we *will have graduated* from college.
Before the end of the semester, we *will have covered* a lot of grammar.
Before we leave Québec City, we *will have seen* all of the tourist attractions.
(Note that the verb in the time clause is in the simple present tense.)

Often, use of the future perfect tense is not absolutely necessary. For instance, the simple future could be used in the above sentences:

By next June, we *will graduate* from college.
Before the end of the semester, we *will cover* a lot of grammar.
Before we leave Québec City, we *will see* all of the tourist attractions.

However, if *already* is used in the sentence, the future perfect is required, as it is in this example:

Incorrect: I *will already go* to bed before you arrive.
Correct: I *will already have gone* to bed before you arrive.

D. THE FUTURE PERFECT PROGRESSIVE TENSE

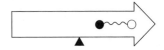

> The seldom used future perfect progressive tense stresses the duration of a future action that is to take place before another future action.

Often, the future perfect progressive and the future perfect tenses have the same meaning, as in the examples below:

Our cousins *will have been studying* English for three months before they arrive in Canada.

Our cousins *will have studied* English for three months before they arrive in Canada.

EXERCISE **28.14**

Fill in the blanks with a future tense of the verb in parentheses. More than one correct answer is possible in some of these sentences. Check your answers against ours on page 562.

1. (you/go) _____ out with me this evening?

2. We are going to be late because of the terrible traffic. By the time we (reach)

    _____ the airport, Miryam's plane (arrive, already) _____.

    She (worry) _____ that something has happened to us.

3. At this pace, we (walk) _____ 30 kilometres by tonight.

4. You were born in _____. By the year 2050, you (live)

    _____ for _____ years. You (see) _____ many changes!

5. I (clean, already) _____ the house by the time you get here.

USING PRESENT TENSES TO INDICATE FUTURE TIME

As if distinguishing among all these tenses is not complicated enough, there is another convention you need to know about. English speakers use the simple present and present progressive tenses to express future time in several circumstances.

1. A few simple present tense verbs—*arrive, begin, close, come, end, finish, leave, open, return, start*—can express that an activity is scheduled in the future.

For ESL Learners: A Review

Usually the sentences contain "future time" words or phrases, like the ones underlined in the three examples below.

Daphne's flight *arrives* <u>at midnight.</u>
School *begins* <u>on September 8 next year.</u>
The stores at the mall *close* <u>at 6 p.m. today.</u>

2. When the sentence contains a time clause (e.g., one beginning with *after* or *before*) or a conditional clause (e.g., one beginning with *if*), the simple present tense is required in that clause even though the verb refers to future or conditional time.

Consider the following examples carefully; the underlined clauses express time or condition, so the verbs must be in the simple present.

Incorrect: I *will take* a vacation <u>after I *will quit* my job.</u>
<u>If the snow *will continue*,</u> the president *will close* the college.

Correct: I *will take* a vacation <u>after I *quit* my job.</u>
<u>If the snow *continues*,</u> the president *will close* the college.

3. The present progressive is often used when a time word or phrase in the sentence indicates the future.

I *am touring* Tuscany <u>next year.</u>
Jess *is having* a baby <u>this spring.</u>

EXERCISE **28.15**

Fill in the blanks with the correct form of the verb in parentheses. Then check your answers against ours on page 562.

1. As soon as Val (graduate) _____, he (leave) _____ for Africa.

2. If the wind (blow) _____ hard, that house (collapse) _____.

3. The café (open) _____ at 6 a.m. every morning.

4. If it (rain) _____ on the weekend, we (cancel) _____ our plans for a beach party.

5. Pierre (be) _____ here in Canada for at least another year before

   he (return) _____ home to France and (get) _____ a job.

Go to Web Exercises 28.7, 28.8

EXERCISE **28.16**

Put the sentences together by matching up the clauses below. Make sure you have the correct verb tense.

Beginning Clauses	**End Clauses**
On my next birthday,	he (fly) _____ for 14 hours
After we (get) _____ married,	I (be) _____ years old.
In a couple of years I (finish) _____ college,	and I (get) _____ a good job.
The teacher (not/finish) _____ marking our tests,	we (have) _____ three children.
When Xavier (arrive) _____ in Toronto tomorrow,	so we (not/know) _____ our grades until next week.

EXERCISE **28.17**

(a) Complete the following fable by inserting the correct past tense form of the verbs in parentheses. (*Speaking/listening tip:* Try to do this exercise orally, on your own, in class, or with a small group, before you pick up your pencil.)

Sour Grapes

   One hot day last summer, a fox (stroll) _____ through an orchard

until he (come) _____ to a bunch of grapes ripening on a vine that (hang)

_____ over a branch. "Just the thing to quench my thirst," he (say)

_____. Drawing back a few paces, he (take) _____ a running jump and just (miss) _____ the grapes. Turning around again, with a "one, two, three," he (try) _____ once more to capture the tasty grapes. At last, he (give) _____ up and (walk) _____ away with his nose in the air, saying, "I am sure those grapes must be sour."

Moral of the story: It is easy to despise what you cannot get.

(b) Complete the following fable by inserting the correct present tense form of the verbs in parentheses.

Sour Grapes

Right this very minute, a fox (stroll) _____ through an orchard until he (come) _____ to a bunch of grapes ripening on a vine that (hang) _____ over a branch. "Just the thing to quench my thirst," he (say) _____. Drawing back a few paces, he (take) _____ a running jump and just (miss) _____ the grapes. Turning around again, with a "one, two, three," he (try) _____ once more to capture the tasty grapes. At last, he (give) _____ up and (walk) _____ away with his nose in the air, saying, "I am sure those grapes must be sour."

Moral of the story: It is easy to despise what you cannot get.

Why does the fox think the "grapes must be sour"? Have you ever heard the phrase "sour grapes" before? What does it mean? Can you think of a situation in which the phrase would be useful?

EXERCISE **28.18**

With a partner (or on your own), read through the exercise below and choose the correct form of the verb in parentheses. Compare your answers with those of another pair of students (or another student). Finally, compare your answers against paragraph 11 of "Many Faiths, One Truth" on page 451. More than one answer may be acceptable.

Let me (tell) _____ you about the Islam I (know) _____. Tibet (have) _____ an Islamic community for around 400 years, although my richest contacts with Islam (be) _____ in India, which (have) _____ the world's second-largest Muslim population. An imam in Ladakh once (tell) _____ me that a true Muslim should love and respect all of Allah's creatures. And in my understanding, Islam (enshrine) _____ compassion as a core spiritual principle, reflected in the very name of God, the "Compassionate and Merciful," that (appear) _____ at the beginning of virtually each chapter of the Koran.

EXERCISE **28.19**

In the following paragraphs, fill in the blanks with the most appropriate verb tenses, choosing from the 12 tenses you have reviewed.

The patriarch of my family (be) _____ my late grandfather Sergei, who was born in 1935 near the Russian city of Moscow. Sergei's parents, Boris and Natasha, (work) _____ hard all their lives, but they never (earn) _____ much money. Sergei (have) _____ two younger sisters and a younger brother, but his sisters (die) _____ during the terrible years of World War II. In 1955, Sergei (come) _____ to Canada as a refugee. Soon he (work) _____ hard at a small furniture factory in Toronto. He (meet) _____ a young Ukrainian woman named Irena, and they (get + marry) _____ in 1958. They (buy) _____ a small house in Toronto after their son, my father, Yuri, was born in 1960. Later, three more children were born. My grandfather always loved music; in fact, he (play) _____ his balalaika (a Russian stringed instrument) when he (pass) _____ away suddenly in 1997. My grandparents (create) _____ a loving and musical family, and I (feel) _____ lucky to (know) _____ them both.

My father, Yuri, (be) _____ a professional musician. He (learn) _____ to play the balalaika from his father when he (be) _____ a child. Now he (play) _____ guitar, and he (make) _____ his living as a rock musician. My father (marry) _____ my mother, Alice, in 1980, but they (divorce) _____ since 1985, the year I was born. My father (travel) _____ a lot because of his work, and I think that it (be) _____ difficult for him to maintain relationships. Nevertheless, he (be + always) _____ a very good father to me. He (teach) _____ me music since I was a little girl. Sometimes, when I'm not in school, I (go) _____ with him on the road.

I (study) _____ at Humber College in the music program for the past two years. Like my father and grandfather, I focus on stringed instruments, mainly the bass. My father (play) _____ rock music, but I (concentrate) _____ on jazz. In the future, I (go) _____ to New York to study and work, and I (hope) _____ to learn from some of the great jazz musicians whom I (admire + always) _____. With my musical heritage, my talent, and my ambition, I (think) _____ that I (be) _____ a great musician someday.

More about Verbs

29

In addition to verb formation and tense, there are four related issues with verbs that often present problems for second-language writers:

- formation of negatives (*not, n't, never*)
- participial adjectives (*interested* or *interesting*?)
- modal auxiliaries (*can, may, must, ought to,* etc.)
- conditional verbs (*if you only knew ...*)

FORMING NEGATIVES

Not expresses a negative idea. In a negative sentence, the word *not* comes immediately after the *be* verb or auxiliary verb.

Auxiliary verbs are helping verbs used to form different tenses. They include the forms of *be, have,* and *do,* and modal auxiliary verbs. (The forms of *be* are *am, is, are, was, were,* and *be.* The forms of *have* are *have, has,* and *had.* The forms of *do* are *do, does,* and *did.*) Modal auxiliary verbs are reviewed on page 370.

Yes, the sun *is out.*	No, the sun *is <u>not</u>* out.
I *have learned* my lesson.	I *have <u>not</u> learned* my lesson.
They *will eat* a whole pizza.	They *will <u>not</u> eat* a whole pizza.
She *might visit* her family.	She *might <u>not</u> visit* her family.

If the main verb in the sentence does not have an auxiliary, the *do* verb is added before *not* when forming the negative; the main verb follows *not*. *Not* can be contracted to *n't*:

is not = isn't	does not = doesn't	had not = hadn't
are not = aren't	do not = don't	cannot = can't
was not = wasn't	did not = didn't	could not = couldn't
were not = weren't	has not = hasn't	would not = wouldn't
will not = won't	have not = haven't	

(*Ain't* is not included in the list because using *ain't* is a grammatical error.)

I *love* him.	I *do not love* him.	I *don't love* him
He *loves* me.	He *does not love* me.	He *doesn't love* me.
I *loved* him.	I *did not love* him.	I *didn't love* him.

Remember that the auxiliary verb picks up the number and tense marker when it precedes the main verb, which reverts to the base form, as in the example above with the third-person singular *-s* ending: "He *loves* me" becomes "He *does* (or *doesn't*) *love* me." ("He *doesn't loves* me" is a grammatical error.) Similarly, the past tense *-d* in *loved* becomes *did not* (or *didn't*) *love* (not "He *didn't loved* me," another grammatical error). Here are three more examples to help you recall this important—but difficult—shift in verb forms:

My friend *works* hard.	My friend *does not work* (or *doesn't work*) hard.
We *finished* the job.	We *did not finish* (or *didn't finish*) the job.
He *came* home last night.	He *did not* (or *didn't*) *come* home last night.

Grammatically, the word *not* is a negative adverb; it isn't part of the verb itself. Other negative adverbs that are used to express negative meanings are *never*, *rarely*, *seldom*, *scarcely (ever)*, *hardly (ever)*, and *barely (ever)*, although these words have slightly different meanings. Here are some examples:

I *never* understand what my boyfriend really wants. (I do not ever understand …)
My wife and I *rarely* go out. (We go out once in a while, but hardly ever.)
The train is *hardly ever* late. (It is usually on time.)
My son *seldom* goes to school. (But rarely he does go.)

The word *no* can be used as an adjective in front of a noun to provide the same meaning as *not*. However, avoid using two negatives, a grammatical error known as a "double negative."

Incorrect: Ali *doesn't have no* problems speaking English.
   (Double negative)

Correct: Ali *doesn't have* problems speaking English.

Ali *has no* problems speaking English.

"Apparently, double negatives are okay in math but not in English."

EXERCISE **29.1**

Change the following sentences into negatives, using both the full and contracted forms of *not*. We've completed an example for you. (*Speaking/listening tip:* Try to do the exercise orally, on your own, in class, or with a small group, before you pick up your pencil. Many of the exercises in this chapter offer good opportunities for speaking practice.) Answers for exercises in this chapter begin on page 563.

Example: I like to listen to music.

I *do not like* to listen to music.

I *don't like* to listen to music.

1. The moon is full tonight.

2. The moon was full last night.

3. Sandy likes vegetables.

4. Ronald and Sandy like vegetables.

5. The teacher wants to help us.

6. The teachers want to help us.

7. The teachers wanted to help us.

8. Is Daphne with you?

9. Will Daphne be with you tomorrow?

10. I have enough money.

EXERCISE 29.2

Rewrite the following sentences to make them negative. Include both the full form and the contracted form of the verbs. We've completed an example for you.

Example: The student needs help from the teacher.

The student *does not* (or *doesn't*) *need* help from the teacher.

ALSO CORRECT: The student *needs no* help from the teacher.

1. I drink milk.

2. You like the teacher.

3. The passengers have their passports.

4. You should have given the students a quiz on negatives.

5. The man looks suspicious to me.

6. Faith bought dinner for us yesterday.

7. We always watch our diet.

8. José and Marta wanted to eat before the movie.

9. Is breakfast ready?

10. The earth goes around the moon.

EXERCISE **29.3**

Rewrite the following sentences to make them negative. Pay close attention to verb tense as you make your changes.

1. Mohammed and Hassan enjoy the winters in Canada.

2. I certainly want to see you.

3. I certainly wanted to see you.

4. There are 14 players on a soccer team.

5. Most of the class attended the reception for international students.

6. The band will stop the music at midnight.

7. Amy looks like her mother.

8. The computer is working very well.

9. The computer was working very well.

10. She came to the meeting alone.

Go to Web Exercises 29.1, 29.2

PARTICIPIAL ADJECTIVES

Participial adjectives are not verbs. They are adjectives that are formed from verbs, and that is why we've included them in the "More about Verbs" chapter. These adjectives present problems for most second-language writers. Am I bored? Or boring? Surprised? Or surprising? Let's try to sort it out with a little story.

Allan and Zeta went out on a date. It didn't go well. The two sentences that follow describe why the evening was not a success, but their meanings are very different.

1. Allan was a *boring* date.
2. Allan was a *bored* date.

Boring and *bored* are adjectives derived from the **participle** forms of the verb *to bore*. *Boring* is the present participle; *bored* is the past participle. Choosing the correct participial adjective is tough. Let's go back to the story.

In sentence 1, Allan is a dull fellow. He is shy and has nothing to talk about. He bored Zeta. She found him *boring*. In sentence 2, Zeta is the dull person with nothing to talk about. Zeta bored Allan, so he was bored and, therefore, a *bored* date.

Are you *confused*? Is the choice *confusing*? Yes. First, we'll explain the principle. Then we'll provide some practice with participial adjectives.

> The **present participle**, the *-ing* form, conveys an active meaning. The noun it describes is or does something.

Allan bores Zeta in sentence 1, so he is *boring*. Participial adjectives often confuse English language learners, so these words are *confusing*.

> The **past participle**, the *-ed* form in regular verbs, conveys a passive meaning. The noun it describes has something done to it.

Zeta bores Allan in sentence 2, so he is *bored*. Participial adjectives confuse English language learners, so these learners are *confused*. Note that the past participles of irregular verbs do not end in *-ed* (for example, a plant is *grown*, not *growed*). See Chapter 11 for the participial forms of irregular verbs, or check your dictionary.

EXERCISE **29.4**

In each of the following sentences, supply the correct present or past participle. The first one has been done for you. (*Speaking/listening tip:* Try to do this exercise orally, on your own, in class, or with a small group, before you pick up your pencil.) Check your answers on page 564 before doing the next exercise.

1. If a new friend *fascinates* you, how would you describe the person? *The friend is fascinating.*

   How would you describe yourself? *I am fascinated.*

2. If your neighbour *annoys* you, how would you describe the neighbour?

   The neighbor is _____. How would you describe yourself? *I am* _____.

3. If an accident *horrifies* you, how would you describe the accident?
The accident is _____. How would you describe yourself? *I am* _____.

4. If a joke *embarrasses* you, how would you describe the joke?
The joke is _____. How would you describe yourself? *I am* _____.

5. If a meal *satisfies* your friend, how would you describe the meal?
The meal is _____. How would you describe your friend? *My friend is*

_____.

6. If the results *disappointed* the boss, how would you describe the results?
The results were _____. How would you describe the boss? *The boss was*

_____.

7. If Jan's job doesn't *bore* her, how would you describe Jan? *Jan isn't*

_____. How would Jan describe her job? *My job isn't* _____.

8. If the music *pleases* you, how would you describe the music?
The music is _____. How would you describe yourself? *I am* _____.

9. If the answer *amazes* your teacher, how would you describe the answer?
The answer is _____. How would you describe your teacher? *The teacher is*

_____.

10. If this class *exhausts* you, how would you describe yourself? *I am* _____.
How would you describe this class? *This class is* _____.

EXERCISE **29.5**

Complete each of the following sentences by filling in the blank with the correct participle of the italicized verb.

1. Hard work *tires* Bob. He is a _____ man.

2. Hard work *tires* Bob. Hard work is _____ for Bob.

3. The movie *interests* the children. The children are _____ .They are

watching an _____ movie.

4. The news *surprised* my brother. He is a _____ man. The news was quite

_____.

5. The garbage in the house *disgusts* me. I am _____. The garbage is

_____.

6. The lecture *stimulated* the students. The lecture was _____. The students

were _____.

7. The task *exhausted* me. I was _____ by this _____ task.

8. The possibility *excites* everyone. The possibility is _____. Everyone is

_____.

9. His story *inspired* the crowd. His story was _____. The crowd was

_____.

10. The test results *shocked* the whole town. The _____ people could hardly

believe the _____ test results.

Go to Web Exercises 29.3, 29.4

MODAL AUXILIARIES

As we have seen, any of the verbs *am, is, are, was, were; do, does, did; has, have,* and *had* can stand alone as the only verb in a sentence.

I *am* strong.   You *are* strong.   He *is* strong.   It *was* strong.   They *were* strong.

We *do* things.   She *does* things.   They *did* things.

I *have* money.   George *has* money.   All of them *had* money.

These verbs can also work in an auxiliary capacity; that is, they can combine with the main verb in a sentence to change the time of an action or to form a negative construction.

I *am working* now.   You *are studying* here.   We *were travelling* last year.

I *don't know* her.   *Does* she *work* hard?   They *didn't call* us.

I *haven't seen* you.   He *has checked* your   They *hadn't told* us.
                          schedule.

There is another kind of auxiliary verb called a **modal auxiliary**. These words provide different shades of meaning or mood to the main verb. The modal auxiliaries are

can	might	should
could	must	will
may	shall	would

Some common verb phrases also function as modals (and are sometimes called *phrasal modals*):

be able to	be supposed to
have to	used to
ought to	

The examples that follow will show you how modal auxiliary verbs change the meaning of the main verb.

Modal	Interpretation
I *can* work.	I am able and willing to do the job.
I *could* work.	I am able to if ...
I *may* work.	I don't know if I will.
I *must* work.	I need to work.
I *should* work.	It is best for me to work.
I *would* work.	I am willing to work if ...
I *used to* work.	In the past, I worked but no more.

The good news about single-word modals is that they are followed by the base form of the verb (e.g., *work*) with no -*s* added to the third-person singular or -*ed* added to the past tense. Unlike *be*, *have*, and *do*, the modal auxiliaries don't change number, and, except for *can/could*, *will/would*, and *shall/should*, they don't change time.

Verb	Modal + verb
I *work*	I *can work*
He *works*	He *must work* (not "He must works")
They *worked*	They *should work* (not "They should worked")

The bad news about modals is that they often suggest subtle changes in meaning that can confuse second-language writers. Traditional grammar texts use a great deal of ink attempting to distinguish "obligation" versus "advisability" and "polite" versus "impolite" requests. The following chart will help you sort out the meanings of modals. But while you're struggling to learn the differences among various modals, keep in mind that almost no native speakers will hear a difference between your telling them that you *may work tomorrow* and you *might work tomorrow*.

Single-Word Modal Auxiliaries

Auxiliary	Meaning	Example (Present/Future)	Example (Past)
can	1. ability	I *can swim* well.	I *could swim* when I was two.
	2. informal request	*Can* I *call* you tonight?	
could	1. past tense of *can*		I *could swim* when I was two.
	2. polite request	*Could* I please *speak* to your wife?	
	3. low level of certainty	It *could rain* tonight, or it *could be* clear.	
may	1. polite request	*May* I please *speak* to your wife?	
	2. low level of certainty	It *may rain* tonight, but it *may* not [*rain*].	
	3. possibility	Harvey says he *may go* with us.	
might	1. low level of certainty	It *might rain* tonight, but it *might* not [*rain*].	
	2. possibility	I *might visit* Paris this summer.	
	3. past tense of *may*		Harvey said he *might go* with us.
must	1. strong necessity	You *must drink* water.	
	2. high level of certainty	The teacher isn't here, so she *must be* ill.	

Auxiliary	Meaning	Example (Present/Future)	Example (Past)
shall	1. polite question	*Shall* I *help* you across the street?	
	2. future (with *I/we*)	I *shall see* you tomorrow. (or *will see* ...)	
should	1. advisable	You *should lose* a few pounds.	
	2. high level of certainty	You study hard, so you *should do* well in the course.	
	3. obligation	He *should support* his children.	
will	1. complete certainty	I'm sure you *will* succeed.	
	2. willingness	I*'ll* be happy to help you.	
	3. polite request	*Will* you please *tell* me what you think?	
would	1. preference (with *rather*)	I *would rather eat* at a restaurant.	
	2. polite request	*Would* you please *tell* me what you think?	
	3. repeated action in past		We *would* always *phone* home on weekends when we lived abroad.

EXERCISE **29.6**

Correct the mistakes in the first five sentences below. Then choose the correct modal auxiliary for the remaining sentences. Check your answers against ours on page 564. (*Speaking/listening tip:* Try to do this exercise orally, on your own, in class, or with a small group, before you pick up your pencil.)

1. Sam should works harder at school so that he can gets into college.

2. Could you showing me the way to the airport?

3. He must buy a new car last week.

4. My best friend may to marry her boyfriend when they finish school.

5. Could you like me to show you my butterfly collection?

Choose the correct modal auxiliary in the following sentences.

6. There _____ be enough room in the classroom for all the students; we'll have to see how many come to class. (*may not, can't*)

7. You _____ pass a tough physical exam if you want to be a police officer. (*could, must*)

8. She isn't answering her cellphone. She _____ have forgotten to bring it with her. (*may, should*)

9. Tell the children they _____ come in the house immediately. (*shall, must*)

10. The team _____ win their last game, but they have been playing so poorly that I don't think they will. (*would, may*)

The chart on page 375 summarizes modal and other auxiliaries that are made up of more than a single word. *Ought to* and *used to* do not require any change in the verb form. Like the single-word modals, they simply precede the base form of the main verb: "I *ought to* see you." "She *used to* love me."

Be able to, *be supposed to*, and *have to* present some challenge. Because they include the verbs *be* or *have*, they require a change in the auxiliary itself to mark tense and number. Study the following examples.

> You *are able to* finish the assignment.
> We *were able to* finish the assignment.
> I *am supposed to* attend a class at noon today.
> She and I *were supposed to* attend a class yesterday.
> He *has to* change his clothes.
> He *had to* change his clothes.

When you are using past participles such as *supposed to* and *used to*, don't forget to include the *-d* at the end of the word. Omitting the *-d* is a common writing error (for native and non-native speakers alike).

Incorrect: The show was **suppose** to begin an hour ago.
                    I **use** to have more money.

Correct: The show was **supposed** to begin an hour ago.
                    I **used** to have more money.

CHAPTER 29 MORE ABOUT VERBS 375

Phrasal Modal Auxiliaries

Auxiliary	Meaning	Example (Present/Future)	Example (Past)
be able to	ability (can)	He *is able to handle* the truck.	He *was able to handle* the truck.
be supposed to	expectation	We *are supposed to meet* them.	We *were supposed to meet* them.
have/has/ had to	necessity (must)	He *has to go* to the bank today.	He *had to go* to the bank on Tuesday.
ought to	1. advisability (should)	We *ought to bring* our raincoats and an umbrella.	
	2. high level of certainty	She studies hard and *ought to do* well in school.	
used to	repeated action in the past		She *used to work* hard in school. He *used to weigh* 100 kilograms.

EXERCISE **29.7**

Fill in each blank with one of the phrasal modal auxiliaries. More than one modal may be correct, but use a different modal in each sentence. Compare your answers against our suggestions on page 564.

1. It may rain later, so you _____ take your umbrella.

2. I _____ go to the United States with just a passport, but now I _____ get a visa.

3. We _____ go to the beach yesterday, but it was too cold. We hope that we _____ go tomorrow.

For ESL Learners: A Review

EXERCISE **29.8**

In each sentence below, choose a modal auxiliary to go with the verb in parentheses. More than one auxiliary may be possible.

1. (visit) I _____ my parents, but we always get into fights when we spend time together. So I rarely see them.

2. (finish) If he works very hard, Paulo _____ the project before the deadline.

3. (complete) He _____ it on time if he wants to get paid.

4. (see, we) _____ the moon tonight, or is it too cloudy?

5. (run) When Oswaldo was younger, he _____ very fast.

6. (love) Felix bought his girlfriend a beautiful engagement ring; he _____ her very much.

7. (drink) Her parents _____ heavily, but they have stopped entirely since joining Alcoholics Anonymous.

8. (pay) Alex _____ back the loan last week, but he hasn't done so.

9. (rain) The sky is getting darker; it _____.

10. (smoke, not) You _____ in public buildings in Canada.

EXERCISE **29.9**

Use a modal auxiliary (one word or a phrase) in each of the blanks. Some sentences require negatives. More than one auxiliary may be possible.

1. I wonder when the boat will arrive. It _____ be here an hour ago.

2. Laura is getting very fat. She _____ eat so much.

3. If you have a food processor, you _____ prepare this salad in a few minutes.

4. I _____ come over and see you if it weren't raining.

5. You _____ be in two places at once.

6. The doctor is not in her office. I'm not sure where she is, but she _____ be at the hospital.

7. Their whole house is decorated in red; they _____ really love the colour!

8. Fred _____ know better than to call me at midnight.

9. Our instructor _____ give us quizzes every day, but now he gives only three a semester.

10. People who drive and text at the same time _____ get tickets from the police.

EXERCISE 29.10

Fill in each blank with an appropriate modal auxiliary.

People choose to immigrate to Canada for many reasons. They _____ want to have more economic opportunity. Or they _____ be looking for a better education for their children. Or they _____ want to _____ to practise their beliefs openly. Perhaps the country where they _____ live denied them certain rights that they _____ enjoy in Canada. Whatever their reasons for coming, immigrants to Canada _____ work very hard to adjust to their new country. They _____ find new homes and jobs, and most of them _____ learn a new language. Immigrating is not an easy process, but new immigrants hope that they _____ build a better life in their new home.

Go to Web Exercises 29.5, 29.6

CONDITIONAL VERBS

Conditional verb structures are tricky for second-language learners because they encompass the confusing territory of "real" versus "unreal" (hypothetical) situations. Since these structures are used frequently in English, it's worth reviewing them. Conditionals are usually signalled by the word *if*, although other words, such as *when*, can also be connected to conditionals. Note that *if* and *when/whenever* have different meanings. "*If* I graduate" suggests that you might do so; "*when* I graduate" implies that you will. The explanation and examples below remind you how conditionals work.

Factual conditionals explain what usually happens in a "real" situation. The simple present tense is used in both the independent and dependent clauses. The dependent clause begins with *if* or *when/whenever* and can come either before or after the independent clause.

(See Chapter 6 for a review of clauses and sentence structure.)

Dependent clause   **Independent clause**
If you *heat* water to 100º Celsius, it *boils*. (simple present tense)

Independent clause **Dependent clause**
I *walk* to work   when (or whenever) I *have* time. (simple present tense)

Present hypothetical conditionals refer to "unreal" situations, those that have not happened and are unlikely to occur. (*Hypothetical* means "not necessarily real or true." A unicorn is a hypothetical animal; your winning a million dollars in the lottery is likely to be a hypothetical occurrence.)

In the present hypothetical mode, the verb in the independent clause is usually in the past tense, and the verb in the dependent clause is a conditional constructed with *would* + the base form. Occasionally, the verb *could* is used in the dependent clause to mean "*would be able to.*"

If I *lived* in China, I *would speak* Chinese. (I don't.)

Tommy *would marry* her if she *had* more money. (She doesn't, so he won't.)

If I *had* wings, I *could* fly. (I don't, so I can't.)

Past hypothetical conditionals refer to "unreal" situations that did not happen or could not have happened in the past. To express this situation, the verb in the independent clause is *would* + *have* + the past participle. The verb in the dependent (*if*) clause is in the past perfect tense.

I *would have come* to see you if I *had known* you were home. (I didn't know and didn't come.)

If Morty *had moved* to Canada as a child, he *would have spoken* English better. (He didn't move earlier, so he can't speak English as well as he might have.)

If you *had worked* harder, you *would have passed* the course. (You didn't work harder, so you didn't pass the course.)

Note that *would* in the conditional structure is often contracted to *'d*: for example, *I'd have come, he'd have spoken, you'd have passed* in the sentences above. The *have* in conditional structures is also frequently shortened: *I would've, I could've, I should've*. (But they aren't "woulda, coulda, shoulda," which is actually an idiom referring to a lost chance. Say the actual contractions aloud, and you'll understand why they sound like "*woulda, coulda, shoulda*.")

Future conditionals predict what may or is likely to happen in the future. The verb in the independent clause is usually *will* + the base form or *be going to* + the base form. The verb in the dependent (*if*) clause is usually in the simple present tense.

My friends *will take* David home if he *asks* them.
If it *rains* tomorrow, we *are going to cancel* the picnic.
If you *find* a four-leaf clover, you*'ll have* good luck.

These examples cover some—but not all—of the permutations in verb form that make up the conditional. Practise using the conditional with the exercises below. (*Speaking/listening tip:* Try to do the following exercises orally, on your own, in class, or with a small group, before you pick up your pencil.)

EXERCISE **29.11**

Complete these sentences with conditional clauses, using *when* or *if*. Compare your answers against ours on pages 565–66.

1. I'll be very angry _____.

2. My mother will be happy _____.

3. She'll be sorry _____.

For ESL Learners: A Review

4. My friends will be disappointed _____.

5. You'll worry about me _____.

6. _____ I become prime minister.

7. _____ you get married.

8. _____ the sun comes up.

9. _____ Fatima finishes college.

10. _____ it doesn't snow tomorrow.

EXERCISE **29.12**

Choose the correct tenses in the sentences below. Some of the sentences are factual conditionals; others are present hypothetical conditionals.

1. You (miss) _____ me if I (move) _____ to Calgary.

2. My husband (eat) _____ eggs for breakfast when he (have) _____ time to cook in the morning.

3. When David (get) _____ home, he (walk) _____ the dog.

4. You (not meet) _____ my new girlfriend if you (stay) _____ home.

5. The dog (bark) _____ whenever he (see) _____ the mail carrier.

6. Peter (get) _____ a bad sunburn today if he (not wear) _____ sunscreen.

7. When the moon (be) _____ full, werewolves (howl) _____.

8. The doctor says if my father (quit) _____ smoking, he (feel) _____ better. But he won't quit.

9. Whenever people (quit) _____ smoking, their overall health (improve) _____.

10. Water (freeze) _____ when it (get) _____ down to a temperature of 0° Celsius.

EXERCISE **29.13**

(a) Fill in the correct verb form, using the past hypothetical conditional mode.

1. Ali failed math. He (pass) _____ the course if he (work) _____ harder.

2. Rhonda found out that she has high blood pressure. If she (learn) _____ about it earlier, she (go) _____ to see a doctor.

3. You lost the race. You (win) _____ if you (run) _____ faster.

4. If we (remember) _____ to lock the door, the burglars (not get) _____ into the house.

5. We (save) _____ some money if we (know) _____ about the sale.

6. If Einstein (not hypothesize) _____ the theory of relativity, someone else (do) _____ it.

(b) Complete the sentences below, using past hypothetical conditional verb forms. Compare your answers with ours on page 566.

7. If I hadn't been so angry, _____.

8. If my parents hadn't met, _____.

9. _____ if he had not moved to Canada.

10. If I had won the lottery, _____.

EXERCISE **29.14**

(a) Fill in the correct verb form, using the future conditional mode.

1. If you (tickle) _____ me, I (laugh) _____.

2. Dana (clean) _____ the kitchen if Louis (do) _____ the laundry.

3. Ann (be) _____ depressed if her boyfriend (not call) _____.

4. If it (not rain) _____ tomorrow, we (go) _____ to the beach.

5. If Jackie (tell) _____ me that joke again, I (scream) _____.

6. You (find) _____ a good job if you (work) _____ hard at it.

7. If his mom (come) _____ to dinner, I (cook) _____ kosher food.

(b) Complete these sentences, using the future conditional.

8. You'll be sorry if _____.

9. I'll work hard if _____.

10. We won't get married if _____.

EXERCISE **29.15**

Complete the sentences below using verbs in the appropriate conditional form.

1. We (eat) _____ dinner at a restaurant tonight if I (not get) _____ home in time to prepare a meal.

2. The baby (cry) _____ whenever he (be) _____ hungry.

3. If I (run) _____ the world, everyone (have) _____ enough to eat.

4. I didn't know the woman we saw last night. If I (know) _____ her name, I (tell) _____ you.

5. If I (speak) _____ French, I (spend) _____ the summer in Quebec. But I don't.

6. Irving lied to me about his work experience. If he (tell) _____ me the truth, I (not hire) _____ him.

7. Tides (be) _____ higher when the moon (be) _____ full.

8. If I (earn) _____ more money, I (buy) _____ you a bigger house.

9. Some people believe that if a person (walk) _____ under a ladder, he (have) _____ bad luck.

10. If the child's parents (not have to) _____ work so hard, they (spend) _____ more time with him.

EXERCISE **29.16**

With a partner (or on your own), read through the exercise below and choose the correct modal, conditional, participial adjective, or negative verb (or ending) to go into the blanks. Compare your answers with those of another team (or another student). Finally, check your answers against the original: the beginning of paragraph 3 of "Career Consciousness" on page 436. More than one answer may be acceptable.

If your career _____ stimulat _____, then chances are good that it

_____ also be reward _____. A good career offers two kinds of

rewards: financial and emotional. Reward _____ work _____ just

happen; it's something you _____ plan for. The first and most important

step is to know yourself. Only if you _____ who you are and what you

need to be happy _____ you consciously seek out career experiences that

_____ bring you satisfaction and steer clear of those that _____ annoy

or stress you.

EXERCISE **29.17**

Edit these sentences to correct the errors in negative constructions, participial adjectives, modal auxiliaries, and conditionals.

1. Claude doesn't very interesting in the movie; he found it bored.

2. All the plants in the office are dying. They may be getting enough sunlight.

3. He ought to been more surprising when I told him the shocked news.

4. You hardly never meet a real prince. Was it an excited experience?

5. If we had arrived early yesterday, we would have find no one at home.

6. They hasn't never been to Europe, but they are suppose to go next year.

7. When people are hear the word *fire*, they usually ran.

8. The whole beach was deserting. We couldn't see nothing but sand.

9. Don't a person has to be rich to lead an excited life?

10. You must knocks before you come into my room if you respect me.

For ESL Learners: A Review

30 Solving Plural Problems

SINGULAR VERSUS PLURAL NOUNS

Nouns in English are words that name people, places, things, or ideas. For example, *Sidney Crosby*, *Saskatchewan*, *alligator*, and *honesty* are all examples of nouns. The first three examples are **concrete** nouns; in other words, they refer to physical objects that we can see or touch. The fourth example, *honesty*, is an **abstract** noun that refers to a concept that exists in our minds; it cannot be seen or touched.

Singular nouns refer to one person, place, thing, or idea: *mother*, *bedroom*, *book*, *justice*. Plural nouns refer to more than one person, place, or thing: *mothers*, *bedrooms*, *books*. Abstract nouns are not often found in the plural form, but some of them can be pluralized.

To form the plural of most nouns, you add *-s* to the singular form.

Singular	Plural
classroom	classrooms
cousin	cousins
ocean	oceans
idea	ideas *(plural abstract noun)*
truck	trucks
umbrella	umbrellas

EXERCISE **30.1**

Rewrite the following sentences in the plural. Make sure that your verbs and pronouns agree with the plural nouns. (Adjectives do not change for plurals.) The first question is done for you. (*Speaking/listening tip:* Try to do the exercise orally, on your own, in class, or with a small group, before you pick up your pencil. Many of the exercises in this chapter are good for speaking practice.) Answers for exercises in this chapter begin on page 567.

1. The book is on her table.

   The books are on their tables.

2. Your little girl loves her new toy.

3. I am going to see my professor.

4. Latanya's brother won the prize.

5. The shark is swimming around the boat.

6. The man visits his girlfriend often.

7. This room is very large.

8. The teacher loves her students.

9. Should my sister find her own apartment?

10. My friend works hard at her job.

Plurals can be particularly tricky for English language learners. Because the rules for forming the plural sometimes depend on the pronunciation of the word (see rules 2 and 4 below), you might want to check a pronunciation dictionary or website (e.g., **www.forvo.com**) to hear how a native speaker would pronounce the word in question. As you probably know, there are many exceptions to the "add -s for plural" rule. The most common exceptions are listed below.

1. Some nouns have irregular plural forms that must be memorized.

Most of the following are very common words that are based on an older form of English. You need to become familiar with their irregular plural forms.

Singular	Plural
child	children
foot	feet
goose	geese
man (woman)	men (women)
mouse	mice
tooth	teeth

2. For nouns ending in "soft" sounds of -s, -x, -z, -ch, -sh, add -es.

Singular	Plural	Singular	Plural
box	boxes	class	classes
buzz	buzzes	dish	dishes
church	churches	kiss	kisses

If the -ch is a "hard" sound—as in *stomach*—add -s only: *stomachs*.

3. For nouns ending in -y preceded by a consonant, change the -y to -i and add -es.

Singular	Plural	Singular	Plural
country	countries	penny	pennies
lady	ladies	reply	replies

Nouns ending in -y preceded by a vowel are regular. Add -s to pluralize them.

Singular	Plural	Singular	Plural
boy	boys	key	keys
delay	delays	valley	valleys

4. For nouns ending in -f or -fe, add -ves if the plural is pronounced with a -v sound.

Note that the word *self* is in this category. This rule has important consequences for the -*self* words.

Singular	Plural	Singular	Plural
calf	calves	himself	themselves
knife	knives	herself	themselves
thief	thieves	myself	ourselves
wife	wives	yourself	yourselves

If the plural noun keeps its -f sound, add only -s.

beliefs	chiefs
chefs	proofs

5. Some nouns ending in *-o* are pluralized by adding *-es*; other nouns ending in *-o* require only *-s*. Use your spell checker or dictionary if you're not sure.

echoes	BUT	pianos
heroes		sopranos
potatoes		studios
tomatoes		zoos

6. Some nouns retain their singular form for the plural.

caribou	elk	salmon
carp	moose	sheep
deer	pickerel	trout

7. Some nouns are used in the plural form only, even though they refer to a single unit.

glasses	pyjamas
jeans	scissors
pants	shorts

8. Some nouns adopted from other languages retain their original plural form.

Singular	Plural	Singular	Plural
analysis	analyses	larva	larvae
criterion	criteria	phenomenon	phenomena
fungus	fungi	stimulus	stimuli
hypothesis	hypotheses	thesis	theses

EXERCISE **30.2**

Fill in the blank with the missing form (singular or plural) of the noun or pronoun. The first one is done for you. Check your answers against ours on page 567.

Singular	Plural
1. one boss	two <u>bosses</u>
2. the woman herself	the _____ _____
3. my country	_____ _____
4. the _____	the men
5. one sheep	many _____
6. my foot	_____ _____
7. an _____	thick eyelashes
8. one _____	many criteria
9. ashamed of yourself	ashamed of _____
10. a photo	several _____
11. the zoo	two _____
12. a _____	many tomatoes
13. one _____	many phenomena
14. the monarch	two _____
15. one thesis	several _____
16. one belief	many _____
17. my husband	my friends' _____
18. his only _____	all your teeth
19. the hero	these _____
20. one chief	two _____

EXERCISE **30.3**

Insert the correct plural forms of the nouns provided in the left column.

woman, salmon   1. The young _____ caught the _____ we ate for dinner.

mushroom, berry   2. Some wild _____ and _____ are poisonous, so be careful about eating them.

"Please, Miss, surely 'trousers' should be singular
at the top and plural at the bottom?"

tree, leaf   3. It is difficult to identify _____ by their bark, but it's

easy if you have some _____ from the tree.

course, quiz   4. We are lucky to have only three _____ this semester

because each of them has weekly _____.

scissors, knife   5. They had to defend themselves with _____ and

_____.

city, community   6. Most Canadian _____ are home to many different

ethnic _____.

inquiry, reply   7. Ming mailed out a dozen _____ about jobs, but she

received only six _____.

potato, yourself   8. The three of you will have to pick the _____ by _____.

child, himself   9. The _____ managed to fix dinner by _____.

cattle, wolf   10. The _____ were threatened by the hungry _____.

Go to Web Exercises 30.1, 30.2

COUNT VERSUS NON-COUNT NOUNS

Count nouns (also known as countable nouns) are words for separate persons, places, or things that can be counted: for example, college, job, meal, student, toy.

Count nouns can be made plural in one of the ways explained in the previous pages. (The regular -*s* ending makes each of the previously mentioned count nouns plural: *colleges, jobs, meals, students, toys*.)

Non-count nouns (also known as uncountable nouns) identify things that cannot be counted: for example, water, granite, information, rain.

Many non-count nouns refer to a "whole" that is made up of different parts. For instance, a room may contain two sofas, three tables, four chairs, and a television. These items can be counted—and the words can be made plural. However, all of these items together can be considered a "whole" and described as *furniture*, which is a non-count noun that is never pluralized.

Incorrect: two chair, all the furnitures
Correct: two chairs, all the furniture

There are several categories of non-count nouns:

- abstract nouns (words for concepts that exist as ideas in our minds): for example, **courage, fun, hatred, health, information** (You acquire *information* as a whole, as you do *knowledge*. You don't say that you have gathered *informations* or *knowledges*. Those abstract nouns cannot be pluralized.)
- words that identify a quantity or mass: for example, **air, coffee, food, rice, salt, sugar, water** (These words identify substances that are made up of particles too numerous to count. You can count *bottles of water* or *bowls of rice*, but you cannot count *water* or *rice*.)
- the names of many sports: for example, **golf, hockey, tennis**
- the names of some illnesses: for example, **diabetes, flu, osteoporosis**
- subjects of study, whether their form is singular (e.g., astronomy, biology, chemistry) or plural (e.g., economics, mathematics, physics)
- weather and other natural phenomena: for example, **electricity, fire, lightning, sunshine**

Understanding the difference between count and non-count nouns is essential to determining whether an article (*a, an, the*) should appear before a noun. Chapter 31 deals with articles and modifiers, so make sure that you understand the difference between count and non-count nouns before going on. For now, keep in mind that you do not add plural endings to non-count nouns, although some of them, such as the academic disciplines listed above, already have an -*s* ending.

Incorrect: I should do my homeworks.
Correct:　I should do my homework.

Incorrect: We always have funs in good weathers.
Correct:　We always have fun in good weather.

Incorrect: My friends and I are concerned about our healths.
Correct:　My friends and I are concerned about our health.

Incorrect: The airline lost our baggages.
Correct:　The airline lost our baggage.

EXERCISE **30.4**

Fill in the blanks in each sentence using the words in the list below. Use each word only once. Write *C* above the added word if it is a count noun; write *NC* above the added word if it is a non-count noun. Make the word plural if necessary. Check your answers against ours on pages 567–68.

For ESL Learners: A Review

advice	suitcase	coffee
health	sugar	dinner
baggage	problem	water
milk	knowledge	vitamin
physics	beef	chemical

1. Put some _____ and _____ in my _____, please.

2. I need your _____ to solve two _____.

3. Your _____ of _____ is better than mine.

4. I love to eat _____ for _____.

5. Please pick up both of my _____ at the _____ claim.

6. The _____ in the lake is full of dangerous _____.

7. You have to take your _____ if you want to regain your _____.

So far, so good, but the count/non-count issue has one further complication. Some nouns can be both count and non-count, depending on how they are used. If the noun has a general, as-a-whole kind of meaning, it is non-count and is not pluralized: for example, "We often eat chicken for dinner." If the noun has a specific, count-them-up kind of meaning, it is a count noun and can be pluralized: for example, "Four chickens were running around in the yard." Therefore, some non-count nouns may also be used in a countable sense and have a plural form. Study the four examples below.

1. Non-count (in a general sense): *Exercise* is good for you.
   Count (a specific movement or example): Do all of the *exercises* and check your answers.

2. Non-count (in a general sense): *Food* is an important part of every culture.
   Count (specific cuisines): There were *foods* from all over the world at the party.

3. Non-count (in a general sense): You need *experience* for this job.
   Count (specific happenings): I had some interesting *experiences* in class this semester.

4. Non-count (in a general sense): When did humans learn to use the power of *fire*?
   Count (specific blazes): We could see several different *fires* on the beach.

Check an advanced learner's dictionary if you are unsure whether a noun is count or non-count. Some dictionaries identify non-count nouns as "uncountable" (abbreviated *U*).

EXERCISE **30.5**

Write the correct form of the word—either singular or plural—in the blanks below. Check your answers against ours on page 568.

money, luck   1. They often win _____ in the lottery, so I guess you could say they have good _____.

luggage, backpack   2. After the _____ arrived at the hotel, we found that two _____ were missing.

piano, furniture   3. Both _____ were too large to fit into the living room because of all the _____.

paper, wood   4. Did you know that _____ is made from _____?

cattle, beef   5. At the slaughterhouse, those _____ will be turned into _____.

light   6. As the sun set and the _____ faded, we turned on all the _____ in the cottage.

time   7. How many _____ do I have to tell you that being on _____ is important?

garbage, work   8. Taking out the _____ every week is not much _____.

advice, rubbish   9. The _____ he gave me was a lot of _____.

apartment, accommodation   10. The two _____ provided good _____ when we were in New York.

EXERCISE **30.6**

Correct the errors in the following sentences.

1. Robert is going bald and wants to know where he can get informations on hairs replacement.

2. I found a couples of hair in my soup.

3. Barney has excellent knowledges of two language: English and French.

4. We want to give you some new cloths to wear as an expression of our thank.

5. The riches get richer, and the poors get poorer.

6. Having two business go bankrupt was a learning experiences.

7. We lost all of our moneys on several bad investment.

8. Did you get any new informations about the computer datas we lost?

9. We didn't hear much laughters coming from the back of the van as we drove through the rush-hour traffics.

10. Money can't buy you loves.

EXERCISE **30.7**

Rewrite the following paragraphs, changing the nouns from singular to plural, as appropriate. Don't forget to make your verbs and pronouns agree with your plural nouns, and prepare to omit some articles (*a, an*)—the subject of Chapter 31. Your paragraph will begin "Sharks are scary animals to most people."

The shark is a scary animal to most people, a killing machine immortalized in movies and books. The shark is actually an ancient species. Its ancestor dates back about 350 million years, as the fossil record shows. In size, the shark ranges from the tiny angel shark that is less than a metre in length to the huge 15-metre whale shark that can weigh 700 kilograms.

The shark is a very effective predator in the ocean. It has very good eyesight, and even in total darkness, the shark can sense the movement of its prey by

means of special pores in its skin that sense another animal's electrical vibra-
tions. In addition, a shark can smell its prey from a long distance. These characteristics make the shark a good killing machine as it hunts for food.

Although the shark is high on the food chain, it usually eats smaller fish,
crabs, seals, and other sea creatures. A shark does not seek out people to eat.
We may fear the shark, but there are only about 100 shark attacks on humans
each year worldwide, and perhaps 25 to 30 of these are fatal. Given our
increasing appetite for shark meat, the truth is that people eat many more
sharks than sharks eat people.

Go to Web Exercises 30.3, 30.4, 30.5

QUANTITY EXPRESSIONS

The English language contains many words and phrases that tell us the quantity or amount of something. For instance, *one prize*, *three prizes*, and *fifty prizes*
state the exact number of prizes; *many prizes*, *several prizes*, and *a few prizes* tell
us that there is more than one prize, but not exactly how many there are. A
noun's status as count or non-count determines the appropriate expression to
quantify the noun. Phrases such as *a lot of* and *some of* are also quantity expressions. Study the examples that follow.

Incorrect: We ate a couple of pizza.
Correct: We ate a couple of pizzas.

Incorrect: She grew a lot of vegetable in the garden.
Correct: She grew a lot of vegetables in the garden.

Incorrect: Some of the picture were very ugly.
Correct: Some of the pictures were very ugly.

Note that it is also correct to omit *of the* in this last sentence, but the noun *pictures* remains plural: "Some pictures were very ugly."

Some quantity expressions are used exclusively with count nouns; some are used exclusively with non-count nouns. Other quantity expressions can be used with both. The following chart uses a count noun (*dollars*) and a non-count noun (*money*) to illustrate how quantity expressions are used with these two noun types.

Quantity Expression	**Count Noun**	**Non-Count Noun**
Singular	*Dollar(s)*	*Money*
one	one dollar	——
each	each dollar	——
every	every dollar	——
Plural		
a couple of	a couple of dollars	——
few/a few	a few dollars	——
a number of	a number of dollars	——
both	both dollars	——
many	many dollars	——
several	several dollars	——
two, three, *etc.*	two dollars, *etc.*	——
a great deal of	——	a great deal of money
a little/little	——	a little money
much	——	much money
all	all dollars	all money
a lot of/lots of	a lot of dollars	a lot of money
hardly any	hardly any dollars	hardly any money
lots of	lots of dollars	lots of money
not any/no	not any/no dollars	not any/no money
most	most dollars	most money
plenty of	plenty of dollars	plenty of money
some	some dollars	some money

EXERCISE **30.8**

Each of the following sentences has a blank indicating where a quantity expression is required. Several choices of quantity expression are given in parentheses following each sentence. Using the information in the chart on page 396, cross out the quantity expressions that *cannot* be used in the blank. Then check your answers against ours on page 569.

1. Roger drinks _____ cocktails every day. (*four, several, much, a great deal of, some, a lot of, too many, a little*)

2. Roger drinks _____ alcohol every day. (*three, some, many, a lot of, several, a great deal of, no, a few, a little, hardly any*)

3. My friend has _____ comfortable chairs on the patio. (*too much, hardly any, four, a few, a great deal of, no, plenty of, some, every*)

4. My friend has _____ comfortable furniture on the patio. (*a few, three, one, some, several, hardly any, much, a lot of, lots of, a couple of*)

Note that *a few* and *few* have different meanings, as do *a little* and *little*. *A few* and *a little* have a positive meaning: for example, "I have a few friends" and "I have a little money" suggest that I have at least some friends and some funds. I'm not completely alone, nor am I completely broke. On the other hand, *few* and *little* have negative connotations. "I have few friends" and "I have little money" suggest that I am a lonely person who has almost no money to spend. Strange twist of meaning, but true.

EXERCISE **30.9**

In the following sentences, fill in each blank either with an appropriate expression of quantity (choose from the list on page 396) or with an appropriate noun. When you've completed this exercise, compare your answers with our suggestions on page 569.

1. _____ extra money is good to have.

2. Several _____ lost money.

3. Roberto has _____ friends here in Canada, so he feels very homesick.

4. Could you please give me _____ help?

5. Very _____ tourists visit the country because of the war.

6. We need only _____ minutes to prepare dinner.

7. _____ of the _____ at the mall is/are open in the evening.

8. _____ of my _____ will be at my party, so we must have

_____ of _____.

9. It takes _____ practice to learn how to ice-skate.

10. _____ of us got home from the game quickly because there was

_____ traffic.

EXERCISE **30.10**

Decide whether *little*, *a little*, *few*, or *a few* is correct in these sentences.

1. The battery of the car is dead, so it is _____ use trying to start it.

2. Only _____ people came to the concert, so many seats were left

empty.

3. The hard-working father spent _____ time with his children.

4. Life in a poor village offers _____ opportunities for people to prosper.

5. It's lucky that I have _____ friends who can help you get a job.

6. My grandmother is feeling _____ better this morning.

7. The girl had _____ friends in the neighbourhood, so she was very lonely.

8. I will need _____ money if I am going to buy a car.

9. After the man regained consciousness, _____ that he said made any

sense; he didn't even know his own name.

10. _____ of us here in the office have gotten together to buy you a

birthday present.

Go to Web Exercises 30.6, 30.7

With a partner (or on your own), read through the exercise below and choose the correct singular or plural form of the word in parentheses or a correct quantifier to fill in the blanks. Compare your answers with those of another pair of students (or another student). Finally, check your answers against the original: paragraph 11 of "Embraced by the Needle" on page 456. More than one answer may be acceptable.

But what of (family) _____ where there was not abuse, but love, where (parent) _____ did their best to provide their children with a secure nurturing home? One also sees addictions arising in such families. The unseen (factor) _____ here is the stress the parents (-*self* word) _____ lived under even if they did not recognize it. That stress could come from relationship (problem) _____, or from outside (circumstance) _____ such as economic pressure or political disruption. The _____ frequent source of hidden stress is the parents' own childhood histories that saddled them with emotional (baggage) _____ they had never become conscious of. What we are not aware of in (-*self* word) _____, we pass on to our children.

Choose the correct word or phrase in the following sentences.

1. (Some/Some of) our (luggage/luggages) arrived on the flight, but the (salmon/ salmons) and (tomatos/tomatoes) we had bought in Vancouver were lost.

2. (Hardly any/most) of the (childs/children) knew how to swim so the teacher couldn't take them to the beach.

3. That house is made of (wood/woods) and (glass/glasses).

4. (One/Each) of the important institutions for ensuring (justice/justices) in this country is the Supreme Court of Canada; there are nine judges or (justice/justices) on the court.

For ESL Learners: A Review

5. Let me give you (some/some of/no) (advice/advices): always do your (homework/homeworks) if you want to pass this course.

6. Did you eat all the (spaghetti/spaghettis) (yourselves/yourselfs)?

7. In (most/much) people's (experience/experiences), (time/times) (pass/passes) very quickly.

8. I must have (few/a few) volunteers to help me move the (furniture/furnitures).

9. (Honesty/Honestys) is the best (policy/policies).

10. Herb is very careful about his (health/healths); he drinks (no/plenty of/some of) liquor or coffee.

Using Articles Accurately

People who learn English as their first language rarely have problems with these three little words: *a*, *an*, and *the*. But if you have learned English as a second (or third or fourth) language, articles are a potential minefield of trouble for you. One reason is that the use or non-use of **articles** often depends on meaning that is implied rather than stated. Look at these sentences, for example:

> *A* woman is waiting in your office.
> *The* woman is waiting in your office.

Both sentences are correct, and the sentence most definitely requires an article ("Woman is waiting in your office" is incorrect). But the meanings of the sentences above are quite different. Whether you choose *a* or *the* is determined by what you know about the woman, not by the grammar of the sentence. If she is an unknown, *indefinite* woman, you use the **indefinite article**, *a*. But if she is a known, *definite* person whom you perhaps expected, you use the **definite article**, *the*. Both articles *can* be used; which one you *should* use depends on what you mean to say. There are few specific rules that govern the use of these troublesome little words. You need to take time to practise until you become familiar with them. There are, however, some general guidelines that will help you use articles correctly. In this chapter, we explain the guidelines and give you practice in applying them.

THE INDEFINITE ARTICLE: *A/An*

The indefinite article marks a non-specific singular noun. In other words, *a/an* is used to refer to a singular (not plural) common noun in a general way.

Here are some examples:

> *A* woman is waiting in your office. (could be any woman)
> I ate *an* apple. (any apple, not a specific apple)
> *A* shark is a dangerous creature. (the whole shark species, not a specific shark)

One rule that always applies (no exceptions) tells you whether to use *a* or *an*: Use *a* if the word that follows begins with a consonant or the sound of a consonant; use *an* if the word that follows begins with the vowel or the sound of a vowel. (If you are unsure about the pronunciation of a sound, check a pronunciation dictionary or a website such as **www.forvo.com** to learn how a native speaker would say the word.)

Consonant or Consonant Sound	**Vowel or Vowel Sound**
a party	an event
a sunset	an umbrella
a great evening	an awful evening
a tiny elf	an ugly elf
a university (*university* begins with a vowel, but it sounds like the consonant -*y*)	an honour (*honour* begins with a consonant, but it sounds like the vowel -*o*)

EXERCISE **31.1**

Insert the correct indefinite article: *a* or *an*. Don't use *the*. (*Speaking/listening tip:* Try to do the exercise orally, on your own, in class, or with a small group, before you pick up your pencil. Many of the exercises in this chapter are good for speaking practice.) Answers for exercises in this chapter begin on page 569.

1. We saw _____ huge dog with _____ old man.

2. _____ zoologist is _____ scientist who studies animals.

3. You should see _____ dentist about your teeth.

4. He made _____ hasty retreat after realizing his error.

5. The president is _____ honest woman.

6. _____ arachnid is _____ insect that has eight legs, such as _____ spider.

7. _____ electrician could fix the problem in _____ hour.

8. _____ European man met us at the airport.

9. After high school, you can study at _____ college or _____ university.

10. The nurse said that Pete needed _____ X-ray to see if he had _____ broken arm.

Now let's look at how to use indefinite articles accurately. Study the five guidelines and examples that follow.

> 1. Use the indefinite article with singular count nouns. (See Chapter 30 for an explanation of count and non-count nouns.)

- *A/an* is never used with plural nouns.
  Incorrect: A women are waiting in your office.
  Correct: Women are waiting in your office.

- *A/an* is never used with non-count nouns.
  Incorrect: We moved a new furniture into the office.
  Correct: We moved new furniture into the office.
  Also correct: We moved a new desk into the office. (*Desk* is a count noun.)

> 2. Many nouns have a count meaning as well as a non-count meaning. The indefinite article *a/an* is required if the noun is being used as a singular count noun.

For example, the noun *life* can be used to refer to the general state of being alive. In this sense, *life* is non-count and is never pluralized: for example, "Life is good." The noun *life*, though, also has a count sense and can be pluralized: for example, "Six lives were lost in the earthquake" or "The hurricane did not take a single life." Also, consider the difference between these two sentences:

Incorrect: Life of poverty is very difficult.
Correct: A life of poverty is very difficult. (*Life* is a singular count noun here because it refers to a particular kind of life.)

Again, the meaning—as well as the grammar of your sentence—determines whether or not you need the article.

There are other nouns usually considered to be non-count that are also used as count nouns: for example, beverages that are held in a container (e.g., *coffee* in a cup). Such count nouns can be used with *a* and can also be pluralized.

Coffee is grown in South America. (*Coffee* is used as a non-count noun.)

Please bring me *a* coffee. (*Coffee* is used as a singular count noun.)

Please bring us two coffees. (*Coffee* is used as a plural count noun.)

For ESL Learners: A Review

3. The indefinite article is used with certain quantity expressions such as *a few, a little,* and *a couple of* (see page 396).

He has *a few* friends in Mumbai.

We have *a couple of* questions for you.

4. The indefinite article is used in certain time expressions, such as *half an hour* and *a half-hour*. The phrases *once an hour, twice a day, three times a week, several times a month,* and similar expressions use *a/an* to express frequency.

Can you meet me in *half an hour*?

Take this medication *three times a day*.

5. Many idioms require the indefinite article.

You should become familiar with the common idioms listed below.

as a rule	lend a hand
do a favour	make a living, make a point of, make a
for a long time	difference, make a fool of
give me a break (informal)	once in a while
have a headache	stand a chance
in a hurry	take a trip, take a break, take a look at
keep an eye on	tell a lie

EXERCISE **31.2**

In the following sentences, fill in the blanks with the correct indefinite article (*a/an*), if it is required. Put a zero (0) in the blanks where *a/an* is not required. Do not use the definite article (*the*) in this exercise. Check your answers against ours on pages 569–70.

1. _____ veterinarian is _____ doctor who treats _____ animals.

2. _____ child learns affection through the love of _____ parents.

3. We were in _____ hurry, so we forgot to bring _____ food.

4. _____ man with _____ big nose and _____ huge feet stepped into the room.

5. As _____ rule, _____ rich person should be prepared to help others who are less fortunate.

6. It is important to see _____ doctor for _____ examination once _____ year.

7. I waited for _____ hours to get _____ ticket to the concert.

8. _____ baby needs to drink _____ milk.

9. Would you please bring me _____ cup of _____ coffee?

10. _____ dog ate your homework? Give me _____ break!

Go to Web Exercises 31.1, 31.2

THE DEFINITE ARTICLE: *The*

The is a word that makes a noun specific or definite. It distinguishes the known from the unknown. In the sentence introduced above, "The woman is waiting in your office," we know the woman isn't a stranger. She is a definite person whose identity the speaker or writer recognizes. Nouns can be particularized—made definite or specific—in several ways. The following guidelines and examples show how nouns are particularized and will help you figure out how to use the definite article.

1. Use the definite article with familiar objects, places, and people in the external environment.

For instance, we speak about *the* North Pole, *the* moon, *the* apartment we live in, *the* school we attend, *the* doctor we consult, and *the* TV shows we watch. All of these things are particularized (made definite) because we are familiar

For ESL Learners: A Review

with them. We know who or what we have in mind when we use the word, and the reader or listener is going to understand the same thing.

The equator divides *the* northern hemisphere from *the* southern hemisphere.

Don't leave *the* keys in *the* car.

2. Nouns can be made definite from the context of the sentence. (This principle is called the anaphoric use—or second mention—of *the*.)

Once you refer to an unknown person, place, or thing using the indefinite article, that person, place, or thing becomes a known—or definite—entity the next time you refer to him, her, or it. Consider this example:

A strange woman is waiting in your office. *The* woman is wearing *an* interesting suit. *The* suit is made of blue silk and has red tassels.

The first time we mention the woman, she is unknown and referred to as *"a woman."* This first mention makes her definite, so we refer to her as *"the woman"* in the second sentence. Can you explain the shift in the articles that modify the suit she is wearing?

EXERCISE **31.3**

Complete the exercise below using *a*, *an*, or *the* correctly in the blanks. Check your answers against ours on page 570.

When you move to _____ new city, you have to think about your housing

needs. If you are going to be there for only _____ short time, you can rent

_____ furnished apartment. _____ apartment should be in _____ conven-

ient location. Perhaps you should locate yourself in _____ downtown area

near public transportation. _____ furnished apartment you rent needs to have

_____ decent kitchen. _____ kitchen should have _____ working stove and

refrigerator. _____ place where you live is _____ important factor in your

adjustment to your new city.

3. The definite article can be used with singular and plural nouns and with count and non-count nouns.

The woman is waiting in your office. (singular noun)

The women are waiting in your office. (plural noun)

We moved *the* new desk into your office. (count noun)

We moved *the* new furniture into your office. (non-count noun)

4. The definite article can also be used with a singular generic noun; that is, it can be used when you are making a generalization about a class of things.

The violin is a difficult instrument to play.

Usually, the indefinite article is also acceptable in such a sentence. Both of the sentences below have the same meaning, and both are correct.

The grizzly bear is dangerous.

A grizzly bear is dangerous.

Do not place *the* before a plural count noun used in the generic sense. Instead, use the plural form with no article: "Grizzly bears are dangerous." If you are referring to specific animals, though, you can use *the* with the plural count noun: "The grizzly bears in my backyard are dangerous."

Below is another example to illustrate the correct use of articles with generic and specific plural count nouns.

Potentially incorrect:	*The* teenagers are often moody and irritable with their parents.
	This use of *the* is incorrect if you are referring to teenagers as a class of people; it is correct if it refers to a specific group of teenagers.
Correct:	Teenagers are often moody and irritable with their parents.
Also correct:	*The* teenagers in that family are often moody and irritable with their parents. (*The* refers to a specific group of teenagers.)

For ESL Learners: A Review

EXERCISE **31.4**

Fill in each blank with *the* or a zero (0) if *the* is not required. Do not use *a/an* in this exercise. Check your answers against ours on page 570.

1. I like _____ classical music, but _____ music he plays late at night disturbs me.

2. _____ children are naturally curious, but _____ children in that class are extraordinarily inquisitive.

3. Do we know who invented _____ wheel?

4. In _____ Far North, _____ sun never sets in _____ June.

5. _____ elephant and _____ whale are both huge animals that give birth to _____ live babies; in other words, they are _____ mammals.

6. _____ books and _____ newspapers are endangered species, thanks to our wired world of e-books and tablet computers.

7. _____ man with _____ dog is married to _____ woman beside you.

8. _____ college students need to spend _____ time studying if they want to be successful.

9. Is _____ money as important as _____ love to you?

10. Thank you for _____ bananas; I love to eat _____ fruit.

Go to Web Exercises 31.3, 31.4

5. The definite article is used in many quantity expressions that contain *of*: for example, *some of the coffee, most of the children, each one of the judges, all of the exams, both of the rings.*

In many of these phrases it is also correct to omit the *of the* part of the phrase.

Many of the models in fashion shows are very young.

Many models in fashion shows are very young.

Both sentences are correct and mean the same thing.

Note that you cannot omit the definite article from a quantity expression without omitting *of* as well.

Incorrect:	Some of people in this building are very wealthy.
Correct:	Some of the people in this building are very wealthy.
Also correct:	Some people in this building are very wealthy.

6. Many idioms use the definite article.

Some common examples are

all the time	play the fool
clear the table	tell the truth
make the beds	wash the dishes

7. Other uses of the definite article are listed below.

- with superlative adjectives: *the* richest man I know
- with number words (ordinals): *the* third child, *the* tenth chapter
- in phrases that specify time or space sequence: *the* next day, *the* beginning, *the* last desk in *the* row, on *the* end
- in phrases that rank things: *the* main reason, *the* only person
- with official titles: *the* prime minister, *the* president (except when the person's name is attached: Prime Minister Harper, President Obama)
- with names of governmental and military bodies, both with common nouns (*the* courthouse, *the* police, *the* army) and with proper nouns (*the* Liberal Party, *the* United Nations, *the* Pentagon)
- with historical periods or events: *the* Renaissance, *the* Ming Dynasty, *the* 1960s
- with legislative bills and acts: *the* Canadian Charter of Rights and Freedoms, *the* Magna Carta

For ESL Learners: A Review

EXERCISE **31.5**

Fill in the blanks in the sentences below with *a*, *an*, or *the*. Do not leave the blank empty. Check your answers against ours on page 570.

1. I want to take _____ trip to _____ West Coast.

2. _____ phases of _____ moon are one of _____ causes of ocean tides.

3. _____ oldest person in _____ world is 114 years old.

4. My friends have two children: _____ boy and two girls. _____ boy is _____ oldest of _____ three.

5. Do you know _____ name of _____ best restaurant in town? I would like to take you out for _____ nice dinner.

6. _____ kind of vacation I enjoy most is _____ long train ride.

7. I don't need _____ special destination when I board _____ train; for me _____ most important thing is _____ journey.

8. _____ economic boom of _____ 1990s turned into _____ Great Recession after _____ financial meltdown of 2008.

9. _____ job requires _____ person with _____ lot of energy, and Danielle is ____ energetic person.

10. In many parts of Canada, _____ college student who begins school in _____ last part of August finishes _____ school year in April.

Go to Web Exercises 31.5, 31.6

NO ARTICLE (ZERO ARTICLE)

No article is used in general statements with non-count and plural nouns unless the noun is particularized or made specific in some way. Study the following guidelines and examples.

1. Do not use an article with non-count nouns:

Water is necessary for life.
Rice is good for you.
Gold is valuable.

No article is required with *water, life, rice,* or *gold* in these sentences.

2. In general statements, no article is required with plural nouns:

We like bananas.
Bears are dangerous.
People need friends.

To decide whether or not you need an article with a plural noun, you must determine whether the word is being used in a general or a specific sense. The following exercise will give you practice in making the correct decision.

EXERCISE **31.6**

Use either *the* or zero (0) article in the blanks below. Do not use *a/an.* Check your answers against ours on page 571.

1. We have had lots of _____ bad weather lately. Do you know what _____

   weather is supposed to be like on _____ weekend?

2. We like _____ food, but _____ most of _____ food at _____ restaurant

   is awful.

3. Everyone has _____ problems in _____ life. _____ problems may be big

   or small, but everyone must find ways to cope with them.

4. Ana is studying _____ Canadian history because she is interested in _____ history of her adoptive country.

5. Some of _____ most important products that Canada buys from India are _____ tea, _____ cotton, and _____ rice.

6. _____ beer is a popular beverage in Canada, and _____ beer brewed here has a high alcohol content.

7. _____ kindness is an attractive quality in people, and _____ kindness of our friend Dana is known to us all.

8. _____ jewellery is a popular gift; my boyfriend loved _____ jewellery that I gave him.

9. Natasha studies _____ art in university, and her specialty is _____ art of _____ Renaissance.

10. _____ boots are a necessary item of winter clothing in Canada, but _____ boots I bought last year are not very warm.

USING *THE* OR NO ARTICLE IN GEOGRAPHICAL NAMES

Why do we use *the* before the names of oceans (*the* Atlantic Ocean) but not before the names of lakes (Lake Ontario)? Who knows? The conventions around article use in geographical names in English are not really consistent. Unfortunately, you just have to get familiar with them. The list and examples below will help you learn some of the patterns.

No (Zero) Article	Examples
Continents	Asia, Australia, Europe, South America
Countries	Canada, China, Italy, Sudan, Mexico
Cities	London, Paris, Penticton, Rio de Janeiro
Lakes, bays, falls	Lake Simcoe, Hudson Bay, Niagara Falls

No (Zero) Article	Examples
Streets and parks	Burrard Street, Portage Avenue, High Park
Colleges and universities with *College* or *University* at end of name	Humber College, Red Deer College, Oxford University, Simon Fraser University
Halls	Carnegie Hall, Convocation Hall, Massey Hall

Definite Article (*the*)	Examples
Plural place names	the Americas, the Balkans, the Maritimes
Countries (or other bodies) that refer to a political union or association	the United Kingdom, the United States
Mountain ranges	the Himalayas, the Rocky Mountains
Groups of islands, *but* not individual islands	the British Isles, the Thousand Islands, the West Indies, *but* Long Island, Manitoulin Island, Vancouver Island
Oceans	the Arctic Ocean, the Atlantic Ocean, the Indian Ocean
Groups of lakes	the Muskokas, the Great Lakes
Rivers, seas, straits	the St. Lawrence River, the Caribbean, the Georgia Strait, the Strait of Juan de Fuca
Colleges and universities that have *of* in the name	the University of Toronto, the University of British Columbia, the University of Saskatchewan
Buildings, towers, bridges, hotels, libraries, museums	the Chrysler Building, the CN Tower, the Granville Street Bridge, the Banff Springs Hotel, the Library of Parliament, the Railway Coastal Museum
Deserts, forests, peninsulas	the Sahara Desert, the Black Forest, the Gaspé Peninsula
Points of the globe or compass	the equator, the Tropic of Capricorn, the Middle East, the North Pole, the southern hemisphere

For ESL Learners: A Review

EXERCISE **31.7**

Use either *the* or zero (0) article in the blanks below. Check your answers against ours on page 571.

Many of _____ geographical names in Canada are derived from _____ languages of Aboriginal peoples who lived here for thousands of _____ years before _____ first European settlers arrived. For example, _____ Manitoulin Island in _____ Lake Huron got its name from _____ Algonquian word *Manitou*, which means "spirit." _____ Queen Charlotte Islands (also known as Haida Gwaii) off _____ coast of _____ British Columbia consist of about 150 islands, _____ largest of which are _____ Graham Island and _____ Moresby Island. _____ province names _____ Saskatchewan and _____ Ontario, _____ Magnetawan River, _____ Lake Okanagan, and even _____ name "Canada" itself are all examples of _____ influence of Aboriginal peoples' languages on Canada's place names.

EXERCISE **31.8**

Use either *the* or zero (0) article in the blanks below.

1. _____ earthquakes sometimes happen in _____ British Columbia, but they rarely occur in _____ Prairie provinces, _____ central Canada, _____ Quebec, or _____ Maritimes.

2. Dora began her studies at _____ Nova Scotia Community College and then transferred to _____ Dalhousie University, but her brother attended _____ University of New Brunswick.

3. _____ Niagara Falls is on _____ Niagara River, which flows from _____ Lake Erie to _____ Lake Ontario.

4. _____ People's Republic of _____ China is also known as _____ China.

5. _____ St. Lawrence River forms _____ boundary between _____ Ontario in _____ Canada and _____ New York in _____ United States.

6. We have done mountain climbing in _____ Rockies, _____ Alps, and _____ Himalayas, but _____ most challenging climb was _____ Mount Kilimanjaro in _____ Africa.

7. _____ Bering Strait is between _____ state of Alaska and _____ former U.S.S.R, now known as _____ Russia.

8. _____ Czech Republic came into being in 1993, when _____ Czechoslovakia was no longer controlled by _____ Soviet Union.

9. _____ capital of _____ Prince Edward Island is _____ Charlottetown.

10. _____ Nile, _____ Amazon, and _____ Yangtze are _____ longest rivers in _____ world.

Go to Web Exercises 31.7, 31.8

EXERCISE **31.9**

Fill in the blanks with *a*, *an*, *the*, or zero article (0).

_____ hurricane is _____ severe tropical storm with winds between 120 and 240 kilometres per hour. Hurricanes are most likely to form in _____ Atlantic Ocean, and they usually blow west across _____ Caribbean and _____ Gulf of Mexico from _____ Africa. Hurricanes gain their energy as they pass over warm ocean waters, so _____ warmest months of _____ year are known as "hurricane season," from _____ June through _____ October. Hurricanes rotate in _____ counter-clockwise direction around _____ "eye." When a hurricane comes onshore, heavy rain, wind, and waves can do _____ tremendous amount of damage to trees, buildings, and people in _____ path of _____ storm.

EXERCISE **31.10**

Correct any misused or missing articles in the paragraph below. There are 10 errors.

Highest place on Earth is an mountain called Mount Everest, which is 8,850 metres high. It is located in Asia, at border of Tibet and Nepal, in a mountain range known as Himalayas. First people to climb Everest were the Edmund Hillary and Tenzing Norgay, who reached peak in 1953. According to a CBC Web site,[1] 2,249 people had climbed the Mount Everest by the end of 2004, but 186 people had died trying. Now there is a small industry of guides who make a good living taking adventurous climbers to the top of Everest. Ascending the mountain is expensive proposition, though. The average cost of a guided climb is about US$65,000. Save your money if you want to make it to top!

EXERCISE **31.11**

With a partner (or on your own), read through the exercise below and insert the appropriate articles (*a, an,* or *the*) in the blanks. Compare your answers with those of another pair of students (or another student). Finally, check your answers against the beginning of paragraph 8 of "Don't Call Me That Word" on page 459. More than one answer may be acceptable.

But does that take the sting out of the word? No. And what's _____ proof of that? We don't use _____ word around our mothers, our teachers, the people we fall in love with, or our children. "Nigger" is _____ word that young black men use on each other. But _____ word still pains most black Canadians. Let me share _____ image of just how much the word hurts.

_____ friend of mine— _____ black woman, community activist and graduate student—was dying to read Kennedy's book. She bought it last week, but couldn't bring herself to start devouring it on _____ subway to work until

---

[1] "Canadians and Mount Everest." *CBC.ca.* Canadian Broadcasting Corporation. 29 May 2006. Web. 20 Aug. 2011.

she had ripped off _____ cover: she wouldn't allow herself to be seen on the subway with the word "nigger" splashed on _____ cover of _____ book, so close to her face.

EXERCISE **31.12**

Fill in the blanks with *a*, *an*, *the*, or zero article (0).

I love _____ travelling and have been to many interesting places around _____ world. My favourite places are _____ China and _____ Morocco because they are very different from Canada in culture, language, architecture, and cuisine. When I go to _____ United States or _____ Great Britain or _____ Australia, I find the experiences much like those here in Canada. In those places, I don't feel that I am far away from _____ home.

In _____ Morocco, I sampled couscous, which is _____ very popular dish in _____ North Africa. In the markets, people wear long, flowing robes and _____ tasselled red hats called fezzes. The buildings are all made of _____ clay, and many of _____ cities are surrounded by large walls.

_____ China, too, is fascinating to me as _____ Canadian because it is so different from my country. _____ Beijing is _____ huge and _____ very interesting city to visit. I also enjoyed a trip to _____ Great Wall. In _____ countryside, oxen are used to plow fields, and bicycles are more common than automobiles. The food is very spicy in some areas of _____ country, and visitors will be surprised by the variety of _____ cuisines in different regions.

_____ Morocco and _____ China are not _____ countries like Canada, where food, dress, and architecture tend to be _____ same wherever you go. Travel is _____ wonderful way to learn about the world.

32 Practising with Prepositions

Prepositions are small words that often cause big problems for second-language learners. People who speak English as a first language are seldom confused by the distinction between *in* and *on* or *from* and *for*. But these little words often puzzle and frustrate second-language learners.

Prepositions have no special endings or inflections that make them easy to identify. (For instance, *-ous* endings usually indicate adjectives, such as *prosperous*, and *-ity* endings suggest nouns, such as *prosperity*.) The only characteristic that prepositions have in common is that *most* of them are short words. Sometimes two prepositions are joined to make a one-word compound (e.g., *into*, *without*, *upon*). English language learners work hard to learn these words and their sometimes multiple meanings.

> A **preposition** is a word that usually provides information about a relationship of time, place, or direction. A preposition comes at the beginning of a group of words known as a **prepositional phrase** (preposition + object).

after lunch	*to* school
during the week	*under* the volcano
in the closet	*inside* the house

In each of these phrases, the italicized word is a preposition. Every prepositional phrase requires an **object** (a noun or pronoun); *lunch*, *week*, *closet*, *school*, *volcano*, and *house* are the objects in the prepositional phrases above.

Below is a list of common prepositions used in English.

about	around	between	from
above	at	beyond	in
across	before	by	inside
after	behind	despite	into
against	below	down	like
along	beneath	during	near
among	beside	for	of

off	past	to	up
on	since	toward	upon
out	through	under	with
outside	throughout	underneath	within
over	till	until	without

We'll break up this long list into four categories to make it easier for you to learn the various uses of prepositions. Each of the four charts on the following pages is organized according to the relationship to which the preposition points. The charts also provide brief definitions and examples of prepositions used correctly.

One of the reasons that prepositions are confusing is that one word can have more than one meaning, so you'll see that some appear in more than one chart (*at*, *by*, and *from*, for example) or more than once in a single chart. Please note that these charts include only the most common prepositions and their meanings. Your dictionary provides more extensive definitions and examples.

Check your understanding of prepositions by doing the exercises that follow each chart. Occasionally, more than one preposition could be used correctly. If you make any mistakes, study the chart again, and do the Web exercises provided.

Prepositions That Indicate Time Relationships		
Preposition	**Uses/Meaning**	**Examples**
after	one event follows another event	We will have dinner *after* the concert.
at	used with a specific time of the day	The bell rang *at* midnight. We have dinner *at* 7:00 p.m.
before	one event comes before (precedes) another	I graduated from college *before* my brother did.
by	no later than	Finish your assignment *by* Friday.
during	indicating a period of time, usually undivided	I usually sleep *during* a long flight.
for	indicating a quantity of time	Could I talk to you *for* a few minutes?
from	indicating the time in the future when something starts	The concert is three days *from* now.

For ESL Learners: A Review

Prepositions That Indicate Time Relationships (cont.)		
Preposition	**Uses/Meaning**	**Examples**
in	used with a part of the day, month, year, or season	I'll see you *in* the morning. My birthday is *in* March. Dahlia was born *in* 2011. Birds fly south *in* the fall.
in	identifying a period of time by which something will happen; also means *during*	I'll see you *in* an hour. Traffic congestion has gotten much worse *in* recent years.
of	used with a date and month	Jessamyn was born on the thirtieth *of* June.
on	used with a day of the week or a specific date	I work *on* Saturday. Passover begins *on* April 7 next year.
since	from one time until now	I have not eaten *since* breakfast.
until, till	as far as the time when another event will occur	I won't have anything to eat *until* dinner.
within	not more than the specified period of time	Call me if you don't receive a cheque *within* a week.

EXERCISE **32.1**

Add *at*, *in*, or *on* to these words or phrases. Answers for exercises in this chapter begin on page 572.

1. _____ 2001

2. _____ Thursday

3. _____ the morning

4. _____ midnight

5. _____ lunchtime

6. _____ the spring

7. _____ work

8. _____ the following day

9. _____ the nick of time

10. _____ December

EXERCISE **32.2**

Fill in the blanks with appropriate prepositions. (*Speaking/listening tip:* Try to do the exercise orally, on your own, in class, or with a small group, before you pick up your pencil. Many of the exercises in this chapter are good for speaking practice.)

1. They were married _____ 1990, so they have been married _____ many years.

2. I hope to hear from him _____ Friday. If I don't, I will wait _____ he calls next week.

3. You have owed me $100 _____ last year. If I don't get the money _____ a week, I will contact your parents.

4. You will finish your degree a year _____ now, and I would like to have a party for you when you graduate _____ June.

5. Randy arrived _____ the summer; he was born _____ noon _____ July 11, 1962.

For ESL Learners: A Review

Go to Web Exercise 32.1

Prepositions That Indicate Place or Position		
Preposition	**Uses/Meaning**	**Examples**
above	directly higher	His apartment is *above* ours.
across	on the other side	She lives *across* the street.
among	included in a group (of more than two)	She sat *among* her 12 grandchildren.
at	indicating a specific location; also used with specific addresses	Maya is *at* school. We live *at* 1500 Bathurst Street.
behind	in back of	The grizzly bear is *behind* you!
below	under; directly lower	Her apartment is *below* ours.
beneath	under	Your coat is *beneath* mine in the pile.
beside	next to	Please sit *beside* me so we can talk.
between	in the middle of two	She sat *between* her two grandchildren.
by	near, beside	He has a house *by* the river.
in	within an area or space	The city of Moose Jaw is *in* Saskatchewan.
near	close to; within a short distance	I live *near* the subway.

Prepositions That Indicate Place or Position (cont.)		
Preposition	**Uses/Meaning**	**Examples**
on	covering or forming part of a surface	Please write *on* the blackboard.
over	higher than something else	The helicopter flew *over* the highway.
under	lower than something else	The subway runs *under* this theatre.
underneath	beneath, close under	Her purse was *underneath* the bed.
within	not farther than the distance from	The school is *within* a kilometre of her apartment.

EXERCISE **32.3**

Fill in the blanks with the appropriate prepositions indicating place or position. Then check your answers against ours on page 573.

1. Either put the dishes _____ the table or put them away _____ the cupboard.

2. What time does my plane land _____ Vancouver? Who will meet me _____ the airport and take me to my hotel, which is _____ the corner of Main and Hastings?

3. Manitoba is _____ Ontario and Saskatchewan.

4. Our house is _____ a valley _____ two hills.

5. Skunks live _____ holes called burrows, and that awful smell suggests you have a skunk burrow _____ a few metres of your back door.

Go to Web Exercise 32.2

Prepositions That Indicate Direction or Movement		
Preposition	**Uses/Meaning**	**Examples**
across	from one side to the other	She walked *across* the room.
around	indicating movement within a larger area; moving past something in a circle	The sprinters ran *around* the track. Jacques sailed *around* the world.
by	moving past someone or something	Michel walked right *by* his ex-wife without speaking. The car drove *by* the restaurant.
down	from a higher to a lower level	I walked quickly *down* the stairs to the basement.
from	indicating place where movement away began	Our flight to Vancouver left *from* Hong Kong.
into	moving to a point inside	Igor dived *into* the cold water.
out of	moving away from	She jumped *out of* bed happily.
past	moving by someone or something	Michel walked right *past* his ex-wife without speaking. The car drove *past* the restaurant.

Prepositions That Indicate Direction or Movement (cont.)		
Preposition	**Uses/Meaning**	**Examples**
through	passing from one side to another	The Assiniboine River flows *through* Winnipeg.
to	movement in the direction of a specific place	She walks *to* school every day.
toward	in the general direction of something	Walk *toward* the ocean and enjoy the beautiful sunset.
up	from a lower to a higher point	I walked quickly *up* the stairs to the attic.

EXERCISE **32.4**

Fill in the blanks with the appropriate prepositions indicating direction or movement. Then check your answers against ours on page 573.

1. We drove _____ your house last night, but we didn't stop because no one seemed to be home.

2. He was _____ the river _____ us when we saw him waving.

3. The woman ran _____ the burning house and rushed _____ the firemen.

4. They'll return next week _____ their vacation _____ Hawaii.

5. The thief climbed _____ the ladder and crawled _____ the house _____ an open upstairs window.

Go to Web Exercise 32.3

For ESL Learners: A Review

Other Prepositional Relationships: Relation, Source, Manner, Possession, Quantity		
Preposition	Uses/Meaning	Examples
about	on the subject of someone or something	This book is *about* love. We know all *about* your past.
about	concerning something	We can do something *about* the problem.
for	indicating the person receiving something	The message is *for* you. What can I do *for* you?
for	with regard to purpose or function	Tara received roses *for* her birthday. He works *for* a car dealership.
from	indicating the source of someone or something; indicating the product or raw material with which something is made	Réné comes *from* the Gaspé. Wine is made *from* grapes.
from	indicating the reason for something	The woman cried *from* frustration.
from	used to make a distinction between two things	English is very different *from* French.
of	belonging to somebody or something	He is a friend *of* mine. Please close the lid *of* the box.
of	concerning, relating to, or showing something	This is a photograph *of* my boyfriend. Do you have a map *of* Mexico?
of	indicating what is measured, counted, or contained	We drank a litre *of* wine.
of	used with *some, many, a few*, etc.	Some *of* the students failed the exam. A few *of* us are coming.

Other Prepositional Relationships: Relation, Source, Manner, Possession, Quantity (cont.)		
Preposition	**Uses/Meaning**	**Examples**
with	in the company of someone or something	I took a vacation *with* my husband. Please leave the keys *with* the parking attendant.
with	having or carrying something	The child *with* the red hair is her son. Take the coffee *with* you.
with	indicating the manner or condition	She did her homework *with* care. He was trembling *with* rage.
with	indicating the tool or instrument used	You can see the stars *with* a telescope.
without	not having, not using	No one can live *without* water. Can you see *without* your glasses?

EXERCISE **32.5**

Fill in the blanks with the appropriate prepositions indicating relation, source, manner, possession, or quantity. Then check your answers against ours on page 573.

1. If you want to spend time _____ him, you should know something _____ his past.

2. After spending a day _____ the twins, we recognized that they are very different _____ one another.

3. It was very kind _____ her to take the children _____ her _____ the party.

4. There were lots _____ adults because many _____ the children came _____ their parents.

For ESL Learners: A Review

5. Spanish-speaking emigrants _____ Mexico often find that working in Canada is difficult _____ a good knowledge of English or French.

Go to Web Exercise 32.4

EXERCISE **32.6**

Fill in the blanks with the appropriate prepositions.

1. We leave school _____ 4 p.m. and usually get home _____ 5 p.m.

2. The old lady _____ the attic is a secret _____ you and me.

3. You remind me _____ your mother, who was always very good _____ me.

4. I'll meet you _____ front of the restaurant that is located _____ the corner _____ Princess and Division Streets _____ Kingston.

EXERCISE **32.7**

1. Make sure that you finish this assignment _____ tomorrow.

2. There was a pool _____ oil _____ the car, so we knew that we would have to take it _____ a mechanic _____ repairs.

3. He ran _____ the house, jumped _____ his car, and sped _____ the street right _____ a police car.

EXERCISE **32.8**

1. _____ tonight's performance, drinks will be sold _____ intermission.

2. If you look _____ the painting _____ the wall, you will find a safe _____ a lot _____ money _____ it.

3. My sister got married _____ a nice man _____ June; she had been living _____ him _____ last year.

4. I work _____ 8:00 _____ the morning _____ 8:00 _____ night,

and I am usually exhausted ___ the end ___ that time.

EXERCISE **32.9**

1. We fixed the hole _____ the ceiling _____ duct tape.

2. I would like to stay _____ you _____ the weekend.

3. The child was standing _____ his father and mother.

4. She studied in France _____ a year.

5. Ana has a very large nose _____ a pair of small, close-set eyes. She

wears a lot _____ heavy makeup _____ her face.

6. They told us all _____ their trip _____ Australia _____ their

return _____ Canada.

7. _____ the opposition _____ the neighbours, the Smiths are going to

go ahead and build a fence _____ the two properties.

8. Even if you have been speaking English _____ a long time, it is easy to

make occasional mistakes _____ prepositions.

Go to Web Exercise 32.5

EXERCISE **32.10**

With a partner (or on your own), read through the exercise below and choose
the correct prepositions to go into the blanks below. Compare your answers
with those of another pair of students (or another student). Finally, check your
answers against paragraph 15 of "Crazy English" on page 445. More than one
answer may be acceptable.

Still, you have to marvel _____ the unique lunacy of the English lan-

guage. Prepositions are spectacularly illogical. You can turn a light ____ and

you can turn a light _____, and you can turn a light _____, but you can't

turn a light in; the sun comes _____ and goes _____, but prices go _____ and come _____. English is a gloriously wiggy tongue in which your house can simultaneously burn _____ and burn _____ and your car can slow up and slow down, in which you fill _____ a form by filling _____ a form, in which your alarm clock goes off by going on, in which you are inoculated for measles by being inoculated against measles, in which you add up a column _____ figures by adding them down, and in which you first chop a tree down—and then you chop it up. And why are actors _____ television but _____ a movie?

EXERCISE 32.11

My friend Karl goes _____ school _____ the Scarborough campus _____ the University _____ Toronto. _____ the same time, he works full-time _____ his family's grocery business. The store is _____ the street _____ the campus, so Karl doesn't have to travel very far _____ school and work. He has to leave school _____ 4 p.m. every day so that he can work _____ the counter of the store selling things _____ customers. _____ September, Karl has been studying computer and business courses, and he puts a lot _____ effort _____ his schoolwork. Because he works every night _____ midnight, he does his homework _____ quiet moments _____ the store. _____ his hard work, Karl's family couldn't keep the store going. Karl is working _____ two important goals: he is determined to succeed _____ his studies, and he is equally determined to help his family prosper.

RAPID REVIEW

Test your mastery of grammar in this unit by choosing the correct options in the following essay. Check your answers on pages 573–75.

[1]You probably (*are/should be/have been*) learning English (*in/for/since*) a number of years now. [2]Maybe you've been living and studying in English for (*much/many*) of your life. [3]Yet perhaps you still (*do/have/don't*) not feel entirely confident about your ability to make yourself understood when you're speaking, particularly when you (*are speak/do speak/are speaking*) to a group of people (*at/with/on*) school or work. [4]You are also not always sure what English speakers mean when they speak (*for/to/beside*) you. [5]Are there any practical ways to improve your fluency in spoken English? [6]Yes, there are. [7]Here are (*some of/few/a few*) tips to help you feel more confident when you are speaking and when you are listening.

[8]One good suggestion for someone who (*is speaking/speak/do speak*) English as a secondary language is to s-l-o-w down. [9]Especially if you are presenting in (*0/a/an/the*) academic or professional situation, it's important to remember to speak more slowly than you normally do. [10]Often what makes your speech difficult to understand isn't the pronunciation of specific sounds ("t" versus "th," for instance), but rather (*0/the*) rhythm that is rooted in your first

language and doesn't sound natural to native English speakers. [11]Sometimes your listeners seem (*frustrated/frustrating*) as they listen to your fast speech and can't understand what you are saying. [12]Slow down and pause frequently (*to/at/on*) appropriate places in your speech or presentation; use transition words such as *next*, *then*, and *in conclusion* to help your listener or reader stay (*by/for/on/with*) you.

[13]If you are preparing (*a/an/the/0*) short presentation, keep in mind that spoken language is simpler than written language. [14]Your sentences and vocabulary (*must been/could have been/should be*) relatively simple. [15]Repeat key points, and use the board or cards to present important vocabulary that you think people might not understand. [16]Try to relax as much as possible, smile occasionally, and look (*by/with/at/from*) the people you're speaking to. [17]Eye contact is important and actually helps to communicate your meaning. [18]If (*you looking/look/are look*) at people, you can usually tell when someone doesn't understand you, and you can repeat or clarify the point you are making.

[19]There are also (*a number/number/some*) of ways that you (*shall/must/can*) improve your comprehension of spoken English. [20]Listening to English radio and TV is helpful. [21]Listen to (*interesting/interested*) programs that you already know something about, whether that is sports, news, celebrity gossip, or fashion. [22]Repeat key phrases to practise (*0/a/the*) rhythm of spoken English.

[23]Listen to recorded phone messages; you might even get native-speaker friends to leave (*complicating/complicated*) messages for you so that you can practise understanding what they are saying. [24]Try to navigate through the phone loops of banks, airlines, or utility companies: "Press 6 if you would like to hear about our payment options."

[25]There are (*many/much/a great deal of*) websites designed to help people learn (*0/a/an/the*) English. [26]A site such as the BBC World Service has (*few/many/much*) resources, including audio and video clips that help people improve their (*listening/listened*) comprehension. [27]Of course, you (*have to/must/may*) find that voices on the BBC have what Canadians call a "British accent." [28]But learning to understand many varieties of spoken English is important to your overall mastery (*of/by/for/in*) the language.

[29]Above all, use your English. [30]Keep yourself immersed in the English-speaking world (*within/beneath/around*) you. [31]Engage people in conversation, listen to what they have to say, and ask questions when you need to. [32]Mastering another language (*was being/is/will have been*) a long and arduous task. [33]Nevertheless, time and (*many/some/a lot*) of practice will give you confidence in your speaking and listening skills.

For ESL Learners: A Review

UNIT 7

Readings

MODEL ESSAY: Brian Green, "Career Consciousness"

Russell Wangersky, "Clinging to the Rock"

Angela Long, "I Believe in Deviled Eggs"

Richard Lederer, "Crazy English"

Jeffrey Moussaieff Masson, "Dear Dad"

Tenzin Gyatso, the 14th Dalai Lama, "Many Faiths, One Truth"

Sun-Kyung Yi, "An Immigrant's Split Personality"

Gabor Maté, "Embraced by the Needle"

Lawrence Hill, "Don't Call Me That Word"

Margaret Wente, "The New Heavyweight Champions"

DOCUMENTED ESSAY: Nell Waldman, "The Second-Language Struggle" (MLA Documentation Style)

Nell Waldman, "The Second-Language Struggle" (APA Documentation Style)

CAREER CONSCIOUSNESS

Brian Green

1   A career can be defined as the employment you prepare for during the first quarter of your life, engage in during the best years of your life, and reap the rewards from when you are least able to enjoy them. Behind the cynicism of this observation lies an important truth: choosing a life's vocation is not a decision to be taken lightly. To justify the time and effort you will invest in your career, it should be stimulating, rewarding, and productive. The better you know yourself, the more likely you are to choose a career you can live with happily.

2   What would a stimulating career be like? Picture yourself getting up in the morning and looking forward to your day with eager anticipation. This may not be the popular image of most jobs, but it is one that can be achieved. Most people participate in leisure activities that they find interesting, even energizing. There's no rule that says you can't be as enthusiastic about your work as you are about your play. Many successful people have turned their interests into careers, thus getting paid for what they like to do. Many career professionals in the arts, for example, make their living by doing what they feel they were born to do: write, act, paint, dance, play or compose music, sing, design, or sculpt. Clive Beddoe loved to fly, and from that passion grew his career as a bush pilot and, later, his founding of one of Canada's most successful airlines, WestJet. Of course, it is not always possible to turn a passion into a career, but to deny what excites you, to relegate it to after-hours activities without trying to incorporate it into your working life, means you will spend most of your life wishing you were doing something else.

3   If your career is stimulating, then chances are good that it can also be rewarding. A good career offers two kinds of rewards: financial and emotional. Rewarding work doesn't just happen; it's something you need to plan for. The first and most important step is to know yourself. Only if you know who you are and what you need to be happy can you consciously seek out career experiences that will bring you satisfaction and steer clear of those that will annoy or stress you. Are you genuinely ambitious, or is power something you seek because you think it is expected of you? The pursuit of status and a high salary brings some people pure pleasure. Many people, however, find leadership positions excruciatingly stressful. Career enjoyment depends to some extent on whether or not you are successful, and success is a state of mind. Consider two graduates from the same college program. One is a technician in a small-town television station who loves his work, takes pride in keeping the station on the air, and delights in raising his family in a community where he is involved in volunteer activities ranging from sports to firefighting. The other is a news director at one of Canada's major television networks. Her work is highly stressful, full of risks, and continually scrutinized by viewers, competitors, and her supervisors.

She thrives on the adrenaline rush of nightly production, and loves the big-city life, the financial rewards of her position, and the national recognition she receives. Which graduate is "successful"? Certainly, both feel their careers are rewarding, according to their individual definitions of the term.

4   A job at which you do not feel useful cannot be either rewarding or stimulating for very long. It is human nature to want to contribute, to feel that your efforts make a difference. Camaraderie with fellow workers, a pleasant daily routine, even a good salary cannot compensate in the long run for a sense that your work is meaningless or unappreciated. Sadly, some people spend their entire working lives at jobs in which their contribution is so insignificant that their absence would scarcely be noticed. Everyone knows people who boast about reading paperback novels on the job, and others who sleep through their night shift so they can spend their days fishing or golfing. Is this the way you want to spend 45 years of your life? All the paperbacks and the rounds of golf don't add up to much without a sense that you are doing something worthwhile. It may take a few years, but when it comes, the realization that your work lacks meaning is soul-destroying.

5   It is not easy to find a career that provides stimulating, enjoyable, and meaningful work. Understanding yourself—your interests, needs, values, and goals—is an essential first step. Making long-term decisions consistent with your values and goals is the difficult second step. Too many people spend their lives in careers that make them miserable because they allow themselves to be governed by parents, friends, or simple inertia. Finally, once you have launched your career, never rest. Actively seek challenges and opportunities that stimulate you. Relish the rewards of meeting those challenges, being productive, and doing your job well. Continually strive to improve, not for the sake of your employer, but for your own sake. Your career will occupy three-quarters of your life, so make the most of it!

QUESTIONS FOR DISCUSSION

1. What kind of attention-getter does the writer use to open his essay? (See pages 305–6 for a discussion of attention-getters.)
2. In paragraph 5, identify the two main parts of the author's conclusion: the summary of the essay's main points and the memorable statement. What kind of memorable statement has he used? Is it appropriate for this essay? Why?
3. In what order has Green arranged his points: chronological, logically linked, climactic, or random? (See pages 271–72 for a discussion of essay organization.) Can you rearrange the points without diminishing the effectiveness of the piece?
4. How do the topic sentences of paragraphs 2, 3, and 4 contribute to the coherence of this essay? Identify three or four transitional words or phrases the author has used within his paragraphs to make them read smoothly.

SUGGESTIONS FOR WRITING

1. How would you define a satisfying career?
2. Who is the most satisfied (dissatisfied) worker you know? What makes him/her happy (unhappy) with the job?
3. If you had enough money invested so that you could live comfortably without paid employment, would you be happy? Why or why not?

CLINGING TO THE ROCK

Russell Wangersky

1   There's life yet in gritty, tightly knit outport communities. In Reefs Harbour on Newfoundland's Northern Peninsula, a handful of fishing sheds, their sides weathered to a uniform silver-grey, stand like forgotten teeth on a half-buried lower jaw. Lobster markers hang from coils of yellow rope inside their dusty windows. A single boat curves in towards the harbour, its engine the only sound in the still air, a solitary fisherman at the stern. Every few seconds, a small wave breaks over the shoals in the harbour, loud enough to drown out the vessel's approach. You can't shake the feeling that Reefs Harbour is asleep, asleep like Rip Van Winkle, breathing slowly through a nap that could last for years.

2   Up and down the island's west coast, with the end of the lobster season, traps are standing in regimented rectangular stacks deep back in the woods, hunkered down as if already waiting for winter—even though it's only early August. In North Harbour, St. Mary's Bay, the small convenience store has closed, the sign gone, and a basketball net is put up in the parking space. The store used to be connected to a family home looking out over the wide, flat bay. Coming in the door at suppertime, you'd smell cabbage and gravy; you'd have to wait a few minutes while someone pushed back from the table and came into the store to ring in your chips and Coke.

3   It's not just North Harbour: it's Sandringham, on the Eastport peninsula nearing central Newfoundland, and Swift Current on the south-reaching Burin Peninsula and many, many more. With shrinking populations in communities, the stores, often known as the "Groc and Conf"—shorthand for their wares in groceries and confectionery—have smaller and smaller margins, their owners working more hours because they can't afford staff. So the signs come down and the inventory goes back. But when it comes to forecasting the demise of outport Newfoundland, you'll meet people in a hurry to tell you that rumours of its death have been greatly exaggerated.

4   Where and when there's a fishery—less frequently now that there's so little cod—it works with such frenzy that people who have never seen it can hardly

---

Reprinted by permission of the author.

imagine. Big fish trucks with grey, yellow and blue fish boxes piled along their flat backs roar down rural roads belching black diesel smoke, heavy with loads of capelin or snow crab. Plants race through shrimp hauls, trying to keep up with the vessels, intent on catching their share before quotas are reached. There are long hours and multiple shifts, with an aging, diminishing workforce.

5   Comment about the struggle of keeping a fish processing plant going, and up above the fine grey sand of the beach at Eastport, a businessman will make a point of almost physically turning you towards the speck in the distance to point out the small town of Salvage and its vibrant fish plant. Go to the town on a Sunday and it's hard to keep from being hit by a forklift on the main street. Comment on the unworldly quiet of the empty side streets in Cape Broyle, just south of St. John's, and you'll get an angry retort telling you that three babies have been born in the last few weeks.

6   What no one should forget is that there are still thousands of outport Newfoundlanders, and these are resilient, hard-working people. It's just that there are fewer of them. Scores have left for greener pastures, to the point that the number of school-aged children in the province has fallen by 30 per cent— or 27,000—in the past decade alone. The stories the travellers send back about drugs and violence and gangs are sometimes daunting, but money can provide an irresistible lure.

7   Outport communities are shaking themselves like a dog, shaking themselves into a new arrangement and then lying down again, changed in fundamental ways. But giving up doesn't really seem to be in their vocabulary: communities are driven, as always, by their people.

8   There are more and more tourists along the Northern Peninsula and across the Avalon, tourists struck by the bare vistas and raw, rugged beauty of the place. If stunning aesthetics are the skin that covers Newfoundland and Labrador, then its people are the sinew. Sometimes they even look the part, strung together with twine and leather, their faces the image of being the next best thing to indestructible.

9   Without cod and with fewer people, the outports are changing forever. Not a requiem yet, perhaps—but still a different, desperate song, sung by fewer voices. They'll admit that in an honest instant at the convenience store—so long as you find one that's still open.

QUESTIONS FOR DISCUSSION

1. Identify on Google Earth or another map several of the Newfoundland towns that Wangersky describes. Do these places have anything in common?

2. What is the main industry in these communities? What is happening to that industry? Identify some of the examples Wangersky uses to communicate the change and its effects to his readers.

3. What is happening to the population of the outport communities? How does Wangersky characterize the people who still live in this part of Newfoundland?

4. Do you think that Wangersky is optimistic or pessimistic about the future of the outport communities? Identify details from the essay to support your view of his opinion.

SUGGESTIONS FOR WRITING

1. Describe a place that is familiar to you: a town, a community, a neighbourhood, even a local hangout. Use enough examples to show how the place defines its inhabitants and the inhabitants reflect the place.

2. What happens to a community when large numbers of its people leave for economic reasons? Who goes and who remains behind? What kind of future is there for such a place?

I BELIEVE IN DEVILED EGGS

Angela Long

1   I confess, I don't know much about religion. I grew up Protestant with a grandfather who was a minister, and I still don't know much about religion. I stopped going to church at the age of 12 when my grandfather died, and up until that point, religion was waking up every Sunday morning to get ready for the 10 o'clock service.

2   Religion was my mother delivering a freshly ironed dress to my bedroom door, and the smell of shoe polish in the kitchen. It was something that interfered with watching cartoons. It was a dark, windowless room in a basement where preteens drew scenes from the life of Jesus with crayons on paper plates. I didn't know much about Jesus except that I could never get his beard right.

3   Religion was the Banquet Burger Combo afterward at the Bo-Peep Restaurant, sometimes accompanied by red Jell-O, sometimes chocolate pudding. It was begging my parents to ask the Bo-Peep hostess if we could sit in the banquet section where the chairs were padded with red faux leather attached by brass studs, the walls covered with dark wood paneling and the stern expressions of British dukes in full hunting regalia.

4   Religion was picnics at the park—deviled eggs, macaroni salad, potato salad, and Dixie Lee chicken. It was escaping the adults when the food was packed away and exploring the perimeters of the forestry station's "experimental forest," a thicket of scraggly trees that invited games of Truth or Dare. Religion was Grandpa giving my two older brothers a dollar to go to the arcade and telling me to help Grandma in the kitchen.

Reprinted by permission of the author. First published in *Geez* magazine, Summer 2008.

5   I never quite realized that only the kneeling, praying, and hymn singing counted as actual religion. I thought they were just things that we did before the real religion—the business of living—began. Don't get me wrong, I knew they were important; I did them voluntarily, with relish even. I even had a favorite hymn—"Onward, Christian Soldiers"—that I'd sing while I walked to school. But the actual words of the hymns were as meaningless to me as my grandfather's sermons. I looked for a catchy tune underlying the words in both. I discovered it by watching the stained-glass windows blaze in the late morning sunshine. I saw how the artist had perfected the curls of a sheep's wool, the gentle gaze of a cow. I discovered it observing the actions of the congregation: the nose picking, the napping, the fondling couples. It was during these moments that I found enlightenment.

6   I wasn't aware that my ignorance of the true meaning of religion was disrespectful or irreverent. The only time I seemed to breach the contract I apparently signed with my baptism was when my grandfather scolded me for exclaiming something remotely blasphemous ("Holy cow!") or too close to the Lord's name ("Geez!"). If you had asked my 12-year-old self if I believed in God, I would have replied yes without a moment's hesitation. Of course I believed in God. At that time, I believed in everything.

7   I especially believed in Sunday—those spring Sundays when crocus shoots appeared, robins pecked at ground still damp from snowmelt, and the scent of rural Ontario filled the air. I believed in the look on my mother's face when I walked down the carpeted stairs in something other than corduroys and a sweatshirt. I believed in the hostess at Bo-Peep as she lifted the barrier to the banquet room and laid five heavy faux-leather-bound menus, one by one, upon the round table. I believed in sitting there, uncomfortable in my dress, passing around the ketchup and not wanting to be anywhere else. And when my older brother, after a week of torturing me in a subtle, big-brotherly fashion, laid his prized slice of dill pickle on the edge of my plate, like an offering, I even believed in miracles.

QUESTIONS FOR DISCUSSION

1. Highlight descriptive details from the essay that appeal to the different senses: sight, smell, touch, sound, taste.
2. What did religion mean to the author when she was a child? What did it have to do with family connections?
3. Yes or no: the author of "I Believe in Deviled Eggs" is a religious person. Why or why not? Support your opinion with details from the essay.

SUGGESTIONS FOR WRITING

1. Would you raise (or are you raising) a child to believe in and practise a particular religion? Why or why not?

2. Describe a specific ritual (religious, family, or traditional) that had significance to you when you were a child. Choose details that communicate the reasons the ritual was so meaningful to you.

CRAZY ENGLISH

Adapted from Richard Lederer's "English Is a Crazy Language"

1   English is the most widely spoken language in the history of our planet, used in some way by at least one out of every seven human beings around the globe. Half of the world's books are written in English, and the majority of international telephone calls are made in English. Sixty percent of the world's radio programs are beamed in English, and more than 70 percent of international mail is written and addressed in English. Eighty percent of all computer texts, including all web sites, are stored in English.

2   English has acquired the largest vocabulary of all the world's languages, perhaps as many as two million words, and has generated one of the noblest bodies of literature in the annals of the human race. Nonetheless, it is now time to face the fact that English is a crazy language—the most loopy and wiggy of all tongues:

In what other language do people drive in a parkway and park in a driveway?

In what other language do people play at a recital and recite at a play?

Why does night fall but never break and day break but never fall?

Why is it that when we transport something by car, it's called *a shipment*, but when we transport something by ship, it's called *cargo*?

Why do we pack suits in a garment bag and garments in a suitcase?

Why do we call it *newsprint* when it contains no printing, but when we put print on it, we call it a *newspaper*?

Why are people who ride motorcycles called *bikers* and people who ride bikes called *cyclists*?

Why—in our crazy language—can your nose run and your feet smell?

3   Language is like the air we breathe. It's invisible, inescapable, and indispensable, and we take it for granted. But when we take the time to step back and explore the paradoxes and vagaries of English, we find that hot dogs can be cold, darkrooms can be lit, homework can be done in school, nightmares can take place in broad daylight while morning sickness and daydreaming can take place at night, tomboys are girls and midwives can be men, hours—especially happy hours and rush hours—often last longer than sixty minutes, quicksand

---

Reprinted by permission of the author. First published in *Crazy English* (Pocketbooks 1998).

works *very* slowly, boxing rings are square, silverware and glasses can be made of plastic and tablecloths of paper, most telephones are dialed by being punched (or pushed), and most bathrooms don't have any baths in them. In fact, a dog can go to the bathroom under a tree—no bath, no room; it's still going to the bathroom. And doesn't it seem a little bizarre that we go to the bathroom in order to go to the bathroom?

4   Sometimes you have to believe that all English speakers should be committed to an asylum for the verbally insane:

In what other language do they call the third hand on the clock the second hand?

Why do they call them *apartments* when they're all together?

Why do we call them *buildings* when they're already built?

Why is it called a *TV set* when you get only one?

Why do they call food servers *waiters*, when it's the customers who do the waiting?

Why is *phonetic* not spelled phonetically? Why is it so hard to remember how to spell *mnemonic*? Why doesn't *onomatopoeia* sound like what it is? Why is the word *abbreviation* so long? Why does the word *monosyllabic* consist of five syllables? Why is there no synonym for *synonym* or *thesaurus*? And why, pray tell, does *lisp* have an *s* in it?

5   English is crazy.

6   If adults commit adultery, do infants commit infantry? If olive oil is made from olives and vegetable oil from vegetables, what do they make baby oil from? If a vegetarian eats vegetables, what does a humanitarian consume? If a television is a TV, shouldn't a telephone be a TP? If a pronoun replaces a noun, does a proverb replace a verb? If *pro* and *con* are opposites, is *congress* the opposite of *progress*?

7   A writer is someone who writes, and a stinger is something that stings. But fingers don't fing, grocers don't groce, hammers don't ham, humdingers don't humding, ushers don't ush, and haberdashers do not haberdash.

8   If the plural of *tooth* is *teeth*, shouldn't the plural of *booth* be *beeth?* One goose, two geese—so one moose, two meese? One index, two indices—one Kleenex, two Kleenices? Why do we wear a pair of pants but, except on very cold days, not a pair of shirts? How can men wear a bathing suit and bathing trunks at the same time? Why is *brassiere* singular but *panties* plural? Why is there a team in Toronto called the *Maple Leafs* and another in Minnesota called the *Timberwolves*?

9   English verbs are crazily unpredictable. If people ring a bell today and rang a bell yesterday, why don't we say that they flang a ball? If they wrote a letter, perhaps they also bote their tongue. If the teacher taught, why isn't it also true that the preacher praught? Why is it that the sun shone yesterday while I shined

my shoes, that I treaded water and then trod on the beach, and that I flew out to see a World Series game in which my favorite player flied out?

10 *A slim chance* and *a fat chance* are the same, as are *a caregiver* and *a caretaker*, *a bad licking* and *a good licking*, and "What's going on?" and "What's coming off?" But *a wise man* and *a wise guy* are opposites. How can *sharp speech* and *blunt speech* be the same and *quite a lot* and *quite a few* the same, while *overlook* and *oversee* are opposites? How can the weather be *hot as hell* one day and *cold as hell* the next?

11 Small wonder that we English users are constantly standing meaning on its head. If *button* and *unbutton* and *tie* and *untie* are opposites, why are *loosen* and *unloosen* and *ravel* and *unravel* the same? If *bad* is the opposite of *good*, *hard* the opposite of *soft*, and *up* the opposite of *down*, why are *badly* and *goodly*, *hardly* and *softly*, and *upright* and *downright* not opposing pairs? If harmless actions are the opposite of harmful actions, why are shameful and shameless behavior the same and pricey objects less expensive than priceless ones? If appropriate and inappropriate remarks and passable and impassable mountain trails are opposites, why are flammable and inflammable materials, heritable and inheritable property, and passive and impassive people the same? How can valuable objects be less valuable than invaluable ones? If *uplift* is the same as *lift up*, why are *upset* and *set up* opposite in meaning? Why are *pertinent* and *impertinent*, *canny* and *uncanny*, and *famous* and *infamous* neither opposites nor the same?

12 English is a crazy language. Let's look at a number of familiar English words and phrases that turn out to mean the opposite or something very different from what we think they mean:

A non-stop flight. Never get on one of these. You'll never get down.

A near miss. *A near miss* is, in reality, a collision. A close call is actually *a near hit*.

A hot water heater. Who heats hot water? This is similar to garbage disposal. Actually, the stuff isn't garbage until after you dispose of it.

A hot cup of coffee. Here again the English language gets us in hot water. Who cares if the cup is hot? Surely we mean *a cup of hot coffee.*

Doughnut holes. Aren't those little treats really *doughnut balls?* The hole is what's left in the original doughnut. (And if a candy cane is shaped like a cane, why isn't a doughnut shaped like a nut?)

A one-night stand. So who's standing? Similarly, to sleep with someone. Who's sleeping?

It's neither here nor there. Then where is it?

Daylight saving time. Not a single second of daylight is saved by this ploy.

Preplan, preboard, preheat, and prerecord. Aren't people who do this simply planning, boarding, heating, and recording? Who needs the pretentious prefix? I have even seen shows "prerecorded before a live audience," certainly preferable to prerecording before a dead audience.

13   Because we speakers and writers of English seem to have our heads screwed on backwards, we constantly misperceive our bodies, often saying just the opposite of what we mean:

Watch your head. I keep seeing this sign on low doorways, but I haven't figured out how to follow the instructions. Trying to watch your head is like trying to bite your teeth.

They're head over heels in love. That's nice, but all of us do almost everything *head over heels*. If we are trying to create an image of people doing cartwheels and somersaults, why don't we say, *They're heels over head in love*?

He's got a good head on his shoulders. What? He doesn't have a neck?

Put your best foot forward. Now let's see ... We have a good foot and a better foot—but we don't have a third—and best—foot. It's our better foot we want to put forward.

Keep a stiff upper lip. When we are disappointed or afraid, which lip do we try to control? The lower lip, of course, is the one we are trying to keep from quivering.

I'm speaking tongue in cheek. So how can anyone understand you?

They did it ass backwards. What's wrong with that? We do *everything* ass backwards.

14   In the rigid expressions that wear tonal grooves in the record of our language, *beck* can appear only with *call*, *cranny* with *nook*, *hue* with *cry*, *main* with *might*, *aback* with *taken*, *caboodle* with *kit*, and *spick* and *span* only with each other. Why must all shrifts be short, all lucre filthy, all bystanders innocent, and all bedfellows strange? I'm convinced that some shrifts are lengthy and that some lucre is squeaky-clean, and I've certainly met guilty bystanders and perfectly normal bedfellows.

15   Still, you have to marvel at the unique lunacy of the English language. Prepositions are spectacularly illogical. You can turn a light on and you can turn a light off, and you can turn a light out, but you can't turn a light in; the sun comes up and goes down, but prices go up and come down. English is a gloriously wiggy tongue in which your house can simultaneously burn up and burn down and your car can slow up and slow down, in which you fill in a form by filling out a form, in which your alarm clock goes off by going on, in which you are inoculated for measles by being inoculated against measles, in which you add up a column of figures by adding them down, and in which you first chop a tree down—and then you chop it up. And why are actors *on* television but *in* a movie?

16   If the truth be told, all languages are a little crazy; they contradict themselves. That's because language is invented by boys and girls and men and women, not created by computers. Language reflects the creative and fearful asymmetry of the human race, which, of course, isn't really a race at all.

QUESTIONS FOR DISCUSSION

1. What introduction strategy does the author use in paragraphs 1 and 2?
2. Why does the author feel that the English language is "crazy"?
3. A *paradox* is a statement that seems logical but actually contradicts itself. Paragraphs 3 and 4 cite examples of common paradoxes in the English language. Identify three or four of your favourites. Can you think of other paradoxical phrases that Lederer hasn't included?
4. What concluding strategy does the author of "Crazy English" employ? Can you think of a more effective strategy?

SUGGESTIONS FOR WRITING

1. Write brief definitions of five of the idiomatic expressions used in paragraph 15.
2. Do you think the author *really* believes that English is crazy, "wiggy," or insane? Why does he repeat this point throughout his essay? What does he think about people who work hard to master the English language?

DEAR DAD

Jeffrey Moussaieff Masson

1   One reason that so many of us are fascinated by penguins is that they resemble us. They walk upright, the way we do, and, like us, they are notoriously curious creatures. No doubt this accounts for our fondness for cartoon images of penguins dressed up at crowded parties, but as fathers, penguins are our superiors.

2   Unlike mammals, male birds can experience pregnancy as an intimate matter, with the father in many species helping to sit (brood) the egg. After all, a male can brood an egg as well as a female can. But in no other species does it reach this extreme.

3   The emperors usually wait for good weather to copulate, any time between April 10 and June 6. They separate themselves somewhat from the rest of the colony and face each other, remaining still for a time. Then the male bends his head, contracts his abdomen, and shows the female the spot on his belly where he has a flap of skin that serves as a kind of pouch for the egg and baby chick. This stimulates the female to do the same. Their heads touch, and the male bends his head down to touch the female's pouch. Both begin to tremble visibly. Then the female lies face down on the ice, partially spreads her wings and opens her legs. The male climbs onto her back and they mate for 10 to 30 seconds.

Reprinted by permission of the author.

4   They stay together afterward constantly, leaning against one another when they are standing up, or if they lie down, the female will glide her head under that of her mate. About a month later, between May 1 and June 12, the female lays a single greenish-white egg. French researchers noted that the annual dates on which the colony's first egg was laid varied by only eight days in 16 years of observation. Weighing almost a pound [.45 kilograms], and measuring up to 131 millimetres long and 86 millimetres wide, this is one of the largest eggs of any bird. The male stays by the female's side, his eyes fixed on her pouch. As soon as he sees the egg, he sings a variation of what has been called the "ecstatic" display by early observers, and she too takes up the melody.

5   She catches the egg with her wings before it touches the ice and places it on her feet. Both penguins then sing in unison, staring at the egg for up to an hour. The female then slowly walks around the male, who gently touches the egg on her feet with his beak, making soft groans, his whole body trembling. He shows the female his pouch. Gently she puts the egg down on the ice and just as gently he rolls it with his beak between his large, black, powerfully clawed feathered feet, and then, with great difficulty, hoists the egg onto the surface of his feet. He rests back on his heels so that his feet make the least contact with the ice. The transfer of the egg is a delicate operation. If it falls on the ice and rolls away, it can freeze in minutes or it might even be stolen. If it is snatched away by a female penguin who failed to find a mate, its chances of survival are slight because the intruder will eventually abandon the egg, since she has no mate to relieve her.

6   With the egg transfer successfully completed, the happy couple both sing. The male parades about in front of the female, showing her his pouch with the egg inside. This thick fold, densely feathered on the outside and bare inside, now completely covers the egg and keeps it at about 95 degrees Fahrenheit, even when the temperature falls to 95 degrees below zero.

7   The female begins to back away, each time a little farther. He tries to follow her, but it is hard, since he is balancing the egg. Suddenly she is gone, moving purposefully toward the open sea. She is joined by the other females in the colony, who, by the end of May or June, have all left for the ocean almost 100 kilometres away. The females have fasted for nearly a month and a half, and have lost anywhere between 17 to 30 per cent of their total weight. They are in urgent need of food.

8   The female must renew her strength and vitality so that she can return with food for her chick. Going to the sea, she takes the shortest route to reach a polynya (open water surrounded by ice). Penguins appear to be able to navigate by the reflection of the clouds on the water, using what has been called a "water sky."

9   The male penguin, who has also been fasting, is now left with the egg balanced on his feet. The first egg was laid on the first of May; a chick will emerge in August. Since the seasons are reversed south of the equator, full winter has

arrived, with many violent blizzards and the lowest temperatures of the year. Emperor penguins are well adapted to the almost unimaginable cold of these 24-hour Antarctic nights: Their plumage is waterproof, windproof, flexible and renewed annually. They may not need tents, but as soon as the bad weather starts, generally in June, the males need some protection from the bitter cold, and nearly all of them find it by forming a *tortue*, which is a throng of very densely packed penguins. When the storms come they move in close to one another, shoulder to shoulder, and form a circle. The middle of the tortue is unusually warm and one would think that every penguin fights to be at the epi-centre of warmth. But in fact what looks like an immobile mass is really a very slowly revolving spiral. The constantly shifting formation is such that every pen-guin, all the while balancing that single precious egg on his feet, eventually winds up in the middle of the tortue, only to find himself later at the periphery.

10   What early French explorers noticed during the two- to three-month incu-bation period is an almost preternatural calm among the males. This is no doubt necessitated by the long fast that is ahead of them. Many of them have already fasted, like the females, for two months or more, and must now face another two months of fasting. And moving about with an egg balanced on one's feet is difficult at the best of times.

11   The only time a father will abandon an egg is if he has reached the maximum limit of his physiological ability to fast, and would die if he did not seek food. Not a small number of eggs are left for this reason, and it would seem that in each case the female is late in returning.

12   In July or August, after being gone for almost three months, the female emperor returns from the sea, singing as she penetrates various groups of birds, searching for her mate and her chick or egg. The males do not move, but make small peeping noises. When she finds her partner, she sings, she makes little dance steps, then she goes quiet and both birds can remain immobile for up to 10 minutes. Then they begin to move around one another. The female fixes her eyes on the incubatory pouch of her partner, while her excitement grows vis-ibly. Finally, if it is the right bird, the male allows the egg to fall gently to the ice, whereupon the female takes it and then turns her back to the male, to whom, after a final duet, she becomes completely indifferent. The male becomes increasingly irritated, stares at his empty pouch, pecks at it with his beak, lifts up his head, groans, and then pecks the female. She shows no further interest in him and eventually he leaves for the open sea, to break his long fast. The whole affair has lasted about 80 minutes....

13   The miracle is that the mothers usually return on the day their chicks hatch. How is it, one wonders, that the female emperor penguin is able to return just in time for the birth of her chick? As Alexander Skutch notes in his wonderful book, *The Minds of Birds*, it is improbable that she has consciously counted the 63 days or whatever the exact number is between the laying of her egg and the

hatching of her chick. "Some subconscious process, physiological or mental, was evidently summing the days to prompt the birds to start homeward when the proper number had elapsed."

14   If the egg has hatched before her arrival and the male already has a chick between his legs, the female is even more excited to hear it peep, and quickly removes it from the male. She immediately regurgitates food to the chick. If she is late in coming, the male, in spite of his near starvation, has a final resource: He regurgitates into the beak of his peeping newborn a substance known as penguin milk, similar to pigeon's milk, or crop milk, which is secreted from the lining of his esophagus. The secretion is remarkably rich, containing essential amino acids, much like the milk of marine mammals such as seals and whales. These feedings allow the young birds to survive for up to two weeks after hatching. Many of these males have now fasted for four and a half months, and have lost up to half of their body weight. It is a sight to see the well-nourished, sleek, brilliantly feathered, healthy-looking females arrive, and the emaciated, dirty, tired males leave.

15   How difficult it is for us to understand the emotions involved in these events. Yet it is hard to resist the anthropomorphic urge. Obviously the male emperor is aware of the loss of what has, after all, been almost a part of his body for two to three months. Is he disappointed, bewildered, relieved, or are his feelings so remote from our own (not inferior, mind you, just different) that we cannot imagine them? We would groan, too, under such circumstances, but the meaning of a penguin's groan is still opaque to us. Yet we, too, are fathers and mothers with babies to protect and comfort, negotiating meals and absences and other obligations, just like our Antarctic cousins. Sometimes, when we are overwhelmed by an emotion, we are hard-pressed to express ourselves. If penguin fathers could speak about this moment in their lives, perhaps they would be at a similar loss for words. Perhaps the songs and groans of the male penguin are all the expression they need.

QUESTIONS FOR DISCUSSION

1. What kind of attention-getter does the author use in the introduction (paragraphs 1 and 2)? (See pages 305–6 for a discussion of attention-getters.)
2. Masson's thesis is implied but not stated in this essay. In your own words, write a thesis statement for this piece.
3. Which paragraphs are developed primarily by means of numerical facts and statistics? Why is this an effective way of supporting the main ideas of these paragraphs?
4. The language of this essay combines scientific terms with words and phrases associated with human emotions, such as "happy couple" in paragraph 6 and "increasingly irritated" in paragraph 12. That is, Masson implies similarities between penguins and humans. Why do you think he

chooses these kinds of phrases? What does the word *anthropomorphic* in paragraph 15 mean?

5. What is the author's attitude toward the emperor penguins? Identify three or four examples to support your opinion.

SUGGESTIONS FOR WRITING

1. Write an essay about a father's role in his young child's life (birth to 24 months). What are the essential responsibilities of a father?

2. Write an essay about being a caregiver. Describe a situation in which you have cared for someone on an ongoing basis. How did you feel about the responsibilities you assumed?

MANY FAITHS, ONE TRUTH

Tenzin Gyatso, the 14th Dalai Lama

1   When I was a boy in Tibet, I felt that my own Buddhist religion must be the best—and that other faiths were somehow inferior. Now I see how naïve I was, and how dangerous the extremes of religious intolerance can be today.

2   Though intolerance may be as old as religion itself, we still see vigorous signs of its virulence. In Europe, there are intense debates about newcomers wearing veils or wanting to erect minarets and episodes of violence against Muslim immigrants. Radical atheists issue blanket condemnations of those who hold to religious beliefs. In the Middle East, the flames of war are fanned by hatred of those who adhere to a different faith.

3   Such tensions are likely to increase as the world becomes more interconnected and cultures, peoples and religions become ever more entwined. The pressure this creates tests more than our tolerance—it demands that we promote peaceful coexistence and understanding across boundaries.

4   Granted, every religion has a sense of exclusivity as part of its core identity. Even so, I believe there is genuine potential for mutual understanding. While preserving faith toward one's own tradition, one can respect, admire and appreciate other traditions.

5   An early eye-opener for me was my meeting with the Trappist monk Thomas Merton in India shortly before his untimely death in 1968. Merton told me he could be perfectly faithful to Christianity, yet learn in depth from other religions

like Buddhism. The same is true for me as an ardent Buddhist learning from the world's other great religions.

6   A main point in my discussion with Merton was how central compassion was to the message of both Christianity and Buddhism. In my readings of the New Testament, I find myself inspired by Jesus' acts of compassion. His miracle of the loaves and fishes, his healing and his teaching are all motivated by the desire to relieve suffering.

7   I'm a firm believer in the power of personal contact to bridge differences, so I've long been drawn to dialogues with people of other religious outlooks. The focus on compassion that Merton and I observed in our two religions strikes me as a strong unifying thread among all the major faiths. And these days we need to highlight what unifies us.

8   Take Judaism, for instance. I first visited a synagogue in Cochin, India, in 1965, and have met with many rabbis over the years. I remember vividly the rabbi in the Netherlands who told me about the Holocaust with such intensity that we were both in tears. And I've learned how the Talmud and the Bible repeat the theme of compassion, as in the passage in Leviticus that admonishes, "Love your neighbor as yourself."

9   In my many encounters with Hindu scholars in India, I've come to see the centrality of selfless compassion in Hinduism too—as expressed, for instance, in the Bhagavad Gita, which praises those who "delight in the welfare of all beings." I'm moved by the ways this value has been expressed in the life of great beings like Mahatma Gandhi, or the lesser-known Baba Amte, who founded a leper colony not far from a Tibetan settlement in Maharashtra State in India. There he fed and sheltered lepers who were otherwise shunned. When I received my Nobel Peace Prize, I made a donation to his colony.

10   Compassion is equally important in Islam—and recognizing that has become crucial in the years since Sept. 11, especially in answering those who paint Islam as a militant faith. On the first anniversary of 9/11, I spoke at the National Cathedral in Washington, pleading that we not blindly follow the lead of some in the news media and let the violent acts of a few individuals define an entire religion.

11   Let me tell you about the Islam I know. Tibet has had an Islamic community for around 400 years, although my richest contacts with Islam have been in India, which has the world's second-largest Muslim population. An imam in Ladakh once told me that a true Muslim should love and respect all of Allah's creatures. And in my understanding, Islam enshrines compassion as a core spiritual principle, reflected in the very name of God, the "Compassionate and Merciful," that appears at the beginning of virtually each chapter of the Koran.

12   Finding common ground among faiths can help us bridge needless divides at a time when unified action is more crucial than ever. As a species, we must embrace the oneness of humanity as we face global issues like pandemics,

economic crises and ecological disaster. At that scale, our response must be as one.

13   Harmony among the major faiths has become an essential ingredient of peaceful coexistence in our world. From this perspective, mutual understanding among these traditions is not merely the business of religious believers—it matters for the welfare of humanity as a whole.

QUESTIONS FOR DISCUSSION

1. What did the Dalai Lama think about his religion when he was a boy in Tibet? How did his view change as he experienced more of the world?
2. Into what categories does the Dalai Lama classify the major religions of the world? In which paragraphs? What does he see as the "unifying thread" (paragraph 7) that they all share?
3. What are the challenges that face everyone in the world, according to the Dalai Lama? What does he think is essential if they are ever to be resolved?

SUGGESTIONS FOR WRITING

1. If you are a person of faith, explain the significance of compassion in your religion.
2. Do you think that in order to feel compassion for others a person must be connected to one of the world's major religions?

AN IMMIGRANT'S SPLIT PERSONALITY

Sun-Kyung Yi

1   I am Korean-Canadian. But the hyphen often snaps in two, obliging me to choose to act as either a Korean or a Canadian, depending on where I am and who I'm with.

2   When I was younger, toying with the idea of entertaining two separate identities was a real treat, like a secret game for which no one knew the rules but me. I was known as Angela to the outside world, and as Sun-Kyung at home. I ate bologna sandwiches in the school lunchroom and rice and kimchee for dinner. I chatted about teen idols and giggled with my girlfriends during my classes, and ambitiously practiced piano and studied in the evenings, planning to become a doctor when I grew up. I waved hellos and goodbyes to my teachers, but bowed to my parents' friends visiting our home. I could also look

Yi, Sun-Kyung. "An Immigrant's Split Personality." *Globe and Mail* 12 April 1992. Print. Reprinted by permission of Sun-Kyung Yi.

straight in the eyes of my teachers and friends and talk frankly with them instead of staring at my feet with my mouth shut when Koreans talked to me. Going outside the home meant I was able to relax from the constraints of my cultural conditioning, until I walked back in the door and had to return to being an obedient and submissive daughter.

3 The game soon ended when I realized that it had become a way of life, that I couldn't change the rules without disappointing my parents and questioning all the cultural implications and consequences that came with being a hyphenated Canadian.

4 Many have tried to convince me that I am a Canadian, like all other immigrants in the country, but those same people also ask me which country I came from with great curiosity, following with questions about the type of food I ate and the language I spoke. It's difficult to feel a sense of belonging and acceptance when you are regarded as "one of them." "Those Koreans, they work hard…. You must be fantastic at math and science." (No.) "Do your parents own a corner store?" (No.)

5 Koreans and Canadians just can't seem to merge into "us" and "we."

6 Some people advised me that I should just take the best of both worlds and disregard the rest. That's ideal, but unrealistic when my old culture demands a complete conformity with very little room to manoeuvre for new and different ideas.

7 After a lifetime of practice, I thought I could change faces and become Korean on demand with grace and perfection. But working with a small Korean company in Toronto proved me wrong. I quickly became estranged from my own people. My parents were ecstatic at the thought of their daughter finally finding her roots and having a working opportunity to speak my native tongue and absorb the culture. For me, it was the most painful and frustrating two and one-half months of my life.

8 When the president of the company boasted that he "operated little Korea," he meant it literally. A Canadianized Korean was not tolerated. I looked like a Korean; therefore, I had to talk, act, and think like one, too. Being accepted meant a total surrender to ancient codes of behaviour rooted in Confucian thought, while leaving the "Canadian" part of me out in the parking lot with my '86 Buick. In the first few days at work, I was bombarded with inquiries about my marital status. When I told them I was single, they spent the following days trying to match me up with available bachelors in the company and the community. I was expected to accept my inferior position as a woman and had to behave accordingly. It was not a place to practice my feminist views, or be an individual without being condemned. Little Korea is a place for men (who filled all the senior positions) and women don't dare speak up or disagree with their male counterparts. The president (all employees bow to him and call him Mr. President) asked me to act more like a lady and smile. I was openly scorned

by a senior employee because I spoke more fluent English than Korean. The cook in the kitchen shook her head in disbelief upon discovering that my cooking skills were limited to boiling a package of instant noodles. "You want a good husband, learn to cook," she advised me.

9   In less than a week I became an outsider because I refused to conform and blindly nod my head in agreement to what my elders (which happened to be everybody else in the company) said. A month later, I was demoted because "members of the workplace and the Korean community" had complained that I just wasn't "Korean enough," and I had "too much power for a single woman." My father suggested that "when in Rome do as the Romans." But that's exactly what I was doing. I am in Canada so I was freely acting like a Canadian, and it cost me my job.

10   My father also said, "It doesn't matter how Canadian you think you are, just look in the mirror and it'll tell you who you *really* are." But what he didn't realize is that an immigrant has to embrace the new culture to enjoy and benefit from what it has to offer. Of course, I will always be Korean by virtue of my appearance and early conditioning, but I am also happily Canadian and want to take full advantage of all that such citizenship confers. But for now I remain slightly distant from both cultures, accepted fully by neither. The hyphenated Canadian personifies the ideal of multiculturalism, but unless the host culture and the immigrant cultures can find ways to merge their distinct identities, sharing the best of both, this cultural schizophrenia will continue.

QUESTIONS FOR DISCUSSION

1. In point form, summarize the main characteristics of the Korean and the Canadian halves of the author's personality.
2. What method of paragraph development does the author use in paragraph 8? (See pages 296–304 for a discussion of paragraph development methods.)
3. Identify five examples of parallel structure in paragraph. How does the author's use of parallelism serve to reinforce her thesis?
4. Identify the summary of main points and the memorable statement in paragraph 10.

SUGGESTIONS FOR WRITING

1. Do you sometimes feel that you are two people trapped inside a single body? Write an essay in which you contrast the two sides of your personality.
2. Contrast three or four significant values of your generation with those of your parents' (or grandparents') generation.

EMBRACED BY THE NEEDLE

Gabor Maté

1   Addictions always originate in unhappiness, even if hidden. They are emotional anesthetics; they numb pain. The first question always is not "Why the addiction?" but "Why the pain?" The answer, ever the same, is scrawled with crude eloquence on the wall of my patient Anna's room at the Portland Hotel in the heart of Vancouver's Downtown Eastside: "Any place I went to, I wasn't wanted. And that bites large."

2   The Downtown Eastside is considered to be Canada's drug capital, with an addict population of 3,000 to 5,000 individuals. I am a staff physician at the Portland, a non-profit harm-reduction facility where most of the clients are addicted to cocaine, to alcohol, to opiates like heroin, or to tranquilizers—or to any combination of these things. Many also suffer from mental illness. Like Anna, a 32-year-old poet, many are HIV positive or have full-blown AIDS. The methadone I prescribe for their opiate dependence does little for the emotional anguish compressed in every heartbeat of these driven souls.

3   Methadone staves off the torment of opiate withdrawal, but, unlike heroin, it does not create a "high" for regular users. The essence of that high was best expressed by a 27-year-old sex-trade worker. "The first time I did heroin," she said, "it felt like a warm, soft hug." In a phrase, she summed up the psychological and chemical cravings that make some people vulnerable to substance dependence.

4   No drug is, in itself, addictive. Only about 8 per cent to 15 per cent of people who try, say alcohol or marijuana, go on to addictive use. What makes them vulnerable? Neither physiological predispositions nor individual moral failures explain drug addictions. Chemical and emotional vulnerability are the products of life experience, according to current brain research and developmental psychology.

5   Most human-brain growth occurs following birth; physical and emotional interactions determine much of our brain development. Each brain's circuitry and chemistry reflects individual life experiences as much as inherited tendencies.

6   For any drug to work in the brain, the nerve cells have to have receptors—sites where the drug can bind. We have opiate receptors because our brain has natural opiate-like substances, called endorphins, chemicals that participate in many functions, including the regulation of pain and mood. Similarly, tranquilizers of the benzodiazepine class, such as Valium, exert their effect at the brain's natural benzodiazepine receptors.

7   Infant rats who get less grooming from their mothers have fewer natural benzo receptors in the part of the brain that controls anxiety. Brains of infant monkeys separated from their mothers for only a few days are measurably deficient in the key neurochemical, dopamine.

8   It is the same with human beings. Endorphins are released in the infant's brain when there are warm, non-stressed, calm interactions with the parenting figures. Endorphins, in turn, promote the growth of receptors and nerve cells, and the discharge of other important brain chemicals. The fewer endorphin-enhancing experiences in infancy and early childhood, the greater the need for external sources. Hence, the greater vulnerability to addictions.

9   Distinguishing skid row addicts is the extreme degree of stress they had to endure early in life. Almost all women now inhabiting Canada's addiction capital suffered sexual assaults in childhood, as did many of the males. Childhood memories of serial abandonment or severe physical and psychological abuse are common. The histories of my Portland patients tell of pain upon pain.

10   Carl, a 36-year-old native, was banished from one foster home after another, had dishwashing liquid poured down his throat for using foul language at age 5, and was tied to a chair in a dark room to control his hyperactivity. When angry at himself—as he was recently, for using cocaine—he gouges his foot with a knife as punishment. His facial expression was that of a terrorized urchin who had just broken some family law and feared draconian retribution. I reassured him I wasn't his foster parent, and that he didn't owe it to me not to screw up.

11   But what of families where there was not abuse, but love, where parents did their best to provide their children with a secure nurturing home? One also sees addictions arising in such families. The unseen factor here is the stress the parents themselves lived under even if they did not recognize it. That stress could come from relationship problems, or from outside circumstances such as economic pressure or political disruption. The most frequent source of hidden stress is the parents' own childhood histories that saddled them with emotional baggage they had never become conscious of. What we are not aware of in ourselves, we pass on to our children.

12   Stressed, anxious, or depressed parents have great difficulty initiating enough of those emotionally rewarding, endorphin-liberating interactions with their children. Later in life such children may experience a hit of heroin as the "warm, soft hug" my patient described: What they didn't get enough of before, they can now inject.

13   Feeling alone, feeling there has never been anyone with whom to share their deepest emotions, is universal among drug addicts. That is what Anna had lamented on her wall. No matter how much love a parent has, the child does not experience being wanted unless he or she is made absolutely safe to express exactly how unhappy, or angry, or hate-filled he or she may feel at times. The sense of unconditional love, of being fully accepted even when most ornery, is

what no addict ever experienced in childhood—often not because the parents did not have it to give, simply because they did not know how to transmit it to the child.

14   Addicts rarely make the connection between troubled childhood experiences and self-harming habits. They blame themselves—and that is the greatest wound of all, being cut off from their natural self-compassion. "I was hit a lot," 40-year-old Wayne says, "but I asked for it. Then I made some stupid decisions." And would he hit a child, no matter how much that child "asked for it"? Would he blame that child for "stupid decisions"?

15   Wayne looks away. "I don't want to talk about that crap," says this tough man, who has worked on oil rigs and construction sites and served 15 years in jail for robbery. He looks away and wipes tears from his eyes.

QUESTIONS FOR DISCUSSION

1. Where does the author live? What is his job? How is his work reflected in this essay?
2. According to the author, what is the cause of addiction to drugs or alcohol? What do addicts have in common?
3. What does the author think happens to a person if he or she does not receive "endorphin-enhancing experiences in infancy and early childhood" (paragraph 8)? What does the phrase in quotation marks mean?
4. How does the author explain the fact that people who grow up in loving and secure homes can also become addicts?

SUGGESTIONS FOR WRITING

1. What do you think are the causes of drug or alcohol addiction? Is addiction rooted in childhood trauma, or does it reflect a lack of personal responsibility?
2. Do you think that the harm-reduction approach to treating addiction is realistic and effective? Why or why not?

DON'T CALL ME THAT WORD

Lawrence Hill

1   Growing up in the 1960s in affluent, almost all-white Don Mills, Ont., I was told by my black father that education and professional achievement were the only viable options for black people in North America. He laid down three rules as if they had been received from the mouth of God: 1) I was to study like the dickens; 2) anything less than complete success in school or at work was to be

regarded as failure; 3) if anybody called me "nigger," I was to beat the hell out of him.

2   This is the legacy of being black in Canada. You overcompensate for the fluke of your ancestry, and stand on guard against those who would knock you down. Over 400 years of black history here, we have had to overcome numerous challenges: the chains of slave vessels, the wrath of slave owners, the rules of segregation, the killing ways of police bullets, our own murderous infighting, and all the modern vicissitudes of polite Canadian oppression.

3   Blacks in Canada, like our metaphorical brothers and sisters all over the world, have a vivid collective memory. We know what our ancestors have been through, and we know what our children still face. Most of us cringe when we hear the word "nigger." No other word in the English language distills hatred so effectively, and evokes such a long and bloody history.

4   These days, more people than ever are talking about the word "nigger," as a result of the publication [in 2003] of the book *Nigger: The Strange Career of a Troublesome Word*, by Randall Kennedy, a black American law professor at Harvard University. It's a fascinating read, but it raises a troublesome argument that I ultimately reject: Kennedy praises "African American innovators" (by which he means comedians and hip hop stylists) for "taming, civilizing, and transmuting 'the filthiest, dirtiest, nastiest word in the English language.'"

5   Some misguided white people have bought into this same way of thinking. We have hit the pinnacle of absurdity when white teenagers sling their arms around black friends and ask, "Whassup my nigger?" And some white people seem to want a piece of that word, and feel the need to apply it to their own difficult experiences. The Irish have been referred to as "the niggers of Europe." In the 1970s, Québécois writer Pierre Vallieres titled one of his books *White Niggers of America*. And just the other night, when I visited a drop-in centre catering mostly to black junior high and high school students in Toronto's Kensington Market area, a white teenager decked out in baggy pants and parroting what he imagined to be blackspeak complained that some kids accused him of being a "wigger"—an insulting term for whites who are trying to act black. Whatever that means.

6   As Randall Kennedy rightly asserts, the word abounds in contemporary black urban culture. True, when it crops up in hip hop lyrics, it's not intended to carry the hate of the racist. It signals an in-group, brotherly, friendly trash talk. This is well known in American culture but it has penetrated black Canadian culture, too. Choclair, a leading black Canadian hip hop artist, uses the word "nigga"— a derivation of "nigger"—frequently in his lyrics.

7   Some people might say that the N-word is making a comeback. That the old-style, racist use of the word has faded into history and that it's now kosher to

use the word in ordinary conversation. This argument fails on two counts. First, racists and racism haven't disappeared from the Canadian landscape. The comeback argument also fails because it suggests that reappropriating the word reflects a new linguistic trend. This is naive. As a way of playing with the English language's most hateful word, black people—mostly young black males—have called themselves "nigger" for generations. The difference now is that these same young blacks have broadcast the word, via music and TV, to the whole world. In the middle-class black cultures I've encountered in Canada and the United States, such a young man usually gets slapped or tongue-lashed by his mother, at just about that point, and he learns that the only time it's safe to use that word is when he's chilling on the street with his buddies. Black people use the word "nigger" precisely because it hurts so much that we need to dance with our own pain, in the same way that blues music dives straight into bad luck and heartbreak. This is very much part of the black North American experience: we don't run from our pain, we roll it into our art.

8   But does that take the sting out of the word? No. And what's the proof of that? We don't use the word around our mothers, our teachers, the people we fall in love with, or our children. "Nigger" is a word that young black men use on each other. But the word still pains most black Canadians. Let me share an image of just how much the word hurts. A friend of mine—a black woman, community activist and graduate student—was dying to read Kennedy's book. She bought it last week, but couldn't bring herself to start devouring it on the subway to work until she had ripped off the cover: she wouldn't allow herself to be seen on the subway with the word "nigger" splashed on the cover of a book, so close to her face.

QUESTIONS FOR DISCUSSION

1. What are the three rules the author's father set for his son? Why do you think he chose this anecdote to introduce his essay?
2. Does Hill think that using the N-word is acceptable now in a time when it is routinely used by black comedians and musicians? Why or why not?
3. According to Hill, what effect does the N-word have on most black Canadians?

SUGGESTIONS FOR WRITING

1. Is it legitimate for someone to use an offensive racial term if the person is of that race? Not of that race? Is there a difference?
2. Are there some words and ideas that are simply too hurtful or dangerous to use? Is it a good idea to ban them because they represent hate speech?

THE NEW HEAVYWEIGHT CHAMPIONS
Margaret Wente

1   Something interesting has happened with many of the couples I know. The wives have now become the major breadwinners. They have high-powered jobs in design, consulting, medicine, public affairs, HR, law and banking. Many of their husbands are underemployed or semi-retired, not always by choice. One works behind the counter in a retail store. Another keeps the books for a small business. One is a freelance writer whose market has nearly dried up, and another husband has gone back to school for a degree. A couple of others work for their wives' businesses. Several of these men also organize the household chores and do the cooking. Thirty years ago, most of these men handily out-earned their wives. But the situation has reversed.

2   Could this be the future? Very likely. At every age and income level, women are more likely than ever before to be the major or sole breadwinner in the family. The reason is not that more women are working, but that fewer men are. Three-quarters of the people who lost their jobs in the U.S. recession were men, and the hardest-hit sectors were the male worlds of construction, manufacturing and finance. Many of those jobs aren't coming back. In the city of Hamilton—once known as Steeltown—just 2 per cent of the population still works in steel. In Sudbury, the town that nickel built, Inco's unionized labour force has shrunk from 12,000 to around 3,300 souls . . . .

3   Back in 2007, something happened in Canada that got almost no attention. We became the first country in the Western world where women outnumbered men in the work force. At first the gap was small—just one half of 1 per cent—but by 2009, the gap had grown to 3.5 per cent. (Note: Statistics Canada's measure doesn't include the self-employed.) This January, the United States followed us across the threshold.

4   All evidence suggests the gender shift is permanent. It would be nice to report that the sons of the nickel workers have gone off to university to become metallurgical engineers. But they have not. Just 18 per cent of Canadian males between 18 and 21 are currently attending university. Their sisters, though, are doing fine. They outperform their brothers in school and are far more focused on getting the credentials that will land them jobs as dental hygienists, bank clerks, office managers and nurses.

5   It's now conventional wisdom that a BA is the new minimum requirement for a good job in the postindustrial economy. Today, 58 per cent of all BAs are earned by women. And nearly all the fields that will yield the most employment

growth over the next couple of decades are ones already dominated by women. (An exception: janitors.)

6   A richly reported story in *The Atlantic* magazine (The End of Men, by Hanna Rosin) argues that these changes in the workplace amount to an unprecedented role reversal, whose cultural consequences will be vast. She notes that even something as fundamental as the sex preferences of parents has changed. Throughout human history, when muscle-power mattered and patriarchy reigned, sons were infinitely more valuable than daughters. But now—from urban America to urban Beijing—people's preferences have tilted toward girls. According to Ms. Rosin, one U.S. outfit that offers sperm selection says requests for girls are running at about 75 per cent.

7   At the heart of the *Atlantic* piece is one highly provocative question. What if the modern, postindustrial economy is simply more congenial to women than to men?

8   It's hard not to answer yes. The modern, postindustrial economy rewards people with a high degree of emotional intelligence who can navigate complex social networks. It rewards people who are flexible, adaptable and co-operative, who have good verbal skills, and who can work diligently, sit still and focus long enough to get the credentials they need to land a job. Women tend to be better at these things than men. They're also good at all the gender-neutral stuff, such as sales and analytical skills. Meantime, as muscle jobs vanish, men are showing little or no interest in becoming dental hygienists, kindergarten teachers or anything else that requires a high degree of people skills and nurturing.

9   It seems that just as women have more aptitude for certain jobs than men, they also have more aptitude for schooling—especially the long years of schooling you've got to put in to finish university. As Torben Drewes, an economics professor at Trent University, discovered, it's no mystery why more girls get in to university than boys. They're more motivated and they work harder in high school. "Fewer males had aspirations for university education than females and this fact might account for the lower levels of effort among them," he wrote. "However, it is also true that males were not able to produce high school averages (and, therefore, the entry requirement for university) as efficiently as females."

10   Men and women also behave differently once they get there. Here's what guys typically do in first-year university: play video games, work out, watch TV, party. Here's what girls do: study.

11   "If men were operating rationally in an economic sense, they should be flooding into higher education," says Tom Mortenson, a senior scholar at the Pell Institute for the Study of Opportunity in Higher Education in Washington. But people don't always operate rationally. And so we have that most modern of stereotypes—the aimless, slacker man-boy who isn't really qualified for anything and can't quite latch on to the job market.

12   As women bring home more and more of the bacon—and sometimes the whole hog—what will men do? How will relationships between the sexes be renegotiated? How will men figure out new ways to be a man? I have no idea. But for the first time since women relied on men to chase away the lions and bring home a tasty side of mastodon, it's all up for grabs.

QUESTIONS FOR DISCUSSION

1. What is a "heavyweight"? Who, according to the author, are the new heavyweights in the working world?
2. What key points do the statistics in paragraphs 2, 3, and 4 support?
3. What are the skills that Wente argues are highly valued in the "postindustrial economy" (paragraph 8)? Are these skills gender-based?
4. Do you agree that women are likely to become the major breadwinners in families of the future? What do you think would be the long-term implications of such an economic and sociological shift?

SUGGESTIONS FOR WRITING

1. Argue for or against the proposition Wente sets out in paragraph 10: in first-year college, boys fool around and girls study.
2. Would you like to be (or have) a househusband who cares for the home and children while the wife works?

THE SECOND-LANGUAGE STRUGGLE
Nell Waldman

Two versions of the same essay follow. The first is an example of a short research paper formatted in MLA style. The annotations point out some features of MLA format and documentation. If your instructor requires a separate title page, ask for guidelines. The second is the same short research paper, formatted in APA style, with annotations that identify features specific to APA documentation and format.

Read the essay your instructor identifies, and then answer the questions at the end of the two versions.

2.5 cm

1.25 cm

Waldman 1 ← *Writer's last name and page number on every page*

2.5 cm

Nell Waldman

Professor L. Rubenstein

En 101-01

30 November 2012

The Second-Language Struggle ← Title centred, not under-lined

Why is it so difficult for us to learn a second language once we are adults?

When we are very young, we learn our first language in a painless process that

we don't even remember. In "Metamorphosis," Sarah Norton describes Jeanie,   *Title and author of source*

an imaginary child who changes from crying infant to talking toddler in the first

eighteen months of her life. This "wondrous transformation" (425) is something   *Page reference (author's name already given)*

all of us accomplish in our native tongue. Learning a second language, however,

especially after the age of puberty, is a painful, time-consuming task. There are

complex physical, intellectual, and emotional factors that make acquiring a   *Thesis statement*

second language difficult.

An important part of acquiring a language is learning to speak, which is a

physical skill. As any athlete will tell you, it is an advantage to start learning a

physical skill at a young age. There are hundreds of muscles used in human

speech: mouth, lips, tongue, larynx, vocal cords, and throat. A young child who

babbles her way to articulate speech is practising the physical skills of her

native language. In addition, young children have a vast capacity for sound

production that is lost as they mature. Hence, even adults who become fluent in

a second language are likely to retain an accent that is a vestige of their first

language.

Double-spaced throughout

Waldman 2

Paragraphs indented five spaces

An adult has intellectual and cognitive skills that a child lacks. An adult can

think abstractly and is able to memorize and use dictionaries (Crystal 373). These

Paraphrase (with author and page reference of source)

skills might seem to make it easier to learn a new language. However, an adult

already has a firmly established first language in her intellectual repertoire, and

the native language actually interferes with mastering the second language.

H. Douglas Brown describes the process whereby remnants of the native

language collide with the new language: "The relatively permanent incorporation

Quotation introduced by complete sentence + colon

of incorrect linguistic forms into a person's second language competence . . . [is]

referred to as *fossilization*" (217). The fossils of our native language tend to keep

turning up as errors in the new language we are struggling to learn.

Emotional factors also complicate the process of learning a second

Ellipses indicate word(s) omitted; square brackets indicate word(s) changed or added

language. Young children are naturally open and lack the self-consciousness

that leads to inhibition. Adults, on the other hand, have a highly developed

language ego; their control of language is bound up with self-esteem. As one

language-learning website observes, "The biggest problem most people face in

Quotation introduced by phrase + comma

learning a new language is their own fear. They worry that they won't say things

correctly or that they will look stupid, so they don't talk at all" ("How to Learn

English"). Making mistakes, as any language learner must do, makes an adult

Website title only (no author identified and no page number)

anxious, shy, and reluctant to communicate in the new language. These

emotions make the process of mastering it even more difficult.

Waldman 3

Many linguists argue that humans are born with an innate capacity for learning language, that we have what is known as a "language acquisition device (LAD) hard-wired into our genetic make-up" (Crystal 234). This LAD is what makes it possible for us to learn our native language with such ease. Knowing more than one language is, of course, an extremely valuable ability. Yet acquiring a second language is a complex and demanding process for most people, especially if they undertake it as adults. Eva Hoffman writes movingly about language and identity and the troubling feelings that accompanied her struggle to master English and transfer her identity, so to speak, from her native Polish language:

> What has happened to me in this new world? I don't know. I don't see what I've seen, don't comprehend what's in front of me. I'm not filled with language anymore, and I have only a memory of fullness to anguish me with the knowledge that, in this dark and empty state, I don't really exist. (110)

Quotation integrated into writer's sentence

Author and page reference of source

Long quotation set off 10 spaces (2.5 cm) from left margin

Waldman 3

Heading is centred, not underlined. → Works Cited

Brown, H. Douglas. *Principles of Language Learning and Teaching.* 3rd ed.

Indent five spaces or 1.25 cm. ←→ Englewood Cliffs, NJ: Prentice Hall, 1994. Print.

Crystal, David. *The Cambridge Encyclopedia of Language.* Cambridge:

Cambridge UP, 1992. Print.

Entries are alphabet- ized. Hoffman, Eva. "Lost in Translation." *Canadian Content.* 5th ed. Ed. Sarah

Norton and Nell Waldman. Toronto: Thomson Nelson, 2003. 309–313. Print.

"How to Learn English." *world-english.* World English. 2004. Web. 18 Aug.

Entries are double- spaced through- out. 2005.

Norton, Sarah. "Metamorphosis." *Canadian Content.* 5th ed. Ed. Sarah Norton

and Nell Waldman. Toronto: Thomson Nelson, 2003. 67–68. Print.

QUESTIONS FOR DISCUSSION

1. In your own words, identify the subject and main points of this essay.
2. How many different kinds of research sources does the essay rely on? How many are used in each paragraph? Are they all quotations?
3. What contrast is the second paragraph based on? Is this contrast developed in any other paragraphs?
4. What kind of concluding strategy does this essay use? Is it effective?

SUGGESTIONS FOR WRITING

1. Have you ever learned (or tried to learn) a new language? Were you successful? Why?
2. What is the value of learning another language as an adult? Why do people choose to make the effort to do so?

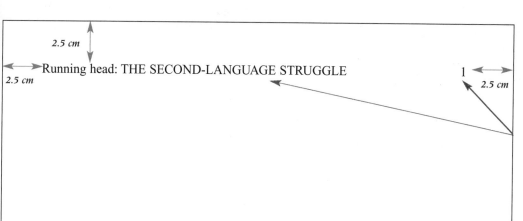

2.5 cm

Running head: THE SECOND-LANGUAGE STRUGGLE

2.5 cm

1

2.5 cm

Running head to appear on every page

The Second-Language Struggle

Nell Waldman

En 101-01

30 November 2012

Essay title and author's name with course code and submission date, centred in the upper half of the page

THE SECOND-LANGUAGE STRUGGLE   2

Double-spaced throughout, 2.5 cm (1 inch) margins

The Second-Language Struggle

Why is it so difficult for us to learn a second language once we are adults?

When we are very young, we learn our first language in a painless process that we

don't even remember. In "Metamorphosis," Sarah Norton (2003) describes Jeanie,

Author of source and date of publication

an imaginary child who changes from crying infant to talking toddler in the first

eighteen months of her life. This "wondrous transformation" (p. 425) is something

all of us accomplish in our native tongue. Learning a second language, however,

Page reference (author's name and date already given)

especially after the age of puberty, is a painful, time-consuming task. There are

complex physical, intellectual, and emotional factors that make acquiring a second

language difficult.

Thesis statement

An important part of acquiring a language is learning to speak, which is a

Paragraphs indented 1.25 cm (0.5 inches)

physical skill. As any athlete will tell you, it is an advantage to start learning a

physical skill at a young age. There are hundreds of muscles used in human

speech: mouth, lips, tongue, larynx, vocal cords, and throat. A young child who

babbles her way to articulate speech is practising the physical skills of her native

language. In addition, young children have a vast capacity for sound production

that is lost as they mature. Hence, even adults who become fluent in a second lan-

guage are likely to retain an accent that is a vestige of their first language.

An adult has intellectual and cognitive skills that a child lacks. An adult can think

Paraphrase followed by author of source, date, and page reference

abstractly and is able to memorize and use dictionaries (Crystal, 1992, p. 373). These

skills might seem to make it easier to learn a new language. However, an adult

THE SECOND-LANGUAGE STRUGGLE   3

already has a firmly established first language in his intellectual repertoire, and the

native language actually interferes with mastering the second language. H. Douglas

Brown (1994) describes the process whereby remnants of the native language collide

with the new language: "The relatively permanent incorporation of incorrect lin-

guistic forms into a person's second language competence … [is] referred to as *fos-

silization*" (p. 217). The fossils of our native language tend to keep turning up as

errors in the new language we are struggling to learn.

Emotional factors also complicate the process of learning a second language.

Young children are naturally open and lack the self-consciousness that leads to

inhibition. Adults, on the other hand, have a highly developed language ego; their

control of language is bound up with self-esteem. As one language-learning web-

site observes, "The biggest problem most people face in learning a new language

is their own fear. They worry that they won't say things correctly or that they will

look stupid, so they don't talk at all" ("How to Learn English," 2004). Making

mistakes, as any language learner must do, makes an adult anxious, shy, and

reluctant to communicate in the new language. These emotions make the process

of mastering it even more difficult.

Many linguists argue that humans are born with an innate capacity for

learning language, that we have what is known as a "language acquisition device

(LAD) hard-wired into our genetic make-up" (Crystal, 1992, p. 234). This LAD is

what makes it possible for us to learn our native language with such ease.

Author of source and year of publication

Quotation introduced by complete sentence + colon

Ellipses indicate word(s) omitted; square brackets indicate word(s) changed or added.

Page number of quotation

Quotation introduced by attribution clause + comma

Abbreviated Web page title (no author identified and no page number) and year of publication

Quotation integrated into writer's sentence

Author of source, date, and page reference

THE SECOND-LANGUAGE STRUGGLE   4

Knowing more than one language is, of course, an extremely valuable ability. Yet

acquiring a second language is a complex and demanding process for most

people, especially if they undertake it as adults. Eva Hoffman (2003) writes mov-

ingly about language and identity and the troubling feelings that accompanied her

struggle to master English and transfer her identity, so to speak, from her native

Polish language:

Long quotation set off 1.25 cm (0.5 inches) from left margin

> What has happened to me in this new world? I don't know. I don't see
>
> what I've seen, don't comprehend what's in front of me. I'm not filled with
>
> language anymore, and I have only a memory of fullness to anguish me
>
> with the knowledge that, in this dark and empty state, I don't really exist.
>
> (p. 110)

THE SECOND-LANGUAGE STRUGGLE   5

References   ◄───────────────────────────── *Heading is centred and bold- faced.*

Brown, H. D. (1994). *Principles of language learning and teaching* (3rd ed.).

　　Englewood Cliffs, NJ: Prentice Hall.   *Entries are alphabet- ized.*

Crystal, D. (1992). T*he Cambridge encyclopedia of language*. Cambridge,

　　England: Cambridge University Press.

Hoffman, E. (2003). Lost in translation. In S. Norton & N. Waldman (Eds.),

　　Canadian content (5th ed., pp. 309–313). Toronto, ON: Thomson Nelson.

How to learn English. (2004). Retrieved from http://world-english.org

Norton, S. (2003). Metamorphosis. In S. Norton & N. Waldman (Eds.), *Canadian*

　　content (5th ed., pp. 67–68). Toronto, ON: Thomson Nelson.

QUESTIONS FOR DISCUSSION

1. In your own words, identify the subject and main points of this essay.
2. How many different kinds of research sources does the essay rely on? How many are used in each paragraph? Are they all quotations?
3. What contrast is the second paragraph based on? Is this contrast developed in any other paragraphs?
4. What kind of concluding strategy does this essay use? Is it effective?

SUGGESTIONS FOR WRITING

1. Have you ever learned (or tried to learn) a new language? Were you successful? Why?
2. What is the value of learning another language as an adult? Why do people choose to make the effort to do so?

Appendixes

A The Fundamentals

Sentences: Kinds and Parts
- Function: Four Kinds of Sentences
- Structure: Basic Sentence Patterns
- The Parts of a Sentence

Parts of Speech
1. Nouns
2. Verbs
3. Pronouns
4. Adjectives
5. Adverbs
6. Prepositions
7. Conjunctions
8. Articles
9. Expletives

B List of Useful Terms

C Answers to Exercises

APPENDIX A
The Fundamentals

This appendix contains a brief overview of the basic building blocks of the English language. At the very least, you should know the kinds and parts of a sentence and the parts of speech before you tackle the complex tasks involved in correcting and refining your writing.

SENTENCES: KINDS AND PARTS

A sentence is a group of words expressing a complete thought. Sentences can be classified in two different ways: by function and by structure.

FUNCTION: FOUR KINDS OF SENTENCES

1. The *declarative* sentence makes a statement or conveys information.

George Clooney starred in *O Brother, Where Art Thou?*, a Coen brothers' film.

He played a character named Ulysses Everett McGill.

2. The *interrogative* sentence asks a question.

Did George Clooney do his own singing in *O Brother, Where Art Thou?*

Was Pete really turned into a frog, or was he turned in to the police?

3. The *imperative* (command) sentence gives an order or a directive.

Stop talking! I'm trying to listen.

The *request* is a modified form of imperative sentence. Its tone is softer:

Let's rent a DVD of *O Brother* and watch it tonight.

4. The *exclamatory* sentence is a strong statement of opinion or warning.

The scene in which Clooney insists on wearing a hair net to bed is hilarious!

Don't answer the phone! This is my favourite part of the movie!

STRUCTURE: BASIC SENTENCE PATTERNS

Every sentence can be classified into one of four patterns, depending on the number and kinds of clauses the sentence contains. (In the examples below, subjects are underlined with one line, verbs with two.)

1. A *simple* sentence consists of one independent clause. It has one subject and one verb, either or both of which may be compound (multiple).

   a. Matt plays hockey for McGill. (single subject, single verb)

   b. Matt and Caro play hockey with their friends on weekends. (compound subject, one plural verb)

   c. Matt and Caro play hockey and drink beer with their friends on weekends. (compound subject, compound verb)

2. A *compound* sentence is made up of two or more independent clauses. The clauses may be joined by a **coordinating conjunction** or by a semicolon. (See Chapters 7 and 18.)

Geoff paid for the flight to Cuba, *and* Kendra paid for their accommodation.

Either or both clauses in a compound sentence may contain a compound subject and/or a compound verb:

Geoff and Kendra flew to Cuba, *but* Matt and Caro stayed home and sulked.

3. A *complex* sentence has one independent clause and one or more dependent clauses introduced by **subordinating conjunctions** (see page 123) or relative clauses introduced by relative pronouns (see pages 197–98).

We flew to Cuba for our vacation *while* my brother stayed home to take care of our dogs.

Matt and Caro stayed home *because* they couldn't afford the trip.

4. The *compound-complex* sentence combines the features of sentence patterns 2 and 3 above. That is, it contains two (or more) independent clauses, together with one or more dependent clauses.

Geoff and Kendra flew to Cuba, *but* Matt and Caro stayed home *because* they couldn't afford the trip and *because* someone needed to care for the dogs.

THE PARTS OF A SENTENCE

Every sentence or independent clause can be divided into two parts: subject and predicate. The subject half contains the **subject** (simple or compound), together with its modifiers. The predicate half contains the **verb** (simple or compound), with its modifiers and any other words or phrases that complete the sentence's meaning. These predicate completers may be **direct objects**, **indirect objects**, or **complements**. In the examples below, direct objects are indicated by a triple underline; indirect objects by a dotted underline; and complements by a broken underline.

1. The **subject** of a sentence is a noun/pronoun (or phrase or clause used as a noun).

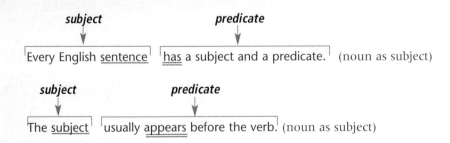

subject	*predicate*
Every English sentence	has a subject and a predicate. (noun as subject)

subject	*predicate*
The subject	usually appears before the verb. (noun as subject)

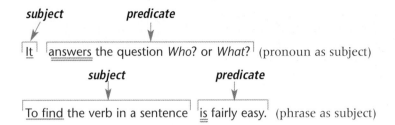

subject   *predicate*

It answers the question *Who?* or *What?* (pronoun as subject)

subject   *predicate*

To find the verb in a sentence is fairly easy. (phrase as subject)

2. The **verb** is the word or phrase that tells the reader what the subject is or does.

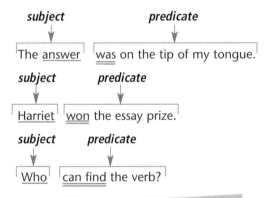

subject   *predicate*

The answer was on the tip of my tongue.

subject   *predicate*

Harriet won the essay prize.

subject   *predicate*

Who can find the verb?

3. The **direct object** is the noun or pronoun that names the receiver of the action of the verb.

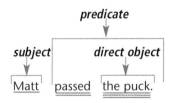

       predicate

subject   *direct object*

Matt passed the puck.

4. The **indirect object** is a noun or pronoun that tells to whom something is (was/will be) done. The indirect object comes before the direct object.

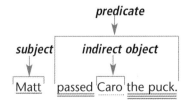

       predicate

subject   *indirect object*

Matt passed Caro the puck.

5. An **object of a preposition** is a noun or pronoun that follows the preposition in a prepositional phrase.

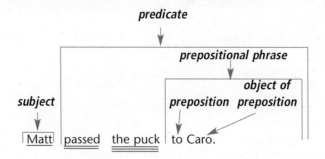

6. A **complement** is a noun, pronoun, or modifier that explains, renames, or describes the subject of a linking verb (e.g., **is, seems, appears, smells, tastes**).

Caro is the captain of the team. (noun complement)
The goal and the game are ours! (pronoun complement)
The crowd went wild. (adjective complement)

PARTS OF SPEECH

The words that make up sentences can be classified into nine grammatical categories or word classes. The function of a word in a sentence determines what part of speech it is. The word *rock*, for example, can belong to any one of three categories, depending on its context.

We stopped to rest in the shadow of an enormous *rock*. (noun)

The baby will usually stop fussing if you *rock* her. (verb)

I used to listen only to *rock* music, but now I prefer rap. (adjective)

Here's another example, illustrating three functions of the word *since*.

We haven't seen Lucy *since* Saturday. (preposition)

We haven't seen Lucy *since* she left. (subordinating conjunction)

We haven't seen Lucy *since*. (adverb)

1. NOUNS

A noun is a word that names a person, place, object, quality, or concept.

A. **Common nouns** are general names for persons, places, and objects: for example, artist, politician; city, suburb; train, computer.
  - **Concrete** nouns name things that can be seen and touched: telephone, sister, puppy.
  - **Abstract** nouns name thoughts, emotions, qualities, or values—things that cannot be seen or touched: for example, ambition, success, honesty.
B. **Proper nouns** name specific persons, places, and things and are capitalized: for example, Queen Elizabeth, Homer Simpson, Bugs Bunny, CN Tower, Calgary, General Motors.
C. **Collective nouns** name groups of people or things that act as a single unit: for example, jury, class, committee, herd.

2. VERBS

A. A verb is a word or phrase that tells what the subject of the clause is or does.

- **Action verbs** tell what the subject does: The driver braked suddenly.
- **Linking** (or *copula*) **verbs** connect the subject to a word or phrase identifying or describing the subject of a sentence: The driver was my older brother. He felt sleepy.

B. All verbs have different forms (called **tenses**) to indicate past, present, or future time.

Our team played badly last night. (action verb in past tense)

Mario thinks that we will win tonight. (present tense, future tense)

I am not so confident. (linking verb in present tense)

C. **Auxiliary** (or **helping**) **verbs** are used with a main verb to show tense or voice.

The auxiliary verbs are *be, have, do, may, can, ought, must, shall, will,* and their various forms.

By November, <u>we</u> <u>will have been</u> in Canada for six months. (future perfect tense)

D. The way verbs interact with their subjects is shown through a quality called **voice**. Active voice and passive voice verbs give different messages to the reader.

- **Active voice** verbs show the subject doing or acting:

  A <u>woman</u> in a BMW <u>took</u> my parking place.

  The <u>tornado</u> <u>destroyed</u> everything in its path.

- **Passive voice** verbs show the subject being acted upon:

  My parking <u>place</u> <u>was taken</u> by a woman in a BMW.

  Our <u>home</u> <u>was destroyed</u> by the tornado.

(See Chapter 11, pages 154–57, for instructions on when to use passive voice verbs.)

3. PRONOUNS

Pronouns are words that substitute for nouns. They can act as subjects or objects. There are seven classes of pronouns:

a. Personal Pronouns	*Singular* (Subject/Object)	*Plural* (Subject/Object)
1st person	I/me	we/us
2nd person	you/you	you/you
3rd person	he, she, it/him, her, it	they/them

We would like *you* to come with *us*, but *they* can fit only four people in the car.

b. Possessive Pronouns

	Singular	*Plural*
1st person	mine	ours
2nd person	yours	yours
3rd person	his, hers, its	theirs

The wonton soup is *yours*; the chicken wings are *hers*; the spareribs are *mine*; and the spring rolls are *ours* to share.

c. Indefinite Pronouns

Singular	*Plural*
any, anyone, anybody, anything	some, all, many
everyone, everybody, everything	some, all, many
someone, somebody, something	some people, some things
no one, nobody, nothing, none (*sing.*)	none (*pl.*)
one	several
each	both
either, neither	few, several, many

Is *no one* curious about *anything someone* is doing for the good of us *all?*

d. Demonstrative Pronouns

Singular	*Plural*
this	these
that	those

This paper is mine; *these* papers are yours.

That is my magazine; I've read *those*, so you can have them if you wish.

e. Relative Pronouns

Singular and Plural
(Subject/Object)

who/whom; whoever/whomever; which/whichever; what/whatever; that; whose

The Order of Canada, *which* was created in 1967, is awarded each year to Canadians *who* have distinguished themselves in the arts and sciences, politics, or community service, and *whose* contributions in *whatever* field are deemed worthy of national honour.

f. Interrogative Pronouns   *Singular and Plural*
                                             (Subject/Object)

                                             who?/whom?
                                             which? what?/which? what?

Jan is the leader on *whom* the team depended. *Who* could take her place? *What* can the team do now?

g. Reflexive/Emphatic
Pronouns   *Singular*   *Plural*

1st person   myself   ourselves
2nd person   yourself   yourselves
3rd person   himself, herself, itself   themselves

We had planned to go by *ourselves,* but since Sharon invited *herself* along, Leo and Jon should have included *themselves* on the outing, too.

4. ADJECTIVES

An adjective is a word that modifies or describes a noun or pronoun.

- Adjectives usually answer one of these questions: *What kind? Which? How many?*

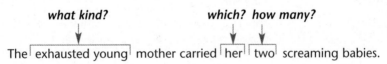

what kind?   which? how many?

The exhausted young mother carried her two screaming babies.

- Pay special attention to the possessive pronoun adjectives: my, our, your, his, her, its, their. These words follow the same rules for agreement that govern the possessive pronouns listed above. See Chapter 15, pages 190–93.
- Most adjectives have three forms:
  1. **positive (base) form:** short, brief, concise
  2. **comparative form:**
     - Add *-er* to one-syllable words: shorter, briefer
     - Use *more* + base form for adjectives of two or more syllables: more concise
  3. **superlative form:**
     - Add *-est* to one-syllable words: shortest, briefest
     - Use *most* + base form for adjectives of two or more syllables: most concise

A few adjectives such as *bad* have irregular comparatives (*worse*) and superlatives (*worst*). Your dictionary will list these irregular forms.

5. ADVERBS

An adverb is a word that modifies or describes a verb, an adjective, or another adverb.

- Adverbs commonly answer the questions *When? Where? How?*
- Adverbs often—but not always—end in *-ly*.

Rocco *foolishly* challenged the police officer. (adverb modifies verb)

The baby is an *extremely* fussy eater. (adverb modifies adjective)

My elderly father drives *very slowly.* (adverb modifies another adverb; adverb phrase modifies verb)

6. PREPOSITIONS

A preposition is a word (or words) such as *in, on, among, to, for, according to,* and *instead of* that introduces a prepositional phrase. A **prepositional phrase** = preposition + object of the preposition (a noun or pronoun).

Prepositional phrases can function as adjectives, adverbs, or nouns.

Celeste is an old friend *of mine* *from Paris.* (prepositional phrases as adjectives modifying noun *friend*)

I'll wait *until seven o'clock.* (prepositional phrase as adverb modifying verb *wait*)

We all hope *for a better world.* (prepositional phrase as noun object of verb *hope*)

7. CONJUNCTIONS

> Conjunctions are connecting words used to join two words, two phrases, or two clauses.

- **Coordinating conjunctions** (and, but, or, for, so, nor, yet) join grammatically equal elements in a sentence (e.g., the two parts of a compound subject; two independent clauses).

  Moreen *and* Gina are coming, *but* Tessa is not.

- **Subordinating conjunctions** are dependent clause cues: because, although, when, since, etc. They link dependent (or subordinate) clauses to independent clauses.

  Tom must go home early *because* he promised to cook dinner.

- **Conjunctive adverbs** are transitional expressions (e.g., however, therefore, nevertheless, in fact) usually used after a semicolon to join two independent clauses.

  I would like to go to the club tonight; *however*, I have no money.

- **Correlative conjunctions** are conjunctions used in pairs: for example, both ... and, not only ... but (also), either ... or, neither ... nor. These constructions are intensifiers. They make the meaning of a statement more emphatic by focusing the reader's attention on each element separately.

  Eva is beautiful *and* intelligent. (coordinating conjunction = statement)

  Eva is *both* beautiful *and* intelligent. (correlative conjunctions = emphatic statement)

  Luca invited all his friends to the party *and* gave everyone a gift. (coordinating conjunction = statement)

  Not only did Luca invite all his friends to the party, *but* (*also*) he gave everyone a gift. (correlative conjunctions = emphatic statement)

8. ARTICLES

An article precedes the noun it modifies. The **definite article**, *the*, may be used with a singular or a plural noun; it denotes a particular person or thing. The **indefinite article** *a/an* is generally used with a singular, countable noun and signals an unspecified one of others. (Use *an* before vowel *sounds*, not just vowels: e.g., an apple, an honest person.)

The student sitting next to you is asleep. (a particular student)

A student in the back row is snoring. (one of a number of students)

A number of factors determine the use or non-use of articles. For a summary of rules governing articles, refer to Chapter 31 or go to "ESL Tips" under More Information on the Student Resources page of our website at **www.bareplus4e.nelson.com**.

9. EXPLETIVES

Here and *there* are expletives, which are words used at the beginning of a sentence to postpone the subject until after the verb and thus emphasize it.

Here is your mail. (= Your mail is here.)

There are hundreds of copies still available. (= Hundreds of copies are still available.)

See Chapter 5, pages 68–69.

APPENDIX B
List of Useful Terms

abstract noun	See **noun**.
action verb	A verb that tells what the subject is doing. See **verb**.
active voice	See **voice**.
adjective	A word that modifies (describes, restricts, makes more precise) a noun or pronoun. Adjectives answer the questions *What kind? How many?* and *Which?* For example, the *competent* student, *five* home runs, my *last* class. When two or more adjectives modify a noun, they may require commas between them. See Chapter 17 for the differences between **coordinate** and **cumulative adjectives**. See also Parts of Speech in Appendix A.
adverb	A word that modifies a verb, adjective, or other adverb. Adverbs answer the questions *When? How? Where? Why?* and *How much?* For example, Matt talks *loudly* (*loudly* modifies the verb *talks*); he is a *very* loud talker (*very* modifies the adjective *loud*); he talks *really* loudly (*really* modifies the adverb *loudly*). Adverbs often—but not always—end in *-ly*. See also Parts of Speech in Appendix A.
agreement	Grammatical correspondence in person and number between a verb and its subject, or in person, number, and gender between a pronoun and its antecedent.
anecdote	A short account of an event or incident, often humorous, that is used to catch the reader's interest and illustrate a point.
antecedent	The word that a pronoun refers to or stands for. Literally, it means "coming before, preceding." The antecedent usually comes before the pronoun that refers to it: My sister thinks she is always right (*sister* is the antecedent of the pronoun *she*).

article	A determiner that precedes a noun. *A/an* is the **indefinite article** that signals an unspecified one of others: *a* stockbroker, *an* accountant, *a* village, *an* animal, *an* opportunity. Use *a/an* with a singular count noun when making a generalization: *A* stockbroker's job is stressful.

The is the **definite article** that signals a particular person, place, or thing that has been singled out from others: *the* stockbroker next door; *the* accountant who audits our books; *the* village where I was born. *The* is used when the speaker or writer and the audience are thinking about the same specific person(s) or thing(s). *The* is also used when an unspecified noun is mentioned a second time: I bought a box of chocolates, and my roommate ate half *the* box.

No article (zero article) is used in general statements with non-count and plural nouns unless the noun is particularized or made specific in some way: *Tea* contains less caffeine than *coffee*. *Diamonds* are a girl's best friend. (Contrast: *The diamond in this ring weighs .50 carats.*) |
attention-getter	One or more sentences that come before the **thesis statement** and that are designed to get the reader interested in what you have to say.
audience	The writer's intended reader or readers. Knowledge of your audience's level of understanding, interests, attitude toward the subject, and expectations of you as a writer is essential to successful communication. Your level of vocabulary, sentence structure, organization of material, the amount of specific detail you include, and tone should all reflect the needs of your audience.
auxiliary verb	A "helping" verb used with a main verb to form different tenses. The auxiliary verbs are *be, have, do, may, can, ought, must, shall, will,* and their various forms.
chronological order	Events or ideas that are arranged in order of time sequence.
clause	A group of words containing a subject and a verb. If the group of words can stand by itself as a complete sentence, it is called an **independent** (or *main*)

clause. If the group of words does not make complete sense on its own but depends on another clause, it is called a **dependent** (or *subordinate*) **clause**. Here's an example: The porch collapsed. This group of words can stand by itself, so it is called an independent clause. Now consider this clause: When Kalim removed the railing with his tractor. This group of words has a subject, *Kalim*, and a verb, *removed*, but it does not make complete sense on its own. For its meaning, it depends on *the porch collapsed*; therefore, it is a dependent clause.

cliché	A phrase that has been used so often it no longer communicates a meaningful idea. See Chapter 1.
climactic order	The arrangement of key ideas in order of importance. The most important or strongest idea comes last. Thus, the paper builds to a climax.
coherence	The logical consistency and stylistic connections between ideas, sentences, and paragraphs in a piece of writing. See Chapter 25.
collective noun	See **noun**.
colloquialism	A word or phrase that we use in casual conversation or in informal writing, but not in formal writing. Steve *flunked* his accounting exam. *Did* you *get* what the teacher said about job placement? I can't believe that *guy* is serious about learning.
command	A sentence that tells the listener or reader to do something. In this type of sentence, no subject appears, but "you" is understood. See Chapter 5. Look up unfamiliar words in the dictionary. Be all that you can be. Sit!
comma splice	The error that results when the writer joins two independent clauses with a comma. The comma splice is an error, it is a kind of run-on sentence.
common noun	See **noun**.
comparison	Writing that points out similarities, showing how two different objects, people, or ideas are alike.

comparison and contrast	Writing that identifies both similarities and differences.
complement	A word or phrase that completes the meaning of a verb. Also called a *subjective completion*, a complement can be a noun, pronoun, or adjective that follows a linking verb.

> Ramani is the *manager*. (noun complement)
> The winner was *she*. (pronoun complement)
> The president's speech was *encouraging*. (adjective complement)

compound	A compound construction is made up of two or more equal parts. Examples:

> Walter and Pieter are brothers. (compound subject)
> Walter came late and left early. (compound verb)
> Pieter is quiet and studious. (compound complement)

compound complement	See **compound**.
compound sentence	A sentence consisting of two or more independent clauses.

> We had no time to warm up, but we won the game anyway.

(See Sentences: Kinds and Parts in Appendix A.)

compound subject	See **compound**.
compound verb	See **compound**.
concrete noun	See **noun**.
conjunction	A word that links two or more words, phrases, or clauses. Conjunctions come in three types: coordinating, correlative, and subordinating. There are seven **coordinating conjunctions**: *and, but, so, or, nor, for,* and *yet*. The **correlative conjunctions** include *either … or, neither … nor, not only … but also,* and *both … and*. Use a coordinating or correlative conjunction when the items being linked are of equal importance in the sentence. When you want to show that one idea is secondary to another, you may use a **subordinating**

conjunction, such as *although, because, since, so that, though,* or *while.* See page 88 for a more comprehensive list of subordinating conjunctions.

conjunctive adverb   A transitional expression usually used after a semicolon to join two independent clauses (e.g., however, therefore, nevertheless, in fact).

consistency   In pronoun use, the maintenance of number, person, and gender. For example, a sentence that begins in the first person but shifts to the second person is incorrect: *We* chose not to drive to Calgary because, these days, *you* just can't afford the gas.

contraction   The combining of two words into one, as in *they're* or *can't.* Contractions are common in conversation and in informal written English. See Chapter 2.

contrast   Writing that points out dissimilarities between things, showing how two objects, people, or ideas differ.

coordinate adjectives   Adjectives that can be arranged in any order and can be separated by the word *and* without changing the meaning of the sentence. Commas come between coordinate adjectives not joined by *and.*

coordinating conjunction   A linking word used to join two or more words, phrases, or clauses of equal importance: *and, but, so, or, nor, for,* and *yet.*

correlative conjunctions   Linking words that appear in pairs and that join two or more words, phrases, or clauses of equal importance: *either ... or, neither ... nor, not only ... but also,* and *both ... and.*

count noun   A common noun that has a plural form and can be preceded by an indefinite article (*a/an*) or a quantity expression such as *one, many, several, a few of, hundreds of* (e.g., car, letter, dollar).

cumulative adjectives   A series of adjectives in which each adjective modifies the word that follows it. No commas are placed between cumulative adjectives.

dangling modifier   A modifier that cannot sensibly refer to any specific word or phrase in the sentence. See Chapter 8.

definite article   See **article**.

dependent clause   A group of words containing a subject and a verb but not expressing a complete idea. It depends on an independent clause for its meaning. Also called a *subordinate clause*. See Chapter 6.

dependent clause cue

A word or phrase that introduces a dependent clause: for example, when, because, in order that, as soon as. Also called a **subordinating conjunction**.

direct object

See **object**.

editing

The correction of errors in grammar, word choice, spelling, punctuation, and formatting.

fused sentence

The error that results when the writer joins two independent clauses without any punctuation between them. See Chapter 7.

The fused sentence is an error it is a kind of run-on sentence.

general level of Standard English

The level of language of educated persons. General-level English is used in college and professional writing. It is non-technical and readily understood by most readers. It uses few if any colloquial expressions, no slang, and few contractions. See Chapter 1.

helping verb

A verb form that adds further meaning to the main verb. Some helping verbs, also called **auxiliary verbs**, show when an action took place (e.g., be, do/did, have/had, will), and some suggest possibility or probability (e.g., can, could, may, might, must, should, would). See Chapter 5 and Chapter 29.

homonyms

Two or more words that are identical in sound (e.g., bear, bare) or spelling (e.g., bank—a place for money; bank—a slope) but different in meaning. See Chapter 2.

indefinite article

See **article**.

independent clause

A group of words containing a subject and a verb and expressing a complete idea. Also called *main clause*. See Chapter 6.

indirect object

See **object**.

informal level of Standard English

The level of language most of us use in conversation and in personal writing. It is casual, includes some slang and colloquial expressions, commonly uses contractions, and is written in first and second person. See Chapter 1.

irregular verb   A verb whose simple past and past participle form are not formed by adding *-ed*: for example, eat (ate, eaten), lay (laid), ride (rode, ridden). See list on pages 147–49.

linking verb   See **verb**.

logically linked order   A pattern of organization that depends on causal connections among the main points. One point must be explained before the next can be understood.

main verb   The verb that follows the helping (auxiliary) verb and tells the action in the sentence. See Chapter 5.

misplaced modifier   A modifier that is next to a word or phrase that it is not meant to modify. A misplaced modifier can change the meaning of your sentence. See Chapter 8.

modal auxiliary   A type of **auxiliary verb** that does not change form regardless of person or number. The modal auxiliaries are *may, might, must, can, could, will, would, shall, should*, and *ought to*.

modifier   A word or group of words that adds information about another word (or phrase or clause) in a sentence. See **adjective**, **adverb**, **dependent clause**, and Chapter 8.

non-count noun   A common noun that cannot be preceded by an indefinite article (*a/an*) or by a quantity expression, such as *one, several, many, a couple of*, and that has no plural form (e.g., traffic, mail, money).

noun   A word that names a person, place, thing, or concept and that has the grammatical capability of being possessive. Nouns are most often used as subjects and objects. There are two classes of nouns: concrete and abstract.

Concrete nouns name things we perceive through our senses; we can see, hear, touch, taste, or smell what they stand for. Some concrete nouns are **proper**: they name people, places, or things and are capitalized—for example, Pierre Elliott Trudeau, Beijing, Canada's Wonderland. Other concrete nouns are **common** (e.g., woman, city, car, coffee); still others are **collective** (e.g., group, audience, crowd, committee).

Abstract nouns name concepts, ideas, characteristics—things we know or experience through our intellect rather than through our senses: for example, truth, pride, prejudice, self-esteem.

object

The "receiving" part of a sentence. The **direct object** is a noun or noun substitute (pronoun, phrase, or clause) that is the target or receiver of the action expressed by the verb. It answers the question *What?* or *Whom?*

> Jai threw the *ball.* (Jai threw *what?*)
> He wondered *where the money went.* (He wondered *what?*)
> Munira loves *Abdul.* (Munira loves *whom?*)

The **indirect object** is a noun or pronoun that is the indirect target or receiver of the action expressed by the verb in a sentence. It is always placed in front of the direct object. It answers the question *To whom?* or *To what?*

> Dani threw *me* the ball. (Dani threw *to whom?*)
> Ian forgot to give his *essay* a title. (Give *to what?*)

The **object of a preposition** is a noun or noun substitute (pronoun, phrase, or clause) that follows a preposition—for example, after the *storm* (*storm* is a noun, object of the preposition *after*); before *signing the lease* (*signing the lease* is a phrase, object of the preposition *before*); he thought about *what he wanted to do* (*what he wanted to do* is a clause, object of the preposition *about*). Notice that what follows a preposition is always its object; that is why the subject of a sentence or clause is never in a prepositional phrase.

parallelism

Consistent grammatical structure. In a sentence, for example, all items in a series would be written in the same grammatical form: words, phrases, or clauses. Julius Caesar's famous pronouncement, "I came, I saw, I conquered," is a classic example of parallel structure. The symmetry of parallelism appeals to readers and makes a sentence read smoothly and rhythmically. Lack of parallelism, on the other hand, is jarring: My favourite sports are *water-skiing, swimming,* and *I particularly love to sail.*

paraphrase	The rephrasing of another writer's idea in your own words. A good paraphrase reflects both the meaning and the tone of the original; it is usually about the same length as or shorter than the original. Whenever you borrow another writer's ideas, you must acknowledge your source. If you don't, you are plagiarizing.
participle	The form of a verb that can be used as an adjective (the *starving* artist, the *completed* work) or as part of a verb phrase (am *working*, have *purchased*).

> The **present participle** of a verb ends in *-ing*.
> The **past participle** of a regular verb ends in *-d* or in *-ed*.
> For a list of **irregular verbs**, see pages 147–49.

passive voice	See **voice**.
past participle	See **participle**.
person	A category of pronouns and verbs. First person refers to the person who is speaking (*I, we*). Second person refers to the person being spoken to (*you*). Third person is the person or thing being spoken about (*he, she, it, they*). Regular verb forms remain constant except in the present tense third-person singular, which ends in *-s*: *I* run; *you* run; *he/she/it* runs; *we* run; *they* run.
person agreement	The consistent use of the first-, second-, or third-person pronoun throughout a sentence or a paragraph.
phrase	A group of meaning-related words that acts as a noun, a verb, an adjective, or an adverb within a sentence. Phrases do not make complete sense on their own because they do not contain both a subject and a verb.

> Please order *legal-size manila file folders.* (phrase acting as noun)
> I *must have been sleeping* when you called. (verb phrase)
> *Sightseeing in Ottawa*, we photographed the monuments *on Parliament Hill.* (phrases acting as adjectives)
> Portaging a canoe *in this weather* is no fun. *(phrase acting as adverb)*

plagiarism	Using someone else's words or ideas in your writing without acknowledging their source.
plural	More than one person or thing.
possession	Ownership, as denoted in writing by the addition of *'s* to a singular noun or just an apostrophe (*'*) to a plural noun ending in *s*. See Chapter 2.

> The writer*'s* goal was to tell as many fallen soldiers*'* stories as she could in one book.

possessive pronoun	A group of words that are already in the possessive form and do not require *'s*. The possessive pronouns are *my, mine, your, yours, his, her, hers, its, our, ours, their, theirs,* and *whose*. See Chapter 3.
prefix	A meaningful letter or group of letters added to the beginning of a word to change either (1) its meaning or (2) its word class.

1. *a* + moral = amoral
   bi + sexual = bisexual
   contra + diction = contradiction
   dys + functional = dysfunctional
2. *a* + board (verb) = aboard (adverb, preposition)
   con + temporary (adjective) = contemporary
     (noun, adjective)
   dis + robe (noun) = disrobe (verb)
   in + put (verb) = input (noun)

Some prefixes require a hyphen, as here:
all-Canadian
de-emphasize
mid-morning

preposition	A word that connects a noun, pronoun, or phrase to some other word(s) in a sentence. The noun, pronoun, or phrase is the **object** of the preposition.

> I prepared the minutes *of the meeting*. (*of* relates *meeting* to *minutes*)
> One *of the parents* checks the children every half hour. (*of* relates *parents* to *One*)

prepositional phrase	A group of grammatically related words beginning with a **preposition** and having the function of a noun, adjective, or adverb. See the list on page 74.

present participle	See **participle**.
pretentious language	Sometimes called *gobbledygook* or *bafflegab*, pretentious language is characterized by vague, abstract, multi-syllable words and long, complicated sentences. Intended to impress the reader, pretentious language is sound without meaning; readers find it irritating, even exasperating.
principal parts	The verb elements we use to construct the various tenses. The principal parts are the infinitive form (*to* + the base verb), the simple past, the present participle (*-ing*), and the past participle. See Chapter 11.
pronoun	A word that functions like a noun in a sentence (e.g., as a subject or as an object of a verb or a preposition). Pronouns usually substitute for nouns, but sometimes they substitute for other pronouns.

He will promote *anything that* brings in money.

Everyone must earn *her* bonus.

There are several kinds of pronouns:

> **personal:** *I, we; you; he, she, it, they; me, us; him, her, them*
> **possessive:** *mine, ours; yours; his, hers, its, theirs*
> **demonstrative:** *this, these; that, those*
> **relative:** *who, whom, whose; which, that*
> **interrogative:** *who? whose? whom? which? what?*
> **indefinite:** all *-one, -thing, -body* pronouns, such as *everyone, something,* and *anybody;* and *each; neither; either; few; none; several*

Note: Possessive pronouns also have adjective forms: *my, our; your; his, her, their*. Possessive adjectives follow the same rules for agreement that govern pronouns. They must agree with their antecedents in person, number, and gender.

> Every young *boy* wants to be the goalie on *his* team. (not *their* team)

pronoun form	Determined by the pronoun's function in a sentence: subject or object. See Chapter 14.

Subject Pronouns		**Object Pronouns**	
Singular	*Plural*	*Singular*	*Plural*
I	we	me	us
you	you	you	you
he, she, it, one	they	him, her, it, one	them

proofreading	The correction of errors in typing or writing that appear in the final draft.
proper noun	See **noun**.
random order	A shopping-list kind of arrangement of main points in a paper. The points could be explained in any order. Random order is appropriate only when all points are equal in significance and are not chronologically or causally connected to one another.
regular verb	A verb whose simple past and past participle form are formed by adding *-ed*, or just *-d* when the verb ends in *-e*. See Chapter 11.
run-on	A sentence with inadequate punctuation between clauses. The two kinds of run-on sentences are **comma splices** and **fused sentences**.
sentence combining	A technique that enables you to produce correct and-pleasing sentences. Sentence combining accomplishes three things: it reinforces your meaning; it refines and polishes your writing; and it results in a style that will keep your reader alert and interested in what you have to say. See Chapter 10.
sentence fragment	A group of words that is punctuated like a sentence but either does not have both a subject and a verb or does not express a complete thought. See Chapter 6.
singular	One person or thing.
slang	Non-standard language used in conversation among people who belong to the same social group. See Chapter 1.
subject	In a sentence, the person, thing, or concept that the sentence is about (see Chapter 5). In an essay, the person, thing, or concept that the paper is about (see Chapter 22).
subordinating conjunction	A word or phrase that introduces a dependent clause: for example, when, because, in order that, as soon as. See page 88 for a more comprehensive list of subordinating conjunctions.

suffix

A letter or group of letters that is added to the end of a word to change (1) its meaning, (2) its grammatical function, or (3) its word class.

1. king + *dom* = kingdom
   few + *er* = fewer
   tooth + *less* = toothless
2. buy (base form) + *s* = buys (third-person singular, present tense)
   eat (base form) + *en* = eaten (past participle)
   instructor + *s* = instructors (plural)
   instructor + *'s* = instructor's (possessive singular)
3. your (adjective) + *s* = yours (pronoun)
   act (verb) + *ive* = active (adjective)
   active (adjective) + *ly* = actively (adverb)
   ventilate (verb) + *tion* = ventilation (noun)

Some words add two or more prefixes and/or suffixes to the base form. Look at *antidisestablishmentarianism*, for example. How many prefixes and suffixes can you identify?

tense

The form of the verb that indicates past, present, or future time. The verb ending (e.g., play**s**, play**ed**) and any helping verbs associated with the main verb (*is* playing, *will* play, *has* played, *had* played, *will have* played) indicate the tense of the verb.

There are simple tenses:

> **present:** *ask, asks*
> **past:** *asked*
> **future:** *will ask*

and perfect tenses:

> **present:** *has (have) asked*
> **past:** *had asked*
> **future:** *will (shall) have asked*

The simple and perfect tenses can also be **progressive**: am asking, have been asking, etc.

thesis

A thesis is the idea or point about a subject that the writer wants to explain or prove to the reader. A summary of the writer's thesis is often expressed in a **thesis statement**. See Chapters 22 and 23.

thesis statement	A statement near the beginning of a paper that announces the paper's subject and scope.
tone	A reflection of the writer's attitude toward his or her topic. For instance, a writer who is looking back with longing to the past might use a nostalgic tone. An angry writer might use an indignant tone or an understated, ironic tone, depending on the subject and purpose of the paper.
topic sentence	A sentence that identifies the main point or key idea developed in a paragraph. The topic sentence is usually found at or near the beginning of the paragraph.
transition	A word or phrase that helps readers to follow the writer's thinking from one sentence to the next or from one paragraph to another. See Chapter 25.
vague reference	A pronoun without a clearly identifiable antecedent. See Chapter 15.
verb	A word or phrase that says something about a person, place, or thing and whose form may be changed to indicate tense (or time). Verbs may express action (physical or mental), occurrence, or condition (state of being). See Chapter 5.

Jessa *hit* an inside curve for a home run. (physical action)

Laurence *believed* the Blue Jays would win. (mental action)

Father's Day *falls* on the third Sunday of June. (occurrence)

Reva eventually *became interested* in English. (condition)

Some verbs are called **linking verbs:** they help to make a statement by linking the subject to a word or phrase that describes it.

William Hubbard *was* Toronto's first Black mayor. (*was* links *William Hubbard* to *mayor*)

Mohammed *looks* tired. (*looks* links *Mohammed* and *tired*)

In addition to am, is, are, was, were, and been, some common linking verbs are appear, become, feel, grow, look, taste, remain, seem, smell, sound.

Another class of verbs is called **auxiliary** or **helping verbs**. They show the time of a verb as future or past (e.g., *will* go, *has* gone) or as a continuing action (*is* reading). They also show the passive voice (*is* completed, *have been* submitted).

voice

Verbs may be **active** or **passive**, depending on whether the subject of the verb is *acting* (active voice) or *being acted upon* (passive voice).

In 2011, the government introduced a new set of tax reforms. (active)

A new set of tax reforms was introduced in 2011. (passive)

wordiness

The use of more words than necessary. Wordiness results when information is repeated or when a phrase is used when a single word will suffice. See Chapter 1.

zero article

See **article**.

APPENDIX C

Answers to Exercises

Answers for Unit 1 Quick Quiz

Note: Triple asterisks (***) indicate that a redundant word or words have been deleted. Each set of triple asterisks counts as one error.. . .

[1]Having decided to buy a new stereo system for my car, I went to Awesome Auto Audio, a store **whose** advertisements in the paper said **their** quality and prices are unbeatable. [2]The salesperson could see that I was a more serious customer **than** the average car radio buyer, and recommended that I consider V3A. [3]Of **course**, I didn't want to let him know that I didn't know what V3A was, so he **led** me to a special showroom where I spotted a sign that read "Voice-Activated Auto Audio (V3A)."

[4]The salesperson switched on the system and demonstrated by saying, "**Louder**," which increased the radio's volume. [5]Then he said, "Techno," and the radio immediately switched to a techno station. [6]I thought this was **excellent**, so, **regardless** of the price, I told him to install it in my car. [7]In *** fact, I had convinced myself that **it's** safer to have a radio that doesn't need to be adjusted manually *** while I was driving. [8]Once I had presented my **credit card** and a **piece** of identification, I went to the parking lot to wait for the installation.

[9]Soon I was driving home and calling out, "Louder" and "**Oldies**" and "Classic rock," and the radio was obeying every command. [10]Suddenly, as I was turning a corner, another driver cut right in front of me. [11]Annoyed, I yelled, "Stupid!" and the radio *** abruptly switched to a call-in talk show.

Answer Key

If you missed the error(s) in sentence ...	see Chapter ...	
[1] *who's, they're*	2	Hazardous Homonyms; 3 The Apostrophe
[2] *then*	2	Hazardous Homonyms
[3] *coarse, lead*	2	Hazardous Homonyms
[4] *"louder"*	4	Capital Letters
[6] *way cool*	1	"Slang" section
[6] *irregardless*	1	"Abusages" section
[7] *In actual fact*	1	"Wordiness" section
[7] *its*	2	Hazardous Homonyms; 3 The Apostrophe
[7] *manually, by hand*	1	"Wordiness" section
[8] *Credit Card*	4	Capital Letters
[8] *peace*	2	Hazardous Homonyms
[9] *"Oldie's"*	3	The Apostrophe
[11] *suddenly and abruptly*	1	"Wordiness" section

Answers for Chapter 1: Choosing the Right Words

Exercise 1.1

1. If you are using a Canadian dictionary, the pronunciation given first is the one favoured in Canada.
2. *Humor.* You must use the root *humor* when adding an ending: for example, *humorous.*
3. Some suggestions: *irrelevant, irrational, irreparable, irrespective, irresponsible, irreverence.*
4. The word is spelled *tattoo* and can be used both as a noun (meaning "artwork on the skin made with a needle and ink") and as a verb (meaning "to create artwork on the skin using a needle and ink).
5. *Program, center, skilful, traveller, judgment.* The preferred spellings in Canada are *program, centre, skilful, traveller,* and *judgment.*

Exercise 1.2

1. ratios	5. crises	9. appendixes
2. criteria	6. data (the singular is *datum*)	(or *appendices*)
3. analyses	7. mothers-in-law	10. formulas
4. personnel	8. nuclei (or *nucleuses*)	(or *formulae*)

Exercise 1.3

1. delayed	5. repayment	8. easier
2. journeys	6. loneliness	9. laziness
3. player	7. policies	10. necessarily
4. destroying		

The root words in 1 to 5 end in a **vowel** plus *y*; these words do not change spelling when you add an ending. The root words in 6 to 10 end in a **consonant** plus *y*; change *y* to *i* when you add an ending to such words.

Exercise 1.4

1. dis-cuss	5. through (Words	7. chal-lenge
2. man-age-ment	of one syllable	8. tech-ni-cian
3. ac-com-mo-date	cannot be divided.)	9. con-science
4. dis-trib-ute	6. cre-ate	10. busi-ness

Exercise 1.7 (suggested answers)

1. A woman has the last word in any argument, and anything a man says is the beginning of a new argument.
2. Each evening at 10, we watch *The National* on CBC.
3. How can we eliminate our debt when we have no choice each month but to spend more than we earn?
4. The city told me that there was little they could do about the raccoons in my backyard.
5. My grandfather impressed me when I asked him if he had lived his whole life in Canada and he replied, "Not yet."

Exercise 1.9 (suggested answers)

Note: Triple asterisks (***) indicate that a word or words have been deleted. Each set of triple asterisks counts as one error.

1. **You** should **be careful** when **using** an axe.

2. We **live** at the **corner** of Maple Street and Rue Érable in *** Sherbrooke.
3. **After** we **looked closely at** the task ***, we knew **we would need help**.
4. When we **saw** storm clouds **ahead**, we knew that **it was going to rain**.
5. My gym teacher **knows** that I **dislike exercise**.

Exercise 1.10 (suggested answers)

We've italicized the clichés in the original and then provided a suggested revision for each item.

1. (a) I'm *just giving you a heads-up* about this problem because *at the end of the day* we're *all in this together*.
   (b) I'm alerting you about this problem because we are partners.
2. (a) *Last but not least*, we want to thank our support staff, whose *thinking outside the box saved the day*.
   (b) Finally, we want to thank our support staff, whose creative thinking saved our project.
3. (a) This is *not rocket science. Ballpark figures* reveal that a small investment now will *reap huge dividends when all is said and done*.
   (b) This is simple. Estimates reveal that a small investment now will result in significant future gains.
4. (a) If I had *cutting-edge* graphics programs on a *state-of-the-art* computer, I could *make the grade* as a game developer.
   (b) If I had superior graphics programs on a powerful computer, I could be a successful game developer.
5. (a) Just when divorce rates have *reached epidemic proportions* and loneliness has become *a fact of life, psychological experts* have agreed that *meaningful* relationships are critical to mental health.
   (b) Just when divorce rates have skyrocketed and loneliness has become commonplace, psychologists have concluded that close relationships are critical to mental health.

Exercise 1.11

Note: Triple asterisks (***) indicate that a word or words have been deleted. Each set of triple asterisks counts as one error.

1. **Many** of my friends are *** happy to be going away to college, but I would rather stay home and live with my family,
2. For this party, you are **supposed** to dress the way you did in primary school.
3. **Regardless** of what you say, I think the mass media **are** generally reliable.
4. Many young people prefer to read the news **on** their smartphones.
5. The **reason** for this preference **is that** smartphones offer *** quick and convenient access to information.
6. Between you and **me**, I rely on television to tell me what's going on in the world.
7. The reason **you** are failing **is that** you **don't do any** homework.
8. Luisa's father isn't **prejudiced**; he can't *** stand **any** of her boyfriends.
9. George shouldn't be driving **anywhere**; we should **have** taken his car keys **from** him.
10. Our instructor doesn't have **any** patience (*or* **has no** patience) with people who should **have** been coming to class and now can't write *** well.

Answers for Chapter 2: Hazardous Homonyms

Exercise 2.1

1. Biology is a **course** that I should be able to pass easily.
2. My sister is a **woman** who **hears** everything and forgets nothing.
3. **Whose** stereo is disturbing our **quiet** meditation time?
4. **They're** still in bed because they stayed up **too** late.
5. This college values **its** students.
6. I'd like to **lose** five kilograms before summer, but I can't resist **desserts**.

Exercise 2.2

1. **It's** the perfect **site** for our annual meeting.
2. Our math teacher won't **accept** assignments submitted **later** than Thursday.
3. Our **morale** was boosted by the **compliments** we received.
4. **Their** love of junk food is having an **effect** on their health.
5. It was the **fourth** quarter of the game, and we **led** by 20 points.

Exercise 2.3

1. Is there anyone **whose advice** you will pay attention to?
2. **Your** confidence in statistics is an **illusion**.
3. My **conscience** sometimes troubles me when I send long **personal** messages on the office computer.
4. It's **your** turn to get more **stationery** from the storeroom.
5. I believe in the **principle** of fairness more **than** the deterrent of punishment.

Exercise 2.4

1. We **led** the relief workers to the **site** of the disaster.
2. She **cited** my writing in her new book on the **effects** of poor grammar.
3. If we **accept** your **counsel**, will you guarantee our success?
4. He was dizzy but **conscious** after falling off his **stationary** bike.
5. At the checkpoint, I was hit on the head and **then** dragged out into the **desert**.

Exercise 2.5

1. **Choose** carefully, because the candidate who is chosen is bound to change **our** environment.
2. This company makes a better product **than** any of **its** competitors does.
3. According to Woody Allen, "The **moral** is that money is better **than** poverty, if only for financial reasons."
4. Rita was **conscious** that Yuri's **compliments** were never sincere.
5. When someone says, "**It's** not the money but the **principle** of the thing," it's the money.

Exercise 2.6

1. Other **than** hope and pray that voters will **choose** our candidate, there is not much more we can do.
2. She's **quite** sure that the committee will **accept** her resumé, even though **it's** late and written on lined **stationery**.
3. The streets were **deserted** and as we drove **through**, we **passed** only a police officer and a stray dog.

4. Not knowing whether to **accept** the company's offer, I asked my lawyer for **advice**; she **cited** previous settlements that convinced me to turn it down.

5. Blindfolded, my wrists and ankles bound with duct tape, I was **led** to the car and driven out into the **desert**, **where** I was left by the side of the road.

Exercise 2.7

1. **Whether** at work or at home, people should **know** it's best to avoid using **coarse** language.

2. All employees, without **exception**, will be fined $20.00 a day until **morale** on the job **site** improves.

3. The **advice** given to us by the personnel firm we hired was to **choose** a **woman whose principal** qualifications were a huge ego and shoes that **complemented** her outfits.

4. Emily is the supervisor **who's** responsible for monitoring the **effects** of automation on assembly-line **personnel**.

Exercise 2.8

I had a hard time **choosing** between two colleges, both of which offered the **courses** I wanted. Both had good placement records, and I just couldn't make up my mind. I asked my friends for **advice**, but they were no help. Several were surprised that any college would even **accept** me! Their negative view of my academic ability did nothing to improve my **morale**; in fact, it **led** me to re-evaluate my selection of friends. My school counsellor, a **woman whose** opinion I respect, didn't think one college was better **than** the other, so she suggested that I choose the school that was located **where** I preferred to live. I followed her advice, and I haven't regretted it.

Exercise 2.9

Many people today are **choosing** a quieter way of life. They hope to live longer and more happily by following the "slower is better" **principle**. Some, on the **advice** of **their** doctors, have been forced to slow down. One heart surgeon, for example, tells his patients to drive only in the slow lane rather **than** use the passing lane. They may arrive a few minutes later, but their blood pressure will not be **affected**. Others don't need to be prompted by their doctors. They **accept** that living at a slower pace doesn't mean **losing** out in any way. In fact, the opposite is true: **choosing** a healthy lifestyle benefits everyone. **Peace** and **quiet** in one's **personal** life lead to increased productivity, higher **morale**, and greater job satisfaction. Sometimes the improvements are **minor**, but as anyone who has **consciously** tried to slow the pace of life can tell you, the slow lane is the fast lane to longevity.

Answers for Chapter 3: The Apostrophe

Exercise 3.1

1. can't
2. she'd
3. he'll
4. we'd
5. who's
6. she'll
7. won't
8. we'll
9. let's
10. I'm

Exercise 3.2

1. they're	5. everyone's	8. you're
2. I'll	6. couldn't	9. we'd
3. it's	7. who's	10. won't
4. can't		

Exercise 3.3

1. **It's** almost certain that **he'll** be late.
2. There **won't** be a problem if **you're** on time.
3. **I'm** sure that contractions **shouldn't** be used in formal writing.
4. **They're** acceptable in conversation and in informal writing.
5. **We'll** help you with your essay, but **you'll** have to get started right away.
6. **It's** not that **I'm** afraid to die; I just **don't** want to be there when it happens.
7. We **haven't** yet decided whom to hire, but **we'll** let you know as soon as possible.
8. In my culture, a **birthday's** the most important day of the year, and anyone **who's** celebrating is the centre of attention.
9. **It's** just too much of a coincidence that **you're** leaving for a two-week holiday the day before your great-aunt Deena arrives for her annual visit.
10. If you **can't** be a good example, maybe **you'll** be a horrible warning.

Exercise 3.4

    I am writing to apply for the position of webmaster for BrilloVision.com that **you have** advertised in the *Daily News*. **I have** the talent and background **you are** looking for. Currently, I work as a web designer for an online publication, Vexed.com, where **they are** very pleased with my work. If you click on their website, I think **you will** like what you see. **There is** little in the way of Web design and application that I **have not** been involved in during the past two years. But **it is** time for me to move on to a new challenge, and BrilloVision.com promises the kind of opportunity **I am** looking for. I guarantee you **will not** be disappointed if I join your team!

Exercise 3.5

1. woman's beauty
2. witness's testimony
3. families' budgets
4. children's school
5. the soldiers' uniforms
6. the book's title
7. everyone's choice
8. the Khans' daughters
9. the oldest child's responsibility
10. our country's flag

Exercise 3.6

1. **Shahn's** greatest fear is his **mother's** disapproval.
2. **Students'** supplies can be expensive, so I buy mine at **Devi's** Dollar Store.
3. My parents would like to know **whose** yogurt has been in **their** fridge for months.
4. After only a **month's** wear, my **son's** jacket had holes in both sleeves.
5. Unfortunately, the **book's** cover was much more interesting than **its** contents.

6. Our **team's** biggest win came at the same time as our **league's** other teams all lost.

7. This **month's** *Fashion* magazine has two pages on **men's** spring clothing and twenty pages on **women's**.

8. This year, our **family's** Thanksgiving celebration will be a quiet one, as we think of other **families'** poverty.

9. Our **country's** healthcare system, one of **its** greatest assets, needs an overhaul if it is to remain affordable.

10. One way of overcoming writer's block is to disconnect **your** computer from **its** monitor so you can't see **your** draft as you type.

Exercise 3.7

1. **I've** heard that **you're** going to quit smoking.
2. **It's** true. My family **doctor's** concerns about my health finally convinced me to quit.
3. **Who's** perfect? I am, at least in my **mother's** opinion.
4. **It's** a fact that most **mothers'** opinions of their children are unrealistically positive.
5. Most **fathers'** opinions of their **daughters'** boyfriends are negative.

Exercise 3.8

1. **Today's** styles and **tomorrow's** trends are featured in this **month's** issue of *Flare* magazine.
2. To find bargains on sale or to sell **your** own unwanted items, try **eBay's** Internet site.
3. **Hockey's** playoff schedule puts the **finals** into the middle of June.
4. **Doctors'** stress levels are high, but **secretaries'** and police **officers'** stress levels are even higher.

Exercise 3.9

1. When you feel like having a snack, you can choose between apples and **Timbits**.
2. **Yolanda's** career took off when she discovered **it's** easy to sell **children's** toys.
3. The Olympic **Games** are held every two years.
4. **Poker's** an easy game to play if you are dealt **aces** more often than your **opponents** are.
5. **Nobody's** perfect, but if you consistently make apostrophe mistakes, you demonstrate that you don't understand possession and **contractions**.

Exercise 3.10

1. **I've** posted a sign on my front lawn: "**Salespersons** welcome. Dog **food's** expensive."
2. The **leaders** of the European Union **countries** meet in Brussels.
3. Three **months'** work was wasted by a few **minutes'** carelessness.
4. In Canada, when it's warm enough to expose **your** skin to the sun, the **insects'** feeding season is at **its** height.

Exercise 3.11

Our well-educated **citizens** are one of our **country's** greatest natural **resources**. Canada can claim the highest percentage of university- and college-educated people of any country. According to the Organization for Economic Co-operation and Development, at 48 percent, Canada topped Japan and New Zealand, **whose** 41 percent tied for second. **It's** interesting to note that the United States (40 percent) and the United

Kingdom (32 percent) placed fourth and tenth respectively, well behind our **nation's** number. Canada owes its high ranking to our **immigrants'** level of education. More than half of our recent immigrants (those who arrived after 2001) came here with a university degree. **That's** more than twice the proportion of degree **holders** among the **country's** native-born population.

Exercise 3.12

An American border guard stopped a Canadian who was crossing the border near Drummondville, Quebec, on his bicycle and carrying two heavy **sacks**. The American demanded to know what was in the sacks, and the **Canadian's** reply was "Sand." The **guard's** response was to search through the bags thoroughly, but all he and his **colleagues** found was sand. On the next **day's** shift, the border guard saw the cyclist with his sacks again and went through the same procedure, with the same result. For several **weeks**, the Canadian carrying sand appeared regularly at the border crossing, and each time the wary **guards** searched the sacks, but they never found anything suspicious. Then the cyclist did not appear for a couple of weeks, and the guard forgot about the mystery until one day, when he was off-duty and visiting Drummondville, he saw the man on the street. He introduced himself and told the man that the guards were convinced he had been smuggling something, but they **couldn't** figure out what it was. Now that the border **crossings** had stopped, he begged the man to tell him what he had been smuggling. The man smiled and replied, "**Bicycles**."

Answers for Chapter 4: Capital Letters

Exercise 4.1

1. **T**he pen is mightier than the sword.
2. Ping hurried back inside and said, "**I**t's too cold to go to school today."
3. **T**aped to the door was a sign that read, "**N**ot to be used as an exit or entrance."
4. **I**n conclusion, I want you to think about the words of Wendell Johnson: "*Always* and *never* are two words you should always remember never to use."
5. Our English teacher told us, "**L**earning standard written English is, for most people, like learning another language."

Exercise 4.2

1. Do you find that **V**isa is more popular than **A**merican **E**xpress when you travel to faraway places such as Mexico, **F**rance, or Jupiter?
2. At **L**oblaws, we argued over the cornflakes. Should we buy Kellogg, **P**ost, **Q**uaker, or **P**resident's **C**hoice?
3. Our stay at the Seaview **H**otel, overlooking the **P**acific **O**cean, was far better than our last vacation at the **B**ates **M**otel, where we faced west, overlooking the city dump.
4. As a member of the Waterloo **A**lumni **A**ssociation, I am working to raise funds from companies such as **D**isney, **T**oyota, **M**icrosoft, and the **CBC**, where our graduates have been hired.

Exercise 4.3

1. The **C**rusades, which were religious wars between **M**uslims and **C**hristians, raged through the **M**iddle **A**ges.

2. The **H**indu religion recognizes and honours many gods; **I**slam recognizes one god, **A**llah; **B**uddhism recognizes none.

3. The **K**oran, the **B**ible, and the **T**orah agree on many principles.

4. The **J**ewish festival of **H**anukkah often occurs near the same time that **C**hristians are celebrating **C**hristmas.

5. After **W**orld **W**ar I, many **J**ews began to immigrate to Palestine, where they and the **M**uslim population soon came into conflict.

Exercise 4.4

1. My favourite months are **J**anuary and **F**ebruary because I love all **w**inter sports.

2. This **M**onday is **V**alentine's **D**ay, when people exchange messages of love.

3. In the summer, big meals seem too much trouble; however, after **T**hanksgiving, we need lots of food to survive the winter cold.

4. A **n**ational **h**oliday named **F**lag **D**ay was once proposed, but it was never officially approved.

5. Thursday is **C**anada **D**ay and also the official beginning of my **s**ummer **v**acation.

Exercise 4.5

1. Don't you think that the authors of this book could have come up with a more imaginative title for this chapter? Why not "**C**onquering **C**apitals," for example?

2. Joseph Conrad's short novel *Heart of Darkness* became the blockbuster movie *Apocalypse Now.*

3. Botticelli's famous painting *Birth of Venus* inspired my poem "**W**oman on the **H**alf **S**hell."

4. The review of my book, *A Happy Vegan,* published in *The Globe and Mail,* was not favourable.

5. Clint Eastwood fans will be delighted that one of the early movies that made him internationally famous, *A Fistful of Dollars,* is now available on **DVD**.

Exercise 4.6

1. I want to take **I**ntroductory **F**rench this term, but it is not offered until **w**inter.

2. Although my favourite subject is **m**ath, I'm not doing very well in Professor Truman's course, **B**usiness **F**inance 101.

3. Correct.

4. Laurie is studying to be a chef and is taking courses called **F**ood **P**reparation, **R**estaurant **M**anagement, and **E**nglish.

5. The prerequisite for Theology 210 is **I**ntroduction to **W**orld **R**eligions, taught by **P**rofessor Singh.

Exercise 4.7

1. Our youth group meets in the **O**ttawa mosque every second **T**hursday.

2. You must take some **s**cience courses, or you'll never get into the program you want at college in the **f**all.

3. Gore Vidal, author of *The Best Man,* once said, "**I**t is not enough to succeed; others must fail."

4. After the game, we went to the **B**urger **P**alace for a late snack and then went home to watch *This Hour Has 22 Minutes* on television.

5. In our **E**nglish course at **C**aribou **C**ollege, we studied *The Englishman's Boy*, a novel about life among the settlers of the **C**anadian **W**est.

Exercise 4.8

Sherlock Holmes and his friend **D**r. **W**atson were on a camping trip in **B**ritish **C**olumbia's **R**ocky **M**ountains. During the night, Holmes awakened his friend and said, "Watson, look up. What do you see?"

Watson replied, "I see millions and millions of stars."

"And what does that tell you?" enquired Holmes.

"If I recall correctly, my **A**stronomy 200 course taught me that there are countless stars, **g**alaxies, and planets. From my knowledge of **a**strology, I observe that **T**aurus is in **S**corpio. From the position of the planets, I deduce it is about 3:30 in the morning, and according to my understanding of **m**eteorology, it will be a lovely **s**ummer day tomorrow."

Holmes was silent for a moment and then said, "**Y**ou **i**diot, Watson, someone has stolen our tent!"

Answers for Unit 1 Rapid Review

Note: Triple asterisks (***) indicate that a redundant word or words have been deleted. Each set of asterisks counts as one error.

[1]In 1908, travellers in the Nova Scotia wilderness reported being **thrilled** by the **sight** of a beaver dam because beavers were almost extinct at that time. [2]What a change 100 years has brought! [3]Now, the beaver is so common and so prolific that **it's** being hunted and trapped as a nuisance across Canada. [4]In fact, Canadian trappers are issued a quota for the number of **beavers** they are **allowed** to trap in their territory, and they must reach that quota or **lose** their trapping licence.

[5]**We're** not alone in our struggle to control these **large,** pesky rodents. [6]A *Canadian Geographic* film called ***The Super Beaver*** documents the **creature's** introduction to Tierra del Fuego, at the tip of South America, which has led to the *** devastation of the ecosystem. [7]The film tells us that only coral and humans have had a greater impact on **Earth's** environment than beavers! [8]They have migrated to the mainland of South America, where without rigorous and expensive government intervention, they threaten to destroy millions of hectares of **Argentina's** land as they expand their territory northward. [9]It's difficult to **accept** the fact that only 100 years ago, travellers in **Canada's** wilderness longed for a glimpse of what was then a rare and exotic animal.

Answer Key

If you missed the error(s) in sentence ...	see Chapter ...
[1] *being blown away*	1 "Slang" section
[1] *cite*	2 Hazardous Homonyms
[3] *its*	2 Hazardous Homonyms; 3 The Apostrophe
[4] *beaver's*	3 The Apostrophe
[4] *aloud*	2 Hazardous Homonyms
[4] *loose*	2 Hazardous Homonyms
[5] *Were*	2 Hazardous Homonyms; 3 The Apostrophe

If you missed the error(s) in sentence ...	see Chapter ...	
[5] *humongous*	1	"Slang" section
[6] *The super beaver*	4	Capital Letters
[6] *creatures*	3	The Apostrophe
[6] *complete and total*	1	"Wordiness" section
[7] *Earths*	3	The Apostrophe
[8] *Argentinas*	3	The Apostrophe
[9] *except*	2	Hazardous Homonyms
[9] *Canadas*	3	The Apostrophe

Answers for Unit 2 Quick Quiz

Note: The superscript numbers refer to the original sentence numbers in the Quick Quiz on pages 62–63.

[1]My heart goes out to anyone struggling to make sense of English idioms. [2]Students are frequently puzzled, often confused, and sometimes **amused** by the thousands of idiomatic expressions **that** give flavour and power to our language. [4]An idiom **is** a phrase whose meaning is difficult to figure out from the meanings of its individual words. [5]For example, **consider** the many idioms involving the word *heart*. [6]We describe a kind, generous person as having a "heart of gold," and a cold, unfeeling person as having a "heart of stone." **These** are relatively simple idioms to understand. [7]But how can we explain the difference between "heartache," which means sorrow or anguish, and "heartburn," which is a term for indigestion? [8]Some "heart" idioms have positive connotations, **others have negative connotations**, and some are neutral. **Many** have to do with love. [9]When falling in love, **we may use** the expression "lost my heart" **or** loving "from the bottom of my heart." [11]But when the relationship ends, we "cry our hearts out" **because** we are "heartbroken" and our former lover is "heartless."

[12]"Heart" idioms apply to many aspects of life other than love. [13]**An example is** learning something "by heart." [14]This phrase means you memorize it. [15]If you want something very badly, you have "your heart set on it." **To** describe someone as "young at heart" means she is youthful in spirit if not in years. [16]To ask someone to "have a heart" **means** to ask for sympathy. [17]**If you are** frightened by a scene in a horror movie, the expression "heart-stopping" comes to mind, and you might have "your heart in your mouth" at the terrifying climax.

[18]English idioms using the word *heart* have a bewildering number of meanings that we discover **only** through experience. [19] People who know the language well understand these phrases automatically. [20]However, if you are still learning English, I advise you to "take heart" and do your best not to "lose heart" when frustrated by our illogical language.

Answer Key

If you missed the error(s) in sentence ...	see Chapter ...	
[2] *sometimes find amusement*	9	The Parallelism Principle
[3] Dependent clause fragment	6	Solving Sentence-Fragment Problems
[4] "Missing piece" fragment	6	Solving Sentence-Fragment Problems
[5] "Missing piece" fragment	6	Solving Sentence-Fragment Problems
[6] Comma splice	7	Solving Run-On Sentence Problems

If you missed the error(s) in sentence ...	see Chapter ...
8 *negative connotations cling to others*	9 The Parallelism Principle
8 Comma splice	7 Solving Run-On Sentence Problems
9 *When falling in love, the expression ...*	8 "Dangling Modifiers" section
10 "Missing piece" fragment	6 Solving Sentence-Fragment Problems
11 Fused sentence	7 Solving Run-On Sentence Problems
13 "Missing piece" fragment	6 Solving Sentence-Fragment Problems
15 Comma splice	7 Solving Run-On Sentence Problems
16 "Missing piece" fragment	6 Solving Sentence-Fragment Problems
17 *Frightened by a scene in a horror movie, the scene ...*	8 "Dangling Modifiers" section
18 *that we only discover ...*	8 "Misplaced Modifiers" section

Answers for Chapter 5: Cracking the Sentence Code

Exercise 5.1

1. Canadians love doughnuts.
2. They eat more doughnuts than people in any other nation.
3. Most malls contain a doughnut shop.
4. Doughnuts taste sweet.
5. Glazed doughnuts are my favourite.
6. Hot chocolate is good with doughnuts.
7. [You] Try a bran doughnut for breakfast.
8. It is good for your health.
9. Doughnut jokes are common on television.
10. Dentists like doughnuts too, but for different reasons.

Exercise 5.2

1. I bought a hybrid car.
2. Hybrids use both electric and gas motors.
3. They normally consume far less gas than other cars.
4. My neighbour drives an SUV.
5. Every day, she takes her children to school.
6. In her SUV, she feels safe in all weather.
7. Last Thursday, it snowed all day long.
8. My neighbour plowed her car into a snowdrift.
9. It became firmly stuck.
10. I drove her children home from school in my little hybrid.

Exercise 5.3

1. Is Tomas still on the team?
2. [You] Consider it done.
3. Here are the answers to yesterday's quiz.
4. Is it your birthday today?
5. Into the pool leaped the terrified cat.
6. Where are the children?
7. There were only two students in class today.
8. Which elective is easier?

9. Are you happy with your choice?
10. Who let the dogs out?

Exercise 5.4

1. Your sister is calling from Mexico.
2. Tia will arrive from Finland tomorrow.
3. Have you arranged accommodation for our guests?
4. The restaurant could have prepared a vegetarian meal.
5. They might have moved away from the city.
6. Xue should have completed her diploma by now.
7. Do you know anything about them?
8. They have visited Venezuela twice.
9. We must have practised enough by now.
10. I will be looking for verbs in my sleep.

Exercise 5.5

1. I am making a nutritious breakfast.
2. It does not include Coca-Cola.
3. You can add fresh fruit to the cereal.
4. The toast should be almost ready now.
5. My doctor has often recommended yogurt for breakfast.
6. I could never eat yogurt without fruit.
7. With breakfast, I will drink at least two cups of coffee.
8. I don't like tea.
9. I simply cannot begin my day without coffee.
10. I should probably switch to decaf.

Exercise 5.6

1. I had never repaired water pipes before.
2. We now get our drinking water by courier.
3. Could you possibly be on time?
4. Have those jeans ever been washed?
5. Money has never come easily to me.
6. Your jokes are not always appreciated.
7. I have sometimes been seen in the library.
8. The librarians have often asked for my ID.
9. There should not be any more delays.
10. Has any turtle ever outlived the shaker of turtle food?

Exercise 5.7

1. Many people in the crowd were confused.
2. Fifty of her friends gave her a surprise party.
3. The official opening of the new city hall will be held tomorrow.
4. In the movies, the collision of two cars always results in a fire.
5. A couple of burgers should be enough for each of us.
6. [You] Please decide on dessert before dinnertime.
7. Only a few of us have finished our homework.
8. After class, the people in my carpool meet in the cafeteria.

9. There is a show ~~about laser surgery on television~~ tonight.

10. ~~In the land of the blind~~, the one-eyed man is king.

Exercise 5.8

1. A party ~~in our neighbours' apartment~~ kept us awake ~~until dawn~~.
2. The meeting ~~of all students in our class~~ solved nothing.
3. ~~From the hallway~~ came the sound ~~of a loud argument~~.
4. ~~According to the news~~, the temperature ~~in Yellowknife~~ fell 20°C overnight.
5. My naps ~~in the afternoon~~ are necessary because ~~of my late-night activities~~.
6. Nothing ~~in this world~~ travels faster than a bad cheque.
7. ~~For many students~~, lack ~~of money~~ is probably their most serious problem.
8. The plural of ~~*choose*~~ should be *cheese*.
9. ~~After my acceptance to this college~~, I became interested ~~in learning about the city~~.
10. My guarantee ~~of an A in this course~~ is valid only ~~under certain conditions~~.

Exercise 5.9

A recent study ~~by Statistics Canada~~ reveals some disturbing facts ~~about the fitness of Canadians~~. ~~According to the study~~, young Canadians spend more than nine hours a day ~~on their backsides~~. Much ~~of this time~~, ~~of course~~, is spent ~~in front of the television~~. As a result ~~of their lack of exercise~~, their physical health is suffering. An example ~~of the influence of television~~ occurred ~~in my son's arithmetic class~~. The teacher was frustrated ~~by the children's lack of attention~~. Finally, ~~in desperation~~, she presented a problem ~~to the class in the hope of stimulating them~~. "What are 2 and 6 and 42 and 31?" One little boy showed enthusiasm ~~by waving~~ his hand ~~in the air~~. ~~With relief for the sudden interest~~, the teacher asked the boy ~~for his answer~~. "NBC, CTV, HBO, and the Sports Network!"

Exercise 5.10

1. The Flames and the Stampeders call Calgary home.
2. My computer freezes and crashes ~~with regularity~~.
3. Books can take you anywhere ~~in the world~~ and have more legroom than airplanes.
4. Poutine, tourtière, Nanaimo bars, and butter tarts constitute Canada's contribution ~~to world cuisine~~.
5. ~~According to some sources~~, hockey, football, lacrosse, and basketball are also Canadian inventions.
6. [You] Measure the ingredients carefully and mix them thoroughly.
7. Many tobacco farmers, cod fishers, and coal miners are retraining ~~for new careers~~.
8. The coyote stopped, stared ~~at the small child~~, and then turned and loped away.
9. You may study my notes and my research results but may not copy my work.
10. Students ~~with good time management skills~~ can research, organize, draft, and revise a first-class paper ~~by the deadline~~.

Exercise 5.11

1. Verbs and subjects are sometimes hard to find.
2. Farmers, loggers, and fishers need and deserve the support ~~of consumers~~.
3. [You] Open the bottle, pour carefully, taste, and enjoy.
4. Where do you and your roommates get the energy ~~for school, work, and fun~~?
5. Werner, Italo, and Pierre discussed and debated recipes all night.
6. ~~During the following week~~, each one chose and prepared a meal ~~for the other two~~.

7. Werner's <u>sauerbraten</u> and Black Forest <u>cake</u> <u>amazed</u> and <u>delighted</u> his friends.
8. <u>Italo</u> <u>chopped</u>, <u>sliced</u>, <u>simmered</u>, and <u>baked</u> a magnificent Italian meal.
9. <u>Pierre</u> and his <u>sister</u> <u>worked</u> ~~in the kitchen for two days~~ and <u>prepared</u> a delicious cassoulet.
10. ~~By the end of the week~~, <u>Pierre</u>, <u>Italo</u>, and <u>Werner</u> <u>were</u> ready ~~for a diet~~.

Exercise 5.12

1. A <u>fool</u> and his <u>money</u> <u>are</u> soon <u>parted</u>.
2. <u>I</u> <u>dream</u> ~~of success~~ and <u>worry</u> ~~about failure~~.
3. <u>Nur</u> and <u>Aman</u> <u>paddled</u> and <u>portaged</u> ~~for 10 days~~.
4. ~~From the back seat of the tiny car~~ <u>emerged</u> a basketball <u>player</u> and a Newfoundland <u>dog</u>.
5. ~~In the mist of early morning~~, a <u>brontosaurus</u> and a <u>tyrannosaurus</u> <u>sniffed</u> the moist air and <u>hunted</u> ~~for food~~.
6. [<u>You</u>] <u>Pack</u> your suitcases and <u>prepare</u> ~~for a magical journey~~.
7. Why <u>are</u> <u>goalies</u> ~~in hockey~~ and <u>kickers</u> ~~in football~~ so superstitious?
8. ~~In my dreams~~, the <u>maid</u>, <u>butler</u>, <u>housekeeper</u>, and <u>chef</u> <u>wash</u> the dishes, <u>vacuum</u> the floors, <u>do</u> the laundry, and <u>make</u> the meals.
9. ~~According to the official course outline~~, <u>students</u> ~~in this English course~~ <u>must take</u> notes ~~during every class~~ and <u>submit</u> their notes ~~to their instructor for evaluation~~.
10. ~~In the opinion of many Canadians~~, the <u>word</u> *politician* <u>is</u> a synonym ~~for "crook."~~

Answers for Chapter 6: Solving Sentence-Fragment Problems

Exercise 6.1

Many different sentences can be made out of the fragments in this exercise. Just be sure that each of your sentences has both a subject and a verb.

1. __F__ One <u>type</u> of sentence-fragment error <u>is called</u> a "missing piece" fragment.
2. __F__ <u>We</u> <u>were</u> glad to be able to help you.
3. __F__ Your <u>mother</u> <u>is hoping</u> to hear from you soon.
4. __F__ The <u>class</u> <u>was saved</u> by the bell from doing yet another exercise.
5. __F__ To prevent a similar tragedy from happening again, a policy and procedures <u>manual</u> <u>will be developed</u>.
6. __F__ <u>It</u> <u>was</u> not a good idea to leave the cat in the same room with the canary.
7. __F__ <u>Attaching</u> a DVD player to the television <u>was</u> a challenge for me.
8. __S__
9. __F__ A new <u>puppy</u>, <u>kitten</u>, or <u>baby</u> <u>gives</u> one no choice but to get up early.
10. __S__

Exercise 6.2

1. F	5. F	9. F
2. F	6. F	10. F
3. F	7. F	
4. F	8. S	

Exercise 6.3 (suggested answers)

1. This apartment suits me in every way**,** **e**xcept for the price. I can't afford it.
2. In track and field, our college is well respected. Our team won the championship last year**,** **s**etting three new provincial records.

3. Whenever I go fishing, the fish aren't biting, but the mosquitoes are. Maybe I should give up fishing **a**nd start collecting insects instead.

4. My son is a genius. On his last birthday, he was given a toy that was guaranteed to be unbreakable. <u>He</u> <u>used</u> it to break all his other toys.

5. We weren't lost, but we were certainly confused. I realized this when we passed City Hall **f**or the third time.

6. We decided to walk downtown to the coffee shop**,** **w**here we both ordered tea, just to be different.

7. My husband and I often go to the hockey arena**,** **n**ot to watch sports but to hear the concerts of our favourite local bands. These concerts give new meaning to the word *cool*.

8. Correct.

9. I enjoy reading travel books **a**bout faraway, exotic places that I have never visited and will probably never get to see. The fun is in the dreaming, not the doing.

10. Spending my days skiing and the nights dining and dancing <u>**is**</u> how I picture my retirement. Unfortunately, by then I'll be too old to enjoy it.

Exercise 6.4

1. S	5. F	8. F
2. F	6. F	9. S
3. F	7. S	10. F
4. F		

Exercise 6.5 (suggested answers)

Note: Triple asterisks (***) indicate that punctuation has been deleted.

David came home from his visit to the doctor *** **looking** very worried. His wife, noticing his worried expression**,** **asked** him what was troubling him. **He replied** that the doctor told him he must take a pill every day for the rest of his life. His wife **was** puzzled by his concern. Lots of people must take a pill a day. Why **was he** worried? David showed her the pill bottle**,** **which** contained only four pills.

Exercise 6.6 (suggested answers)

1. F (After) class is over.
2. F (Until) I hear from the hiring committee.
3. S
4. F (Once) the batteries are charged.
5. F (Who) encouraged us to keep trying.
6. S
7. F (Even if) there is an earthquake.
8. F (If) your form has been filled out correctly.
9. F (Where) you left your keys?
10. F (Although) he was weak from hunger and exhausted from lack of sleep.

Exercise 6.7 (suggested answers)

1. After class is over**,** I <u>am meeting</u> Manuel for coffee.
2. Until I hear from the hiring committee, I <u>am keeping</u> my fingers crossed.
3. Correct.
4. Once the batteries are charged**,** <u>you</u> <u>can use</u> the sweeper.
5. It <u>was</u> our captain who encouraged us to keep trying.
6. Correct.

7. Even if there is an earthquake **,** <u>we</u> <u>should be</u> safe in our mountain retreat.
8. If your form has been filled out correctly, the <u>committee</u> <u>will be</u> in touch with you.
9. How <u>should</u> <u>I</u> <u>know</u> where you left your keys?
10. Although he was weak from hunger and exhausted from lack of sleep, <u>he</u> <u>managed</u> to crawl to the refrigerator.

Exercise 6.8

1. Rain doesn't bother me. I like to stay inside and read. When the weather is miserable.
2. Walking is probably the best form of exercise there is. Unless you're in the water. Then swimming is preferable.
3. Whenever Kiki gets the opportunity. She loves to dance. But her boyfriend hates dancing, so she seldom gets the chance to show off her moves.
4. Please try this curry. After you've tasted it. I am sure you'll be able to tell me what's missing.
5. The report identifies a serious problem that we need to consider. Whenever our website is revised or updated. It is vulnerable to hackers.

Exercise 6.9

1. I keep the temperature in my apartment very low. In order to save money. My friends have to wear sweaters when they visit.
2. Your idea that we should ask for directions was a good one. We would still be lost now. If we had relied on the map.
3. Home decoration isn't difficult. When you don't have enough money for furniture, carpets, or curtains. You have no choice but to be creative.
4. I believe that honesty is the best policy. If I found a million dollars in the street and discovered it belonged to a poor, homeless person. I'd give it right back.
5. The names of many Canadian landmarks have been changed over the years. The Oldman River, for example, which runs through Lethbridge, used to be called the Belly River. Until local residents petitioned for a change to a more dignified name.

Exercise 6.10
Corrections to the fragments in Exercise 6.8:

1. Rain doesn't bother me. I like to stay inside and read **when** the weather is miserable.
2. Walking is probably the best form of exercise there is **unless** you're in the water. Then swimming is preferable.
3. Whenever Kiki gets the opportunity **, she** loves to dance. But her boyfriend hates dancing, so she seldom gets the chance to show off her moves.
4. Please try this curry. After you've tasted it **, I** am sure you'll be able to tell me what's missing.
5. The report identifies a serious problem that we need to consider. Whenever our website is revised or updated **, it** is vulnerable to hackers.

Corrections to the fragments in Exercise 6.9:

1. I keep the temperature in my apartment very low **in** order to save money. My friends have to wear sweaters when they visit.

2. Your idea that we should ask for directions was a good one. We would still be lost now **if** we had relied on the map.

3. Home decoration isn't difficult. When you don't have enough money for furniture, carpets, or curtains, **y**ou have no choice but to be creative.

4. I believe that honesty is the best policy. If I found a million dollars in the street and discovered that it belonged to a poor, homeless person, **I**'d give it right back.

5. The names of many Canadian landmarks have been changed over the years. The Oldman River, for example, which runs through Lethbridge, was called the Belly River **until** local residents petitioned for a change to a more dignified name.

Exercise 6.11 (suggested answers)

Here are some basic truths about the differences between men and women. While a woman marries a man expecting that he will change, **h**e won't. While a man marries a woman expecting that she will not change, **s**he will. A woman worries about the future **until** she gets a husband. A man never worries about the future **until** he gets a wife. A woman will dress up, do her hair, and apply makeup to go shopping, get the mail, put out the garbage, water the plants, or go to the gym **while** a man gets dressed up only for weddings and funerals. When it comes to her children, **a** woman knows all about them. **She** remembers their dental appointments and secret fears, best friends and romances, favourite foods, and hopes and dreams. A man, on the other hand, is vaguely aware of some short people living in the house. And finally, **there is** the matter of arguments. A woman has the last word in any argument. If a man says anything after the woman has the last word, **h**e starts a new argument.

Answers for Chapter 7: Solving Run-On Sentence Problems
Exercise 7.1

1. Press on the wound; that will stop the bleeding.
2. Don't let your worries kill you. **L**et the church help.
3. I can't read it **because** the print is too small.
4. Here is my number. **G**ive me a call.
5. Correct.
6. You'll love our new bikinis! **T**hey are simply the tops!
7. Eat sensibly; exercise regularly; die anyway.
8. That was a great dive, **so** you get a perfect 10.
9. Listen to this man play. **H**e's a jazz–blues musician who calls himself Dr. John.
10. While you were out, you received one phone call; it was from a telemarketer.

Exercise 7.2

1. I hate computers; they're always making mistakes.
2. I'm trying to stop playing computer games, **for** they take up too much of my time.
3. My watch has stopped, **so** I don't know what time it is.
4. I'm innocent. **T**his is a case of mistaken identity.
5. I'm going to stay up all night **because** I don't want to miss my 8:30 class.
6. The microwave oven is the most important appliance in my home; without it, I'd starve.
7. Money may not be everything, **but** it is far ahead of whatever is in second place.
8. Correct.

9. Teachers are coming across more and more students who went from printing straight to a keyboard**.** **T**hey have never learned cursive script.

10. These students are at a huge disadvantage during exams, **for** it takes far longer to print block capitals than it does to write cursive script.

Exercise 7.3

1. My favourite music is the blues **because** it complements my usual mood.
2. This restaurant is terribly slow**.** **I**t will be suppertime when we finally get our lunch.
3. I am pushing 60**.** **T**hat's enough exercise for me.
4. **If you** smile when you speak, you can get away with saying almost anything.
5. Correct.
6. That's the dumbest joke I've ever heard**;** it makes no sense.
7. The fine art of hitting an electronic device to get it to work again is called "percussive maintenance**.**" **N**ine times out of ten, it works.
8. The English language makes no sense**.** **W**hy do people recite at a play and play at a recital?
9. I write in my journal every day**.** **W**hen I'm 90, I want to read about all the important events in my life.
10. We have not inherited the Earth from our ancestors**;** we are borrowing it from our children.

Exercise 7.4 (suggested answers)

Last year, an exchange student from the south of France came to live with us**.** **H**er name was Simone, **and** she came to Canada to practise her English and learn something about our culture. Simone was amazed by ice hockey**;** she had never seen the game before and thought it was very exciting. In her first months here, Simone was surprised by what she perceived as Canadians' devotion to everything American, from television shows to sports events to music to fast food**.** **S**he confessed that she couldn't see much that was uniquely Canadian**.** **S**he was disappointed by our lack of a distinct culture, **but** after she made a week-long trip to Chicago, she began to understand some of the differences between the two countries**.** **T**he relative cleanliness of Canada's cities, our support of multiculturalism, and our respect for law and order impressed her**.** **T**he vastness of our country, with its huge expanses of untouched wilderness, intimidated her a little. Although she was homesick, especially in the first few weeks, Simone enjoyed her year in Canada**.** **W**hen she was packing up to return to Provence, she was already planning her next visit**.** **S**he wants to go camping on Prince Edward Island.

Exercise 7.5 (suggested answers)

Patience is a rare virtue in our "instant gratification" society**.** **E**ven in our written communication, we're so impatient that now we use short forms and initials instead of writing out words. Half a century ago, we might have written a letter (in ink on paper), put it in an envelope, and taken it to the nearest post office**.** **E**ventually our letter would arrive at its destination, and if a reply was necessary, we might receive it within two weeks. Now the same communication takes seconds, so it is no wonder that our attention spans have shrunk to nanoseconds**.** **T**his explains the popularity of short-form communications like those used on Twitter**.** **I**nstant social media make it almost impossible for teachers to hold the attention of students who are used to receiving information in tiny, seconds-long bursts.

Patience, however, is a useful virtue. **W**hen we are impatient, we might remember the story of the snail that entered a bar and asked for a beer. The bartender, without a word, picked up the snail and threw it out of the bar. **I**t rolled across the street into a ditch. Ten years passed. **P**eople were born and people died. **C**ountries appeared and disappeared. **E**conomies rose and fell. **W**ar followed peace, and peace followed war. The snail entered a bar and said, "Why did you do that?"

Exercise 7.6
1. The snow continues to fall. **I**t hasn't let up for three days.
2. Eagles may soar, **but** weasels don't get sucked into jet engines.
3. Computers are not intelligent; if they were, they wouldn't allow humans to touch their keyboards.
4. Going through the interview process **is** a valuable experience **even** if you don't get the job.
5. A cup of coffee in the morning gets me started; another at midday helps keep me alert after lunch.
6. CRNC is the home of the million-dollar guarantee. **Y**ou give us a million dollars, **and** we guarantee to play any song you want.
7. Television is a mass medium. **T**here is an old saying that it is called a medium because it rarely does anything well.
8. After studying the menu in my favourite vegetarian restaurant, my carnivorous husband observed, "This isn't food; this is what food eats."
9. The first sign of adulthood is the discovery that the volume knob also turns to the left. **F**or some people, this realization takes years.
10. The newspaper tells us that the weekend set records, both for high temperatures and for traffic accidents. **T**he two records are probably connected.

Answers for Chapter 8: Solving Modifier Problems
Exercise 8.1
1. They closed **just** before five.
2. We were splashed with mud by **almost** every car that passed.
3. She was exhausted after walking **only** 300 metres.
4. The French drink wine with **nearly** every meal, including lunch.
5. The suspect gave the police **scarcely** any information.
6. He was underwater for **nearly** two minutes before surfacing.
7. **In August** we went camping in a national park with lots of wildlife.
8. We will sell gas **in an approved container** to anyone for cash.
9. **Wearing her bikini**, Minnie shampooed and groomed her dog.
10. After the fire, she took her clothes **with the most smoke damage** to the cleaners.

Exercise 8.2
1. The manager fired **only** those who had not met their sales quotas.
2. I have **nearly** been fired every week that I have worked here.
3. I had answered **scarcely** 12 of the 25 questions when time was up.
4. This is a book **with real depth** for serious readers.
5. We provide computers **that are constantly crashing** to all our staff.
6. Canadians enjoy **practically** the highest standard of living in the world.

7. We bought toys **with batteries included** for the children.

8. Matti couldn't force the **loudly braying** donkey to take a single step.

9. **With your book closed**, tell me what you have read.

10. **With her binoculars**, Daisy crouched in the long grass and watched the lioness.

Exercise 8.3 (suggested answers)

1. Travelling in Quebec, **you** will find that knowing even a little French is useful.

2. Her saddle firmly cinched, **the mare** was led out of the barn.

3. After being seasick for two days, **we** were relieved when the ocean became calm.

4. Standing in the water for more than an hour, **he** was numbed to the bone by the cold.

5. Being very weak in math, **I** found the job was out of my reach.

6. **When you are looking for a job**, a good resumé is essential.

7. After spending two weeks constantly quarrelling, **they** decided to end their relationship.

8. In less than a minute after applying the ointment, **I** found the pain began to ease.

9. **When I was coming home on the bus**, my wallet was stolen.

10. Having had the same roommate for three years, **I** was urged by my parents to look for another.

Exercise 8.4 (suggested answers)

1. As a college teacher, **I** find dangling modifiers annoying.

2. **When we left the movie theatre**, the sky was dark and a storm threatened.

3. Hoping to miss the rush-hour traffic, **I** set the alarm for 5:00 a.m.

4. **Because our guests arrived an hour late**, dinner was both overcooked and cold.

5. Driving recklessly, **André** was stopped at a roadblock by the police.

6. Dressed in a new miniskirt, **Ping** looked terrific to her boyfriend.

7. After waiting for 20 minutes, **we** finally got the attention of the server.

8. Having been convicted of breaking and entering, **Bambi** was sentenced to two years in prison.

9. After revising her resumé, filling out the application, and going through the interview, **she** was disappointed to learn the position was given to someone else.

10. **After I scored the winning goal in overtime**, the fans began chanting my name and wouldn't stop, even during the trophy presentation.

Exercise 8.5 (suggested answers)

1. The sign said that **only** students were admitted to the pub.

2. As a responsible pet owner, **I walk my dog** at least twice a day.

3. The lion was recaptured **by the trainer** before anyone was mauled or bitten.

4. Swimming isn't a good idea if **the water is** polluted.

5. **When the bus driver suddenly slammed on the brakes**, several passengers were thrown to the floor.

6. Employees who are **often** late are dismissed without notice. (*Or* Employees who are late are **often** dismissed without notice.)

7. **After we waited for you for over an hour**, the evening was ruined.

8. **Since we'd been munching on chicken wings during the game**, our appetites for dinner were ruined.

9. **Because of her experience**, we hired the first designer who applied.
10. **For 20 minutes**, the president spoke glowingly of the retiring workers who had worked long and loyally.

Exercise 8.6 (suggested answers)

1. **Just before I left home**, my cellphone rang.
2. **While we were relaxing on the back porch**, the mosquitoes became increasingly annoying.
3. Startled by a loud knock on the door, **Daniel** nicked his chin with his razor.
4. My mother taught me how to drive a tractor **when I was five**.
5. **While we were sitting on the patio outside the restaurant**, my brother drove by in my car and waved.
6. As a college student constantly faced with new assignments, **I** sometimes find the pressure intolerable.
7. **Since we have been to Cuba twice and Spain once**, Jaime, who has never been outside the province, was fascinated by our travel stories.
8. **When she dived away from the inside pitch**, the ball hit her on the elbow.
9. We bought fish and chips, **wrapped in newspaper and smelling deliciously of malt vinegar**, from a street vendor on the beach. (*Or* **From a street vendor on the beach**, we bought fish and chips **wrapped in newspaper and smelling deliciously of malt vinegar**.)
10. **Under the Greek sun, wearing as little as the law allowed**, they soon forgot the Winnipeg winter they had left behind.

Answers for Chapter 9: The Parallelism Principle
Exercise 9.1

1. This is a book to read, enjoy, and **remember**.
2. The new brochure on career opportunities is attractive and **informative**.
3. Gracefully but **carefully**, Bonita descended the stairs in her floor-length gown and five-inch heels.
4. He ate his supper, did the dishes, watched television, and **went to bed**.
5. Barking dogs and **screaming children** keep me from enjoying the park.
6. Ali was discouraged by the low pay, **the long hours**, and the office politics.
7. In this clinic, we care for the sick, the injured, and **the homeless**.
8. If she wasn't constantly eating chips, playing bingo, and **smoking cigarettes**, she'd have plenty of money for groceries.
9. If I can't be an RCMP officer, I want to be a chef, an architect, or **a stand-up comic**.
10. So far, the countries I have enjoyed most are China for its people, France for its food, and Brazil **for its beaches**.

Exercise 9.2

1. Being unable to speak the language, I was confused, frustrated, and **embarrassed**.
2. Trying your best and **succeeding** are not always the same thing.
3. I hold a baseball bat right-handed but **hold a hockey stick** left-handed. (*Or* I **play baseball** right-handed but hockey left-handed.)
4. A good student attends all classes and **finishes all projects** on time.

5. A good teacher motivates with enthusiasm, informs with sensitivity, and **counsels with compassion**.
6. A good college president has the judgment of Solomon, **the wisdom of Plato**, and the wit of Rick Mercer.
7. Licking one's fingers and **picking one's teeth** in a restaurant are one way to get attention.
8. To succeed in this economy, small businesses must be creative and **flexible**.
9. Canadians must register the cars they drive, the businesses they own, the contracts they make, the houses they buy, and **the guns they possess**.
10. This course requires you to complete three major assignments: write a research paper on a Canadian author, **read three contemporary Canadian novels**, and **see two Canadian plays**.

Exercise 9.3 (suggested answers)
1. understand
2. rinsing, flossing (*or* to brush, rinse, floss)
3. loosen
4. engineering
5. knowledge
6. well educated
7. entertainment
8. exploring fully
9. punctual, organized
10. without value, meaning, or interest (*or* valueless, meaningless, uninteresting)

Exercise 9.5 (suggested answers)

The dictionary is a useful educational resource. Everyone knows that its three chief functions are to check the spelling, **meanings, and pronunciations of words**. Few people, however, use the dictionary for discovery as well as learning. There are several ways to use the dictionary as an aid to discovery. One is randomly looking at words, another is **reading** a page or two thoroughly, and still another is **skimming** the text looking for unfamiliar words. By this last method I discovered the word *steatopygous*, a term I now try to use at least once a day. You can increase your vocabulary significantly by using the dictionary, and, of course, a large and varied vocabulary can be used to baffle your colleagues, **impress your employers**, and **surprise your English teacher**.

Exercise 9.6 (suggested answers)
1. A coach has four responsibilities:
   - To encourage and motivate
   - To teach skills and techniques
   - To develop teamwork and cooperation
   - To build physical and mental strength
2. The college will undertake the following steps to conserve energy:
   - Lowering building temperatures by two degrees in winter
   - Putting lights in all rooms on motion sensors
   - Raising building temperatures by two degrees in summer
   - Replacing all windows with high-efficiency glass

3. In selecting a location for the new college residence, we must be mindful of transportation factors:
   - Convenient access to mass transit
   - Ample parking for all residents with cars
   - Easy connections to major highways
   - Immediate access to the bicycle-path network
   - On-site availability of pedestrian walkways
4. New programming guidelines for the college radio station prescribe the following:
   - Alternate and independent music to be played exclusively
   - No advertising to be aired between 6 p.m. and midnight
   - Newscasts to include only local and college material
   - Show hosts to keep their talk between songs to less than 30 seconds
   - Station regulations regarding obscenity and swearing to be strictly observed
   - Station identification to be given hourly
5. The following regulations regarding the use of communication devices such as cellphones, personal digital assistants, iPads and tablets, smartphones, and netbooks will apply from 1 April 2013:
   - No communication devices will be permitted in any exam rooms
   - Ring tones, alarms, and audio will be turned off in all lectures, seminars, and labs
   - Communication devices may be used only in designated areas of the college
   - Only specified classwork is permitted in lectures, seminars, and labs

Answers for Chapter 10: Refining by Combining

Exercise 10.1
1. Our town may be small, **but** (*or* **yet**) it is not backward.
2. Our final exam will be held on **either** Friday afternoon **or** Monday morning.
3. This book promises to help me manage my money, **so** I will buy it.
4. I have completed all the exercises, **and** my sentence skills are gradually improving.
5. This man is **neither** my father **nor** my husband.

Exercise 10.2
1. My favourite team is the Vancouver Canucks **although** my father prefers the Montreal Canadiens. (*Or* **Although** my favourite team is the Vancouver Canucks, my father prefers the Montreal Canadiens.)
2. We will take a picnic to the ballgame today **if** the rain stays away. (*Or* **If** the rain stays away, we will take a picnic to the ballgame.)
3. Our vacation this year will be in October, **when** we will visit Nova Scotia to see the autumn colours.
4. My Facebook page says I am a good dancer **even though** my favourite type of music is opera.
5. Art is long, **but** life is short.

Exercise 10.A
1. Although the test was difficult, I passed it. (*Or* The test was difficult, but I passed it.)
2. After eating our lunch, we went back to work on our project. (*Or* We ate our lunch, then we went back to work on our project.)

3. Correct.
4. Since our essay is due tomorrow, we must stay up late tonight. (*Or* Our essay is due tomorrow, so we must stay up late tonight.)
5. Even though the pictures are good, I hate seeing myself. (*Or* The pictures are good, yet I hate seeing myself.)
6. Correct.
7. Though having a car would be convenient, I need the money for other things. (*Or* Having a car would be convenient, but I need the money for other things.)
8. If this book will help me, I will buy it. (*Or* This book will help me, so I will buy it.)
9. When you find a mistake, you must correct it.
10. Although that program frequently crashes, this program is stable. (*Or* That program frequently crashes, but this program is stable.)

Exercise 10.B
1. I have a teacher who is always losing his glasses.
2. This is the computer that is always crashing.
3. I am enrolled in an art class that meets Wednesday evenings.
4. That singer whose name I always forget just won a Grammy.
5. The cellphone that you gave me is broken.
6. My plant, which you forgot to water, is dead.
7. The parcel that I was waiting for finally arrived.
8. Lisa babysits for a man whose wife speaks only Japanese.
9. The taxi driver who took me to the airport drove 20 kilometres over the speed limit all the way.
10. My roommate whose snoring keeps me awake is finally moving out.

Exercise 10.3
1. **Because** the tortoise is slow but steady, it will win the race.
2. The calendar says it is April, **but** it feels like February.
3. Nicole used the wi-fi from her neighbour's apartment **until** he changed the password.
4. I sometimes have bad dreams, **but** they don't usually bother me unless I eat pepperoni pizza as a late-night snack.
5. Gregor procrastinates by playing video games **while** his essay remains unfinished. *Or* **While** his essay remains unfinished, Gregor procrastinates by playing video games. (Remember that a subordinate clause can be placed either before or after an independent clause.)

Exercise 10.4
1. The Nissan Juke, **which** is a small SUV, has received excellent reviews.
2. The iPad is on my wish list, **so** I'm hoping I get it as a birthday present.
3. **Because** parking downtown is impossible, we are moving to the suburbs. (*Or* We are moving to the suburbs **because** parking downtown is impossible.)
4. **Although** I don't mind doing this exercise, I'll be glad when it's finished.
5. Carson, **who** thinks all his thoughts are interesting, blogs incessantly. (*Or* Carson, **who** blogs incessantly, thinks all his thoughts are interesting.)

Exercise 10.5

1. Our apartment is large and comfortable, yet it is reasonably priced.
2. Some people believe that alien spacecraft are observing Earth.
3. Our company will sponsor a marathon runner, but one of the employees must enter the race.
4. Hybrid cars are becoming more popular even though they cost more than comparable gas-powered models.
5. Heidi's grades improved when she followed her study schedule.
6. Your outfit is not appropriate for the office, but it would look just right in an after-hours club.
7. Although I love the taste of strong, black coffee, it keeps me awake.
8. The chef who wrote this book owns a restaurant just down the street.
9. You have the freedom to do all the things you wanted just when you are too old to enjoy them.
10. (a) I don't eat meat or poultry.
    (b) I eat neither meat nor poultry.

Exercise 10.6 (suggested answers)

1. The village that I grew up in is very small.
2. My car is in the repair shop because it needs a new alternator.
3. The gates are down and the lights are flashing, but (*or* yet) a train is not coming.
4. After I read this book from cover to cover and completed all the exercises, my writing skills improved.
5. You are polite and considerate of the feelings of others, but you should be more assertive.
6. My wife enjoys watching hockey, but I prefer soccer, which is the world's most popular spectator sport.
7. This movie, which Meiling shot on her cellphone, edited on her iPad, and posted on YouTube, is not very good.
8. My ex-girlfriend, who broke up with me on Twitter and deleted me from her friends list, is a cruel person.
9. My vacation in Florida was disappointing, for the weather was cold, and I don't like shopping malls, which are everywhere in Florida
10. This restaurant is very expensive, but I don't mind paying the price for good food and excellent service.

Exercise 10.7 (suggested answers)

1. I was born in the small town of Weyburn, Saskatchewan, but I have not lived there since I was a baby.
2. Hanna, who can find her way anywhere, is very good at reading a map, but she cannot fold it properly.
3. While Justin Bieber is a pop phenomenon, most talented musicians never make it, so it is safer to go to college and work toward a career.
4. I should have unplugged my computer or backed up my files because I lost them all when my hard drive was destroyed by a lightning strike.
5. Even though the car had many of the features she was looking for and was the right price, Ying decided not to buy it because it was the wrong colour.

6. Vijay's father, who is a surgeon, bought a new car that Vijay is allowed to wash but not to drive.

7. Tina is a Canadian citizen who was born in Halifax; she has American citizenship too because her mother was born in Chicago.

8. My clothes don't fit because I lost weight, so I need to buy a new wardrobe, but I don't have the money to buy the clothes I like.

9. Jenn, who is fit and athletic, hates winter weather, so she vacations every spring break in Mexico, where she likes to run on the beach.

10. In most of the Middle East, young people are in the majority, but there is high unemployment and little opportunity, which lead to unrest and rebellion.

Answers for Unit 2 Rapid Review

Note: The superscript numbers in the following revision indicate the original sentence numbers in the Unit 2 Rapid Review.

[1]Last year, while driving through rural Alberta, **I spotted** [*or* **saw** *or equivalent*] a sign at the end of a farmer's lane: "FOR SALE: TALKING DOG. $15." [2]Curious, **I had hardly stopped my car** before rushing out to ask the farmer about the dog. [3]He directed me to a kennel behind the house. **There** was a beautiful golden retriever dozing in the warm sun. [4]Kneeling down beside him and making sure no one was looking, I quietly asked him if he could really talk. [6]He opened one eye and **yawned** and said, "Of course."

[7]I must have fainted from the shock. **The** dog was licking my face when I regained consciousness. [8]When I recovered my composure, I asked him how he had come to be here in a farmyard in Alberta. [9]His tale was both complicated and **interesting**. [10]He told me that when he discovered he could talk, he volunteered to help the RCMP in their canine unit. **The** police quickly discovered he was too valuable for that task and assigned him to undercover work. [11]He would curl up near a suspect and eavesdrop, thus catching many criminals, earning the admiration of his police comrades, and **winning** many medals. [12]He was reassigned to Canada's spy agency, CSIS, **but** the stress of constant travelling and spying on world leaders and suspected enemies **soon** tired him out. [13]At only eight years old, **he was advised by** a military veterinarian that the stress of his undercover life had weakened his heart and **he should retire**. [14]The veterinarian had a brother in Alberta who would give the dog a comfortable home where he could enjoy a peaceful retirement. [15]"So here I am," the dog concluded.

[16]I couldn't wait to return to the farmer and offer to buy this heroic dog. **I** couldn't resist asking why he wanted **only** $15 for such an amazing animal. [17]The farmer shrugged and replied, "Because he's a liar, that's why. He never did any of those things."

Answer Key

If you missed the error(s) in sentence ...	see Chapter ...
[1] *while driving ..., a sign*	8 "Dangling Modifiers" section
[2] *Curious, my car had hardly stopped before rushing ...*	8 "Dangling Modifiers" section
[3] Run-on sentence	7 "Comma Splices" section
[4] Sentence fragment	6 "Dependent Clause Fragments" section
[6] *He opened one eye and yawning and said ...*	9 The Parallelism Principle

If you missed the error(s) in sentence ...   **see Chapter ...**

7 Run-on sentence	7 "Comma Splices" section
9 *His tale was both complicated and full of interest.*	9 The Parallelism Principle
10 Run-on sentence	7 "Comma Splices" section
11 *catching ... earning ... and won many medals*	9 The Parallelism Principle
12 Run-on sentence	7 "Comma Splices" section
12 *tired him out soon*	8 "Misplaced Modifiers" section
13 *At only eight years old, a military veterinarian*	8 "Dangling Modifiers" section
13 *retirement should be his choice*	9 The Parallelism Principle
16 Run-on sentence	7 "Fused Sentences" section
16 *he only wanted $15 ...*	8 "Misplaced Modifiers" section

Answers for Unit 3 Quick Quiz (page 142)

[1]Every generation **has** one or two defining moments **that** are so significant that everyone remembers precisely where **he or she was** when the event occurred. [2]Most of the events that have **become** part of our consciousness were tragic, but there **are** exceptions. [3]Nobody **who** was alive when the Allied victory that ended World War II was declared **is** likely to forget the mingled joy and relief of that occasion. [4]**All** Canadian hockey **fans**, even if they were not watching the game at the time, remember The Goal: Paul Henderson's winner in the 1972 series against the Soviet Union. [5]Neither of these glorious moments **is** going to fade from the memories of those who experienced them. [6]Memorable tragic moments, however, are more common than joyful ones, and somehow they **seem** more important to us as we look back. [7]My contemporaries and **I** all remember exactly where we were when President John F. Kennedy was shot, while those who were born after 1980 will never forget the destruction of the World Trade Center in New York City in 2001. [8]No one **who** saw the televised images of the twin towers as they collapsed and crumbled **is** ever likely to forget the horror of those moments.

Answer Key

If you missed the error(s) in sentence ...   **see Chapter ...**

1 *generation have*	12 "Singular and Plural" section
moments which	15 "Relative Pronouns" section
everyone ... they	15 "Pronouns Ending in -*one*, -*body, -thing*" section
everyone ... were	12 "Singular and Plural" section
2 *have became*	11 "The Principal Parts of Irregular Verbs" section; 13 Keeping Your Tenses Consistent
there's	12 "Singular and Plural" section
3 *Nobody that*	15 "Pronouns Ending in -*one*, -*body, thing*" section
Nobody ... are	12 "Singular and Plural" section
4 *Every fan ... they*	15 "Pronoun–Antecedent Agreement" section

If you missed the error(s) in sentence ...   see Chapter ...

⁵ *Neither ... are*	12 "Four Special Cases" section
⁶ *are ... seemed*	13 Keeping Your Tenses Consistent
⁷ *contemporaries and me*	14 "Subject and Object Pronouns" section
while them	14 "Subject and Object Pronouns" section
⁸ *No one that*	15 "Relative Pronouns" section
No one ... are	12 "Four Special Cases" section

Answers for Chapter 11: Choosing the Correct Verb Form

Exercise 11.1

1. wear   You **wore** your good hiking boots only once, but after you have **worn** them several times, you won't want to take them off.
2. give   The tourists **gave** Tania a tip after she had **given** them directions to the hotel.
3. begin   After the project had **begun**, the members of the team soon **began** to disagree on the procedure to follow.
4. eat   I **ate** as though I had not **eaten** in a month.
5. cost   The vacation in Cuba **cost** less than last year's trip to Jamaica had **cost** and was much more fun.
6. bring   If you have **brought** your children with you, I hope you also **brought** enough toys and movies to keep them occupied during your stay.
7. grow   The noise from the party next door **grew** louder by the hour, but by midnight I had **grown** used to it, and went to sleep.
8. sit   Marc **sat** in front of the TV all morning; by evening he will have **sat** there for eight hours—a full workday!
9. write   After she had **written** the essay that was due last week, she **wrote** emails to all her friends.
10. pay   I **paid** off my credit cards, so I have not **paid** this month's rent.

Exercise 11.2

1. ride   I had never **ridden** in a stretch limo until I **rode** in one to Xue's wedding.
2. sing   She **sang** a little song that her mother had **sung** to her when she was a baby.
3. teach   Harold had been **taught** to play poker by his father, and he **taught** his daughter the same way.
4. find   He **found** the solution that hundreds of mathematicians over three centuries had not **found**.
5. fly   Suzhu had once **flown** to Whitehorse, so when she **flew** north to Tuktoyaktuk, she knew what to expect.
6. feel   At first, they had **felt** silly in their new pink uniforms, but after winning three games in a row, they **felt** much better.
7. lie   The cat **lay** right where the dog had **lain** all morning.
8. go   We **went** to our new home to find that the movers had **gone** to the wrong address to deliver our furniture.
9. lose   The reason you **lost** those customers is that you have **lost** confidence in your ability to sell our product.

10. steal   I **stole** two customers away from the sales representative who earlier had **stolen** my best account.

Exercise 11.3

1. think   I had **thought** that you were right, but when I **thought** more about your answer, I realized you were wrong.

2. buy   If we had **bought** this stock 20 years ago, the shares we **bought** would now be worth a fortune.

3. do   They **did** what was asked, but their competitors, who had **done** a better job, got the contract.

4. show   Today our agent **showed** us a house that was much better suited to our needs than anything she had **shown** us previously.

5. hurt   Budget cuts had **hurt** the project, but today's decision to lay off two of our workers **hurt** it even more.

6. throw   The rope had not been **thrown** far enough to reach those in the water, so Mia pulled it in and **threw** it again.

7. lay   Elzbieta **laid** her passport on the official's desk where the other tourists had **laid** theirs.

8. put   I have **put** your notebook in the mail, but your pen and glasses I will **put** away until I see you again.

9. fight   My parents **fought** again today, the way they have **fought** almost every day for the past 20 years.

10. break   She **broke** the Canadian record only six months after she had **broken** her arm in training.

Exercise 11.5

1. __A__ Our professor checks our homework every day.
2. __P__ The report is being prepared by the marketing department.
3. __P__ The limousine was driven by a chauffeur.
4. __A__ Eva will invite Tariq to the party.
5. __P__ The CN Tower is visited by hundreds of people every day.
6. __A__ Sula designed and made this jewellery.
7. __P__ *The English Patient* was written by Canadian author Michael Ondaatje.
8. __A__ Hollywood made the book into a successful movie.
9. __P__ The song was performed by Eminem.
10. __P__ Two metres of snow had to be shovelled off the driveway.

Exercise 11.6

1. Our homework is checked by our professor every day.
2. The marketing department is preparing the report.
3. A chauffeur drove the limousine.
4. Tariq will be invited to the party by Eva.
5. Hundreds of people visit the CN Tower every day.
6. This jewellery was designed and made by Sula.
7. Canadian author Michael Ondaatje wrote *The English Patient*.
8. The book was made into a successful movie by Hollywood.
9. Eminem performed the song.
10. We had to shovel two metres of snow off the driveway.

Exercise 11.7

1. The delicious curry filled our hungry stomachs.
2. Lisa bought the gas for the trip.
3. Our houseguests washed the dishes.
4. The sales representative gave me his business card.
5. Our computer made an error in your bill.
6. You have not formatted your essay in APA style, as required.
7. On our first anniversary, a professional photographer took our portrait.
8. Canadians do not always understand American election practices.
9. In today's class, all of you will work on your research papers.
10. This book contains all the information you need to become a competent writer.

Exercise 11.8

1. Lola told the professor that she was finding the course too difficult. (Active voice is more effective.)
2. This meal was prepared by a master chef. (Passive voice is more effective; the person who prepared the meal is unknown.)
3. Three firefighters carefully entered the burning building. (Active voice is more effective.)
4. Someone had left the lights on the whole time we were away. (Passive voice is more effective because it places the emphasis on the lights—the object affected by the action—rather than on the unknown person who performed the action.)
5. In the final ceremony, a biathlete carried the Olympic flag. (Passive voice is more effective because it puts the focus on the Olympic flag, an enduring symbol, rather than on the unknown athlete who happened to carry it in this particular ceremony.)
6. The last thing my kids ever did to earn money was lose their baby teeth. (Active voice is more effective.)
7. My brother uses his bookcase to hold his bowling trophies and empty fast-food containers. (Active voice is more effective.)
8. The provincial government has declared a state of emergency and set up a special fund to aid the flood victims. (Active voice is more effective for two reasons: the doer of the action is known and so should occupy the subject position, and the passive construction is too wordy for easy reading.)
9. Poor communication among the members of the team delayed the project. (Active voice is more effective. Projects are often delayed, but we don't always know why they are delayed. So the emphasis on the "actors" gives useful information.)
10. Electronic devices will never replace newspapers for two reasons: one can't line a birdcage with a TV, and one can't serve fish and chips in a smartphone. (This sentence is a real challenge: the main clause is more effective in active voice [it's less wordy], but the two clauses following the colon are more effective in passive voice because they are examples of reasons 1 and 2 on page 156.)

Answers for Chapter 12: Mastering Subject–Verb Agreement
Exercise 12.1

1. key
2. invoices
3. people
4. Professor Kersey
5. Jupiter, Saturn

Exercise 12.2

1. has
2. succeeds
3. shows
4. talks
5. has

Exercise 12.3

1. My <u>paper</u> <u>is</u> due on Tuesday.
2. A <u>skier</u> <u>loves</u> cold weather and heavy snowfalls.
3. A snow <u>shoveller</u> <u>does</u> not.
4. <u>Has</u> the lucky <u>winner</u> <u>collected</u> the lottery money?
5. The <u>article</u> in this journal <u>gives</u> you the background information you need.
6. Why <u>does</u> a <u>teenager</u> <u>fall</u> in love?
7. Only recently <u>has</u> our track <u>coach</u> <u>become</u> interested in chemistry.
8. So far, only <u>one</u> of your answers <u>has been</u> incorrect.
9. The <u>pressure</u> of schoolwork and part-time work <u>has caused</u> many students to drop out.
10. Under our back porch <u>lives</u> a <u>family</u> of skunks.

Exercise 12.4

1. A good <u>example</u> <u>is</u> hockey players.
2. <u>Sardines</u> <u>are</u> a healthy type of oily fish.
3. An important <u>supplier</u> of oxygen to the Earth <u>is</u> trees.
4. Noisy <u>speedboats</u> on our quiet lake <u>are</u> what irritates us.
5. An important <u>part</u> of a balanced diet <u>is</u> fresh fruits and vegetables.

Exercise 12.5

A dog seems to understand the **mood** of **its owner. It is** tuned in to any **shift** in emotion or **change** in health of the **human it lives** with. **A doctor** will often suggest adding **a pet** to **a household** where there **is someone** (*or* **a person**) suffering from depression or **an** emotional **problem. A dog is a** sympathetic **companion.** The **mood** of **a person** in **a** retirement **home** or even **a** hospital **ward** can be brightened by **a visit** from **a** pet **owner** and **a dog. A dog** never **tires** of hearing about the "good old days," and **it is** uncritical and unselfish in giving affection. **A doctor** will often encourage **an** epilepsy **sufferer** to adopt **a** specially trained **dog.** Such **a dog is** so attuned to the health of **its owner** that **it** can sense when **a seizure is** about to occur long before **its owner** can. The **dog** then **warns** the **owner** of the coming attack, so the **owner is** able to take safety precautions.

Exercise 12.6

1. is
2. deters
3. fascinates
4. influence
5. signs

Exercise 12.7

1. wants
2. has
3. promises
4. is
5. don't

Exercise 12.8

1. loves
2. thinks
3. recommends
4. want
5. were

Exercise 12.9

1. holds
2. is
3. goes
4. was
5. seems

Exercise 12.10

1. The amount of government money directed toward job creation **is** enormous.
2. Not the weekly quizzes but the final exam **is** what I'm worried about.
3. Everyone within four blocks of the crime scene **was** interviewed by the detectives.
4. Either the tires or the alignment **is** causing the steering vibration.
5. There's no good **reason** for skipping lunch. (*Or* There **are** no good reasons for skipping lunch.)
6. This province, along with six others, **has** voted in favour of a federally supported drug program.
7. When Yusuf emptied his pockets, he found that $2.00 **was** all he had left to buy lunch.
8. The band, together with the backup players, the roadies, and the producers, **is** staying in a motel near the concert site.
9. We'd better fill up with gas: 400 kilometres of mountain roads **lies** ahead.
10. It seems that in every group project, one of the team members **gets** stuck with most of the work.

Exercise 12.11

1. Each day that passes **brings** us closer to the end of term.
2. Members of the Quechua tribe, who live in the Andes Mountains, **have** two or three more litres of blood than people living at lower elevations.
3. The swim team **have** been billeted with host families during their stay in Seattle.
4. Neither fame nor riches **are** my goal in life.
5. The original model for the king in a standard deck of playing cards **is** thought to be King Charles I of England.
6. A large planet together with two small stars **is** visible on the eastern horizon.
7. The lack of things to write about **is** my problem.
8. One faculty member in addition to a group of students **has** volunteered to help us clean out the lab.
9. Not only cat hairs but also ragweed **makes** me sneeze.
10. Everyone who successfully completed these exercises **deserves** high praise.

Exercise 12.12

Most jobs now require computer skills, but the digital revolution has not improved our quality of life. Since a desktop computer, complete with headphones for sound-based functions, **exists** in every office, work should be simpler. However, neither increased efficiency nor improved employee morale **has** resulted from our switch from paper to computers. Indeed, each worker's tasks **have** become more complex. In the past, for example, one invoice or two purchase orders **were** needed to complete a request for supplies. The process, including online confirmation, now **requires** five separate documents. The result of this unnecessary complication, not surprisingly, **is** frustration and curses. Everyone, including the supervisors, **is** fed up with the extra work. When our division **implements** a new computer system next month, I expect at least two of my co-workers to quit. Fifteen hours of training **is** needed to learn the new system, and that is more time than any of us **has** to waste.

Exercise 12.13

1. plural
2. singular
3. plural
4. singular
5. singular
6. singular
7. singular
8. plural
9. singular
10. singular

Answers for Chapter 13: Keeping Your Tenses Consistent

Exercise 13.1

1. Your professor is in a meeting until 4 p.m., so you **have** to wait to see her.
2. Giles tried to laugh, but he **was** too upset even to speak.
3. After his fiancée broke up with him, she **refused** to return his ring.
4. Correct.
5. The rebellion failed because the people **did** not support it.
6. I enjoy my work, but I **am** not going to let it take over my life.
7. Prejudice is learned and **is** hard to outgrow.
8. A Canadian is someone who thinks that an income tax refund **is** a gift from the government.
9. Piers went to Laval for his vacation every summer and **stayed** with his aunt and uncle on a farm.
10. Shahn likes to play cricket with his Canadian friends even though most of them **don't** understand the rules.

Exercise 13.2

A young businesswoman *decides* that the best way to ensure success in her new business is to rent impressive office space. She **looks** around at what is available and eventually **selects** a corner suite in a new downtown office tower. She then **decides** to install fine furniture: a walnut desk, leather chairs, and brushed-steel fixtures. Last, she **finishes** the office decor with expensive carpets and fine art.

On her first day in her beautiful new office, she **sees** a man come into the reception area, and, wanting to make a good impression, **picks** up the phone and **pretends** to speak to a customer. She **sees** that her visitor **is** looking at her with interest, so she **begins** to talk to her imaginary customer as though she **is negotiating** a huge deal. She **mentions** enormous sales numbers and huge sums of money, and finally **concludes** the "conversation" and hangs up the phone. She then **turns** to her visitor and **asks** how she could help him. The man replies, "I am here to install the phone."

Exercise 13.3

A large, scruffy-looking man *walked* into a Cadillac dealership on Bay Street in Toronto and **proceeded** to stroll around the showroom, studying the cars on display. The salesman, taking note of the battered black cowboy hat, scuffed western boots, and weathered leather vest, **decided** to ignore him. The man **spent** ten minutes or so looking at each model, frequently checking to see if the salesman would help him. The salesman **didn't** move from his desk at the back of the showroom, but he **watched** the big man carefully.

Finally, obviously annoyed, the man **gave** an exaggerated tip of his weather-beaten hat in the direction of the salesman and **walked** out of the dealership. About an hour later, a sleek Mercedes-Benz sedan **pulled** up to the Cadillac dealership, and the driver **honked** the horn until the salesman **looked** over. It **was** the same scruffy man, now driving a car worth more than any of the Cadillacs in the showroom. The man **blew** a kiss at the salesman and **drove** away. The bearded man in the shabby clothes **was** Ronnie Hawkins, the great blues/rockabilly/alternative country singer who **had** just made a fortune from his latest hit album.

Answers for Chapter 14: Choosing the Correct Pronoun Form
Exercise 14.1
1. There's nobody in the building but **us**.
2. My mother and **she** cannot agree on anything.
3. Except for Vikram and **her**, no one knows how to enter the data manually.
4. **Anton and I** are best friends.
5. The work will go much faster if **he** and Roland do it by themselves.
6. Sami and **he** wrote, shot, and edited the entire film.
7. It will be difficult to choose between **her** and **me**.
8. Every year, my grandmother knits sweaters for my brother and **me**.
9. Surely your sister wasn't serious when she said that **they** and their children were coming to stay with us for three weeks.
10. **He and I** have completely different tastes in music.

Exercise 14.2
1. Have you and **she** ever tried rock climbing?
2. **He** and Alex take the same math class.
3. It is not up to you or **me** to discipline your sister's children.
4. Living with our parents isn't easy, either for **them** or **us**.
5. **He** and his mother get along fine, but **he** and his father are constantly arguing.
6. Was it **he** who served you? Or was it **she**?
7. **He** and Marie finished on time; except for **them** and their staff, no one else met the deadline.
8. Susana and **I** are going to be your trainers for the next month.
9. In terms of career potential, I don't think there's much difference between **them** and **us**.
10. For once, there was no one ahead of Trina and **me** in the lineup outside the registrar's office.

Exercise 14.3
1. The prize is sure to go to Omar and [to] **her**.
2. No one likes our cooking class more than **I** [do].
3. In fact, nobody in the class eats as much as **I** [do].
4. It's not surprising that I am much bigger than **they** [are].
5. My mother would rather cook for my brother than [for] **me** because he never complains when dinner is burned or raw.
6. At last I have met someone who loves barbecued eel as much as **I** [do]!
7. More than **I** [do], Yuxiang uses the computer to draft and revise his papers.

8. He doesn't write as well as **I** [do], but he does write faster.
9. Only a few Mexican food fanatics can eat as many jalapeno peppers as **he** [does].
10. I think you have as much trouble with English as **I** [do].

Answers for Chapter 15: Mastering Pronoun–Antecedent Agreement
Exercise 15.1

1. The caller refused to leave **a** message.
2. Can anyone bring **a** car?
3. Each player on the team has **her** strengths.
4. . . . every team member played below **his** ability.
5. It seemed that everyone in the mall was talking on **a** cellphone.
6. Would someone kindly lend **a** copy of the textbook to Lisa?
7. A bandleader is someone who is not afraid to face **the** music.
8. Everyone is expected to pay **a** share of the expenses.
9. We will try to return to **its** owner anything we find in the locker room.
10. Anyone who wants a high mark for **this** essay should see me after class and write **a** cheque payable to me.

Exercise 15.2 (suggested answers)

Note: Triple asterisks (***) indicate that a word or words have been deleted. Each set of triple asterisks counts as one error.

1. Everyone is a product of *** environment as well as heredity.
2. No one as capable as you needs to have help with **this** assignment.
3. Each car in all categories will be judged on **its** bodywork, engine, and interior.
4. Every movie-, theatre-, and concertgoer knows how annoying it is to have **an** evening's enjoyment spoiled by a ringing cellphone.
5. Put the sign at the curb so anyone looking for our yard sale won't have to waste *** time driving around the neighbourhood.
6. Everyone who pays **the** membership fee in advance will receive a free session with a personal trainer.
7. A smart husband knows enough to think twice before **he says** anything.
8. Ultimate is a game in which **all players enjoy** themselves, whether their team finishes first or last.
9. No one on the football team has been able to convince **his** parents to donate **their** house for the party.
10. **All children want** to grow up as fast as possible, but once they reach adulthood, they wish they could go back.

Exercise 15.3 (suggested answers)

1. Every time Hassan looked at the dog, **it** barked.
2. What did Mei say to her mother before **her mother** (*or* **Mei**) hung up the phone?
3. Karla didn't hear my question **because** she was eavesdropping on the couple in the next booth.
4. I lost my temper and slammed my fist on the table, breaking **my hand** (*or* **the table**).
5. Some of our friends are already parents, but we're not in a hurry to have **a child**.

6. My wife was annoyed when I didn't notice she had fallen overboard; **I was distracted** because I was concentrating on landing my fish.

7. When I learned that smoking was the cause of my asthma, I gave up **cigarettes** for good.

8. Kevin told Yu to leave the books on the table beside **Kevin's** (*or* **Yu's**) computer.

9. **Our college strictly enforces** the "no smoking" policy.

10. Being on time is a challenge for my girlfriend, so I'm getting her **a watch** for her birthday.

Exercise 15.4

1. Chi Keung is the technician **who** can fix your problem.

2. I would have won, except for one judge **who** placed me fourth.

3. A grouch is a person **who** knows himself and isn't happy about what he knows.

4. The sales clerk **who** sold me my DVD player didn't know what he was talking about.

5. Everyone **who** was at the party had a good time, though a few had more punch than was good for them.

6. The open-office concept sounds good to anyone **who** has worked in a stuffy little cubicle all day.

7. I wish I could find someone in our class **who** could help me with my homework.

8. I regularly order supplies from companies **that** are located in cities all across the country.

9. The tests **that** we wrote today were designed to discourage anyone **who** didn't have the knowledge, preparation, and stamina to endure them.

10. My roommate has just started on the term paper, **which** was assigned a month ago, for her political science course.

Exercise 15.5

North Americans seem obsessed with showing their grasp of useless information. Trivia games have been hugely popular for decades, and they continue to attract large audiences. **Trivia players are** expected to have at their fingertips all sorts of obscure information, from sports statistics to popular music, from world geography to the film industry. Team trivia contests have become important fundraising events for charity. Teams of eight to ten players answer trivia questions in competition with other teams. Each member of a team is expected to have **a** particular area of expertise and to help **the** team gain points by answering the questions in that area. At the end of the contest, the winning team will usually have answered correctly more than 80 percent of the questions called out by the quizmaster.

Another forum for trivia is the television shows in which **contestants** must demonstrate their knowledge individually in a high-pressure, game show format. Alone, each contestant faces the show's host, who may give *** assistance if **the contestant asks** for it. In other games, **contestants play against each other** and must demonstrate superior knowledge if they want to win. Playing trivia at home is also popular, and many households have **a game**.

Whether you play alone, with friends, on a team, or on television, **you** should keep the game in perspective. After all, the object of any trivia game is to reward the players **who** demonstrate that they know more about unimportant and irrelevant facts than anyone else in the game!

Answers for Chapter 16: Maintaining Person Agreement

Exercise 16.1

1. If you want to be a rock star, **you** should start developing a stage personality early.
2. A person can succeed at almost anything if **he or she has** talent and determination.
3. When we laugh, the world laughs with **us**.
4. You can save a great deal of time if **you fill** out the forms before going to the passport office.
5. Clarify the question before beginning to write, or **you** may lose your focus.
6. Our opinions will never be heard unless **we try** to communicate them in logical order.
7. I wish that **we** had a few more options to choose from.
8. **You** should not question Professor Snape in class because he loses his temper, and you don't want that to happen.
9. Anyone with a telephone can get **his or her** voice heard on the radio.
10. Call-in programs give everyone the opportunity to make sure the whole world knows **one's** ignorance of the issues.

Exercise 16.2 (suggested answers)

1. The faster **you go**, the more you need good brakes. (The faster one goes, the more **one needs** good brakes.)
2. One is never too old to learn, but **one is** never too young to know everything. (**You are** never too old ...,)
3. One always removes **one's** shoes when entering a mosque.
4. The speed limit is the speed **you** go as soon as you see a police car.
5. When **you visit** Beijing, you must see the Great Wall, the Forbidden City, and the Temple of Heaven.
6. Experience is that marvellous thing that enables us to recognize a mistake when **we** make it again. (F.P. Jones)
7. If you can't cope with the pressure, **you** must expect to be replaced by someone who can.
8. We all believed his story because **we** couldn't believe he would lie.
9. Diaries are places to record **your** private thoughts, and you ought to be brutally honest when making your entries.
10. Most people enjoy eating when **they** are with good friends in relaxed surroundings.

Exercise 16.3

Those of us who enjoy baseball find it difficult to explain **our** enthusiasm to non-fans. We baseball enthusiasts can watch a game of three hours or more as **we follow** each play with rapt attention. We true fans get excited by a no-hitter—a game in which, by definition, nothing happens. **We** claim that the game is about much more than mere action, but non-fans must be forgiven if **they** don't get the point. To them, watching a baseball game is about as exciting as watching paint dry.

Exercise 16.4 (suggested answers)

When **we are** at the beginning of our careers, it seems impossible that **we** may one day wish to work less. The drive to get ahead leads many of us to sacrifice **our** leisure, **our** community responsibilities, even **our** family life for the sake of **our** careers.

Normally, as **we** age, **our** priorities begin to change, and career success becomes less important than quality of life. Not everyone, however, experiences this shift in priorities. Indeed, some people work themselves to death, while others are so committed to their work throughout their lives that they die within months of retirement—presumably from stress caused by lack of work. The poet Robert Frost once observed, "By working faithfully eight hours a day, you may eventually get to be a boss. Then **you** can work twelve hours a day." Those of **us** who are living and working in the early years of the 21st century would be wise to take Frost's words to heart.

Answers for Unit 3 Rapid Review

[1]A professor at our college **began** the last week of term by giving a demonstration to her business administration students. [2]For 15 weeks, she had **spoken** about the need for balance in life, but she felt that she had not yet gotten her message across. [3]She suspected that most of the students **who** sat before her **were** still primarily focused on money and career advancement. [4]"People in business," she began, "sometimes have a hard time remembering **their** true priorities." [5]She placed a large glass jar on the desk and **filled** it with golf balls and asked the students if the jar was full. [6]**All** of the students nodded their heads. [7]She then **poured** pebbles into the jar, **filling** up the spaces around the golf balls. [8]"Is it full now?" she asked. [9]**The students** all laughed and said that they thought it was full. [10]**The professor then poured sand** into the jar, filling it to the brim. [11]Everyone **who** was watching agreed that the jar was now full. [12]Then the professor poured two cups of coffee into the jar. [13]She brought the demonstration to a close with this explanation: [14]"The golf balls **represent** the important things in your life: health, family, and relationships. [15]The pebbles are the less important things such as jobs, hobbies, cars, and houses. [16]And the sand is the small, unimportant stuff. [17]If I had filled the jar with sand, there wouldn't have been room for anything else. [18]The same thing is true in life: if you fill your life with small stuff, **you'll** have no room for the important things. [19]Take care of the important things first; there is always room for the small stuff."

[20]One student asked what the coffee **represented**. [21]"No matter how full your life may seem," the professor replied with a smile, "there's always room for a cup of coffee with a friend!"

Answer Key

If you missed the error(s) in sentence ...	see Chapter ...
[1] *begun*	11 "The Principal Parts of Irregular Verbs" section
[2] *spoke*	11 "The Principal Parts of Irregular Verbs" section
[3] *students ... that*	15 "Relative Pronouns" section
most ... was	16 "Singular and Plural" section
[4] *People ... one's*	16 Maintaining Person Agreement
[5] *placed ... fills*	13 Keeping Your Tenses Consistent
[6] *Each ... their*	15 "Pronoun–Antecedent Agreement" section *See also:* 12"Four Special Cases" section

If you missed the error(s) in sentence ...	see Chapter ...
[7] *pours*	13 Keeping Your Tenses Consistent
which	15 "Vague References" section
[9] *Everyone ... they*	15 "Pronouns Ending in -*one*, -*body*, -*thing*" section
[10] *Then sand was poured ...*	11 "Choosing between Active and Passive Voice" section
[11] *Everyone that ...*	15 "Relative Pronouns" section
[14] *golf balls ... represents*	12 "Singular and Plural" section
[18] *you ... we'll*	16 Maintaining Person Agreement
[20] *asked ... represents*	13 Keeping Your Tenses Consistent

Answers for Unit 4 Quick Quiz

Note: Triple asterisks (***) indicate that a word or words have been deleted. Each set of triple asterisks counts as one error.

[1]When we go to a movie **,** most of us like to sit back, munch away on a bucket of popcorn, and get lost in a good story. [2]Some people **,** however **,** delight in examining each frame to see if the producers of the film have made mistakes called "bloopers." [3]One kind of blooper is an anachronism. [4]An anachronism is something that is inconsistent with the time period in which the movie is set. [5]For example **,** in *Pirates of the Caribbean: Curse of the Black Pearl* **,** when Jack is shouting at his men **,** a film-crew member in a white T-shirt and tan cowboy hat is clearly visible over his shoulder. [6]In *Gladiator*, Russell Crowe walks past a field marked with tractor-tire tracks. [7]Filter-tipped cigarettes in *Titanic* **,** a Volkswagen Beetle in *The Godfather*, and white *** canvas sneakers in *The Ten Commandments* are other glaring examples of anachronisms. [8]Whoops **!**

[9]Another kind of blooper is *** the continuity mistake. [10]This kind of slip-up involves inconsistencies from one film sequence to the next. [11]For example, if a character drinks from a glass in one shot, the glass must contain less liquid, not more, in the next. [12]Continuity problems abound **:** cigarettes get longer instead of shorter or appear and disappear from an actor's hand, hair changes style or length, and jewellery changes location. [13]Did you notice any of these bloopers when you watched the following films **?** [14]In *The Aviator*, the canopy on Leonardo DiCaprio's airplane pops on and off from sequence to sequence. [15]In *Lord of the Rings: Return of the King*, Frodo's scar moves several times from the right side of his face to the left and back again. [16]In *Harry Potter and the Order of the Phoenix*, while Harry is having a nightmare in bed **,** his shirt changes from short-sleeved to long-sleeved.

[17]When we encounter a work of art, we want to experience what the poet Coleridge called **"**the willing suspension of disbelief.**"** [18]We need to believe because getting lost in the story is the essence of a great movie. [19]Bloopers can interfere with this belief **,** but so can looking too hard for mistakes!

Answer Key
If you missed the error(s) in sentence ...   see Chapter ...

[1] *When we go to a movie most*	17 The Comma (Rule 3)
[2] *people however delight*	17 The Comma (Rule 4)

If you missed the error(s) in sentence ...	see Chapter ...
[5] *For example in* Pirates ...	17 The Comma (Rule 3)
Black Pearl *when Jack is shouting at his* *men a film-crew member*	17 The Comma (Rule 4)
[7] *Filter-tipped cigarettes in* Titanic *a*	17 The Comma (Rule 1)
Volkswagen Beetle and white, canvas sneakers	17 The Comma (Rule 5)
[8] *Whoops.*	21 "The Exclamation Mark" section
[9] *is: the continuity mistake*	19 The Colon
[12] *problems abound;*	18 The Semicolon; 19 The Colon
[13] *the following films.*	21 "The Question Mark" section
[16] *while Harry is having a nightmare in bed* *his shirt*	17 The Comma (Rule 4)
[17] *the willing suspension of disbelief*	20 Quotation Marks
[19] *belief but*	17 The Comma (Rule 2)

Answers for Chapter 17: The Comma

Exercise 17.1

1. My favourite philosophers are Rick Mercer, Tina Fey, and Don Cherry.
2. If you ignore my terrible accent, poor grammar, and limited vocabulary, my French is excellent.
3. Wei held two aces, a King, a Queen, and a Jack in his hand.
4. Cambodian food is spicy, colourful, nourishing, and delicious.
5. In Canada, the seasons are spring, summer, fall, winter, winter, and winter.
6. Correct.
7. The successful applicant will have excellent communication and computer skills, a friendly disposition, and a willingness to work hard.
8. Sleeping through my alarm, dozing during sociology, napping in the library after lunch, and snoozing in front of the TV are all symptoms of my overactive nightlife.
9. Of Paris, Moscow, Sydney, Madrid, and Beijing, which is not a national capital?
10. Both my doctor and my nutritionist agree that I should eat better, exercise more, and stop smoking.

Exercise 17.2

1. Rudi and I are good friends, yet we often disagree.
2. Correct.
3. Please pay attention, for the topic of today's lesson will be on the exam.
4. Money can't buy happiness, but it makes misery easier to live with.
5. Honesty may be the best policy, but it is not the cheapest.
6. Correct.
7. The power went out at work today, so we packed up early and went home.
8. Pack an extra jacket or sweater, for evenings in September can be cold.
9. This is my first full-time job, and I don't want to mess it up.
10. Noah had the last two of every creature on his ark, so why didn't he swat those mosquitoes?

Exercise 17.3

1. First, do no harm.
2. Before we begin, we need to understand what an independent clause is.

3. According to my stomach, lunchtime came and went about an hour ago.
4. In the end, we will be judged by how much happiness we have given others.
5. If you live by the calendar, your days are numbered.
6. No matter how much I practise, my singing never improves.
7. When you are right about something, it's considered polite not to gloat.
8. When everything is coming your way, you are in the wrong lane.
9. Until I went to France, I didn't think I could remember a word of my high school French.
10. Correct.

Exercise 17.4

1. Commas, like capitals, are clues to meaning.
2. Our hope, of course, is that the terrorists will be caught and punished.
3. Our family doctor, like our family dog, never comes when we call.
4. Our adventure began in Barcelona, which is the site of a famous unfinished cathedral designed by Gaudi.
5. Gaudi, who in his 50s was killed by a bus, began the cathedral as atonement for the sins of mankind.
6. Correct.
7. Our car made it all the way from Thunder Bay to Saskatoon, a piece of good luck that surprised us all.
8. Correct.
9. My bike, despite its age and rust, gets me around town efficiently and cheaply.
10. A compliment, like a good perfume, should be pleasing but not overpowering.

Exercise 17.5

1. Correct.
2. Correct.
3. Correct.
4. Toronto in the summer is hot, smoggy, and humid.
5. This month's *Road and Track* features a car made of lightweight, durable aluminum.
6. Our new uniforms are surprisingly contemporary, comfortable, and flattering.
7. This ergonomic, efficient, full-function tablet comes in a variety of eye-popping colours.
8. We ordered a nutritious, low-calorie salad for lunch and then indulged in apple pie topped with vanilla ice cream for dessert.
9. When she retired, my mother bought herself a large, comfortable leather reclining chair, which is almost exclusively used by my father.
10. We survived the long, high-velocity descent but almost didn't survive the jarring, unexpected crash landing.

Exercise 17.6

1. No words in the English language rhyme with *month*, *orange*, *silver*, or *purple*.
2. I call my salary "take-home pay," for home is the only place I can afford to go on what I make.
3. Unless the union intervenes, tomorrow will be my last day on the job.

4. James went to the bank to withdraw enough money to pay for his tuition, his books, and the student activity fee.
5. In a moment of foolish optimism, I invested my life savings in a software development company.
6. The happiest years of my life, in my opinion, were the years I spent in college.
7. Sabina dances all night in the clubs, and she sleeps all day in bed.
8. Doing punctuation exercises is not very exciting, but it's cleaner than tuning your car.
9. This year, instead of the traditional gold watch, we will be giving retiring employees a framed photograph of our company's president.
10. Iqaluit, which was called Frobisher Bay until 1987, is a major centre on Baffin Island in Canada's eastern Arctic region.

Exercise 17.7

One of Canada's former prime ministers was John Diefenbaker. According to John Robert Colombo, author of many books about Canada, this was Diefenbaker's favourite story:

Two English ladies were travelling across Canada by train. They admired the Maritime provinces, loved Quebec and Ontario, and were fascinated by the Prairies. As they travelled across the Prairie provinces, they were amazed by the vast openness of the landscape. The bright red sunsets and endless hectares of golden wheat impressed and moved them. Eventually, however, they began to wonder where they were. One of them decided to ask the conductor, so she left the compartment to find him. Having checked the bar car, the baggage car, and the observation car, she finally found him in the dining car and asked for the name of the nearest town. He replied, "Saskatoon, Saskatchewan." When she returned to her compartment, her companion asked her if she had learned where they were. She replied, "No, I still don't know where we are, but wherever it is, they don't speak English!"

Answers for Chapter 18: The Semicolon
Exercise 18.1

2. Correct.   7. Correct.
3. Correct.   10. Correct.
4. Correct.

Exercise 18.2

Note: Triple asterisks (***) indicate that a word or words have been deleted. Each set of triple asterisks counts as one error.

1. We'll have to go soon; *** it's getting late. (*Or* We'll have to go soon, for it's getting late.)
5. My brother and I have not spoken in almost three years, which is how long we have had text-messaging.
6. If a tree falls in the woods where no one can hear it, does it make a noise?
8. Invented by a Canadian in the late 19th century, basketball is one of the world's most popular sports.
9. My neighbour works for a high-tech company, but he can't program his own VCR.

Exercise 18.3

Note: Triple asterisks (***) indicate that a punctuation mark has been deleted.

1. We're late again**;** this is the third time this week.
2. My boyfriend always buys me jewellery that I don't like**;** however, Harold the Gold Buyer is always happy to see me.
3. I need to replace my computer ******* because it continually freezes.
4. When life hands you lemons**,** make lemonade.
5. If you ever need a loan or a helping hand**,** just call Michel.
6. Travelling in Italy broadens the mind**;** eating Italian food broadens the behind.
7. North America's oldest continuously run horse race**,** the Queen's Plate, predates the Kentucky Derby by 15 years.
8. We can't afford dinner at an expensive restaurant**,** so let's have spaghetti and salad at home.
9. I am a marvellous housekeeper**;** every time I leave a man**,** I keep his house.
10. A man has to do what a man has to do**;** a woman must do what he can't.

Exercise 18.4

1. Concluding that we weren't really welcome**,** we left and went to Tim Hortons for coffee.
2. Horton was a native of Cochrane, Ontario**;** there's a very popular Tim Hortons shop in his hometown.
3. He played hockey for the Toronto Maple Leafs at a time when they were league champions**;** he was a key player on their defensive line.
4. Correct.
5. Horton ended his career playing for the Buffalo Sabres**;** nevertheless**,** it is as a member of the Toronto Maple Leafs that he is best remembered.
6. Correct.
7. Correct.
8. Deep-fried in fat and made from starch and sugar, doughnuts tend to pack on the pounds**;** some Tim Hortons outlets have been obliged to install reinforced seating for their customers.
9. When Tim Hortons became smoke-free, long-time patrons fumed since cigarettes and coffee were thought to go together as naturally as Don Cherry and bad suits**;** however, the concept actually increased the chain's popularity.
10. It's sad but true that this icon of the Canadian way of life, named for one of Canada's hockey heroes, is no longer a Canadian corporation**;** Wendy's bought it in 1995.

Answers for Chapter 19: The Colon

Exercise 19.1

1. Correct.	4. Correct.
3. Correct.	8. Correct.

Exercise 19.2

Note: Triple asterisks (***) indicate that a punctuation mark has been deleted.

2. Here is a good example of what I mean**:** Starbucks.
5. My car is so badly built that, instead of a warranty, it came with ******* an apology.

6. There are many species of fish in this lake, including ******* pike, bass, and walleye.

7. Two common causes of failure are ******* poor time management and inadequate preparation.

9. This apartment would be perfect if it had more storage: there aren't enough closets, bookshelves, or even drawers.

10. The difference between Canadians and Americans is that ******* Canadians know there is a difference.

Exercise 19.3

Note: Triple asterisks (***) indicate that a punctuation mark has been deleted.

1. Our dog knows only one trick: pretending to be deaf.

2. Let me give you an example of a female role model: Adrienne Clarkson.

3. If at first you don't succeed, become a consultant and teach someone else.

4. There is nothing we can do about our incompetent manager: she's the owner's daughter.

5. Leila spends too much time *** shopping at the malls, talking on the phone, and watching TV.

6. Your research paper lacks three important features: a title page, a references page, and some content in between.

7. The shortstop on our baseball team caught only one thing all season: a cold.

8. My mother always wanted a successful son, so I did my part: I urged her to have more children.

9. Looking forward to a good horror story, I was disappointed in Margaret Atwood's book *Negotiating with the Dead: A Writer on Writing.*

10. Of course, I have no one to blame but myself: I should have read the subtitle before buying the book.

Exercise 19.4

A class of Grade 4 students was studying Laura Secord, one of Canada's heroes. They learned how she lived in the village of Queenston, a community that had been taken over by the Americans during their invasion in 1813. American officers were billeted at her house; this is how she found out that the invaders were about to launch an attack against a small force led by Lieutenant Fitzgibbon in nearby Beaver Dams. Without regard for her own safety, Secord set out on a 30-kilometre trek through mosquito-infested bush and swamp, across enemy lines, over the Niagara Escarpment to warn the British officer and his Aboriginal allies. After 18 hours of hard travel, she stumbled across her rescuers, a band of Aboriginals who agreed to take her to Fitzgibbon. Having been warned by Secord, Fitzgibbon and his 50 soldiers and their 400 Aboriginal allies were able to prepare for a fight that would go down in history: the Battle of Beaver Dams. The American column was destroyed: of 500 men, 100 were killed and the rest were taken prisoner. Thanks to her heroism, the American invasion was stopped, Fitzgibbon and his men were safe, and Secord's name would become famous.

At the end of the lesson, the teacher asked what would have happened if Laura Secord had not showed such courage. Robbie, the class clown, had a ready reply: "We'd be eating Martha Washington chocolates instead of Laura Secords!"

Answers for Chapter 20: Quotation Marks

Exercise 20.1

1. The most famous quotation in the history of Canadian sports is Foster Hewitt's "He shoots! He scores!"
2. Michael Kesterton describes Canada's national animal, the beaver, as "a distant relative of the sewer rat."
3. "All we want," said Yvon Deschamps, "is an independent Québec within a strong and united Canada."
4. In the opinion of writer Barry Callaghan, "We Canadians have raised being boring to an art form."
5. Will and Ian Ferguson sum up Canadian cuisine as follows: "If you let a Canadian anywhere near a piece of food, [he or she is] sure to fling it into a deep fryer. Or cover it with sugar. Or fling it into a deep fryer and *then* cover it with sugar."

Exercise 20.2

1. Oscar Wilde had witty observations about almost everything, including age: "The old believe everything; the middle-age suspect everything; the young know everything."
2. "I've been on a constant diet for the past two decades," complains Erma Bombeck. "I've lost a total of 789 pounds. By all accounts, I should be hanging from a charm bracelet."
3. "The only reason I wear glasses," said Woody Allen, "is so that I can drive my car—or find it."
4. Roseanne Barr thinks job titles are important: "I don't like to be called 'housewife.' I prefer 'domestic goddess.'"
5. Historian and journalist Pierre Berton summed up the difference between Canadians and Americans as follows: "You ask an American how he's feeling, and he cries, 'Great!' You ask a Canadian, and he answers, 'Not bad,' or 'Pas mal.'"

Exercise 20.3

1. You can find my article, "What's Wrong with the Entire World," in the April edition of my blog, *The Ghastly Truth*.
2. The cooking column of England's *Daily Mail* newspaper had rather startling advice: "One can peel tomatoes easily by plunging in boiling water for a minute."
3. Last night, we rented the hit Québec-produced movie *C.R.A.Z.Y.*, in which Patsy Cline's classic song "Crazy" is a recurring theme.
4. Two books have influenced my life recently: Jonathan Safran Foer's *Eating Animals* has changed what I eat, and Richard Carlson's *Don't Sweat the Small Stuff* has helped me put things in perspective.
5. Canada's national anthem is derived from a French song, "Chant national," which was first performed in Québec City in 1880.
6. "O Canada," the English version of "Chant national," was written by R. Stanley Weir, a Montréal judge and poet, and was first performed in 1908.
7. When I read the review of *Daybreakers*, a vampire movie with a twist, I wanted to go right out and see it, but then I decided to wait to get it on Netflix so I could dress in my vampire clothes and eat ketchup sandwiches while I watched it.

8. Britney Spears, who is at least as famous for her behaviour as she is for songs like "Toxic" and "Till the World Ends," revealed in an interview that she might have been a geography major: "I like travelling to overseas places, like Canada."

9. When asked what the best thing he had read all year was, Justin Timberlake, writer/singer of "Girlfriend," "Gone," "Like I Love You," and others, replied, "You mean, like a book?"

10. Eric Deggans, the critic for the ***St. Petersburg Times***, comments on the phenomenon of game show reruns such as ***Jeopardy*** and ***Wheel of Fortune*** in his blog, ***The Feed***.

Answers for Chapter 21: Question Marks, Exclamation Marks, and Punctuation Review

Exercise 21.1

1. If the game ends in a tie, who will win the series?
2. Can you explain what a rhetorical question is?
3. I want to know what's going on here.
4. Why do they bother to report power outages on TV?
5. Are you aware that half the population is below average?
6. If olive oil comes from olives, and corn oil comes from corn, I wonder where baby oil comes from.
7. I read your report carefully, and I question your conclusions.
8. I'm curious about the human being who first decided that eating snails was a good idea.
9. I also wonder if that person would have found snails edible, let alone delectable, if they hadn't been buried under quantities of butter and garlic.
10. Do you know another word for *thesaurus*?

Exercise 21.2

1. I quit. (*Or*, if you want emphasis, I quit!)
2. Stop, thief!
3. This salsa is scorching!
4. He's on the stairway, right behind you! (*Or*, if you are describing a non-threatening scene, He's on the stairway, right behind you.)
5. We won! I can't believe it!
6. The crowd chanted triumphantly, "Go, Habs, go!"
7. Waving her new credit card, Tessa raced through the mall shouting, "Charge it!"
8. Take the money and run. (*Or*, if this is a dramatic situation, Take the money and run!)
9. Help! My brain is overloaded with punctuation and is about to explode!
10. This music is horrible! I'm going home.

Exercise 21.3

[1]What a day! [2]My daughter was scheduled to make a presentation to her Grade 3 class, and the entire family was stressed. [3]She and her mother had come up with a topic but hadn't shared it with me. [4]Why, I don't know. [5]Aren't fathers supposed to be supportive and encouraging, even if they don't have a clue what the female portion of the household is doing? [6]Anyway, my wife took our daughter off to school to do the big

demonstration, and when they left, I discovered some celery, raisins, and peanut butter on the kitchen counter. [7]What was I supposed to do? [8]I smeared the peanut butter on the celery and put the raisins in the peanut butter. [9]Was it ever a good breakfast! [10]Just as I finished eating, the car zoomed up the driveway and screeched to a stop; mother and daughter dashed into the house and ran into the kitchen. [11]"Where are the raisins and celery and peanut butter?" they screamed. [12]I told them I had eaten it and asked what the fuss was about. [13]There was more screaming. [14]I had eaten my daughter's demonstration. [15]The teacher told them later that was the first time she had heard the excuse, "My daddy ate my homework!"

Exercise 21.4

[1]I wonder why it is that I cannot dance. [2]My girlfriend would go out dancing every night of the week if she didn't have morning classes. [3]And can she ever dance! [4]When she is really into the music, I've seen her receive applause from an entire club as she leaves the dance floor. [5]They applaud me, too, but it's because they're glad to see me sit down. [6]Why is it that every part of my body moves to a different rhythm? [7]When my hips find the beat, my feet are half a beat behind, and my shoulders move around on their own as if I had some horrible nervous disorder. [8]Is it because I'm tall, and nerve impulses have to travel a long way to get from one part of my frame to another? [9]I've been told that, when dancing, I look like a stork with an uncontrollable itch in a vital part of its anatomy. [10]Talk about embarrassing! [11]"What can I do?" I ask myself. [12]Should I subject myself to weeks of torture and take dancing lessons when I suspect they wouldn't help in the least? [13]Is there no medical cure for my condition? [14]I must have been born without a rhythm gene! (*Or* .) [15]I wonder if it's too late to get a transplant.

Exercise 21.5

Note: Triple asterisks (***) indicate that a punctuation mark has been deleted.

1. If you want to make your living as a comedian, you must *** remember the punch line.
2. Good health, according to my doctor, should be defined as *** "the slowest possible rate at which one can die."
3. The fast pace of life doesn't bother me; it's the sudden stop at the end that has me worried.
4. This new fad diet can be summed up in a single sentence: "If it tastes good, don't eat it."
5. Being a news junkie, I rely on the radio to keep me informed; however, I also read a national newspaper, subscribe to ***Maclean's***, and watch ***The National*** on CBC each night.
6. "Don't worry about avoiding temptation," advised Winston Churchill. "As you grow older, it will avoid you."
7. The directions are simple: preheat the oven to 350° Fahrenheit, take the lasagna out of the box, remove the foil from the top, put the lasagna in the oven, and ignore it for 45 minutes.
8. In spite of what my partner says, I'm really quite an elegant dresser. On formal occasions, for example, I insist that the trouser cuffs of my formal pants just brush the tops of my sandals.

9. Columbus first encountered turkeys, which were unknown in Europe in his time, on an island off the coast of Honduras; he was served roast turkey by the Aboriginal peoples. According to Margaret Visser, author of **The Rituals of Dinner**, "At ceremonial feasts, the Spaniards were served huge tamales containing a whole turkey each."

10. George Bernard Shaw sent an invitation to his new play, **Major Barbara**, to Winston Churchill, along with a note saying, "Here are two tickets to opening night. Bring a friend ... if you have one." Churchill replied, "I cannot attend the first night but will come on the second ... if there is one."

Answers for Unit 4 Rapid Review

[1]A Member of Parliament was asked to give a major speech to the executives of Canada's banks and investment companies. [2]Since his staff included a professional speechwriter, he called her into his office and explained the importance of his audience, the government policies he wanted to talk about, and the tone and approach he thought would be appropriate for the occasion. [3]The speechwriter asked only one question: she wanted to know how long the speech should be. [4]The MP told her the speech should be no longer than 20 minutes. [5]Knowing how important this address would be for her boss, the writer went right to work; she stayed late to draft what she thought was a masterpiece.

[6]On the day after the big speech, the writer was at her desk early; she was eager to learn how her speech had been received. [7]When her boss called, she could tell from the tone of his voice that he was angry. [8]"The speech was a disaster!" he bellowed. [9]"I asked for a 20-minute speech, not a 60-minute speech! [10]Before I was finished, half the audience had left the hall, and most of the others were asleep!" [11]The writer thought for a minute before replying that she had given him exactly what he had asked for: notes for a 20-minute speech and two copies.

Answer Key

If you missed the error(s) in sentence ...	see Chapter ...
[2] *speechwriter he*	17 The Comma (Rule 3)
audience the	17 The Comma (Rule 1)
about and	17 The Comma (Rule 1)
[3] *question she*	19 The Colon
[5] *boss the*	17 The Comma (Rule 3)
to work she	18 The Semicolon
[6] *big speech the*	17 The Comma (Rule 3)
her desk early she	18 The Semicolon
[7] *called she*	17 The Comma (Rule 3)
[8] *The speech was a disaster*	20 Quotation Marks *and*
	21 "The Exclamation Mark" section
[9] *I asked ... speech*	20 Quotation Marks
[10] *had left the hall and most ...*	17 The Comma (Rule 2)
were asleep	21 "The Exclamation Mark" section
[11] *asked for notes*	19 The Colon

Answers for Chapter 22: Finding Something to Write About

Exercise 22.1

1. Not specific
2. Not significant: every child knows what they are
3. Not significant
4. Not single
5. Not significant
6. Not single
7. Not specific or supportable
8. Not specific or supportable
9. Not single
10. Not specific

Exercise 22.2

1. Not specific. If limited, the subject could yield several possibilities: for example, "Bottled water is an environmental catastrophe," "Bottled water is a waste of money," "The water bottling industry is depleting Canada's sources of pure water."
2. Not specific. You could limit this subject in several ways so that it passes the 4-S test: for example, "What makes a male (or female) attractive to Canadian adolescents?" or "How the notion of physical attractiveness has changed between my parents' generation and mine."
3. Not significant, and it's hard to imagine how you could make it so.
4. Not specific. What about it? Also not supportable without significant research.
5. Possible, but too broad. You could make the topic significant by applying one or more limiting factors to it. For example, "How predatory mites and spiders protect organic wheat farms." (Obviously, this topic would require most students to do considerable research.)
6. Not significant.
7. Neither significant nor supportable. It needs limiting: for example, "Weather forecasting is becoming more precise" or "Basic palm-reading techniques."
8. Not single. Choose one hero from one war.
9. Not specific. What about them? How to use them? Why they are useful? What they are used for?
10. Not specific. Limit the discussion to one kind of Internet piracy: for example, "The impact of Internet piracy on the gaming software industry."

Exercise 22.6

1. Better looks: not distinct; overlaps with "improved appearance."
2. Alcohol: not relevant to subject; it is not a reason for drug abuse.
3. Buying a wardrobe for summer and winter: not distinct; overlaps with "adjusting to the climate."
4. The Oprah Winfrey Network: not relevant; it's a network of shows, not a kind of show.
5. Poor sleep: not distinct; included in "fatigue and insomnia."
6. Eye strain from video screens: not relevant; it's not an advantage.
7. Sometimes have to pay more: not relevant; it's not a reason to buy Canadian products. Get product protection or warranty may not be relevant, either. Most products manufactured around the world come with warranties of some sort.
8. Coal: not relevant to the subject. It has been a mainstream source of energy for centuries, so it cannot be considered an "alternative" source.

9. High cost of cigarettes: not distinct; overlaps with "financial savings."
10. Keep a record of all purchases: not distinct; overlaps with "keep track of income and spending."

Exercise 22.8

Subject	**Main Points**

1. How to prepare for a job interview (chronological)

  _1_ Visit the company's website.
  _4_ Dress appropriately.
  _2_ Prepare answers to standard interview questions.
  _3_ Ask a friend to role-play the interview with you.

2. Reasons for student financial struggles (climactic)

  _1_ They lack family assistance.
  _2_ They lack government assistance.
  _4_ They can't manage money effectively.
  _3_ They can't find part-time work.

3. How to write a research paper (chronological)

  _3_ Read and take notes on selected research sources.
  _4_ Draft the paper.
  _2_ Compile a working bibliography of research sources.
  _1_ Define the subject.
  _7_ Type and proofread the final draft.
  _5_ Insert source citations and reference list.
  _6_ Revise the paper.

4. Effects of malnutrition (logical)

  _3_ Malnutrition affects the productivity and prosperity of nations as a whole.
  _1_ Malnutrition impedes the mental and physical development of children.
  _2_ Undernourished children become sickly adults unable to participate fully in their society.

5. Why pornography should be banned (chronological)

  _1_ It degrades those who make it.
  _3_ It brutalizes society as a whole.
  _2_ It desensitizes those who view it.

6. Why young people don't vote (climactic)

  _2_ The voting process is intimidating.
  _3_ The politicians and politics seem corrupt or irrelevant.
  _1_ They lack interest in political issues.

7. How to vote (chronological)

  _1_ Make sure you are on the voting list.
  _3_ Present your voter card.

Subject	Main Points
	_2_ Go to the specified polling station on election day.
	_4_ Take your ballot to the private voting station.
	_7_ Put your ballot through the slot in the ballot box.
	_5_ Mark an X in the circle next to your candidate of choice.
	_6_ Fold the ballot and return to the election officer's table.
	_8_ Follow the results on TV or radio.
8. How public transit benefits society as a whole (climactic)	_3_ It allows city planners to develop commercial corridors.
	_2_ It frees up core space for parks and development.
	_1_ It moves people to and from city centres quickly.
	_4_ It reduces pollution by taking cars off the roads.
9. Stock market cycles (logical)	_4_ Prices stabilize and begin to rise.
	_1_ Overeager investors create "bubbles."
	_2_ Investors realize that bubbles do not reflect worth and begin selling.
	_3_ The sell-off becomes widespread and can create panic, causing prices to fall.
10. How technology benefits humankind (climactic)	_2_ Knowledge: virtually all of human knowledge is accessible on a computer.
	_1_ Entertainment: a vast array of programming and gaming opportunities are available.
	_4_ Democracy: technology enables everyone to express opinions, acquire information, and communicate with others around the world.
	_3_ Communication: technology enables us to be instantly in touch with one another, at any time, in any place.

Answers for Chapter 23: The Thesis Statement

Exercise 23.1

1. Three essential components of a strong and lasting relationship are good communication, sexual compatibility, and mutual respect.
2. If I were you, I would avoid eating in the cafeteria because the food is expensive, tasteless, and unhealthy.
3. Behavioural psychologists classify parents into four different types : indulgent, authoritarian, indifferent, and authoritative.
4. Fad diets are not the quick and easy fixes to weight problems that they may seem to be ; in fact, they are often costly, ineffective, and even dangerous.
5. Aerobic exercise, strength and endurance training, and flexibility exercises are the essential components of a total fitness program. (Note that main points sometimes appear before the statement of subject.)
6. The responsibilities of a modern union include protecting the jobs of current employees, seeking to improve their working conditions and compensation, and protecting the pensions and benefits of pensioners.
7. Because they lack basic skills, study skills, or motivation, some students run the risk of failure in college.
8. Hollywood is in financial trouble. Even well-known stars, stunning technical effects, and a hugely expensive advertising campaign no longer guarantee a blockbuster movie.
9. *The Simpsons* amuses and provokes viewers with its depiction of a smart-alecky, underachieving son; a talented, overachieving daughter; and a hopeless, blundering father.
10. In order to prosper in the decades to come, Canada must lessen its dependence on a resource-based economy, cultivate a spirit of entrepreneurship, increase productivity, and encourage immigration.

Exercise 23.2

1. ✓
2. (Not parallel)
3. (Not parallel)
4. (Not parallel)
5. (Not parallel)

Exercise 23.3

1. Correct.
2. Good writing involves applying the principles of organization, sentence structure, spelling, and **punctuation**.
3. Our company requires employees to be knowledgeable, **honest**, disciplined, and **reliable**.
4. Hobbies are important because they provide us with **recreation**, stimulation, and **relaxation**.
5. Some of the negative effects of caffeine are heart palpitations, nervousness, and **sleeplessness**.

Exercise 23.4 (suggested answers)

1. The four kinds of essay writing are description, **narration**, **exposition**, and argumentation. (parallelism)

2. Intramural sports offer students a way to get involved in their school, an opportunity to meet friends, and **a way to keep fit**. (parallelism and significance: "uniforms" is a trivial point)

3. Increasingly, scientists are finding links between the weather and diseases such as colds, **arthritis**, and cancer. (parallelism and relevance—aging isn't a disease)

4. The most prolific producers of pretentious language are politicians, educators, **advertising copywriters**, and sportswriters. (overlap between *teachers and administrators* and *educators*; parallelism)

5. There are three categories of students whom teachers find difficult: those who skip class, **those who sleep through class**, and those who disrupt class. (parallelism—and wordiness! *Better:* **skippers**, **sleepers**, and **disrupters**)

Exercise 23.5 (suggested answers)

1. To succeed in college, a student requires several essential qualities.
   - Living in a college residence rather than one's own home is not a quality needed for success. It is a choice based on personal circumstances and preferences.
   - B. Three essential qualities students require to succeed in college (are) good academic skills, organizational skills, and motivation.

2. Some forms of electronic communication can improve a student's social life.
   - instant messaging *(Yes, this service helps people to stay in touch.)*
   - iPods *(No. If anything, once you're plugged into an iPod, you are isolated from the social life around you.)*
   - blogging *(Yes, you can communicate with people who have similar interests.)*
   - expensive gadgets *(No. Many are available, but by themselves, they have nothing to do with the subject. How you use them is what may or may not have an impact on your social life.)*
   - Internet dating *(Yes, people date people they meet online.)*
   - A. Some forms of electronic communication can improve a student's social life; (for example), Internet dating, instant messaging, and blogging.
   - B. Some forms of electronic communication that can improve a student's social life (are) Internet dating, instant messaging, and blogging.

3. Living in Canada has some advantages over living in the United States.
   - universal medical care *(Yes, good point.)*
   - pleasant climate *(No, not true. Canada's climate is cold and snowy for much of the year.)*
   - less crime *(Yes.)*
   - tundra *(No. The tundra is an Arctic region where no trees grow.)*
   - more affordable post-secondary education *(Yes, generally true.)*
   - multicultural environment *(No. Both countries are immigrant societies made up of people from many cultures.)*
   - A. There are at least three advantages to living in Canada rather than in the United States (:) universal medical care, more affordable post-secondary education, and less crime.

B. Living in Canada has some advantages over living in the United States (because) Canada has <u>universal medical care</u>, <u>more affordable post-secondary education</u>, and <u>less crime</u>.

4. Thesis: Immigration benefits Canada.
   - Immigrants must often learn a new language. *(While this is true, it is not related to the thesis.)*
   - Immigrants may find it difficult to adjust to life in Canada. *(Again, this is sometimes true, but it does not support the thesis.)*

   A. Immigration benefits Canada (because) <u>immigrants supply talents and skills our country lacks</u>, <u>they are needed to maintain our workforce numbers</u>, and <u>they enrich Canadian cultural life</u>.

   B. Immigrants to Canada benefit our country in many ways , (such as) <u>supplying talents and skills we lack</u>, <u>maintaining our workforce numbers</u>, and <u>enriching Canadian cultural life</u>.

5. Maintaining a healthy lifestyle
   - balanced diet
   - adequate exercise
   - (Your choice)

   A. (Main points first) <u>A balanced diet</u>, <u>adequate exercise</u>, and _____ (are) essential to maintaining a healthy lifestyle .

   B. Answers will vary.

Answers for Chapter 25: Paragraphs

Exercise 25.1

1.

Topic sentence ⟶ → Distinguishing skid row addicts is the extreme degree of stress they had to endure early in life . Almost all women now inhabiting Canada's addiction capital suffered sexual assaults in childhood, as did many of the males. Childhood memories of serial abandonment or severe physical and psychological abuse are common. The histories of my Portland patients tell of pain upon pain .

Supporting sentences develop topic by examples.

Conclusion

2.

Topic sentence ⟶ → Something interesting has happened with many of the couples I know. The wives have now become the major breadwinners . They have high-powered jobs in design, consulting, medicine, public affairs, HR, law and banking. Many of their husbands are underemployed or semi-retired, not always by choice. One works behind the counter in a retail store. Another keeps the books for a small business. One is a freelance writer whose market has nearly dried up, and another husband has gone back to school for a degree. A couple of others work for their wives' businesses. Several of these men also organize the household chores and do the cooking. Thirty years ago, most of these men handily out-earned their wives. But the situation has reversed .

Supporting sentences develop topic by examples.

Conclusion

3.

Topic sentence—

Supporting sentences develop topic through explanation and details.

Conclusion

Some people might say that the N-word is making a comeback. That the old-style, racist use of the word has faded into history and that it's now kosher to use the word in ordinary conversation. This argument fails on two counts. First, racists and racism haven't disappeared from the Canadian landscape. The comeback argument also fails because it suggests that reappropriating the word reflects a new linguistic trend. This is naive. As a way of playing with the English language's most hateful word, black people—mostly young black males—have called themselves "nigger" for generations. The difference now is that these same young blacks have broadcast the word, via music and TV, to the whole world. In the middle-class black cultures I've encountered in Canada and the United States, such a young man usually gets slapped or tongue-lashed by his mother, at just about that point, and he learns that the only time it's safe to use that word is when he's chilling on the street with his buddies. Black people use the word "nigger" precisely because it hurts so much that we need to dance with our own pain, in the same way that blues music dives straight into bad luck and heartbreak. This is very much part of the black North American experience: we don't run from our pain, we roll it into our art.

Exercise 25.7

1. Descriptive details
2. Quotation
3. Specific details
4. Series of steps/stages
5. Definition + contrast
6. Specific numerical details
7. Paraphrase
8. Examples
9. Statistical details
10. Quotation + contrast

Exercise 25.10

Those who support fighting in hockey argue that "It's part of the game" or "It's what fans want" or "It prevents dangerous, dirty play." Even a quick look at the facts shows that such arguments are baseless. Like hockey, sports such as football, soccer, and basketball are fast, aggressive, and violent, but fighting is banned in all of them. If fighting was what fans demanded, then there would be few viewers for the Olympics or for World Championship tournaments. The fact that these events draw unequalled ratings demonstrates that hockey fans do not need fights to draw them to the game. Meanwhile, NHL ratings are in decline in Canada, and the rest of the world views hockey as a third-rate sport. Hockey can be beautiful, fast, skilful, and creative, but when players whose only skill is fighting are sent into the game, it becomes nothing more than a brutal brawl.

Answers for Chapter 26: Revising Your Paper

Exercise 26.5 (suggested answers)

Note: Triple asterisks (***) indicate that a word or words have been deleted.

Do you find it a struggle to pay the bills every month**?** When **you live** beyond your means, even a small shortfall at the end of each month can quickly add up to a

significant debt. To **overcome** this problem**,** you **can *** choose** to spend less or **earn** more. At first, the former may seem the more **difficult** choice**. Cutting** back on what you spend may mean giving up some of the things you "need**,**" such as eating out, **going to** movies, or **buying** the latest fashions. Doing without such expensive pleasures, however, often **produces** significant savings**. You** may even save enough to balance the monthly books.

Earning more money ***** and continuing** to spend at your present pace may seem like a more attractive **option**, but is it realistic**? First,** there is the challenge of finding another job that pays better **or** adding part-time work to the job you already have**. Either** way**, you're** going to **lose** even more of your already scarce study and leisure time. **Second,** it **is a** fact that most people continue to spend at the same rate, regardless of how much money **they** make**. So it's** likely that, even with additional income, you'll still be **overdrawn** at the end of the month. The best solution to the end-of-month budget blues is likely a combination of cutting costs where practical and adding to income where possible.

Answers for Chapter 27: Using Research Resources Responsibly

Exercise 27.1

1. This "paraphrase" is plagiarism. The writer has made little attempt to rethink or rewrite the author's original. Many of the phrases in this attempt at paraphrasing have been taken word for word from the original source.
2. This paragraph is an acceptable paraphrase. Not only does it cite the author's article appropriately, but it expresses the ideas in the writer's style, not Maté's, and presents the points in an original order.
3. Good try, but this paragraph is closer to plagiarism than it is to paraphrase. While the writer has made an effort to reword the author's ideas, she hasn't been entirely successful. Her paragraph begins well, but after a strong start she drifts into echoing the original author's words (e.g., sentence 3 is virtually identical to Wente's sentence 5; the last sentence in the student's paragraph is a shortened version of Wente's last two sentences). The student presents the author's ideas and examples in the same order as the original.

Answers for Unit 6 Quick Quiz

[1]People learn their first language when they are very young. [2]Most of us understand spoken words and respond to them **by** the time we are two or three years old. [3]It takes another few years for us to learn how to read and write, but we acquire our first language easily. [4]**For** most of us, however, learning a second language is a slow and exasperating process. [5]Most people who study English as a second language are especially **frustrated** by three of its peculiarities: its disorderly pronunciation, its inconsistent spelling, and its enormous vocabulary.

[6]English **has** sounds that are difficult for speakers of other languages. [7]The *th* sound is one of them. [8]Why is it pronounced differently in words such as *this* and *think*? [9]The consonant sounds *l*, *r*, and *w* also present problems. [10]Many new English speakers don't hear the differences between *light*, *right*, and *white*, so they pronounce them as the same word. [11]There are also more vowel sounds in English than in most other **languages**. [12]The *a* sound in the words *bat* and *mat* is peculiar to English, so second-language learners often pronounce *bet*, *bat*, and *but* identically. [13]To native speakers of English, these words **have** quite distinct sounds that many second-language learners do not hear and so cannot

pronounce. [14]Many English language **learners** find it difficult to pronounce the unusual vowel sounds that occur in the words *bird, word,* and *nurse.* [15]The fact that the same sound occurs in words with three different vowels—*i, o,* and *u*—is **an** example of **the** second major difficulty with English: its inconsistent spelling system.

[16]Most native speakers would agree that English spelling is difficult. [17]Why do *tough* and *stuff* rhyme when their spellings are so different? [18]Shouldn't *tough* rhyme with *cough*? [19]But *cough* rhymes with *off.* [20]Why does *clamour* rhyme with *hammer* while *worm* and *storm,* which should rhyme, don't rhyme? [21]There **is no** single answer. [22]Because English has absorbed many words, sounds, and spellings from other languages, it has some wacky spelling patterns. [23]Almost 75 percent of English words are spelled regularly. [24]Unfortunately, the 25 percent of English words spelled in unpredictable ways are the most commonly used **words** in the language: for example, *Wednesday, answer, knee.* [25]All of us, second-language learners and native speakers alike, simply have to learn to spell.

[26]English also has a huge vocabulary, in part because it borrows freely from other languages. [27]The roots of English are Germanic, but the Celts, Romans, French, and many others have contributed heavily to the language. [28]The gigantic *Oxford English Dictionary* lists about 500,000 words and does not include about another half-million technical and scientific **words**.

[29]English is **a** difficult language for all of these **reasons**, but it's a rich and **satisfying** one that is worth the effort to learn.

Answer Key

If you missed the error(s) in sentence ...	see Chapter ...
[2] *along the time*	32 Practising with Prepositions
[4] *By most of us*	32 Practising with Prepositions
[5] *especially frustrating*	29 "Participial Adjectives" section
[6] *English is having sounds*	28 Choosing the Correct Verb Tense
[11] *most other language*	30 "Quantity Expressions" section
[13] *these words are having*	28 Choosing the Correct Verb Tense
[14] *Many English language learner*	30 "Quantity Expressions" section
[15] *is example*	31 "The Indefinite Article: *A/An*" section
of second major difficulty	31 "The Definite Article: *The*" section
[21] *isn't no single answer*	29 "Forming Negatives" section
[24] *commonly used word*	30 Solving Plural Problems
[28] *scientific word*	30 "Quantity Expressions" section
[29] *is difficult language*	31 "The Indefinite Article: *A/An*" section
these reason	30 Solving Plural Problems
satisfied one	29 "Participial Adjectives" section

Answers for Chapter 28: Choosing the Correct Verb Tense

Exercise 28.1

1. He *has* been *going.*   He *has* been *seeing.*
2. I was **going.**   I was **seeing.**
3. He **goes.** They **go.**   He **sees.** They **see.**

4. You **are going**.   You **are seeing**.
5. We **went**.   We **saw**.
6. She **will** be **going**.   She **will** be **seeing**.
7. It **has gone**.   It **has seen**.
8. We had **gone**.   We had **seen**.
9. You **will go**.   You **will see**.
10. Someone had **been going**.   Someone had **been seeing**.

Exercise 28.2

1. He will **be** going with us. (future progressive)
2. The business **has been** doing very well this year. (present perfect progressive)
3. My parents **have** always **been** good to me. (present perfect)
4. I **am** leaving for Vancouver a week next week. (present progressive expressing future)
5. My friend **had** lived in Canada for two years, but he returned to Poland last week. (past perfect)
6. You **have been** working very hard, so why not take a break? (present perfect progressive)
7. The movie **had been** playing for 30 minutes by the time we got there. (past perfect progressive)
8. We **were** playing tennis yesterday when the rain began. (past progressive)
9. I **am** taking off my running shoes right now because they **are** killing my feet. (present progressive)
10. Linsey **was** eating dinner when the phone rang. (past progressive)

Exercise 28.3

1. It **is snowing** again today. In my country, it often **rains**, but it never **snows**.
2. My father usually **comes** to see my games, but tonight he **is working** a late shift.
3. I **study** almost every night, but tonight I **am going** to visit some friends.
4. A ticket home **costs** so much that I **doubt** I can afford the trip.
5. I **know** you can get a college degree if you **work** hard.
6. My boyfriend usually **texts** me after work, but it is now 10 p.m., and I **am still waiting** for his message. I wonder what he **is doing**.
7. The baby **is crying** again. He always **cries** when his mother **leaves**.
8. What **is she doing** right now? She **is appearing** in a Broadway play.
9. The little girl **looks** tired, but right now she **is looking** at her favourite storybook.
10. Wanda **wants** to get a good job, but she **has** to finish her college education first.

Exercise 28.4

1. Does Rahim like to travel?
   Yes, he does. He **has gone** to many different places during his life. He **has visited** both Asia and Africa **since** 2006.
2. Are you taking an ESL course this semester?
   No, I **have already taken** it. I **have studied** English **for** 11 years.
3. Do you love me?
   Yes, I **have always loved** you. I **have known** you **since** I was young, and I **have never loved** anyone but you.

4. Does Amir like to cook?

Yes, he loves to cook. He made us a delicious tajine last night. He **has prepared** a wonderful meal every night this week.

5. When did you move to Canada?

I moved here in ___. I **have been** here **for** ___ years.

Exercise 28.5

1. It **has been snowing** all day.
2. They **have been studying** physics for three days straight.
3. We **are looking** for a new house right now.
4. She **has been answering** all of the email messages.
5. The phone **has been ringing** all morning.

Exercise 28.6

1. It **has been raining** (*or* **has rained**) all night, and the basement is flooded.
2. There **have been** four big rainstorms already this week.
3. I always **have done** my homework carefully, and for the past two months, I also **have been working** with a tutor.
4. Lorenzo **has not seen** his father since 2006.
5. How long **have you lived** (*or* **have you been living**) in Canada?

Exercise 28.7

1. Three of us **were smoking** in the upstairs washroom when the boss **walked** in.
2. The cat **was hiding** behind the fish tank when I **saw** his tail twitch and **caught** him.
3. While their sister **was preparing** their lunch, the children **ran** into the house and **turned** on the television.
4. When we **were working** outside in the yard last night, we **felt** the jolt of a small earthquake.
5. Rick **was trying** to do his homework when his girlfriend **came** over. He never **finished** his work.
6. While we **were watching** television, the telephone **rang**.
7. The professor **was teaching** an important lesson when two men **came** in late and **disturbed** the class.
8. I **did not hear** you arrive last night because I **was sleeping**.
9. **Were** you **eating** breakfast this morning when I **phoned**?
10. While I **was looking** at my boyfriend's Facebook profile, I **noticed** that his relationship status said "Married."

Exercise 28.8

1. Tyshawn was late for class. The professor **had just given** a quiz when he **got** there.
2. Yesterday my friend Ronit **saw** an old friend whom she **had not seen** in years.
3. I almost missed my flight. Everyone **had already boarded** the plane by the time I **rushed** in.
4. They **had** scarcely **eaten** anything when the waiter **removed** their plates.
5. The movie **had** hardly **started** when the audience **walked** out.

Exercise 28.9

1. It is 6 p.m. I **have been working** for 10 hours straight, so it is time to go home.

2. It was 6 p.m. I **had been working** for 10 hours straight, so it was time to go home.
3. I woke up feeling strange this morning because I **had been dreaming** about dinosaurs all night.
4. Kyle **had been riding** his bicycle for two hours by the time he **got** home.
5. They **had been dating** for a year before they broke up.

Exercise 28.10

1. By the time I **realized** that I needed an elective to graduate, I **had already dropped** my history course.
2. The child **was playing** outside when her babysitter **arrived** yesterday.
3. Karin's sister **arrived** about 10 minutes after Karin **had left** (*or* **left**).
4. I **wasn't listening** when they **made** the announcement.
5. By the time Kim **had been working** (*or* **had worked**) the night shift for three months, she **thought** that she would never have a social life again.
6. We **had been looking** forward to our vacation for months when my wife **got** a promotion, and we **had** to cancel our plans.
7. If I **had known** how difficult this course **was**, I would have signed up for something easier.
8. Ana **had been living** (*or* **had lived**) in California for three years when she **opened** her first business.
9. My parents **gave** me a thousand dollars when they **came** to visit me last year.
10. Kim **never thought** about her friend's feelings; she **was** (*or* **was being**) very selfish when she made the decision.

Exercise 28.11

1. When I **got** home last night, everyone **had already eaten** dinner.
2. We **had gone** (*or* **went**) to sleep before the roof **collapsed**.
3. Julia **has been working** (*or* **has worked**) in this office for a year, and now she **is getting** a raise and a promotion.
4. Hockey **has always been** Canadians' favourite sport; we **have been playing** (*or* **have played**) the game for more than 150 years.
5. Although Ali **has lived** (*or* **has been living**) in Toronto since he was 10, he **has never visited** the CN Tower.
6. While Igor **was talking** on the phone, the bathtub **overflowed**.
7. They **had been waiting** (*or* **had waited** *or* **waited**) for two years to adopt a child, and their baby **has just arrived**.
8. **Have** you **finished** your homework yet?
9. Yesterday my father **made** me go to the barber who **has been cutting** (*or* **has cut**) his hair for the past 20 years.
10. While I **was waiting** (*or* **waited**) for my turn, I **noticed** that I **was** the only person under 50 in the shop.

Exercise 28.12

1. He **is going to arrive** tonight, but I **won't be** here.
2. Tomorrow is his birthday, so he **is going to have** dinner with friends.
3. Since you **are going to take** an elective course next semester, I suggest you sign up for sociology. You **will enjoy** Professor Singh's sense of humour.

4. Our neighbours **are going to build** an addition onto their home next summer. I hope we **will be** on vacation when the construction begins.

5. Raoul **is going to buy** a computer because he hopes that his children **will send** him emails and pictures.

Exercise 28.13

1. I have no idea where I **will be working** next week, but I **will let** you know as soon as I find out.

2. This time tomorrow, we **will be sitting** on a beach with margaritas in our hands.

3. I **won't have** (*or* **will not have**) time to talk on the phone this afternoon because I **will be cooking** a traditional dinner for 14 people.

4. Ravi says that he **is going to teach** in Tokyo next year.

5. We **won't stay** (*or* **will not stay**) at this hotel again.

Exercise 28.14

1. **Will** you **go** out with me this evening?

2. We are going to be late because of the terrible traffic. By the time we **reach** the airport, Miryam's plane **will already have arrived**. She **will be worrying** (*or* **will worry**) that something has happened to us.

3. At this pace, we **will have walked** 30 kilometres by tonight.

4. You were born in ___. By the year 2050, you **will have lived** (*or* **will have been living**) for ___ years. You **will have seen** (*or* **will see**) many changes!

5. I **will have already cleaned** the house by the time you get here.

Exercise 28.15

1. As soon as Val **graduates**, he **will leave** (*or* **is leaving** *or* **will be leaving**) for Africa.

2. If the wind **blows** hard, that house **will collapse**.

3. The café **opens** at 6 a.m. every morning.

4. If it **rains** on the weekend, we **will cancel** (*or* **are going to cancel**) our plans for a beach party.

5. Pierre **will be** here in Canada for at least another year before he **returns** home to France and **gets** a job.

Exercise 28.16

On my next birthday, I **will be** ___ years old.

After we **get** married, we **are going to have** (*or* **will have**) three children.

In a couple of years I **will finish** (*or* **will have finished**) college, and I **will get** a good job.

The teacher **has not finished** marking our tests, so we **won't know** our grades until next week.

When Xavier **arrives** in Toronto tomorrow, he **will have been flying** for 14 hours.

Exercise 28.17

(a) One hot day last summer, a fox **was strolling** through an orchard until he **came** to a bunch of grapes ripening on a vine that **was hanging** over a branch. "Just the thing to quench my thirst," he **said**. Drawing back a few paces, he **took** a running jump and just **missed** the grapes. Turning around again, with a "one, two, three," he **tried** once more to capture the tasty grapes. At last, he **gave** up and **walked** away with his nose in the air, saying, "I am sure those grapes must be sour."

(b) Right this very minute, a fox **is strolling** through an orchard until he **comes** to a bunch of grapes ripening on a vine that **is hanging** over a branch. "Just the thing to quench my thirst," he **says.** Drawing back a few paces, he **takes** a running jump and just **misses** the grapes. Turning around again, with a "one, two, three," he **tries** once more to capture the tasty grapes. At last, he **gives** up and **walks** away with his nose in the air, saying, "I am sure those grapes must be sour."

Answers for Chapter 29: More about Verbs
Exercise 29.1
1. The moon **is not (isn't)** full tonight.
2. The moon **was not (wasn't)** full last night.
3. Sandy **does not (doesn't) like** vegetables.
4. Ronald and Sandy **do not (don't) like** vegetables.
5. The teacher **does not (doesn't) want** to help us.
6. The teachers **do not (don't) want** to help us.
7. The teachers **did not (didn't) want** to help us.
8. **Is** Daphne **not** with you? **Isn't** Daphne with you?
9. **Will** Daphne **not be** with you tomorrow? **Won't** Daphne **be** with you tomorrow?
10. I **do not (don't) have** enough money.

Exercise 29.2
1. I **do not (don't) drink** milk. (*Or* I **drink no** milk.)
2. You **do not (don't) like** the teacher.
3. The passengers **do not (don't) have** their passports. (*Or* The passengers **have no** passports.)
4. You **should not (shouldn't) have given** the students a quiz on negatives.
5. The man **does not (doesn't) look** suspicious to me.
6. Faith **did not (didn't) buy** dinner for us yesterday. (*Or* Faith **bought no** dinner for us yesterday.)
7. We never **watch our** diet. (*Or* We **do not (don't) watch** our diet.)
8. José and Marta **did not (didn't) want** to eat before the movie.
9. **Isn't** breakfast ready?
10. The earth **does not (doesn't) go** around the moon.

Exercise 29.3
1. Mohammed and Hassan **do not (don't) enjoy** the winters in Canada.
2. I certainly **do not (don't) want** to see you.
3. I certainly **did not (didn't) want** to see you.
4. There **are not (aren't)** 14 players on a soccer team.
5. Most of the class **did not (didn't) attend** the reception for international students.
6. The band **will not (won't) stop** the music at midnight.
7. Amy **does not (doesn't) look** like her mother.
8. The computer **is not (isn't)** working very well.

9. The computer **was not (wasn't)** working very well.
10. She **did not (didn't) come** to the meeting alone.

Exercise 29.4

2. annoying; annoyed
3. horrifying; horrified
4. embarrassing; embarrassed
5. satisfying; satisfied
6. disappointing; disappointed
7. bored; boring
8. pleasing; pleased
9. amazing; amazed
10. exhausted; exhausting

Exercise 29.5

1. He is a **tired** man.
2. Hard work is **tiring** for Bob.
3. The children are **interested**. They are watching an **interesting** movie.
4. He is a **surprised** man. The news was quite **surprising**.
5. I am **disgusted**. The garbage is **disgusting**.
6. The lecture was **stimulating**. The students were **stimulated**.
7. I was **exhausted** by this **exhausting** task.
8. The possibility is **exciting**. Everyone is **excited**.
9. His story was **inspiring**. The crowd was **inspired**.
10. The **shocked** people could hardly believe the **shocking** test results.

Exercise 29.6

1. Sam should **work** harder at school so that he can **get** into college.
2. Could you **show** me the way to the airport?
3. He **had to** buy a new car last week. (*Or* He **must have** bought a new car last week.)
4. My best friend **may marry** her boyfriend when they finish school.
5. **Would** you like me to show you my butterfly collection?
6. There **may not** be enough room in the classroom for all the students; we'll have to see how many come to class.
7. You **must** pass a tough physical exam if you want to be a police officer.
8. She isn't answering her cellphone. She **may** have forgotten to bring it with her.
9. Tell the children they **must** come in the house immediately.
10. The team **may** win their last game, but they have been playing so poorly that I don't think they will.

Exercise 29.7 (suggested answers)

1. It may rain later, so you **ought to** take your umbrella.
2. I **used to** go to the United States with just a passport, but now I **have to** get a visa.
3. We **were supposed to** go to the beach yesterday, but it was too cold. We hope that we **are able to** go tomorrow.

Exercise 29.8 (suggested answers)

1. I **should** (*or* **ought to**) **visit** my parents, but we always get into fights when we spend time together. So I rarely see them.

2. If he works very hard, Paulo **may** (*or* **might** *or* **will**) **finish** the project before the deadline.

3. He **must** (*or* **has to**) **complete** it on time if he wants to get paid.

4. **Will** we **be able to see** the moon tonight, or is it too cloudy?

5. When Oswaldo was younger, he **could run** very fast.

6. Felix bought his girlfriend a beautiful engagement ring; he **must love** her very much.

7. Her parents **used to drink** heavily, but they have stopped entirely since joining Alcoholics Anonymous.

8. Alex **was supposed to pay** back the loan last week, but he hasn't done so.

9. The sky is getting darker; it **may** (*or* **might**) **rain.**

10. You **can't** (*or* **must not**) **smoke** in public buildings in Canada.

Exercise 29.9 (suggested answers)

1. I wonder when the boat will arrive. It **was supposed to** be here an hour ago.

2. Laura is getting very fat. She **shouldn't** eat so much.

3. If you have a food processor, you **can** prepare this salad in a few minutes.

4. I **would** come over and see you if it weren't raining.

5. You **can't** be in two places at once.

6. The doctor is not in her office; I'm not sure where she is, but she **may** (*or* **might**) be at the hospital.

7. Their whole house is decorated in red; they **must** really love the colour!

8. Fred **should** know better than to call me at midnight.

9. Our instructor **used to** give us quizzes every day, but now he gives only three a semester.

10. People who drive and text at the same time **ought to** (*or* **should**) get tickets from the police.

Exercise 29.10

People choose to immigrate to Canada for many reasons. They **may** (*or* **might**) want to have more economic opportunity. Or they **might** (*or* **may**) be looking for a better education for their children. Or they **may** (*or* **might**) want to **be able** to practise their beliefs openly. Perhaps the country where they **used to** live denied them certain rights that they **can** (*or* **are able to**) enjoy in Canada. Whatever their reasons for coming, immigrants to Canada **must** (*or* **have to**) work very hard to adjust to their new country. They **must** (*or* **have to**) find new homes and jobs, and most of them **have to** (*or* **must**) learn a new language. Immigrating is not an easy process, but new immigrants hope that they **will** build a better life in their new home.

Exercise 29.11 (suggested answers)

1. I'll be very angry *if I lose my job.*

2. My mother will be happy *when I graduate from college.*

3. She'll be sorry *when I move out of the house.*

4. My friends will be disappointed *if I don't go to their party.*

5. You'll worry about me *when I go skydiving.*

6. *Canada will be a different place if* I become prime minister.

7. *You'll live happily ever after when* you get married.

8. *We'll take the dog for a walk when* the sun comes up.

9. *The family will move when* Fatima finishes college.

10. *I'll go to school if* it doesn't snow tomorrow.

Exercise 29.12

1. You **would miss** me if I **moved** to Calgary. You **will miss** me if I **move** to Calgary.

2. My husband **eats** eggs for breakfast when he **has** time to cook in the morning.

3. When David **gets** home, he **walks** the dog.

4. You **won't meet** my new girlfriend if you **stay** home.

5. The dog **barks** whenever he **sees** the mail carrier.

6. Peter **will get** a bad sunburn today if he **isn't wearing** sunscreen.

7. When the moon **is** full, werewolves **howl**.

8. The doctor says if my father **quit** smoking, he **would feel** better. But he won't quit.

9. Whenever people **quit** smoking, their overall health **improves**.

10. Water **freezes** when it **gets** down to a temperature of 0° Celsius.

Exercise 29.13

(a) 1. Ali failed math. He **would have passed** the course if he **had worked** harder.

2. Rhonda found out that she has high blood pressure. If she **had learned** about it earlier, she **would have gone** to see a doctor.

3. You lost the race. You **would have won** if you **had run** faster.

4. If we **had remembered** to lock the door, the burglars **would not have gotten** into the house.

5. We **would have saved** some money if we **had known** about the sale.

6. If Einstein **hadn't hypothesized** the theory of relativity, someone else **would have done** it.

(b) 7. If I hadn't been so angry, *I would have talked to them.*

8. If my parents hadn't met, *I would not have been born.*

9. *He would have lived happily in Katmandu* if he had not moved to Canada.

10. If I had won the lottery, *I would have bought a new house.*

Exercise 29.14

(a) 1. If you **tickle** me, I**'ll laugh**.

2. Dana **will clean** the kitchen if Louis **does** the laundry.

3. Ann **will be** depressed if her boyfriend **doesn't call**.

4. If it **doesn't rain** tomorrow, we **will go** to the beach.

5. If Jackie **tells** me that joke again, I**'ll scream**.

6. You**'ll find** a good job if you **work** hard at it.

7. If his mom **comes** to dinner, I**'ll cook** kosher food.

(b) 8. You'll be sorry if *he dumps you.*

9. I'll work hard if *I get the job.*

10. We won't get married if *you don't love me anymore.*

Exercise 29.15

1. We**'ll eat** dinner at a restaurant tonight if I **don't get** home in time to prepare a meal.

2. The baby **cries** whenever he **is** hungry.

3. If I **ran** the world, everyone **would have** enough to eat.

4. I didn't know the woman we saw last night. If I **had known** her name, I **would have told** you.

5. If I **spoke** French, I **would spend** the summer in Quebec. But I don't.

6. Irving lied to me about his work experience. If he **had told** me the truth, I **would not have hired** him.

7. Tides **are** higher when the moon **is** full.

8. If I **earned** more money, I **would buy** you a bigger house.

9. Some people believe that if a person **walks** under a ladder, he **will have** bad luck.

10. If the child's parents **didn't have to** work so hard, they **would be able to spend** (*or* **could spend**) more time with him.

Answers for Chapter 30: Solving Plural Problems
Exercise 30.1

2. Your little **girls love their** new **toys.**

3. **We are** going to see **our professors.**

4. Latanya's **brothers** won the **prizes.**

5. The **sharks are** swimming around the **boats.**

6. The **men visit their girlfriends** often.

7. **These rooms are** very large.

8. The **teachers love their students.**

9. Should **our sisters** find **their** own **apartments?**

10. **Our friends work** hard at **their jobs.**

Exercise 30.2

2. women themselves	9. yourselves	16. beliefs
3. our countries	10. photos	17. husbands
4. man	11. zoos	18. tooth
5. sheep	12. tomato	19. heroes
6. their feet	13. phenomenon	20. chiefs
7. eyelash	14. monarchs	
8. criterion	15. theses	

Exercise 30.3

1. women, salmon	6. cities, communities
2. mushrooms, berries	7. inquiries, replies
3. trees, leaves	8. potatoes, yourselves
4. courses, quizzes	9. children, themselves
5. scissors, knives	10. cattle, wolves

Exercise 30.4

	NC	NC	NC
1.	milk	sugar	coffee

	NC	C
2.	advice	problems

	NC	NC
3.	knowledge	physics

	NC	C
4.	beef	dinner

	C	NC
5.	suitcases	baggage

	NC	C
6.	water	chemicals

	C	NC
7.	vitamins	health

Exercise 30.5

1. money, luck
2. luggage, backpacks
3. pianos, furniture
4. paper, wood
5. cattle, beef
6. light, lights
7. times, time
8. garbage, work
9. advice, rubbish
10. apartments, accommodation

Exercise 30.6

1. Robert is going bald and wants to know where he can get **information** on **hair** replacement.
2. I found a **couple** of **hairs** in my soup.
3. Barney has excellent **knowledge** of two **languages**: English and French.
4. We want to give you some new **clothes** to wear as an expression of our **thanks**.
5. The **rich** get richer, and the **poor** get poorer.
6. Having two **businesses** go bankrupt was a learning **experience**.
7. We lost all of our **money** on several bad **investments**.
8. Did you get any new **information** about the computer **data** we lost?
9. We didn't hear much **laughter** coming from the back of the van as we drove through the rush-hour **traffic**.
10. Money can't buy you **love**.

Exercise 30.7

Note: Triple asterisks (***) indicate that a word or words have been deleted. These words are often articles, which are the subject of Chapter 31.

    *** Sharks are *** scary **animals** to most people, ******* killing **machines** immortalized in movies and books. ***** Sharks are** actually an ancient species. **Their ancestors date** back about 350 million years, as ***** fossil records show**. In size, ***** sharks range** from ***** tiny angel sharks** that **are** less than a metre in length to ******* huge 15-metre whale **sharks** that can weigh 700 kilograms.

    *** Sharks are *** very effective **predators** in the **oceans**. **They have** very good eyesight, and even in total darkness, ***** sharks** can sense the movement of **their** prey by means of special pores in **their** skin that sense **other animals'** electrical vibrations. In addition, ***** sharks** can actually smell **their** prey from ***** long distances**. These characteristics make ***** sharks ***** good killing **machines** as **they hunt** for food.

    Although ***** sharks are** high on the food chain, **they** usually **eat** smaller fish, crabs, seals, and other sea creatures. ***** Sharks do** not seek out people to eat. We may fear ***** sharks**, but there are only about 100 shark attacks on humans each year worldwide, and perhaps 25 to 30 of these are fatal. Given our increasing appetite for shark meat, the truth is that people eat many more sharks than sharks eat people.

Exercise 30.8

1. Roger drinks _____ cocktails every day. (*four, several, ~~much~~, ~~a great deal of~~, some, a lot of, too many, ~~a little~~*)
2. Roger drinks _____ alcohol every day. (*~~three~~, some, ~~many~~, a lot of, ~~several~~, a great deal of, ~~no~~, ~~a few~~, a little, ~~hardly any~~*)
3. My friend has _____ comfortable chairs on the patio. (*~~too much~~, hardly any, four, a few, ~~a great deal of~~, no, plenty of, some, ~~every~~*)
4. My friend has _____ comfortable furniture on the patio. (*~~a few~~, ~~three~~, ~~one~~, some, ~~several~~, hardly any, much, a lot of, lots of, ~~a couple of~~*)

Exercise 30.9 (suggested answers)

1. **A little** extra money is good to have.
2. Several **businesses** lost money.
3. Roberto has **few** friends here in Canada, so he feels very homesick.
4. Could you please give me **some** help?
5. Very **few** tourists visit the country because of the war.
6. We need only **a few** minutes to prepare dinner.
7. **Some** of the **stores** at the mall **are** open in the evening.
8. **Many** of my **friends** will be at my party, so we must have **lots** of **food**.
9. It takes **a lot of** practice to learn how to ice-skate.
10. **Both** of us got home from the game quickly because there was **hardly any** traffic.

Exercise 30.10

1. The battery of the car is dead, so it is **little** use trying to start it.
2. Only **a few** people came to the concert, so many seats were left empty.
3. The hard-working father spent **little** time with his children.
4. Life in a poor village offers **few** opportunities for people to prosper.
5. It's lucky that I have **a few** friends who can help you get a job.
6. My grandmother is feeling **a little** better this morning.
7. The girl had **few** friends in the neighbourhood, so she was very lonely.
8. I will need **a little** money if I am going to buy a car.
9. After the man regained consciousness, **little** that he said made any sense; he didn't even know his own name.
10. **A few** of us here in the office have gotten together to buy you a birthday present.

Answers for Chapter 31: Using Articles Accurately

Exercise 31.1

1. **a** huge dog, **an** old man
2. **A** zoologist, **a** scientist
3. **a** dentist
4. **a** hasty retreat
5. **an** honest woman
6. **An** arachnid, **an** insect, **a** spider
7. **An** electrician, **an** hour
8. **A** European man
9. **a** college, **a** university
10. **an** X-ray, **a** broken arm

Exercise 31.2

1. **A** veterinarian, **a** doctor, **(0)** animals
2. **A** child, **(0)** parents

3. **a** hurry, **(0)** food
4. **A** man, **a** big nose, **(0)** huge feet
5. As **a** rule, **a** rich person
6. **a** doctor, **an** examination, **a** year
7. **(0)** hours, **a** ticket
8. **A** baby, **(0)** milk
9. **a** cup of **(0)** coffee
10. **A** dog, **a** break

Exercise 31.3

When you move to **a** new city, you have to think about your housing needs. If you are going to be there for only **a** short time, you can rent **a** furnished apartment. **The** apartment should be in **a** convenient location. Perhaps you should locate yourself in **the** downtown area near public transportation. **The** furnished apartment you rent needs to have **a** decent kitchen. **The** kitchen should have **a** working stove and refrigerator. **The** place where you live is **an** important factor in your adjustment to your new city.

Exercise 31.4

1. I like **(0)** classical music, but **the** music he plays late at night disturbs me.
2. **(0)** Children are naturally curious, but **the** children in that class are extraordinarily inquisitive.
3. Do we know who invented **the** wheel?
4. In **the** Far North, **the** sun never sets in **(0)** June.
5. **The** elephant and **the** whale are both huge animals that give birth to **(0)** live babies; in other words, they are **(0)** mammals.
6. **(0)** Books and **(0)** newspapers are endangered species, thanks to our wired world of e-books and tablet computers.
7. **The** man with **the** dog is married to **the** woman beside you.
8. **(0)** College students need to spend **(0)** time studying if they want to be successful.
9. Is **(0)** money as important as **(0)** love to you?
10. Thank you for **the** bananas; I love to eat **(0)** fruit.

Exercise 31.5

1. I want to take **a** trip to **the** West Coast.
2. **The** phases of **the** moon are one of **the** causes of ocean tides.
3. **The** oldest person in **the** world is 114 years old.
4. My friends have two children: **a** boy and two girls. **The** boy is **the** oldest of **the** three.
5. Do you know **the** name of **the** best restaurant in town? I would like to take you out for **a** nice dinner.
6. **The** kind of vacation I enjoy most is **a** long train ride.
7. I don't need **a** special destination when I board **a** (*or* **the**) train; for me **the** most important thing is **the** journey.
8. **The** economic boom of **the** 1990s turned into **the** Great Recession after **the** financial meltdown of 2008.
9. **The** job requires **a** person with **a** lot of energy, and Danielle is **an** energetic person.
10. In many parts of Canada, **a** college student who begins school in **the** last part of August finishes **the** school year in April.

Exercise 31.6

1. We have had lots of **(0)** bad weather lately. Do you know what **the** weather is supposed to be like on **the** weekend?
2. We like **(0)** food, but **(0)** most of the food at **the** restaurant is awful.
3. Everyone has **(0)** problems in **(0)** life. **The** problems may be big or small, but everyone must find ways to cope with them.
4. Ana is studying **(0)** Canadian history because she is interested in **the** history of her adoptive country.
5. Some of **the** most important products that Canada buys from India are **(0)** tea, **(0)** cotton, and **(0)** rice.
6. **(0)** Beer is a popular beverage in Canada, and **the** beer brewed here has a high alcohol content.
7. **(0)** Kindness is an attractive quality in people, and **the** kindness of our friend Dana is known to us all.
8. **(0)** Jewellery is a popular gift; my boyfriend loved **the** jewellery that I gave him.
9. Natasha studies **(0)** art in university, and her specialty is **the** art of **the** Renaissance.
10. **(0)** Boots are a necessary item of winter clothing in Canada, but **the** boots I bought last year are not very warm.

Exercise 31.7

Many of **the** geographical names in Canada are derived from **the** languages of Aboriginal peoples who lived here for thousands of **(0)** years before **the** first European settlers arrived. For example, **(0)** Manitoulin Island in **(0)** Lake Huron got its name from **the** Algonquian word *Manitou*, which means "spirit." **The** Queen Charlotte Islands (also known as Haida Gwaii) off **the** coast of **(0)** British Columbia consist of about 150 islands, **the** largest of which are **(0)** Graham Island and **(0)** Moresby Island. **The** province names **(0)** Saskatchewan and **(0)** Ontario, **the** Magnetawan River, **(0)** Lake Okanagan, and even **the** name "Canada" itself are all examples of **the** influence of Aboriginal peoples' languages on Canada's place names.

Exercise 31.8

1. **(0)** Earthquakes sometimes happen in **(0)** British Columbia, but they rarely occur in **the** Prairie provinces, **(0)** central Canada, **(0)** Quebec, or **the** Maritimes.
2. Dora began her studies at **(0)** Nova Scotia Community College and then transferred to **(0)** Dalhousie University, but her brother attended **the** University of New Brunswick.
3. **(0)** Niagara Falls is on **the** Niagara River, which flows from **(0)** Lake Erie to **(0)** Lake Ontario.
4. **The** People's Republic of **(0)** China is also known as **(0)** China.
5. **The** St. Lawrence River forms **the** boundary between **(0)** Ontario in **(0)** Canada and **(0)** New York in **the** United States.
6. We have done mountain climbing in **the** Rockies, **the** Alps, and **the** Himalayas, but **the** most challenging climb was **(0)** Mount Kilimanjaro in **(0)** Africa.
7. **The** Bering Strait is between **the** state of Alaska and **the** former U.S.S.R., now known as **(0)** Russia.
8. **The** Czech Republic came into being in 1993, when **(0)** Czechoslovakia was no longer controlled by **the** Soviet Union.

9. **The** capital of **(0)** Prince Edward Island is **(0)** Charlottetown.

10. **The** Nile, **the** Amazon, and **the** Yangtze are **the** longest rivers in **the** world.

Exercise 31.9

A hurricane is **a** severe tropical storm with winds between 120 and 240 kilometres per hour. Hurricanes are most likely to form in **the** Atlantic Ocean, and they usually blow west across **the** Caribbean and **the** Gulf of Mexico from **(0)** Africa. Hurricanes gain their energy as they pass over warm ocean waters, so **the** warmest months of **the** year are known as "hurricane season," from **(0)** June through **(0)** October. Hurricanes rotate in **a** counter-clockwise direction around **an** (*or* **the**) "eye." When a hurricane comes onshore, heavy rain, wind, and waves can do **a** tremendous amount of damage to trees, buildings, and people in **the** path of **the** storm.

Exercise 31.10

The highest place on Earth is **a** mountain called Mount Everest, which is 8,850 metres high. It is located in Asia, at **the** border of Tibet and Nepal, in a mountain range known as **the** Himalayas. **The** first people to climb Everest were **(0)** Edmund Hillary and Tenzing Norgay, who reached **the** peak in 1953. According to a CBC website, 2,249 people had climbed **(0)** Mount Everest by the end of 2004, but 186 people had died trying. Now there is a small industry of guides who make a good living taking adventurous climbers to the top of Everest. Ascending the mountain is **an** expensive proposition, though. The average cost of a guided climb is about US$65,000. Save your money if you want to make it to **the** top!

Answers for Chapter 32: Practising with Prepositions

Sometimes more than one preposition can be used in the context of a sentence. The answers we have provided are those that usually apply in the context; the alternatives given in parentheses are also common and correct responses. Other answers may also be correct. If your answers differ from ours, check with your instructor (or with a native-English-speaking friend).

Exercise 32.1

1. **in** 2001
2. **on** Thursday
3. **in** the morning (possible to use *on* with a specific event: for example, *on* the morning of our wedding)
4. **at** midnight
5. **at** lunchtime
6. **in** the spring
7. **at** work
8. **on** the following day
9. **in** the nick of time (an idiom meaning "just in time")
10. **in** December

Exercise 32.2

1. in, for
2. on (*or* by), until
3. since, within
4. from, in
5. in (*or* during), at, on

Exercise 32.3

1. on, in
2. in, at, at (*or* on)
3. between
4. in, between
5. in, within

Exercise 32.4

1. by (*or* past)
2. across, from
3. out of (*or* from), toward (*or* to)
4. from, in
5. up, into, through

Exercise 32.5

1. with, about
2. with, from
3. of, with, to
4. of, of, with
5. from, without

Exercise 32.6

1. at (*or* by *or* before), around (*or* at *or* by *or* before)
2. in, between
3. of, to
4. in, at (*or* on), of, in

Exercise 32.7

1. by (*or* before)
2. of, under (*or* underneath *or* beneath), to, for
3. out of, into (*or* in), up (*or* down), by (*or* past)

Exercise 32.8

1. At, during (*or* at)
2. behind (*or* under), on, with, of, in
3. to, in, with, since
4. from, in, till (*or* until *or* to), at, by (*or* at), of

Exercise 32.9

1. in, with
2. with, for (*or* on)
3. between
4. for
5. between, of, on
6. about, to, after (*or* on *or* upon), to
7. Despite (In spite of), of, between
8. for, with

Answers for Unit 6 Rapid Review

[1]You probably **have been** learning English **for** a number of years now. [2]Maybe you've been living and studying in English for **much** of your life. [3]Yet perhaps you still **do** not feel entirely confident about your ability to make yourself understood when you're speaking, particularly when you **are speaking** to a group of people **at** school or work. [4]You are also not always sure what English speakers mean when they speak **to** you. [5]Are there any practical ways to improve your fluency in spoken English? [6]Yes, there are. [7]Here are **a few** tips to help you feel more confident when you are speaking and when you are listening.

[8]One good suggestion for someone who **is speaking** English as a secondary language is to s-l-o-w down. [9]Especially if you are presenting in **an** academic or professional situation, it's important to remember to speak more slowly than you normally do. [10]Often what makes your speech difficult to understand isn't the pronunciation of specific sounds ("t" versus "th," for instance), but rather **the** rhythm that is rooted in your first language and doesn't sound natural to native English speakers. [11]Sometimes your listeners seem

frustrated as they listen to your fast speech and can't understand what you are saying. [12]Slow down and pause frequently **at** appropriate places in your speech or presentation; use transition words such as *next, then*, and *in conclusion* to help your listener or reader stay **with** you.

[13]If you are preparing **a** short presentation, keep in mind that spoken language is simpler than written language. [14]Your sentences and vocabulary **should be** relatively simple. [15]Repeat key points, and use the board or cards to present important vocabulary that you think people might not understand. [16]Try to relax as much as possible, smile occasionally, and look **at** the people you're speaking to. [17]Eye contact is important and actually helps to communicate your meaning. [18]If you **look** at people, you can usually tell when someone doesn't understand you, and you can repeat or clarify the point you are making.

[19]There are also **a number** of ways that you **can** improve your comprehension of spoken English. [20]Listening to English radio and TV is helpful. [21]Listen to **interesting** programs that you already know something about, whether that is sports, news, celebrity gossip, or fashion. [22]Repeat key phrases to practise **the** rhythm of spoken English. [23]Listen to recorded phone messages; you might even get native-speaker friends to leave **complicated** messages for you so that you can practise understanding what they are saying. [24]Try to navigate through the phone loops of banks, airlines, or utility companies: "Press 6 if you would like to hear about our payment options."

[25]There are **many** websites designed to help people learn **(0)** English. [26]A site such as the BBC World Service has **many** resources, including audio and video clips that help people improve their **listening** comprehension. [27]Of course, you **may** find that voices on the BBC have what Canadians call a "British accent." [28]But learning to understand many varieties of spoken English is important to your overall mastery **of** the language.

[29]Above all, use your English. [30]Keep yourself immersed in the English-speaking world **around** you. [31]Engage people in conversation, listen to what they have to say, and ask questions when you need to. [32]Mastering another language **is** a long and arduous task. [33]Nevertheless, time and **a lot** of practice will give you confidence in your speaking and listening skills.

Answer Key

If you missed the error(s) in sentence ...	see Chapter ...	
[1]	*have been*	28 Choosing the Correct Verb Tense
	for	32 Practising with Prepositions
[2]	*much*	30 "Quantity Expressions" section
[3]	*do*	29 "Forming Negatives" section
	are speaking	28 Choosing the Correct Verb Tense
	at	32 Practising with Prepositions
[4]	*to*	32 Practising with Prepositions
[7]	*a few*	30 "Quantity Expressions" section
[8]	*is speaking*	28 Choosing the Correct Verb Tense
[9]	*an*	31 Using Articles Accurately
[10]	*the*	31 Using Articles Accurately
[11]	*frustrated*	29 "Participial Adjectives" section
[12]	*at*	32 Practising with Prepositions
	with	32 Practising with Prepositions

If you missed the error(s) in sentence ...	see Chapter ...
13 *a*	31 Using Articles Accurately
14 *should be*	29 "Modal Auxiliaries" section
16 *at*	32 Practising with Prepositions
18 *look*	28 Choosing the Correct Verb Tense
19 *a number*	30 "Quantity Expressions" section
can	29 "Modal Auxiliaries" section
21 *interesting*	29 "Participial Adjectives" section
22 *the*	31 Using Articles Accurately
23 *complicated*	29 "Participial Adjectives" section
25 *many*	30 "Quantity Expressions" section
(0)	31 Using Articles Accurately
26 *many*	30 "Quantity Expressions" section
listening	29 "Participial Adjectives" section
27 *may*	29 "Modal Auxiliaries" section
28 *of*	32 Practising with Prepositions
30 *around*	32 Practising with Prepositions
32 *is*	28 Choosing the Correct Verb Tense
33 *a lot*	30 "Quantity Expressions" section

INDEX

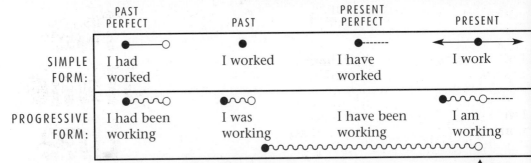

	PAST PERFECT	PAST	PRESENT PERFECT	PRESENT
SIMPLE FORM:	I had worked	I worked	I have worked	I work
PROGRESSIVE FORM:	I had been working	I was working	I have been working	I am working

NOW

Legend:

▲ indicates *now*, the present moment.

● represents *a completed action or state of being.*

○ indicates *an event that occurred or will occur sometime after the action represented by the black dot took place.*

⌣ represents *a continuing action or condition*, both of which are expressed by the progressive forms of a verb.

--- indicates that *the action or condition* may continue into the future.

SIMPLE

Simple Present

Expresses an action or condition that regularly or usually exists. It exists now, has existed in the past, and will probably exist in the future.

I *work* all week.
Sami *does* his homework every day.

Simple Past

Expresses an action or condition that began and ended in the past.

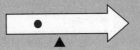

I *worked* last night.
Sami *did* his homework yesterday.

Simple Future

Expresses an action or condition that will happen some time after the present moment.

I *will work* hard on the project.
Sami *will do* his homework tomorrow.

(Alternative form: I *am going to work* hard on the project. Sami *is going to do* his homework tomorrow.)

PROGRESSIVE

Present Progressive

Expresses an action or condition that is in progress or that is taking place at this moment.

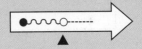

I *am working* on the project.
Sami *is doing* his homework now.

Past Progressive

Expresses an action or condition that began, continued for a period of time, and ended in the past.

I *was working* all night.
Sami *was doing* his homework when I called.

Future Progressive

Expresses an action or condition that will begin some time in the future and will continue for a period of time.

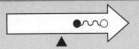

I *will be working* next week.
Sami *will be sleeping* during tomorrow's class.